Little Lulu®

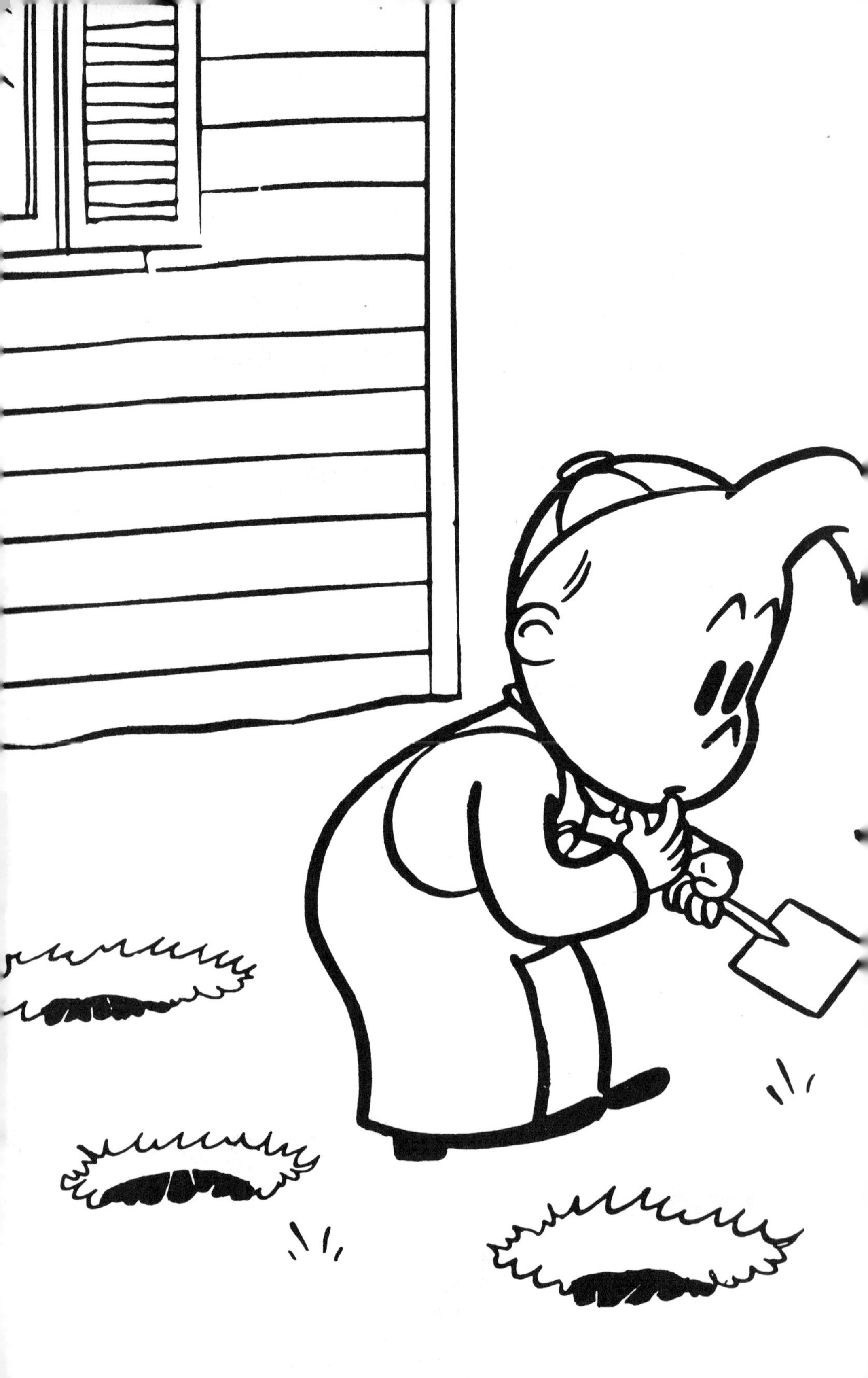

Little Lulu ®

Sunday Afternoon

Story and Art
John Stanley
and
Irving Tripp

Based on the character
created by
Marge Buell

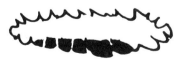

DARK HORSE BOOKS™

Publisher
Mike Richardson

Editor
Shawna Gore

Editorial Assistants
Rachel Miller
Gina Gagliano

Collection Designer
Debra Bailey

Art Director
Lia Ribacchi

Published by
Dark Horse Books
A division of Dark Horse Comics, Inc.
10956 SE Main Street
Milwaukie, OR 97222

Little Lulu : Sunday Afternoon, June 2005. Published by Dark Horse Comics, Inc., 10956 SE Main Street, Milwaukie, Oregon 97222. Little Lulu Copyright © 2005 by Classic Media, Inc. LITTLE LULU is a registered trademark of Classic Media, Inc. All Rights Reserved. Dark Horse Comics® is a trademark of Dark Horse Comics, Inc., registered in various categories and countries. All rights reserved. No portion of this publication may be reproduced or transmitted, in any form or by any means, without the express written permission of Dark Horse Comics, Inc. Names, characters, places, and incidents featured in this publication either are the product of the author's imagination or are used fictitiously. Any resemblance to actual persons (living or dead), events, institutions, or locales, without satiric intent, is coincidental.

First edition June 2005
ISBN: 1-59307-345-3

1 3 5 7 9 10 8 6 4 2
Printed in U.S.A.

A note about Lulu

Little Lulu came into the world through the pen of cartoonist Marjorie "Marge" Henderson Buell in 1935. Originally commissioned as a series of single-panel cartoons by *The Saturday Evening Post*, Lulu took the world by storm with her charm, smarts, and sass. Within ten years, she not only was the star of her own cartoon series, but a celebrity spokesgirl for a variety of high-profile commercial products.

Little Lulu truly hit her stride as America's sweetheart in the comic books published by Dell Comics starting in 1945. While Buell was solely responsible for Lulu's original single-panel shenanigans, the comic-book stories were put into the able hands of comics legend John Stanley. Stanley wrote and laid out the comics while artist Irving Tripp provided the finished drawings. After a number of trial appearances in Dell Comics, Lulu's appeal was undeniable, and she was granted her very own comic-book series, called *Marge's Little Lulu*, which was published regularly through 1984.

This volume contains every comics story from Dell Comics issues 131, 139, 146, and 158.

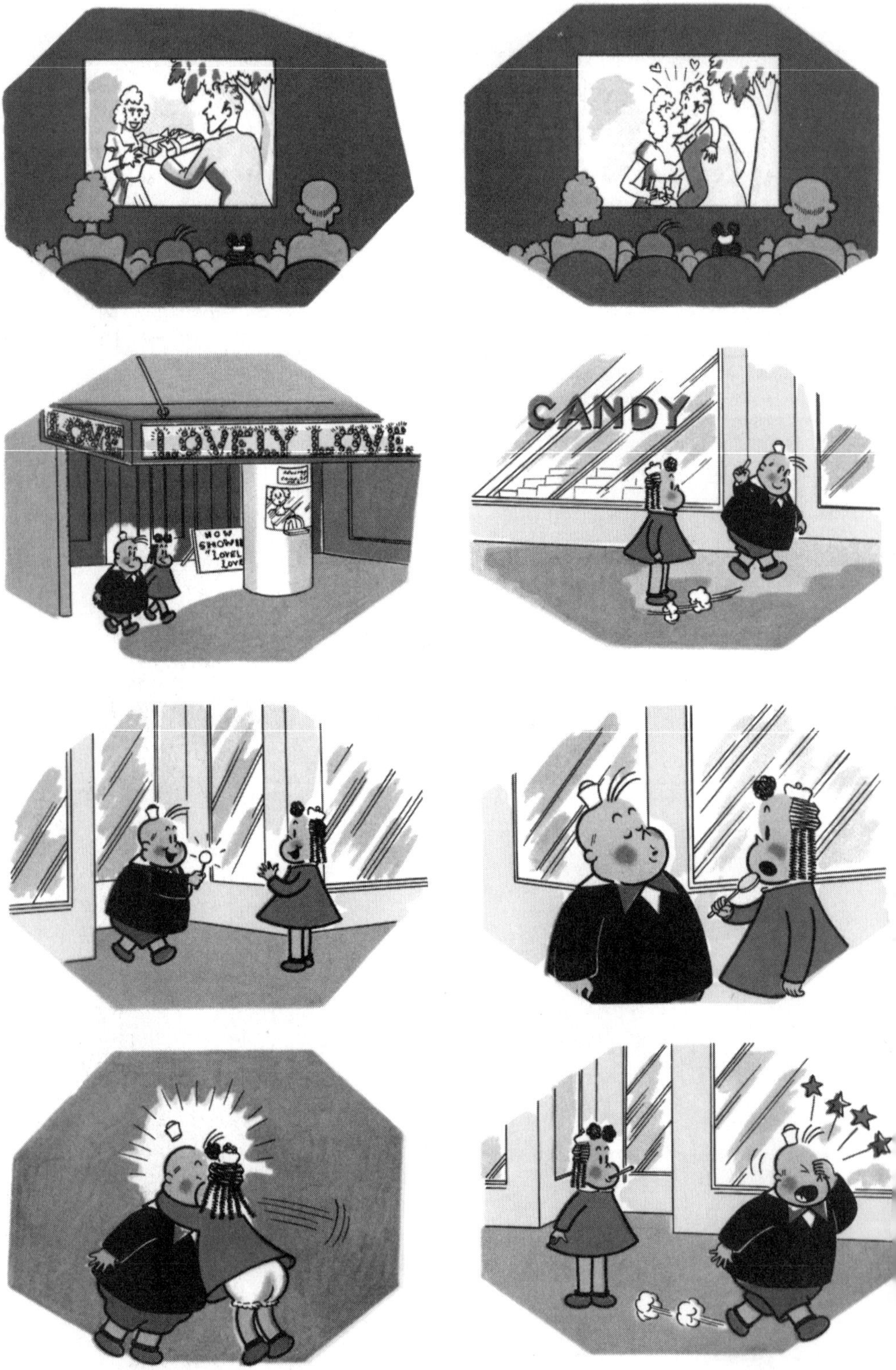
LOVE
LOVELY LOVE
CANDY

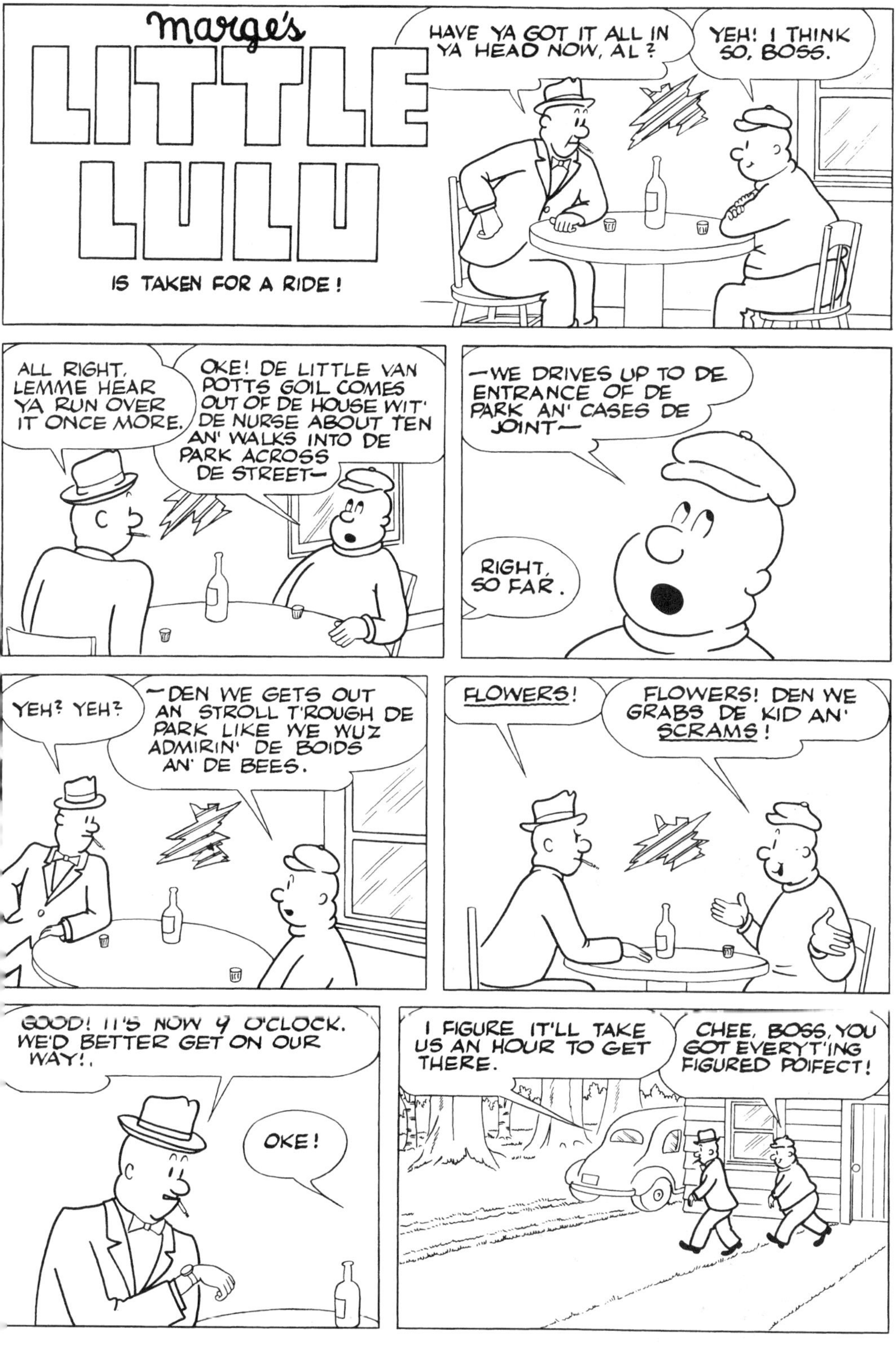
marge's
LITTLE LULU
IS TAKEN FOR A RIDE!
HAVE YA GOT IT ALL IN YA HEAD NOW, AL?
YEH! I THINK SO, BOSS.
ALL RIGHT. LEMME HEAR YA RUN OVER IT ONCE MORE.
OKE! DE LITTLE VAN POTTS GOIL COMES OUT OF DE HOUSE WIT' DE NURSE ABOUT TEN AN' WALKS INTO DE PARK ACROSS DE STREET—
—WE DRIVES UP TO DE ENTRANCE OF DE PARK AN' CASES DE JOINT—
RIGHT, SO FAR.
YEH? YEH?
—DEN WE GETS OUT AN STROLL T'ROUGH DE PARK LIKE WE WUZ ADMIRIN' DE BOIDS AN' DE BEES.
FLOWERS!
FLOWERS! DEN WE GRABS DE KID AN' SCRAMS!
GOOD! IT'S NOW 9 O'CLOCK. WE'D BETTER GET ON OUR WAY!.
OKE!
I FIGURE IT'LL TAKE US AN HOUR TO GET THERE.
CHEE, BOSS, YOU GOT EVERYT'ING FIGURED POIFECT!

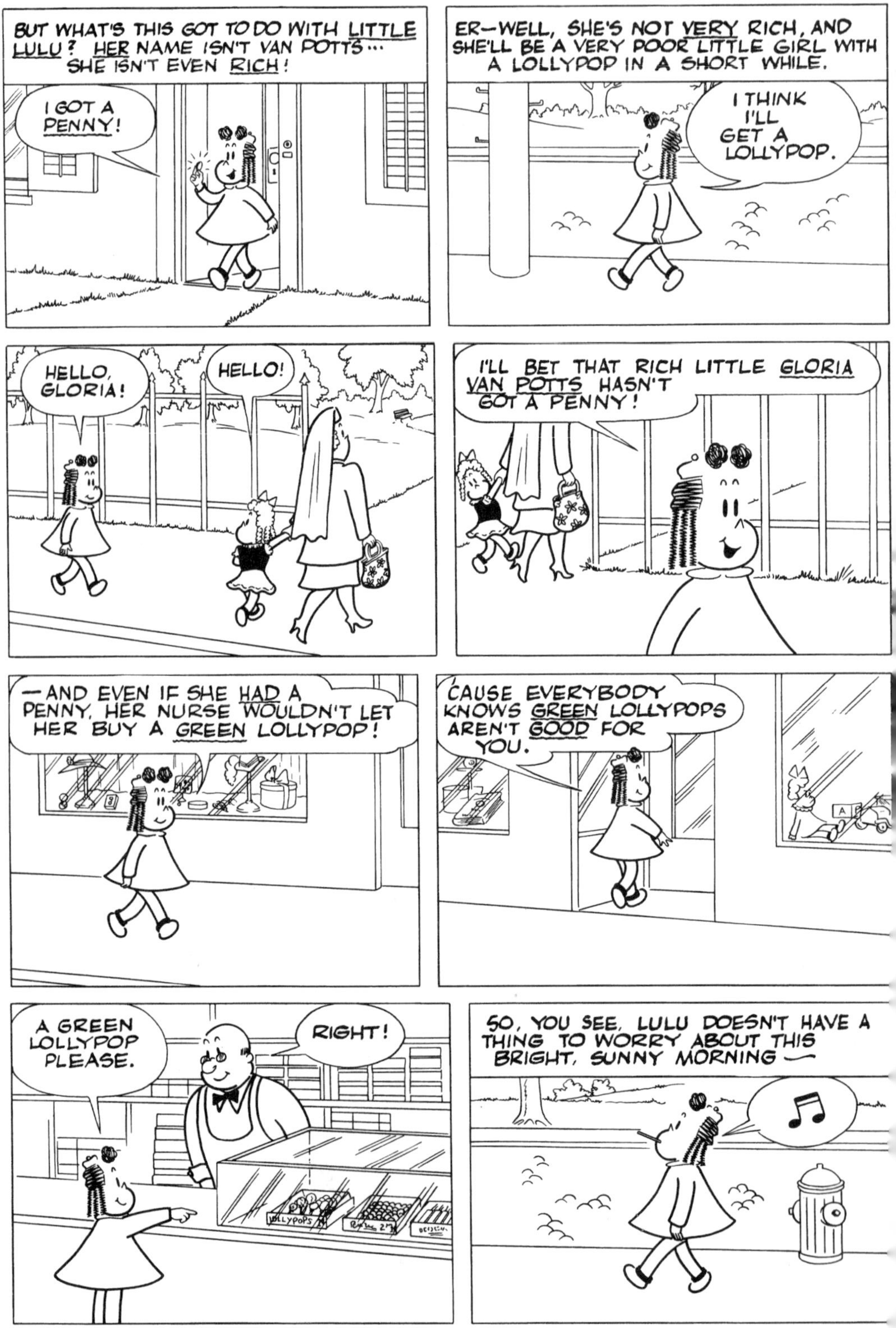
BUT WHAT'S THIS GOT TO DO WITH LITTLE LULU? HER NAME ISN'T VAN POTTS... SHE ISN'T EVEN RICH!
I GOT A PENNY!
ER—WELL, SHE'S NOT VERY RICH, AND SHE'LL BE A VERY POOR LITTLE GIRL WITH A LOLLYPOP IN A SHORT WHILE.
I THINK I'LL GET A LOLLYPOP.
HELLO, GLORIA!
HELLO!
I'LL BET THAT RICH LITTLE GLORIA VAN POTTS HASN'T GOT A PENNY!
—AND EVEN IF SHE HAD A PENNY, HER NURSE WOULDN'T LET HER BUY A GREEN LOLLYPOP!
'CAUSE EVERYBODY KNOWS GREEN LOLLYPOPS AREN'T GOOD FOR YOU.
A GREEN LOLLYPOP PLEASE.
RIGHT!
LOLLYPOPS
SO, YOU SEE, LULU DOESN'T HAVE A THING TO WORRY ABOUT THIS BRIGHT, SUNNY MORNING—

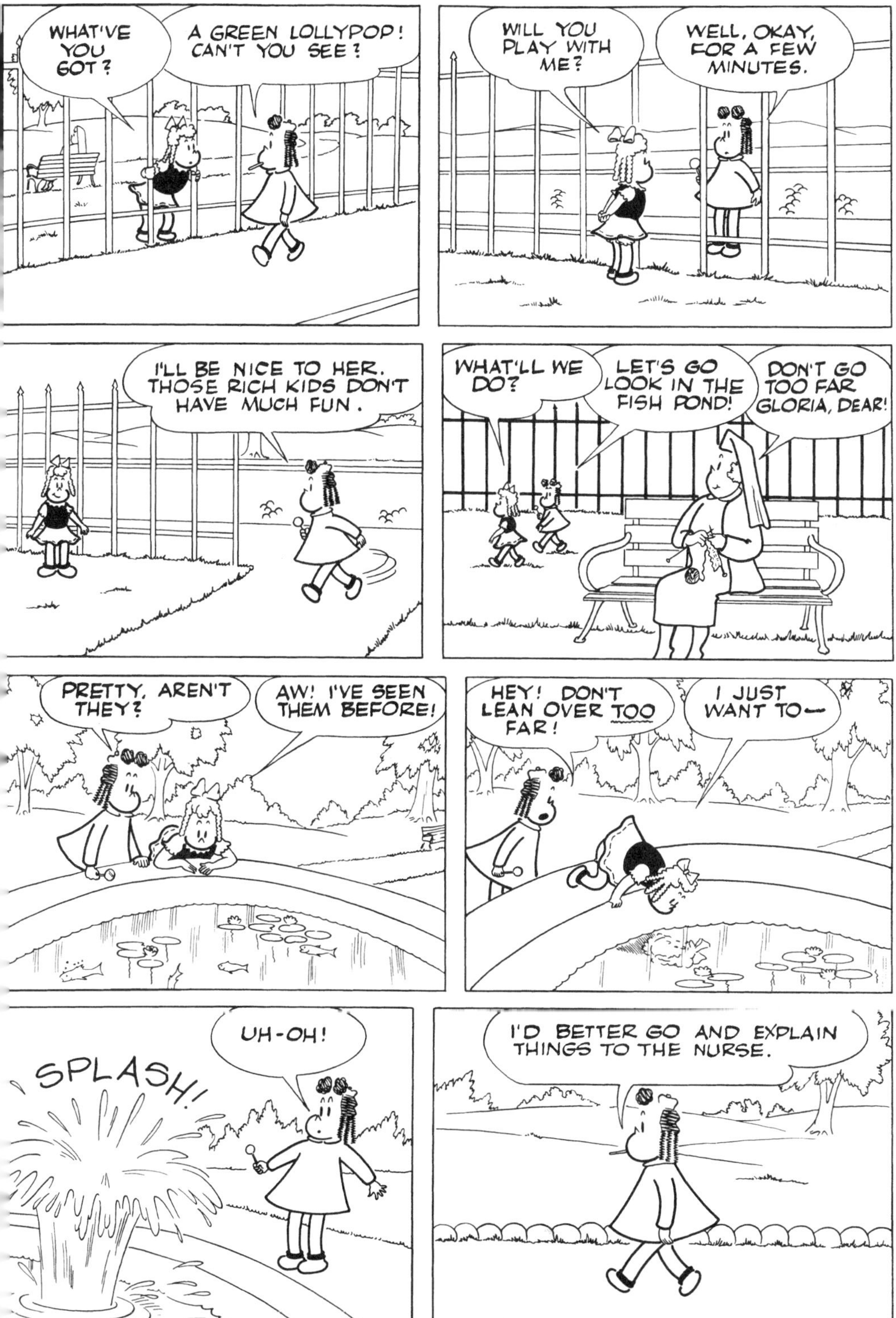
WHAT'VE YOU GOT?
A GREEN LOLLYPOP! CAN'T YOU SEE?
WILL YOU PLAY WITH ME?
WELL, OKAY, FOR A FEW MINUTES.
I'LL BE NICE TO HER. THOSE RICH KIDS DON'T HAVE MUCH FUN.
WHAT'LL WE DO?
LET'S GO LOOK IN THE FISH POND!
DON'T GO TOO FAR GLORIA, DEAR!
PRETTY, AREN'T THEY?
AW! I'VE SEEN THEM BEFORE!
HEY! DON'T LEAN OVER TOO FAR!
I JUST WANT TO—
SPLASH!
UH-OH!
I'D BETTER GO AND EXPLAIN THINGS TO THE NURSE.

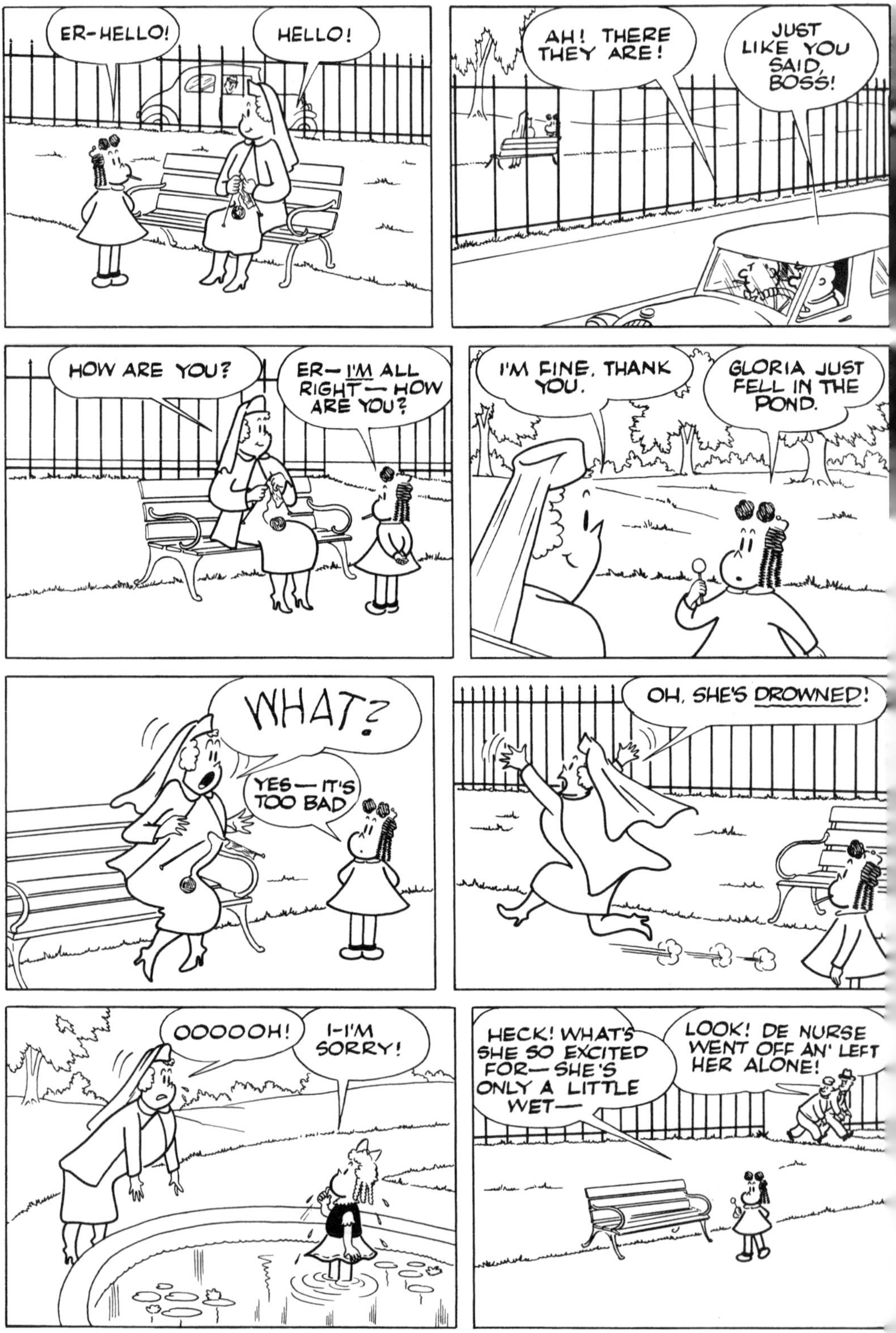
ER-HELLO!
HELLO!
AH! THERE THEY ARE!
JUST LIKE YOU SAID, BOSS!
HOW ARE YOU?
ER—I'M ALL RIGHT—HOW ARE YOU?
I'M FINE, THANK YOU.
GLORIA JUST FELL IN THE POND.
WHAT?
YES—IT'S TOO BAD
OH, SHE'S DROWNED!
OOOOOH!
I-I'M SORRY!
HECK! WHAT'S SHE SO EXCITED FOR—SHE'S ONLY A LITTLE WET—
LOOK! DE NURSE WENT OFF AN' LEFT HER ALONE!

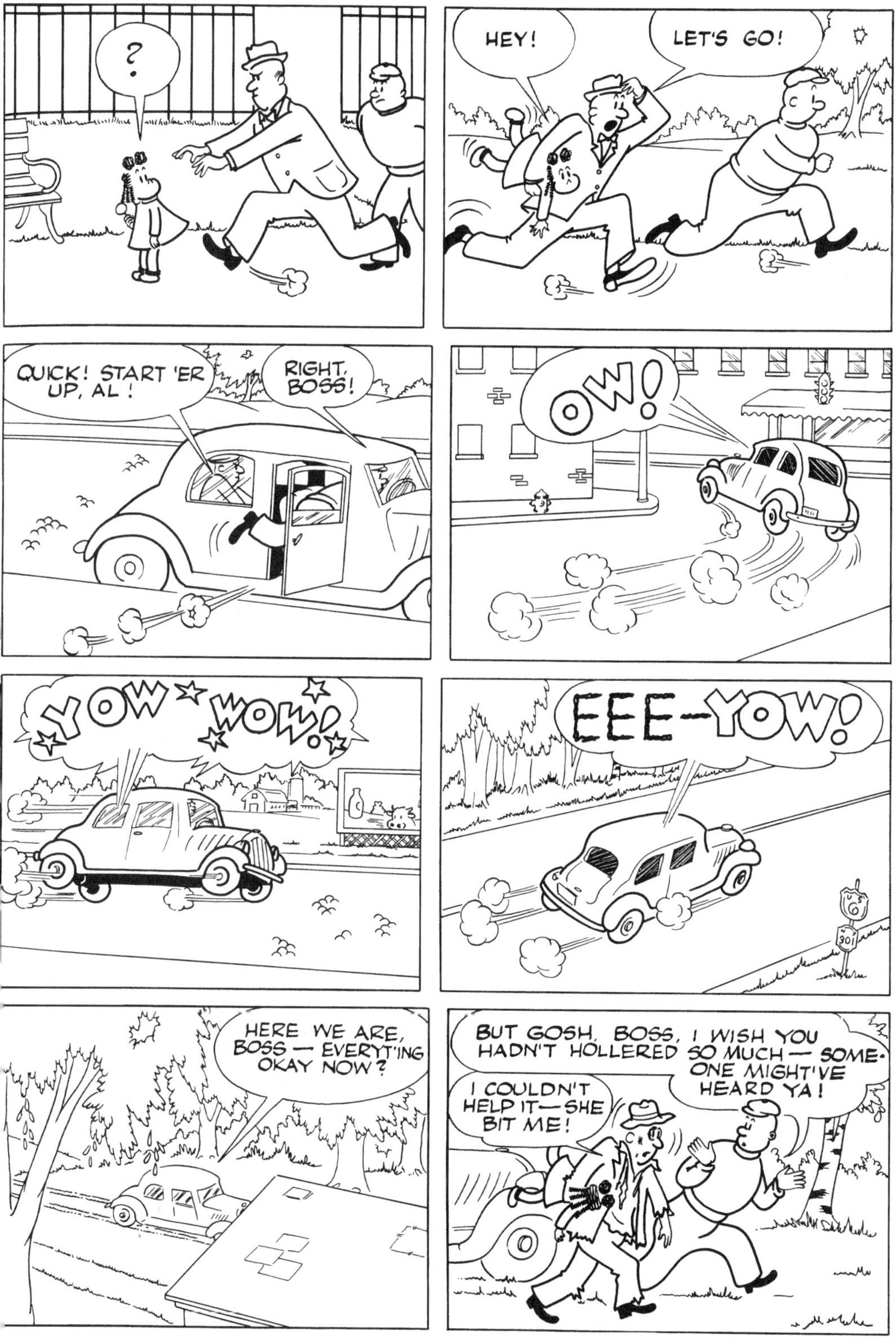
?
HEY!
LET'S GO!
QUICK! START 'ER UP, AL!
RIGHT, BOSS!
OW!
YOW WOW!
EEE-YOW!
HERE WE ARE, BOSS — EVERYT'ING OKAY NOW?
BUT GOSH, BOSS, I WISH YOU HADN'T HOLLERED SO MUCH — SOME-ONE MIGHT'VE HEARD YA!
I COULDN'T HELP IT — SHE BIT ME!

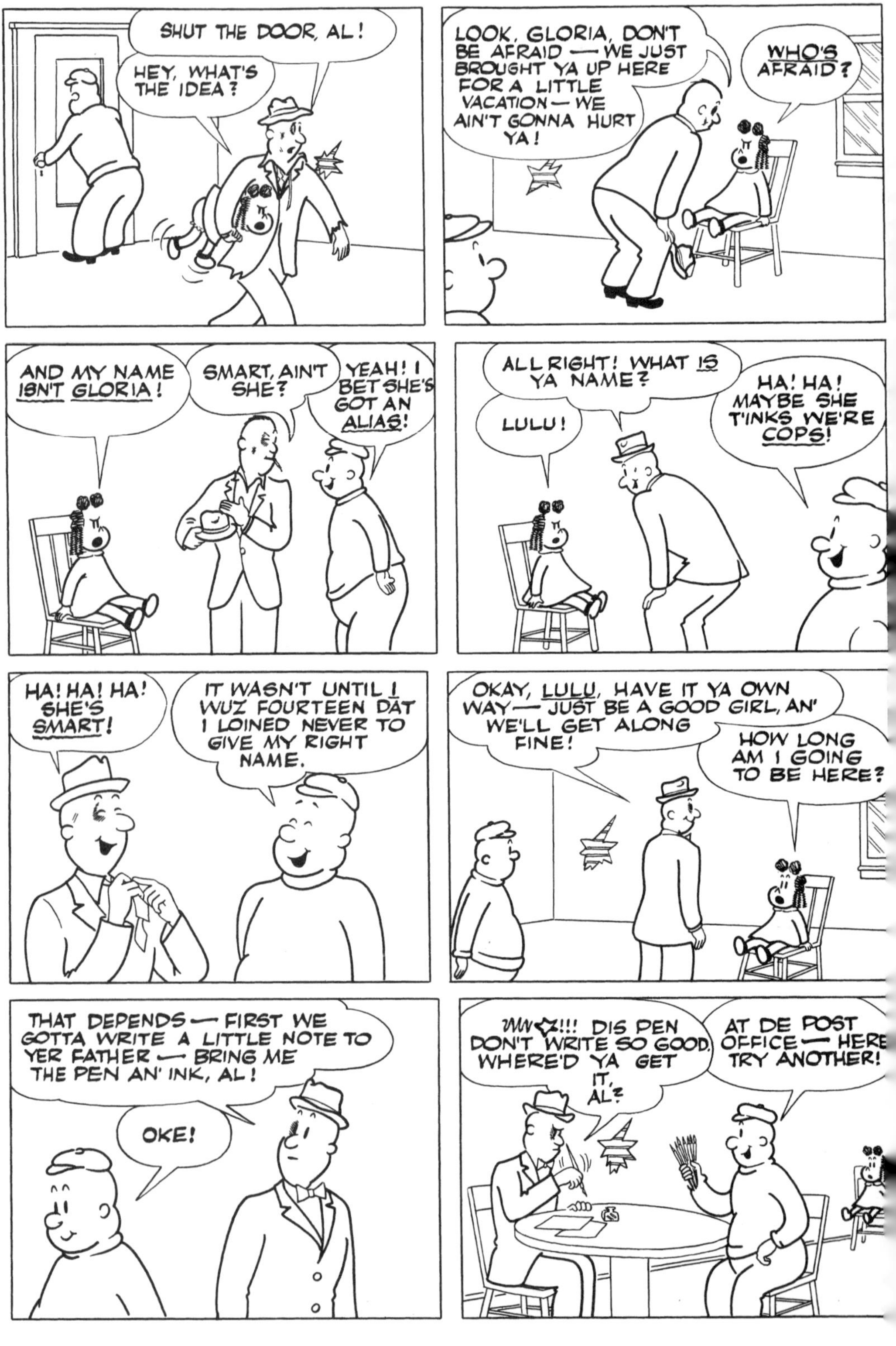
SHUT THE DOOR, AL!
HEY, WHAT'S THE IDEA?
LOOK, GLORIA, DON'T BE AFRAID — WE JUST BROUGHT YA UP HERE FOR A LITTLE VACATION — WE AIN'T GONNA HURT YA!
WHO'S AFRAID?
AND MY NAME ISN'T GLORIA!
SMART, AIN'T SHE?
YEAH! I BET SHE'S GOT AN ALIAS!
ALL RIGHT! WHAT IS YA NAME?
LULU!
HA! HA! MAYBE SHE T'INKS WE'RE COPS!
HA! HA! HA! SHE'S SMART!
IT WASN'T UNTIL I WUZ FOURTEEN DAT I LOINED NEVER TO GIVE MY RIGHT NAME.
OKAY, LULU, HAVE IT YA OWN WAY— JUST BE A GOOD GIRL, AN' WE'LL GET ALONG FINE!
HOW LONG AM I GOING TO BE HERE?
THAT DEPENDS— FIRST WE GOTTA WRITE A LITTLE NOTE TO YER FATHER — BRING ME THE PEN AN' INK, AL!
OKE!
!!! DIS PEN DON'T WRITE SO GOOD. WHERE'D YA GET IT, AL?
AT DE POST OFFICE — HERE TRY ANOTHER!

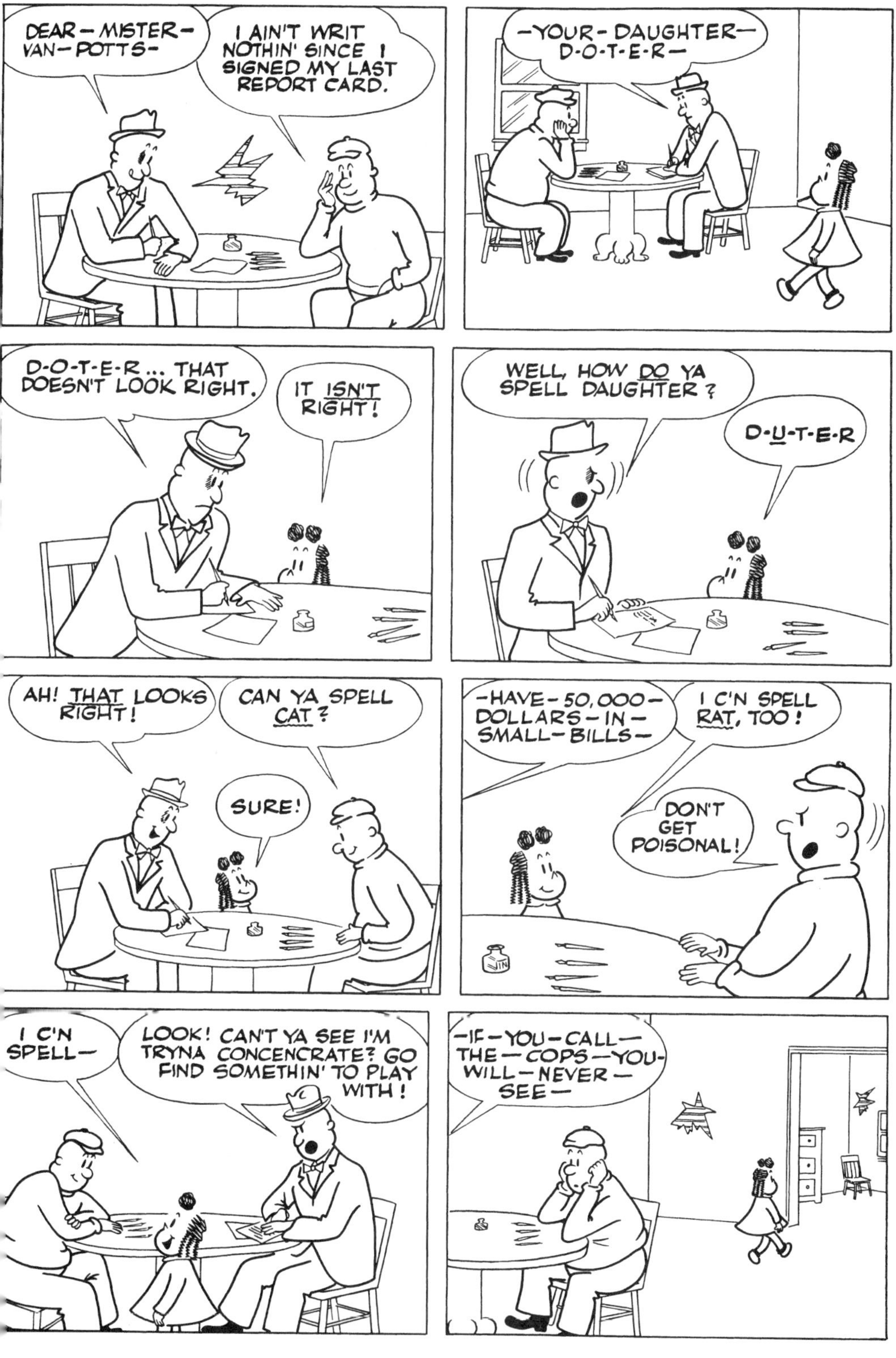
DEAR—MISTER—VAN—POTTS—
I AIN'T WRIT NOTHIN' SINCE I SIGNED MY LAST REPORT CARD.
—YOUR—DAUGHTER—D-O-T-E-R—
D-O-T-E-R... THAT DOESN'T LOOK RIGHT.
IT ISN'T RIGHT!
WELL, HOW DO YA SPELL DAUGHTER?
D-U-T-E-R
AH! THAT LOOKS RIGHT!
CAN YA SPELL CAT?
SURE!
—HAVE—50,000—DOLLARS—IN—SMALL—BILLS—
I C'N SPELL RAT, TOO!
DON'T GET POISONAL!
I C'N SPELL—
LOOK! CAN'T YA SEE I'M TRYNA CONCENCRATE? GO FIND SOMETHIN' TO PLAY WITH!
—IF—YOU—CALL—THE—COPS—YOU—WILL—NEVER—SEE—

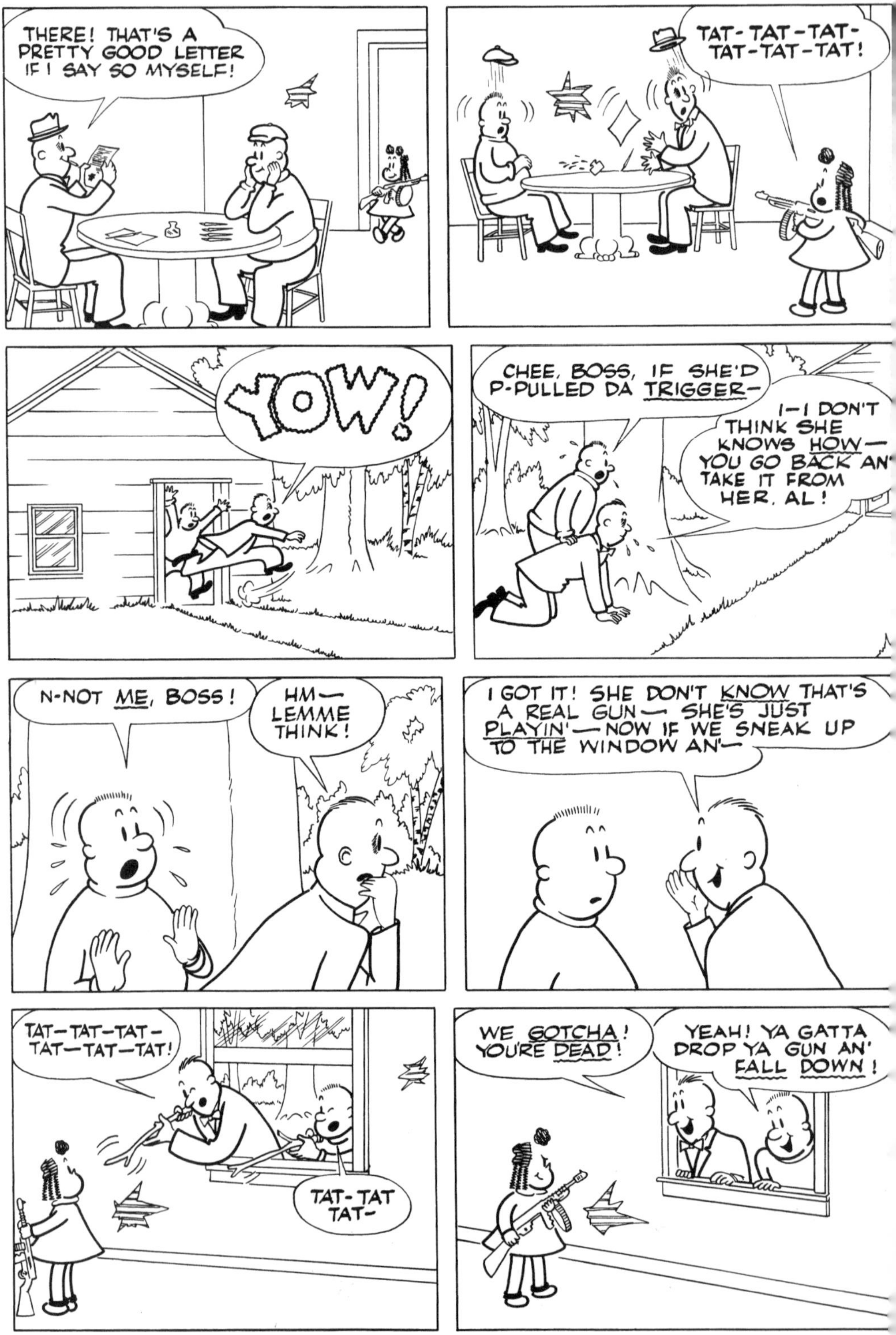
THERE! THAT'S A PRETTY GOOD LETTER IF I SAY SO MYSELF!
TAT-TAT-TAT-TAT-TAT-TAT!
YOW!
CHEE, BOSS, IF SHE'D P-PULLED DA TRIGGER—
I—I DON'T THINK SHE KNOWS HOW—YOU GO BACK AN' TAKE IT FROM HER, AL!
N-NOT ME, BOSS!
HM—LEMME THINK!
I GOT IT! SHE DON'T KNOW THAT'S A REAL GUN— SHE'S JUST PLAYIN'—NOW IF WE SNEAK UP TO THE WINDOW AN'—
TAT—TAT—TAT—TAT—TAT—TAT!
TAT-TAT TAT-
WE GOTCHA! YOU'RE DEAD!
YEAH! YA GATTA DROP YA GUN AN' FALL DOWN!

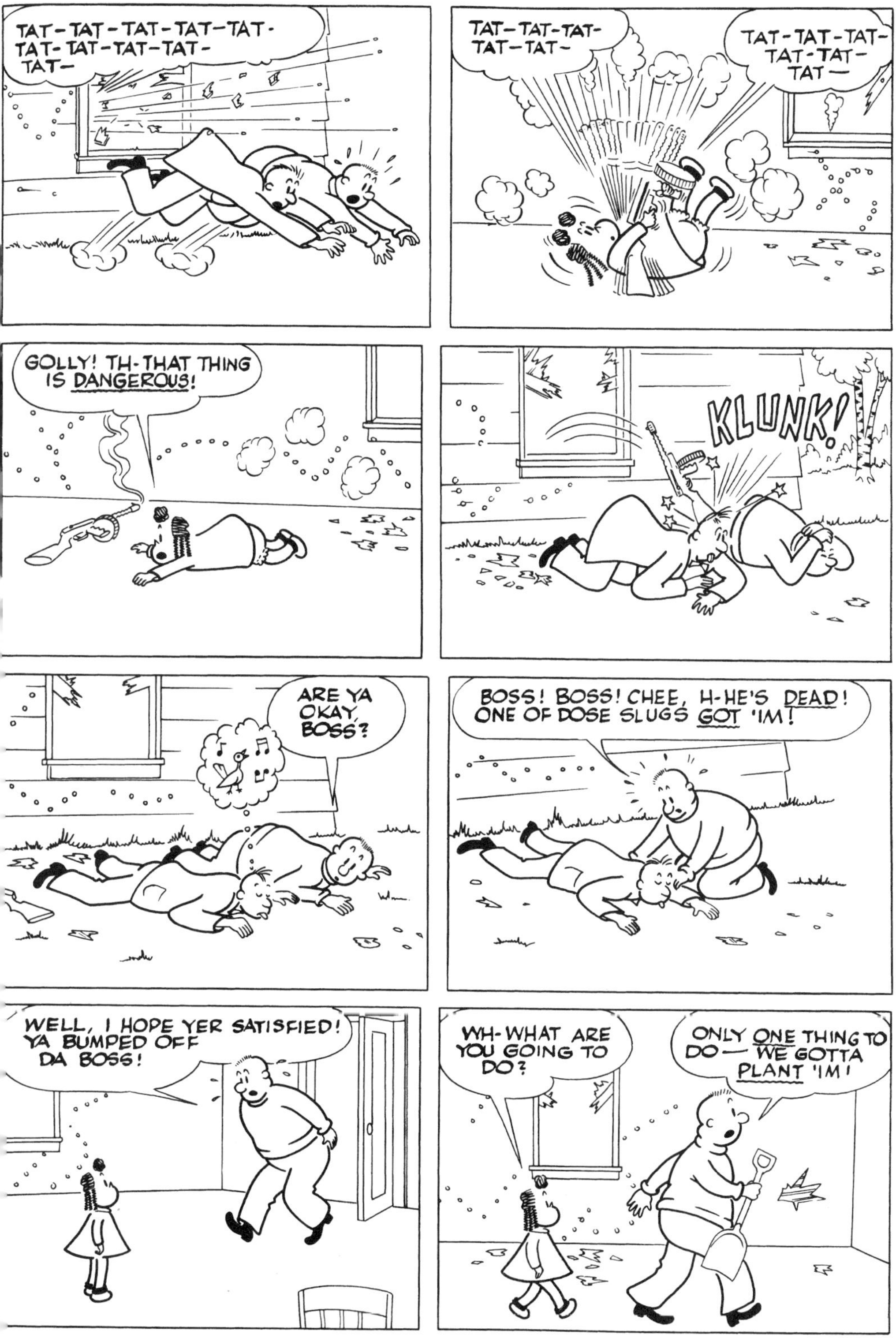
TAT-TAT-TAT-TAT-TAT-
TAT-TAT-TAT-TAT-
TAT—
TAT-TAT-TAT-
TAT-TAT-
TAT-TAT-TAT-
TAT-TAT-
TAT—
GOLLY! TH-THAT THING IS DANGEROUS!
KLUNK!
ARE YA OKAY, BOSS?
BOSS! BOSS! CHEE, H-HE'S DEAD! ONE OF DOSE SLUGS GOT 'IM!
WELL, I HOPE YER SATISFIED! YA BUMPED OFF DA BOSS!
WH-WHAT ARE YOU GOING TO DO?
ONLY ONE THING TO DO— WE GOTTA PLANT 'IM!

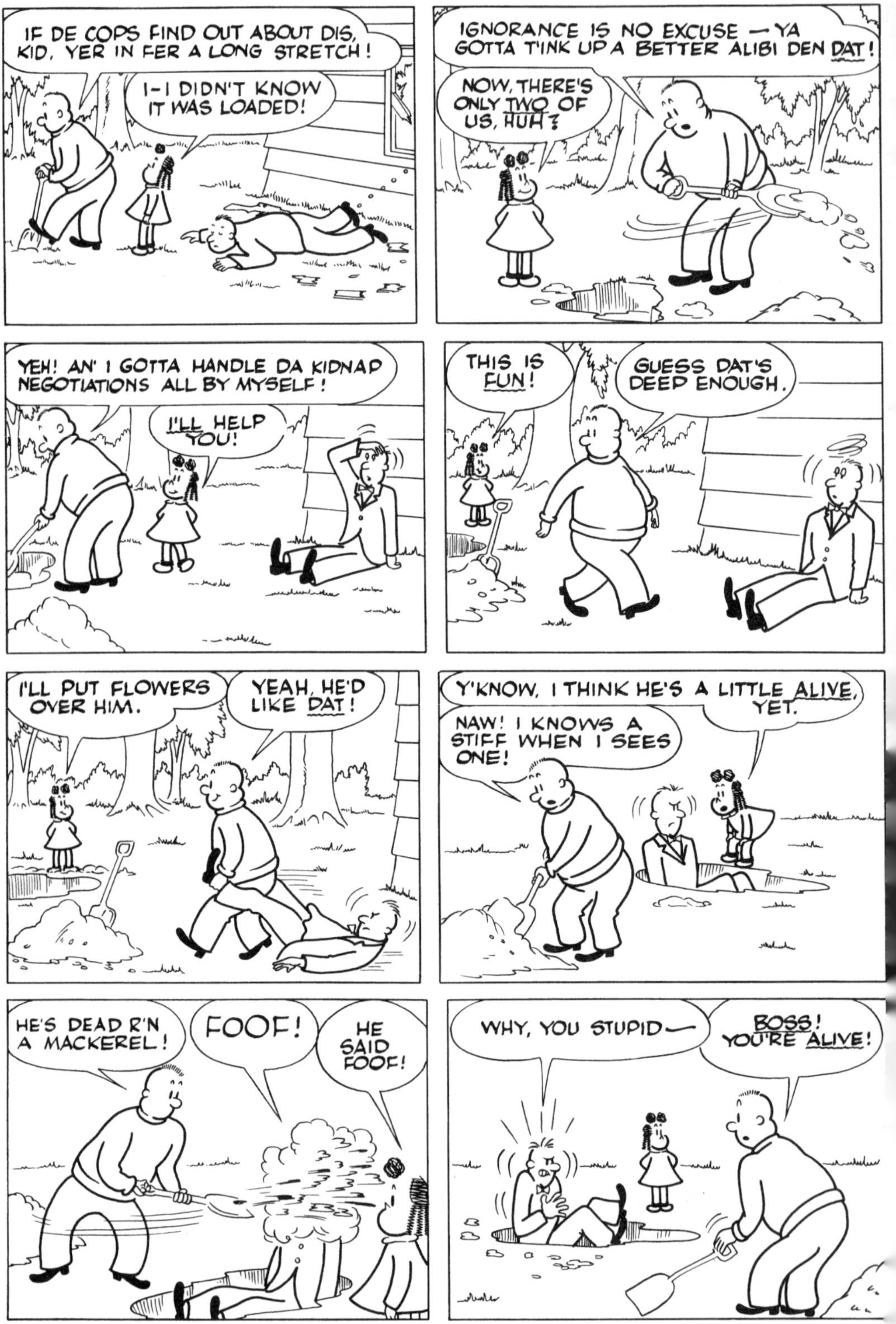
IF DE COPS FIND OUT ABOUT DIS, KID, YER IN FER A LONG STRETCH!
I-I DIDN'T KNOW IT WAS LOADED!
IGNORANCE IS NO EXCUSE — YA GOTTA T'INK UP A BETTER ALIBI DEN DAT!
NOW, THERE'S ONLY TWO OF US, HUH?
YEH! AN' I GOTTA HANDLE DA KIDNAP NEGOTIATIONS ALL BY MYSELF!
I'LL HELP YOU!
THIS IS FUN!
GUESS DAT'S DEEP ENOUGH.
I'LL PUT FLOWERS OVER HIM.
YEAH, HE'D LIKE DAT!
Y'KNOW, I THINK HE'S A LITTLE ALIVE, YET.
NAW! I KNOWS A STIFF WHEN I SEES ONE!
HE'S DEAD R'N A MACKEREL!
FOOF!
HE SAID FOOF!
WHY, YOU STUPID—
BOSS! YOU'RE ALIVE!

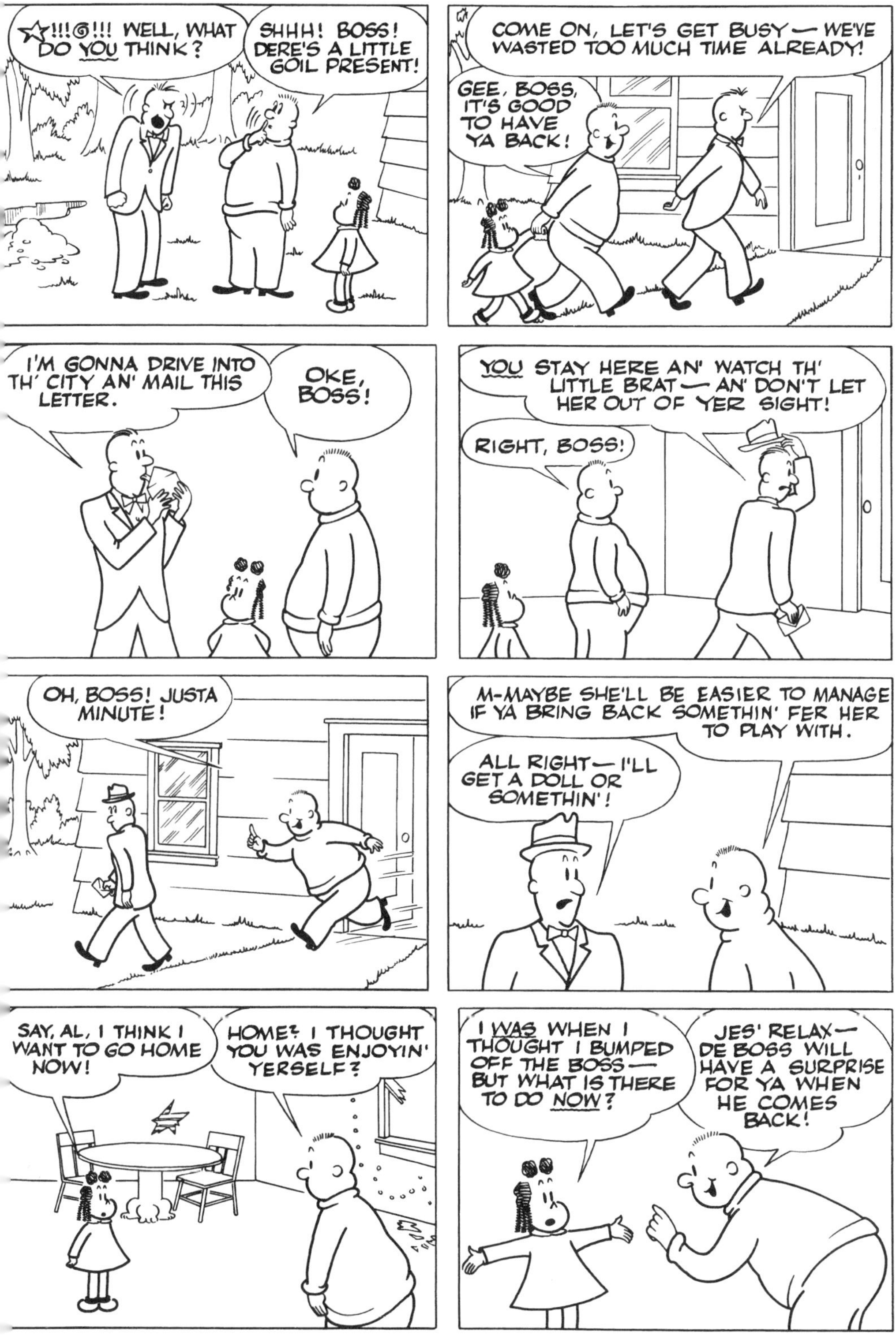
☆!!!@!!! WELL, WHAT DO YOU THINK?
SHHH! BOSS! DERE'S A LITTLE GOIL PRESENT!
COME ON, LET'S GET BUSY — WE'VE WASTED TOO MUCH TIME ALREADY!
GEE, BOSS, IT'S GOOD TO HAVE YA BACK!
I'M GONNA DRIVE INTO TH' CITY AN' MAIL THIS LETTER.
OKE, BOSS!
YOU STAY HERE AN' WATCH TH' LITTLE BRAT — AN' DON'T LET HER OUT OF YER SIGHT!
RIGHT, BOSS!
OH, BOSS! JUSTA MINUTE!
M-MAYBE SHE'LL BE EASIER TO MANAGE IF YA BRING BACK SOMETHIN' FER HER TO PLAY WITH.
ALL RIGHT — I'LL GET A DOLL OR SOMETHIN'!
SAY, AL, I THINK I WANT TO GO HOME NOW!
HOME? I THOUGHT YOU WAS ENJOYIN' YERSELF?
I WAS WHEN I THOUGHT I BUMPED OFF THE BOSS — BUT WHAT IS THERE TO DO NOW?
JES' RELAX — DE BOSS WILL HAVE A SURPRISE FOR YA WHEN HE COMES BACK!

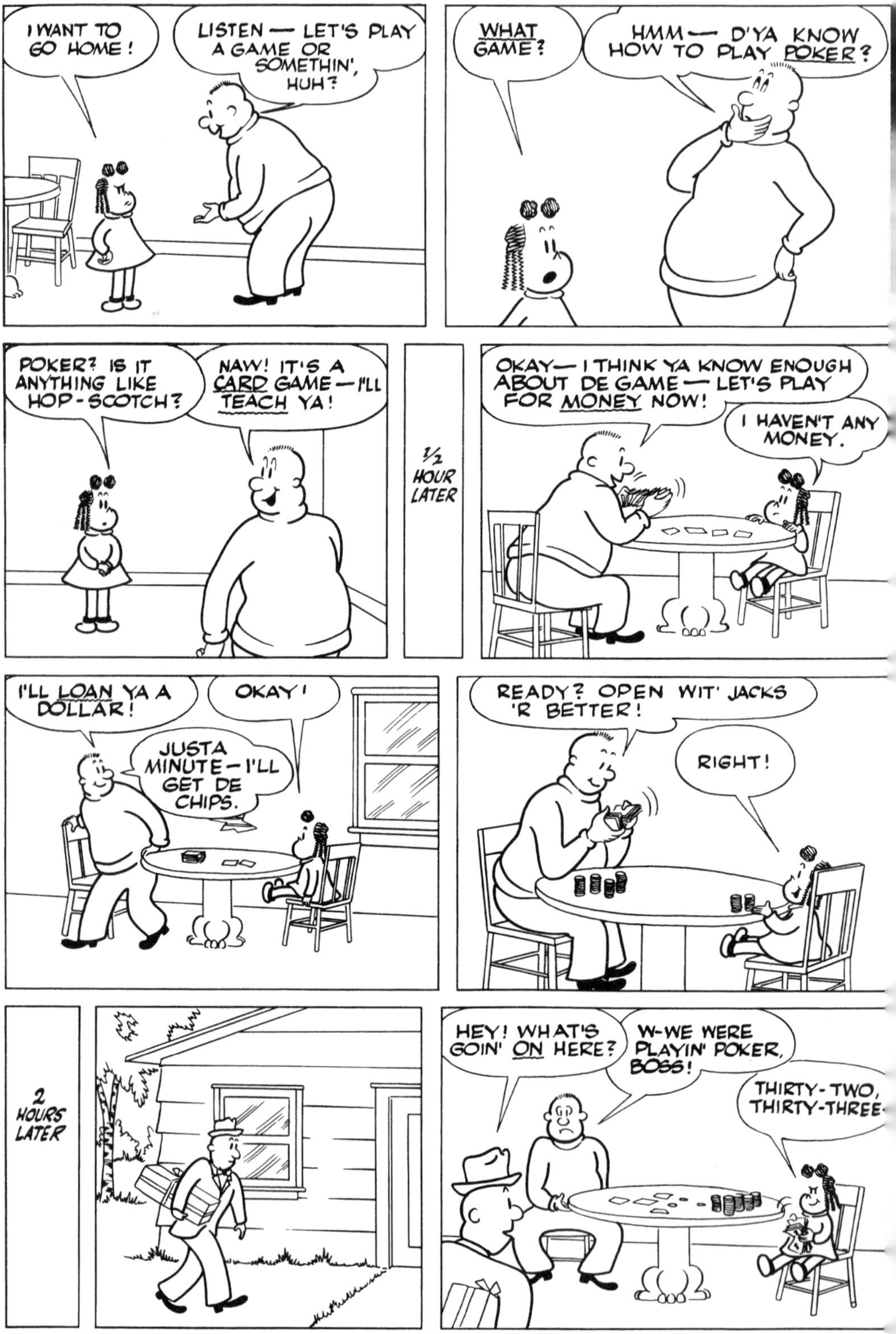
I WANT TO GO HOME!
LISTEN — LET'S PLAY A GAME OR SOMETHIN', HUH?
WHAT GAME?
HMM — D'YA KNOW HOW TO PLAY POKER?
POKER? IS IT ANYTHING LIKE HOP-SCOTCH?
NAW! IT'S A CARD GAME — I'LL TEACH YA!
1/2 HOUR LATER
OKAY — I THINK YA KNOW ENOUGH ABOUT DE GAME — LET'S PLAY FOR MONEY NOW!
I HAVEN'T ANY MONEY.
I'LL LOAN YA A DOLLAR!
OKAY!
JUSTA MINUTE — I'LL GET DE CHIPS.
READY? OPEN WIT' JACKS 'R BETTER!
RIGHT!
2 HOURS LATER
HEY! WHAT'S GOIN' ON HERE?
W-WE WERE PLAYIN' POKER, BOSS!
THIRTY-TWO, THIRTY-THREE-

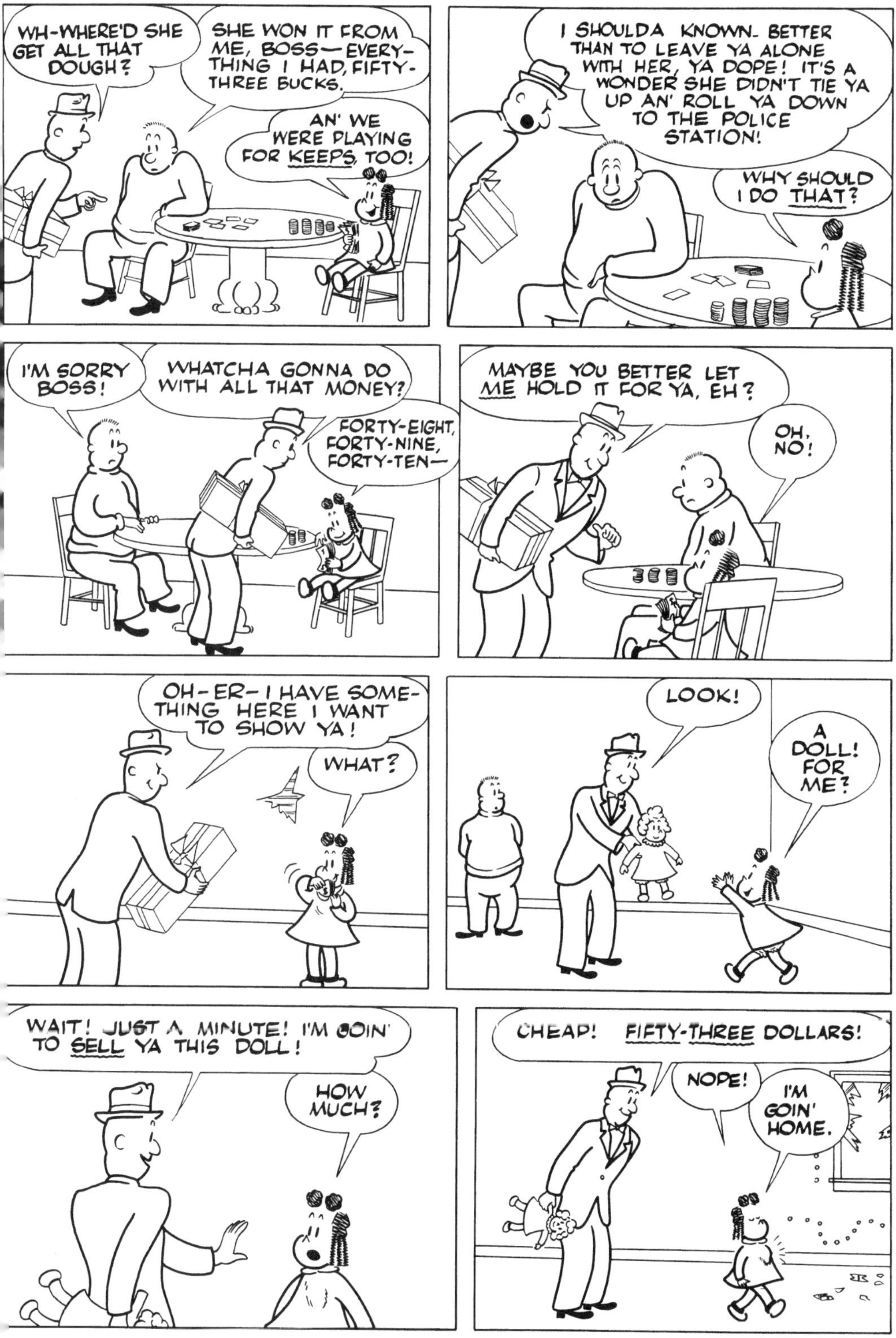
WH-WHERE'D SHE GET ALL THAT DOUGH?
SHE WON IT FROM ME, BOSS—EVERYTHING I HAD, FIFTY-THREE BUCKS.
AN' WE WERE PLAYING FOR KEEPS, TOO!
I SHOULDA KNOWN BETTER THAN TO LEAVE YA ALONE WITH HER, YA DOPE! IT'S A WONDER SHE DIDN'T TIE YA UP AN' ROLL YA DOWN TO THE POLICE STATION!
WHY SHOULD I DO THAT?
I'M SORRY BOSS!
WHATCHA GONNA DO WITH ALL THAT MONEY?
FORTY-EIGHT, FORTY-NINE, FORTY-TEN—
MAYBE YOU BETTER LET ME HOLD IT FOR YA, EH?
OH, NO!
OH-ER-I HAVE SOMETHING HERE I WANT TO SHOW YA!
WHAT?
LOOK!
A DOLL! FOR ME?
WAIT! JUST A MINUTE! I'M GOIN' TO SELL YA THIS DOLL!
HOW MUCH?
CHEAP! FIFTY-THREE DOLLARS!
NOPE!
I'M GOIN' HOME.

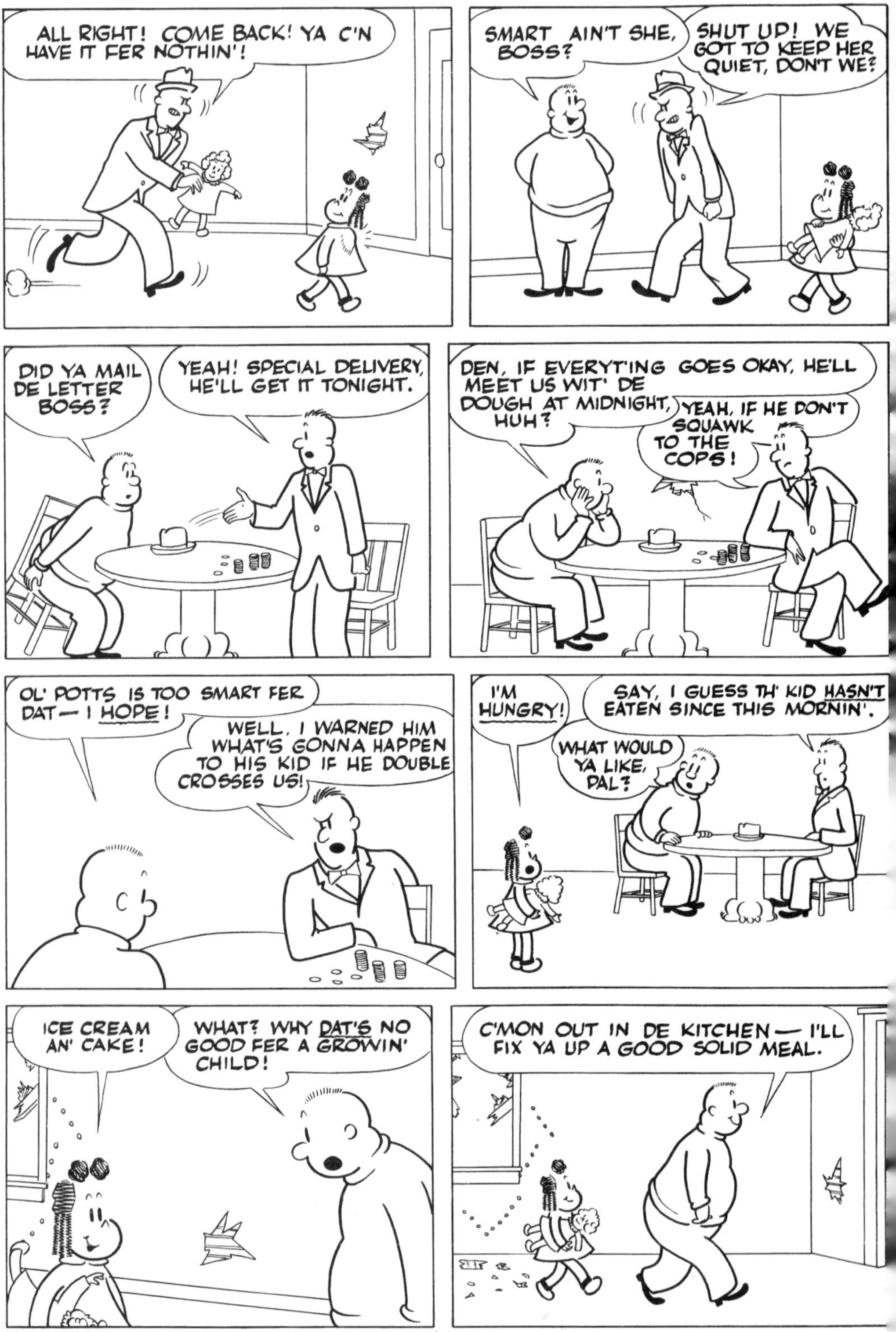

ALL RIGHT! COME BACK! YA C'N HAVE IT FER NOTHIN'!
SMART AIN'T SHE, BOSS?
SHUT UP! WE GOT TO KEEP HER QUIET, DON'T WE?
DID YA MAIL DE LETTER BOSS?
YEAH! SPECIAL DELIVERY, HE'LL GET IT TONIGHT.
DEN, IF EVERYT'ING GOES OKAY, HE'LL MEET US WIT' DE DOUGH AT MIDNIGHT, HUH?
YEAH, IF HE DON'T SQUAWK TO THE COPS!
OL' POTTS IS TOO SMART FER DAT— I HOPE!
WELL, I WARNED HIM WHAT'S GONNA HAPPEN TO HIS KID IF HE DOUBLE CROSSES US!
I'M HUNGRY!
SAY, I GUESS TH' KID HASN'T EATEN SINCE THIS MORNIN'.
WHAT WOULD YA LIKE, PAL?
ICE CREAM AN' CAKE!
WHAT? WHY DAT'S NO GOOD FER A GROWIN' CHILD!
C'MON OUT IN DE KITCHEN— I'LL FIX YA UP A GOOD SOLID MEAL.

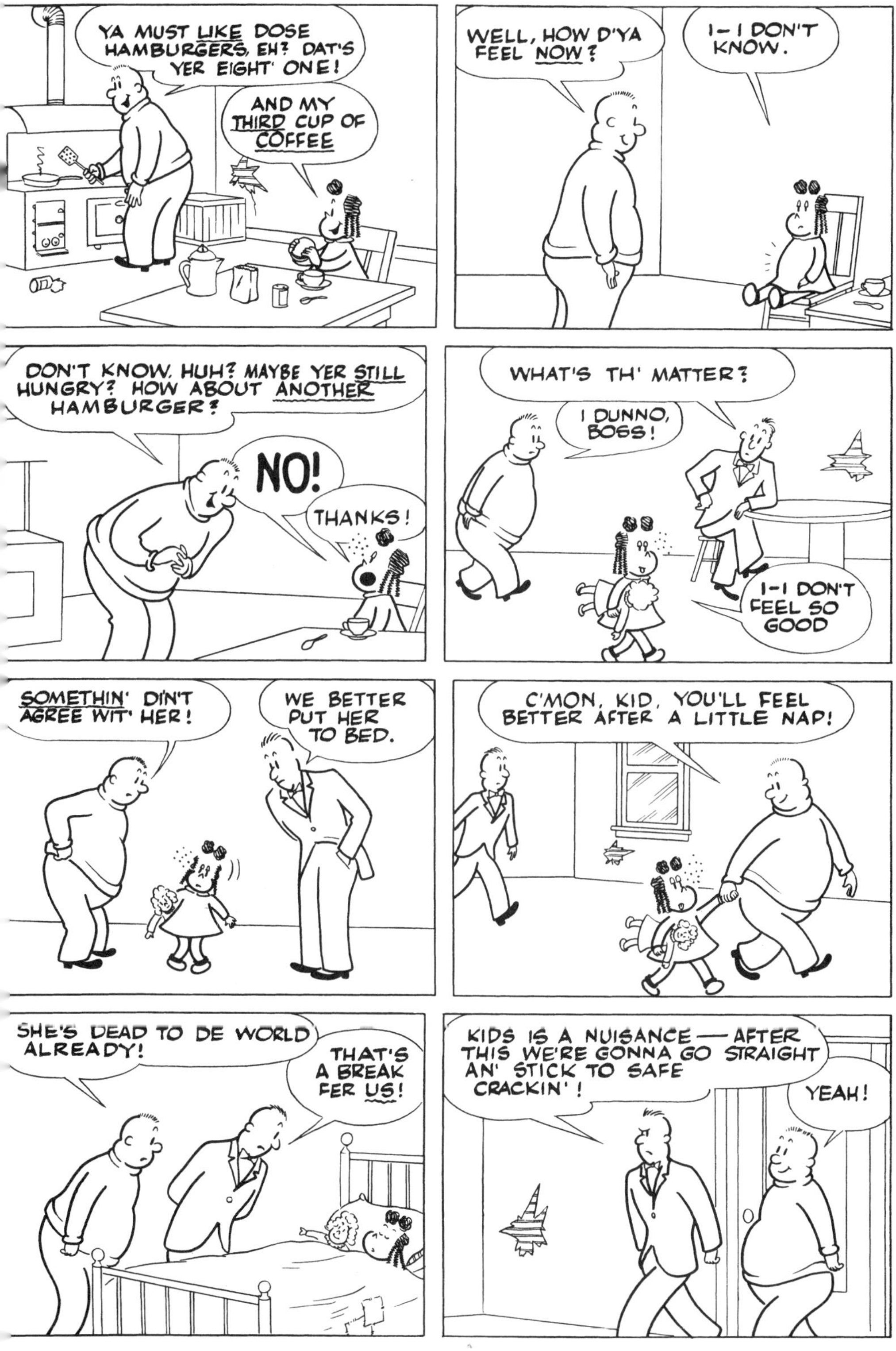
YA MUST LIKE DOSE HAMBURGERS, EH? DAT'S YER EIGHT' ONE!
AND MY THIRD CUP OF COFFEE
WELL, HOW D'YA FEEL NOW?
I-I DON'T KNOW.
DON'T KNOW, HUH? MAYBE YER STILL HUNGRY? HOW ABOUT ANOTHER HAMBURGER?
NO!
THANKS!
WHAT'S TH' MATTER?
I DUNNO, BOSS!
I-I DON'T FEEL SO GOOD
SOMETHIN' DIN'T AGREE WIT' HER!
WE BETTER PUT HER TO BED.
C'MON, KID, YOU'LL FEEL BETTER AFTER A LITTLE NAP!
SHE'S DEAD TO DE WORLD ALREADY!
THAT'S A BREAK FER US!
KIDS IS A NUISANCE — AFTER THIS WE'RE GONNA GO STRAIGHT AN' STICK TO SAFE CRACKIN'!
YEAH!

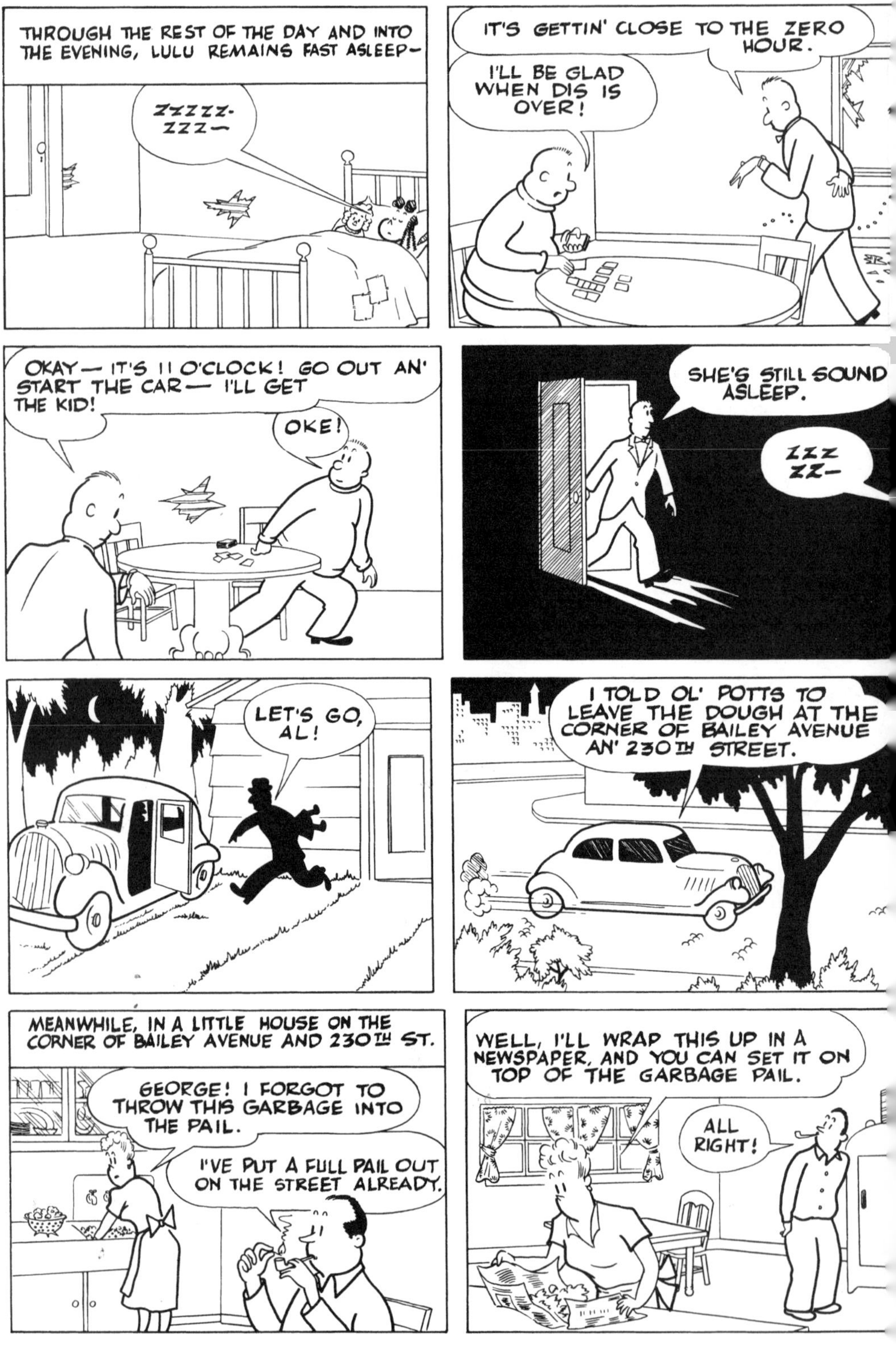
THROUGH THE REST OF THE DAY AND INTO THE EVENING, LULU REMAINS FAST ASLEEP—
ZZZZZ-ZZZ—
IT'S GETTIN' CLOSE TO THE ZERO HOUR.
I'LL BE GLAD WHEN DIS IS OVER!
OKAY— IT'S 11 O'CLOCK! GO OUT AN' START THE CAR— I'LL GET THE KID!
OKE!
SHE'S STILL SOUND ASLEEP.
ZZZ ZZ—
LET'S GO, AL!
I TOLD OL' POTTS TO LEAVE THE DOUGH AT THE CORNER OF BAILEY AVENUE AN' 230TH STREET.
MEANWHILE, IN A LITTLE HOUSE ON THE CORNER OF BAILEY AVENUE AND 230TH ST.
GEORGE! I FORGOT TO THROW THIS GARBAGE INTO THE PAIL.
I'VE PUT A FULL PAIL OUT ON THE STREET ALREADY.
WELL, I'LL WRAP THIS UP IN A NEWSPAPER, AND YOU CAN SET IT ON TOP OF THE GARBAGE PAIL.
ALL RIGHT!

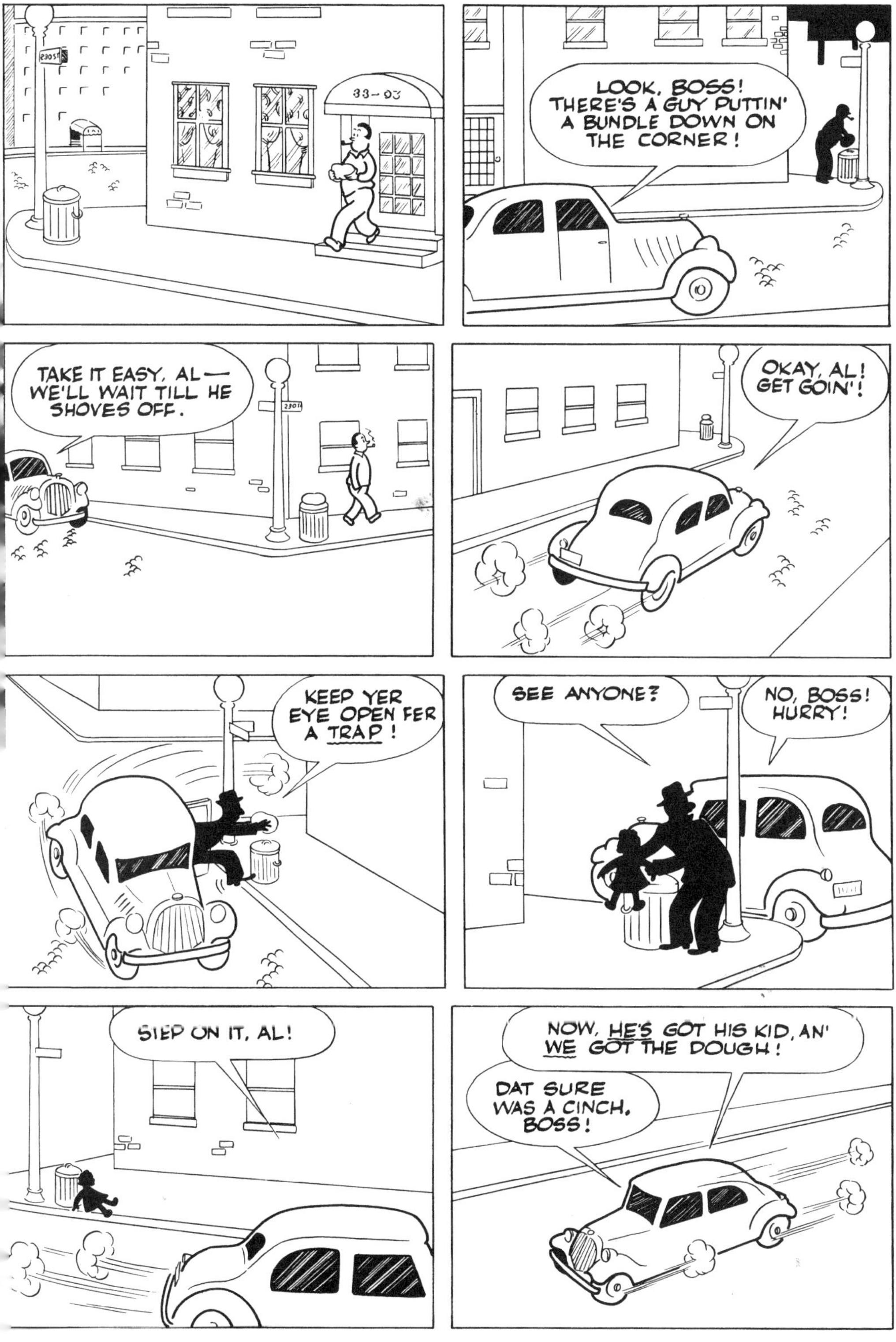
230 ST
33-93
LOOK, BOSS! THERE'S A GUY PUTTIN' A BUNDLE DOWN ON THE CORNER!
TAKE IT EASY, AL— WE'LL WAIT TILL HE SHOVES OFF.
OKAY, AL! GET GOIN'!
KEEP YER EYE OPEN FER A TRAP!
SEE ANYONE?
NO, BOSS! HURRY!
STEP ON IT, AL!
NOW, HE'S GOT HIS KID, AN' WE GOT THE DOUGH!
DAT SURE WAS A CINCH, BOSS!

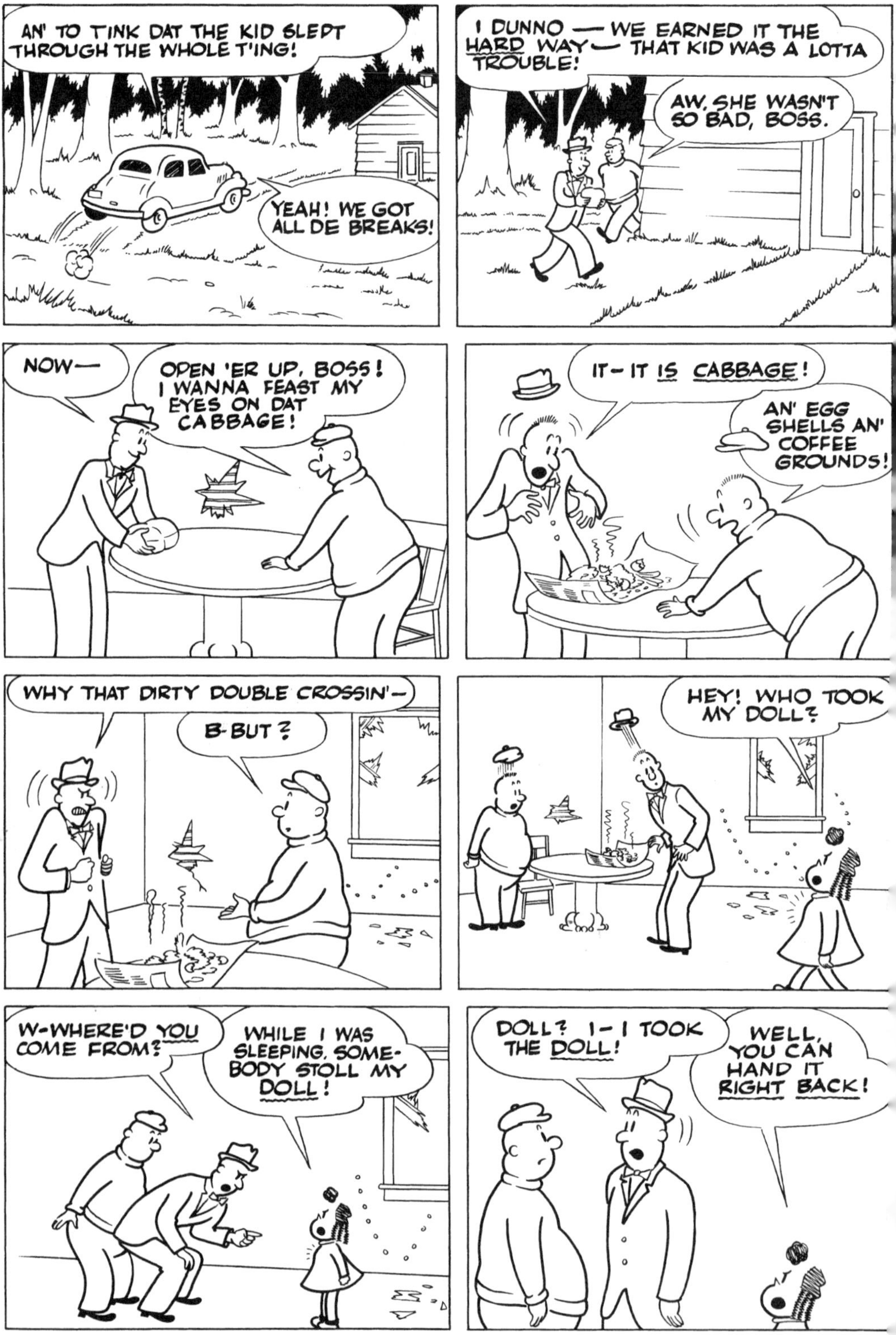
AN' TO TINK DAT THE KID SLEPT THROUGH THE WHOLE T'ING!
YEAH! WE GOT ALL DE BREAKS!
I DUNNO — WE EARNED IT THE HARD WAY — THAT KID WAS A LOTTA TROUBLE!
AW, SHE WASN'T SO BAD, BOSS.
NOW—
OPEN 'ER UP, BOSS! I WANNA FEAST MY EYES ON DAT CABBAGE!
IT-IT IS CABBAGE!
AN' EGG SHELLS AN' COFFEE GROUNDS!
WHY THAT DIRTY DOUBLE CROSSIN'—
B-BUT?
HEY! WHO TOOK MY DOLL?
W-WHERE'D YOU COME FROM?
WHILE I WAS SLEEPING, SOMEBODY STOLL MY DOLL!
DOLL? I-I TOOK THE DOLL!
WELL, YOU CAN HAND IT RIGHT BACK!

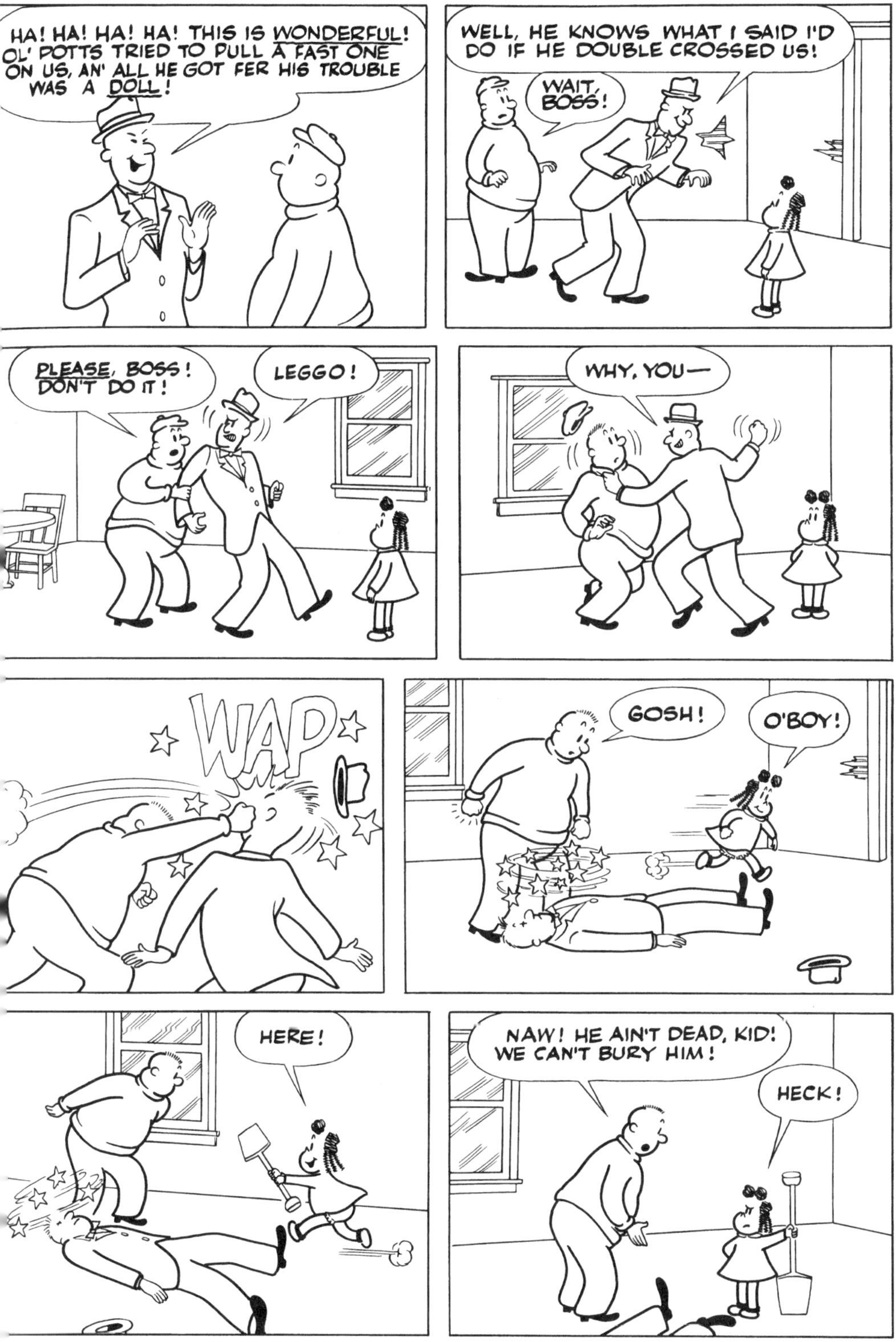
HA! HA! HA! HA! THIS IS WONDERFUL! OL' POTTS TRIED TO PULL A FAST ONE ON US, AN' ALL HE GOT FER HIS TROUBLE WAS A DOLL!
WELL, HE KNOWS WHAT I SAID I'D DO IF HE DOUBLE CROSSED US!
WAIT, BOSS!
PLEASE, BOSS! DON'T DO IT!
LEGGO!
WHY, YOU—
WAP
GOSH!
O'BOY!
HERE!
NAW! HE AIN'T DEAD, KID! WE CAN'T BURY HIM!
HECK!

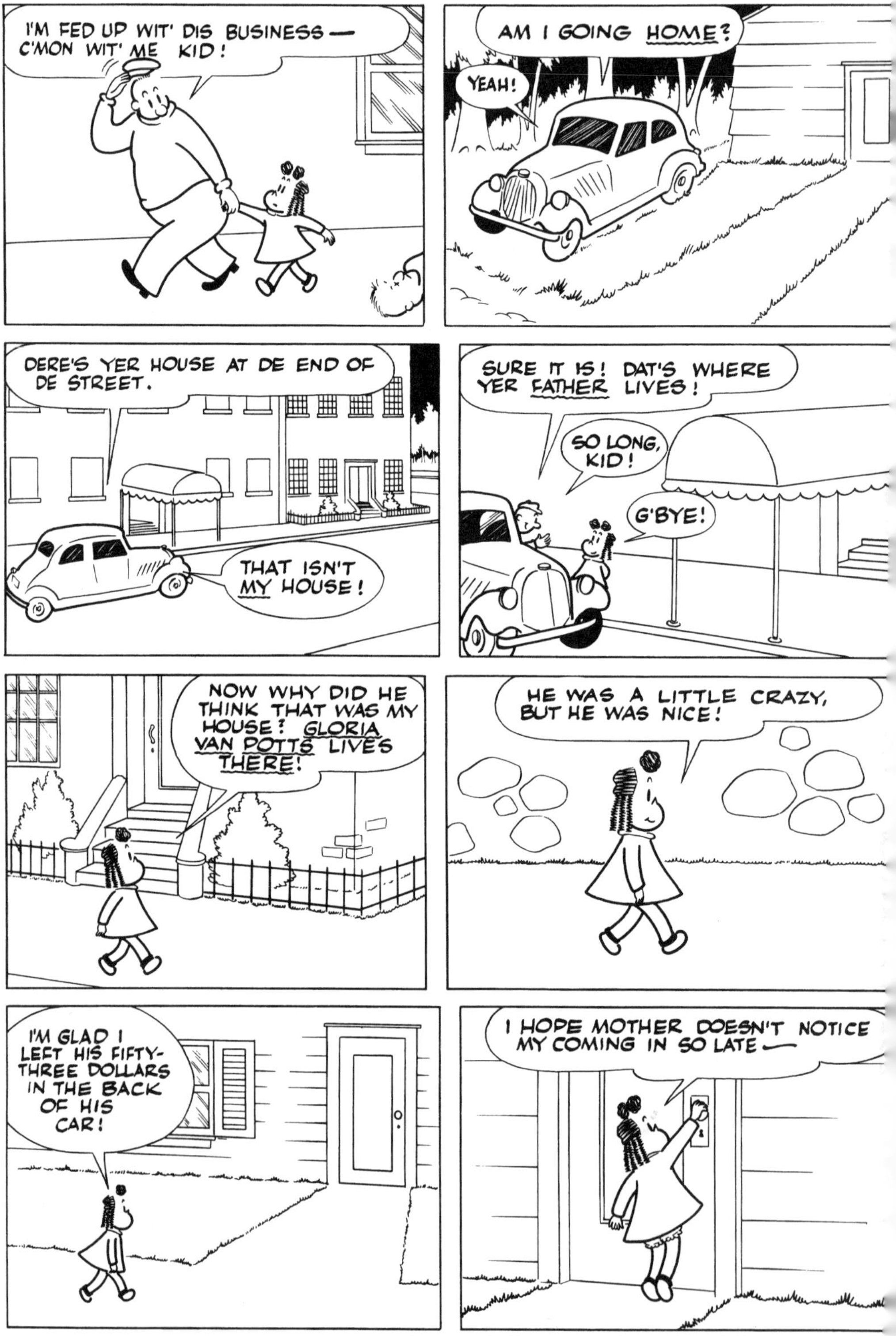
I'M FED UP WIT' DIS BUSINESS— C'MON WIT' ME KID!
AM I GOING HOME?
YEAH!
DERE'S YER HOUSE AT DE END OF DE STREET.
THAT ISN'T MY HOUSE!
SURE IT IS! DAT'S WHERE YER FATHER LIVES!
SO LONG, KID!
G'BYE!
NOW WHY DID HE THINK THAT WAS MY HOUSE? GLORIA VAN POTTS LIVES THERE!
HE WAS A LITTLE CRAZY, BUT HE WAS NICE!
I'M GLAD I LEFT HIS FIFTY-THREE DOLLARS IN THE BACK OF HIS CAR!
I HOPE MOTHER DOESN'T NOTICE MY COMING IN SO LATE—

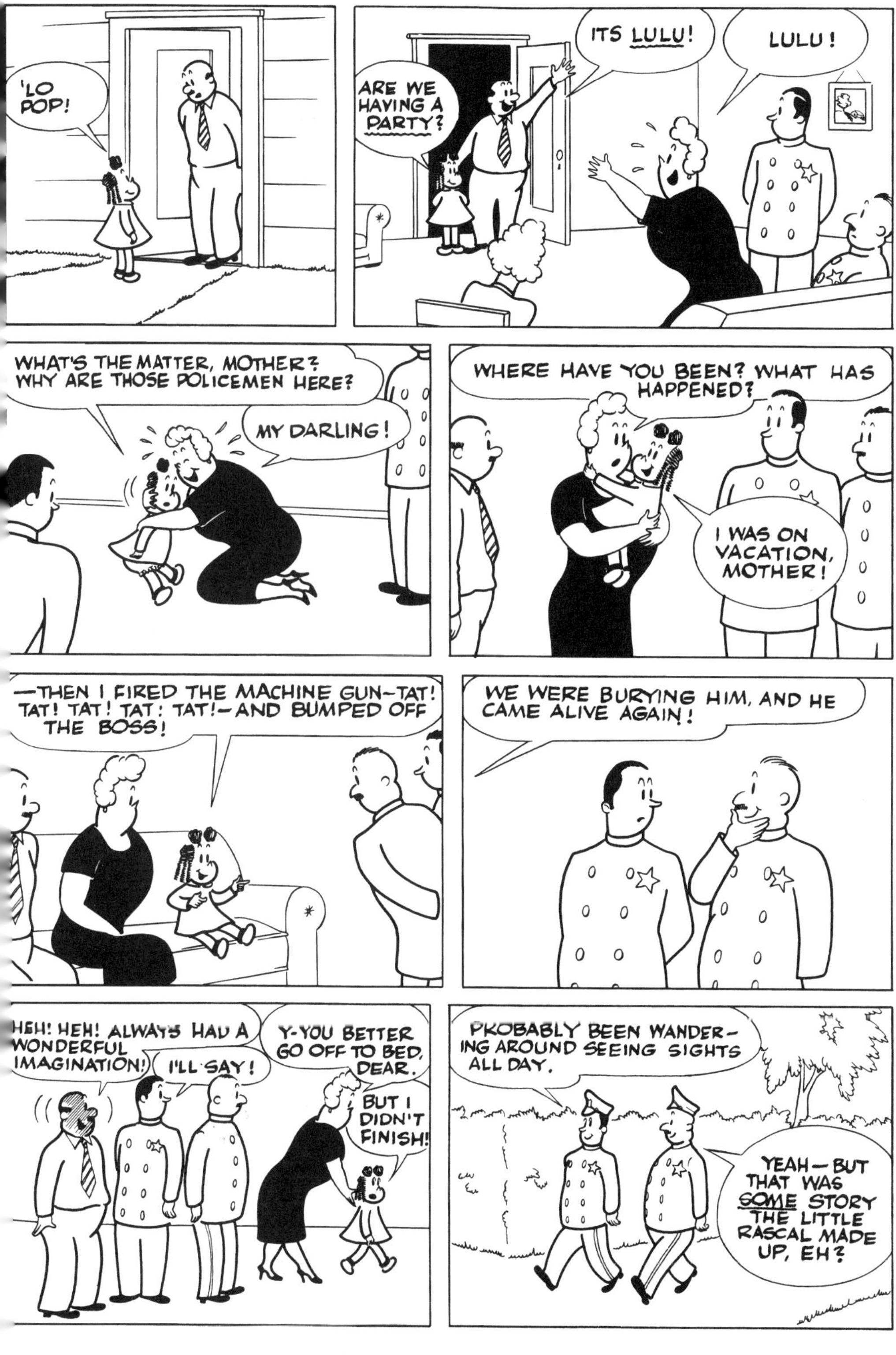

'LO POP!
ARE WE HAVING A PARTY?
ITS LULU!
LULU!
WHAT'S THE MATTER, MOTHER? WHY ARE THOSE POLICEMEN HERE?
MY DARLING!
WHERE HAVE YOU BEEN? WHAT HAS HAPPENED?
I WAS ON VACATION, MOTHER!
—THEN I FIRED THE MACHINE GUN—TAT! TAT! TAT! TAT: TAT!—AND BUMPED OFF THE BOSS!
WE WERE BURYING HIM, AND HE CAME ALIVE AGAIN!
HEH! HEH! ALWAYS HAD A WONDERFUL IMAGINATION!
I'LL SAY!
Y-YOU BETTER GO OFF TO BED, DEAR.
BUT I DIDN'T FINISH!
PROBABLY BEEN WANDERING AROUND SEEING SIGHTS ALL DAY.
YEAH—BUT THAT WAS SOME STORY THE LITTLE RASCAL MADE UP, EH?

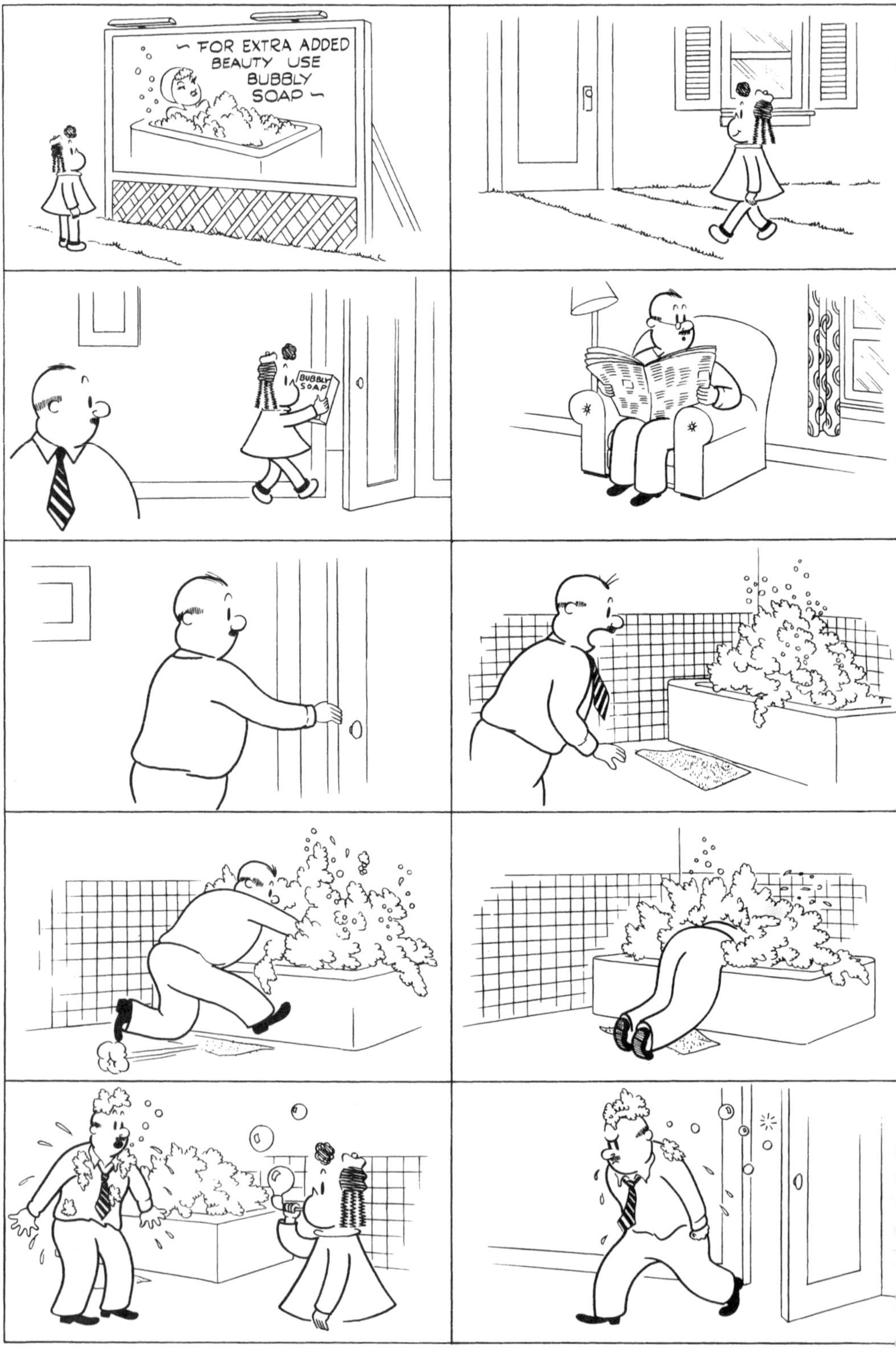

FOR EXTRA ADDED BEAUTY USE BUBBLY SOAP
BUBBLY SOAP

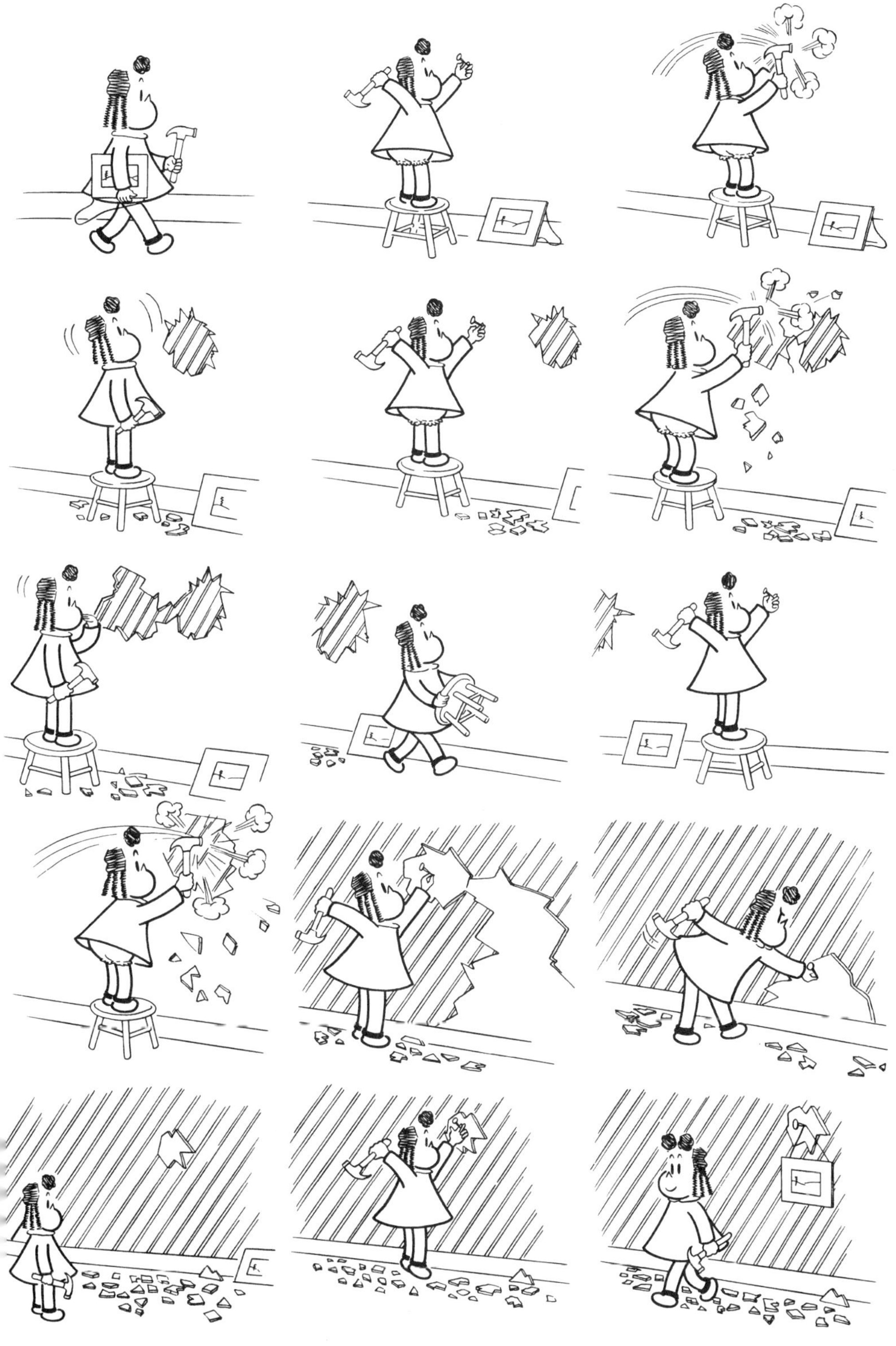

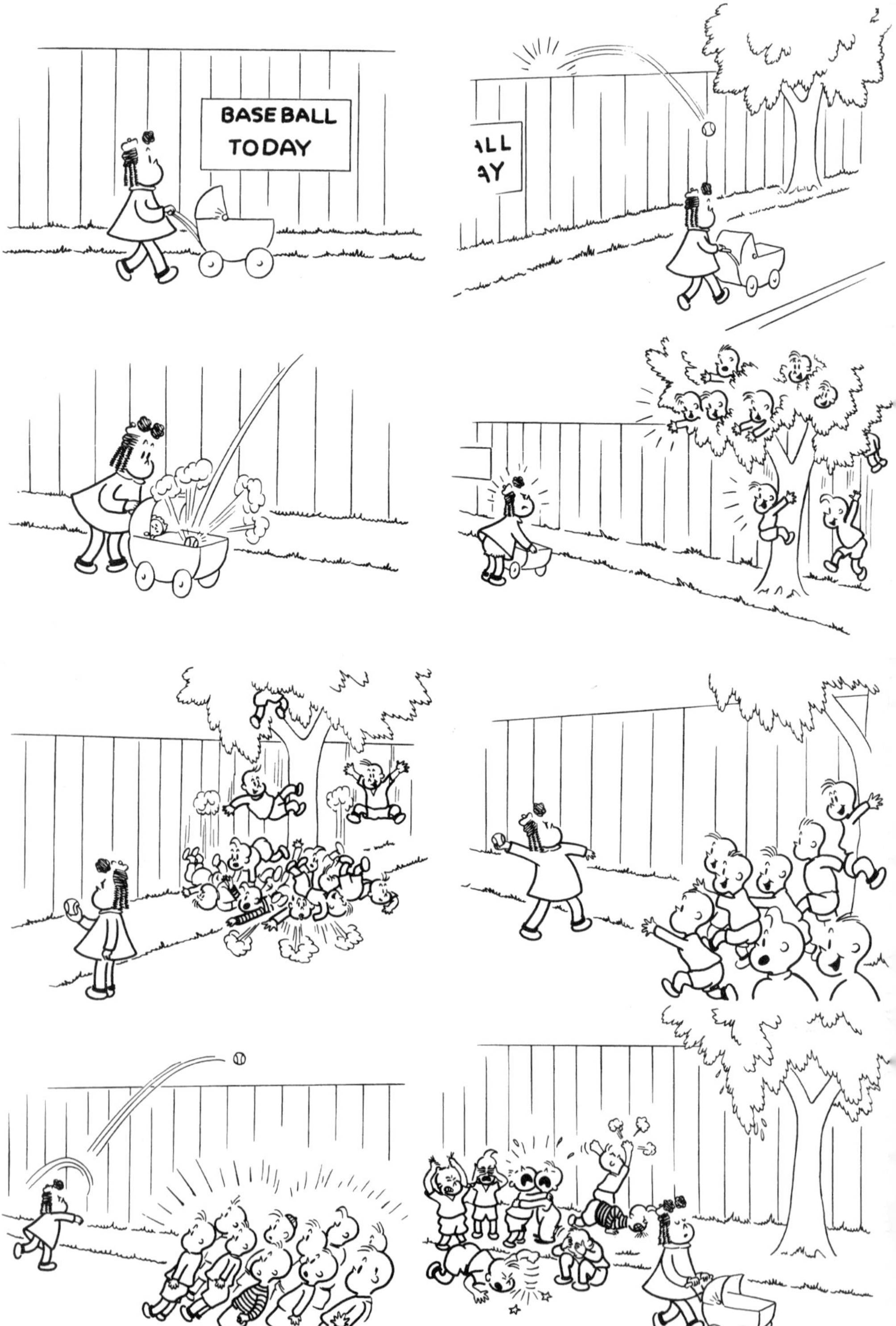

BASE BALL
TODAY

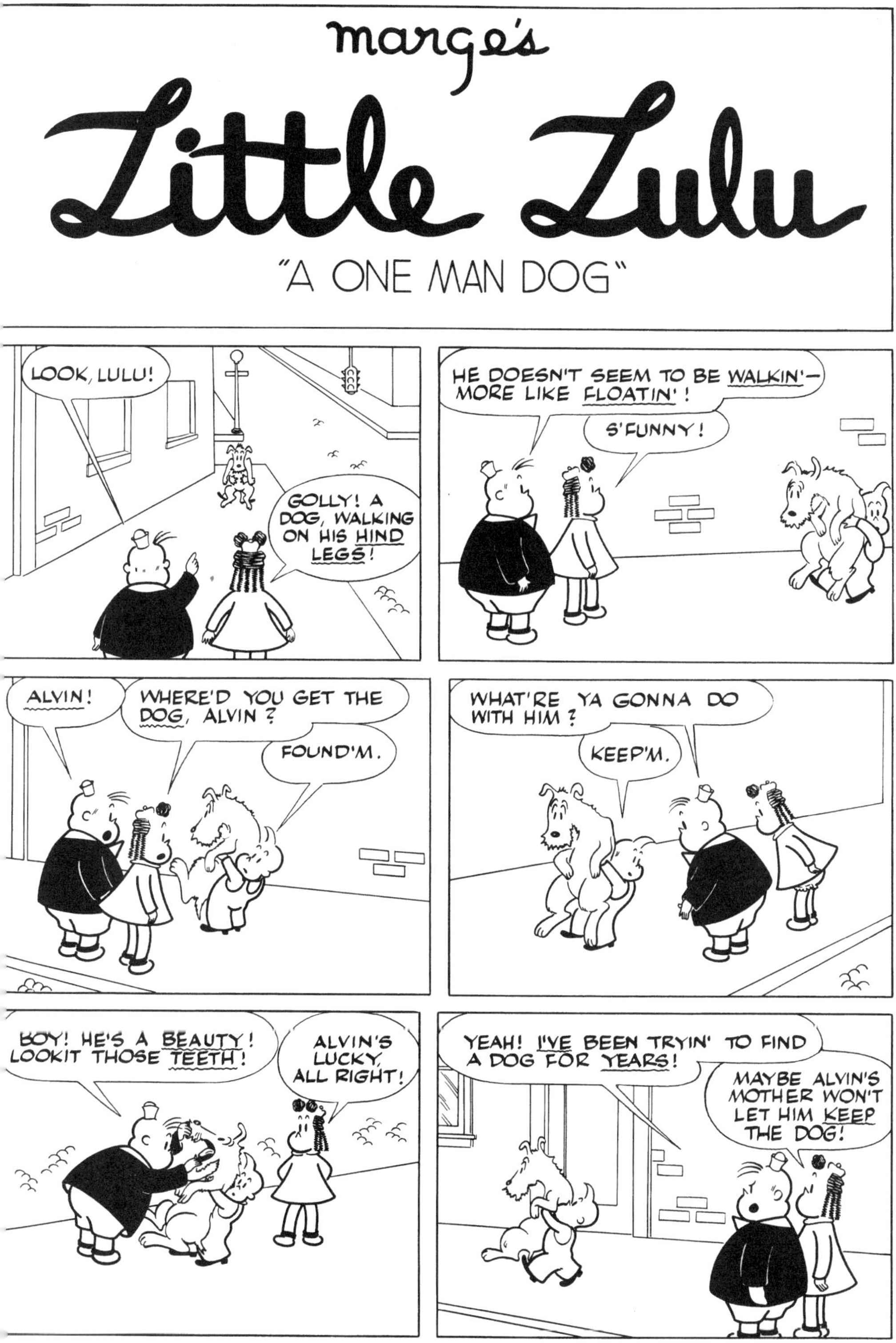
marge's
Little Lulu
"A ONE MAN DOG"
LOOK, LULU!
GOLLY! A DOG, WALKING ON HIS HIND LEGS!
HE DOESN'T SEEM TO BE WALKIN'— MORE LIKE FLOATIN'!
S'FUNNY!
ALVIN!
WHERE'D YOU GET THE DOG, ALVIN?
FOUND'M.
WHAT'RE YA GONNA DO WITH HIM?
KEEP'M.
BOY! HE'S A BEAUTY! LOOKIT THOSE TEETH!
ALVIN'S LUCKY, ALL RIGHT!
YEAH! I'VE BEEN TRYIN' TO FIND A DOG FOR YEARS!
MAYBE ALVIN'S MOTHER WON'T LET HIM KEEP THE DOG!

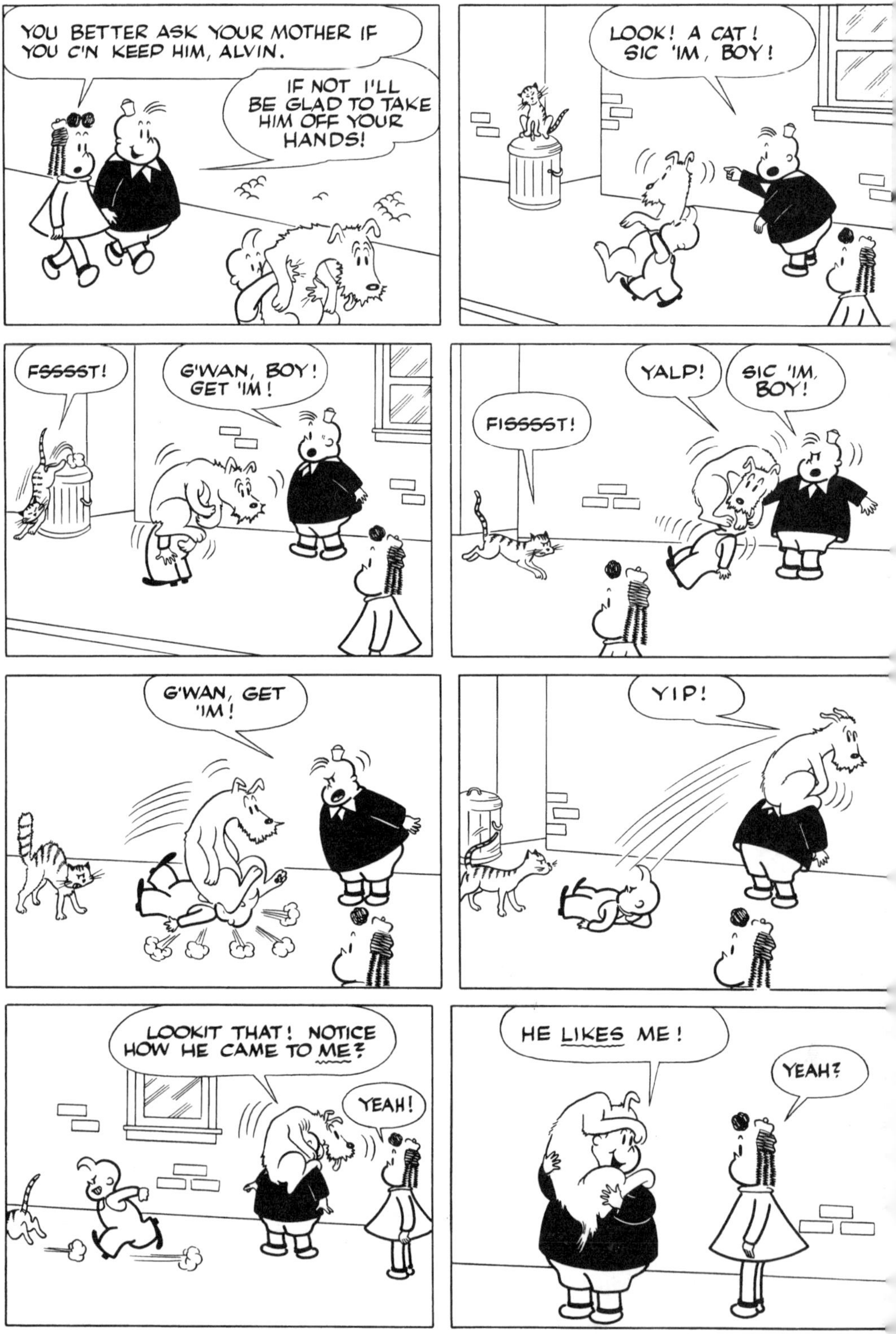
YOU BETTER ASK YOUR MOTHER IF YOU C'N KEEP HIM, ALVIN.
IF NOT I'LL BE GLAD TO TAKE HIM OFF YOUR HANDS!
LOOK! A CAT! SIC 'IM, BOY!
FSSSST!
G'WAN, BOY! GET 'IM!
FISSSST!
YALP!
SIC 'IM, BOY!
G'WAN, GET 'IM!
YIP!
LOOKIT THAT! NOTICE HOW HE CAME TO ME?
YEAH!
HE LIKES ME!
YEAH?

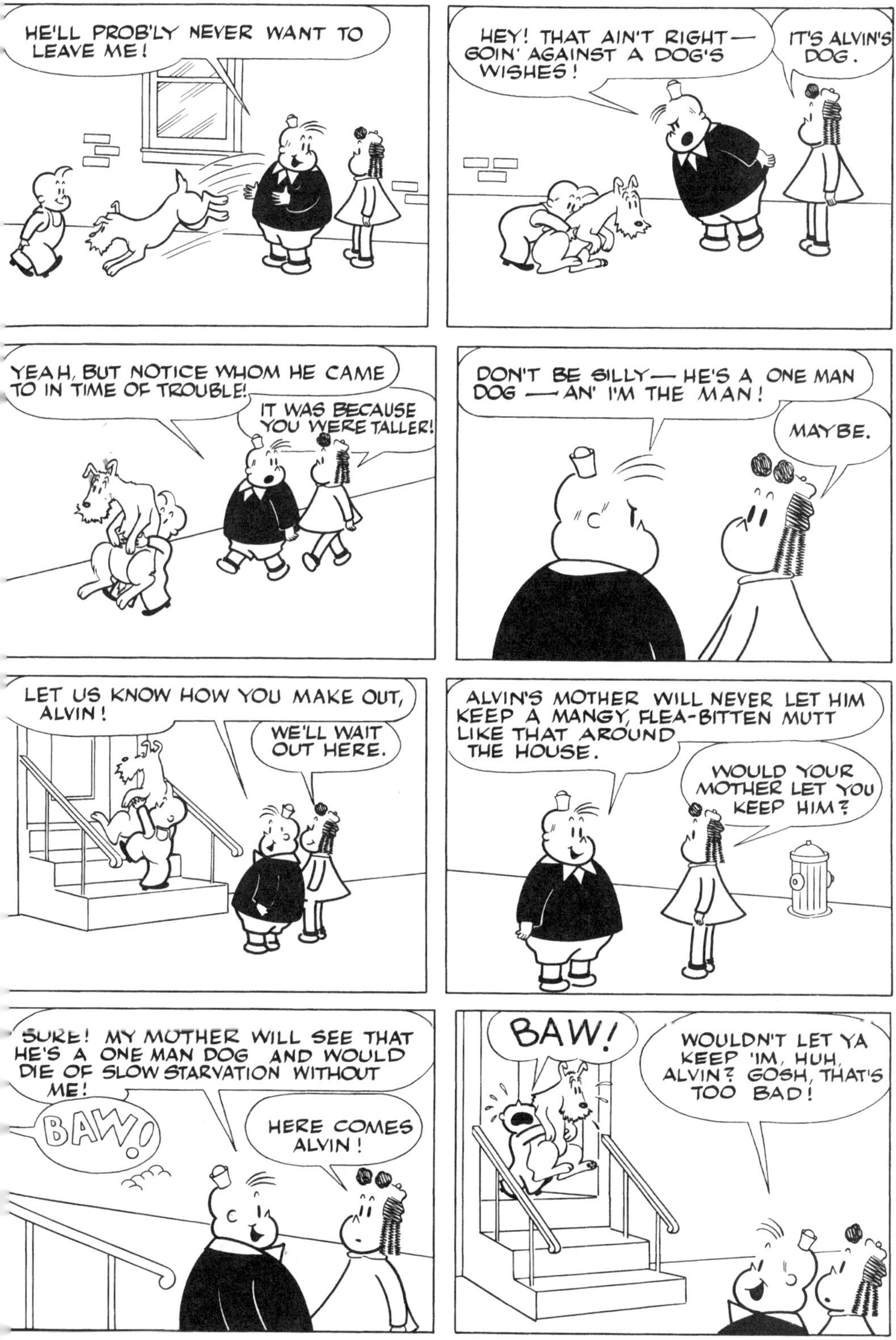
HE'LL PROB'LY NEVER WANT TO LEAVE ME!
HEY! THAT AIN'T RIGHT— GOIN' AGAINST A DOG'S WISHES!
IT'S ALVIN'S DOG.
YEAH, BUT NOTICE WHOM HE CAME TO IN TIME OF TROUBLE!
IT WAS BECAUSE YOU WERE TALLER!
DON'T BE SILLY— HE'S A ONE MAN DOG — AN' I'M THE MAN!
MAYBE.
LET US KNOW HOW YOU MAKE OUT, ALVIN!
WE'LL WAIT OUT HERE.
ALVIN'S MOTHER WILL NEVER LET HIM KEEP A MANGY, FLEA-BITTEN MUTT LIKE THAT AROUND THE HOUSE.
WOULD YOUR MOTHER LET YOU KEEP HIM?
SURE! MY MOTHER WILL SEE THAT HE'S A ONE MAN DOG AND WOULD DIE OF SLOW STARVATION WITHOUT ME!
BAW!
HERE COMES ALVIN!
BAW!
WOULDN'T LET YA KEEP 'IM, HUH, ALVIN? GOSH, THAT'S TOO BAD!

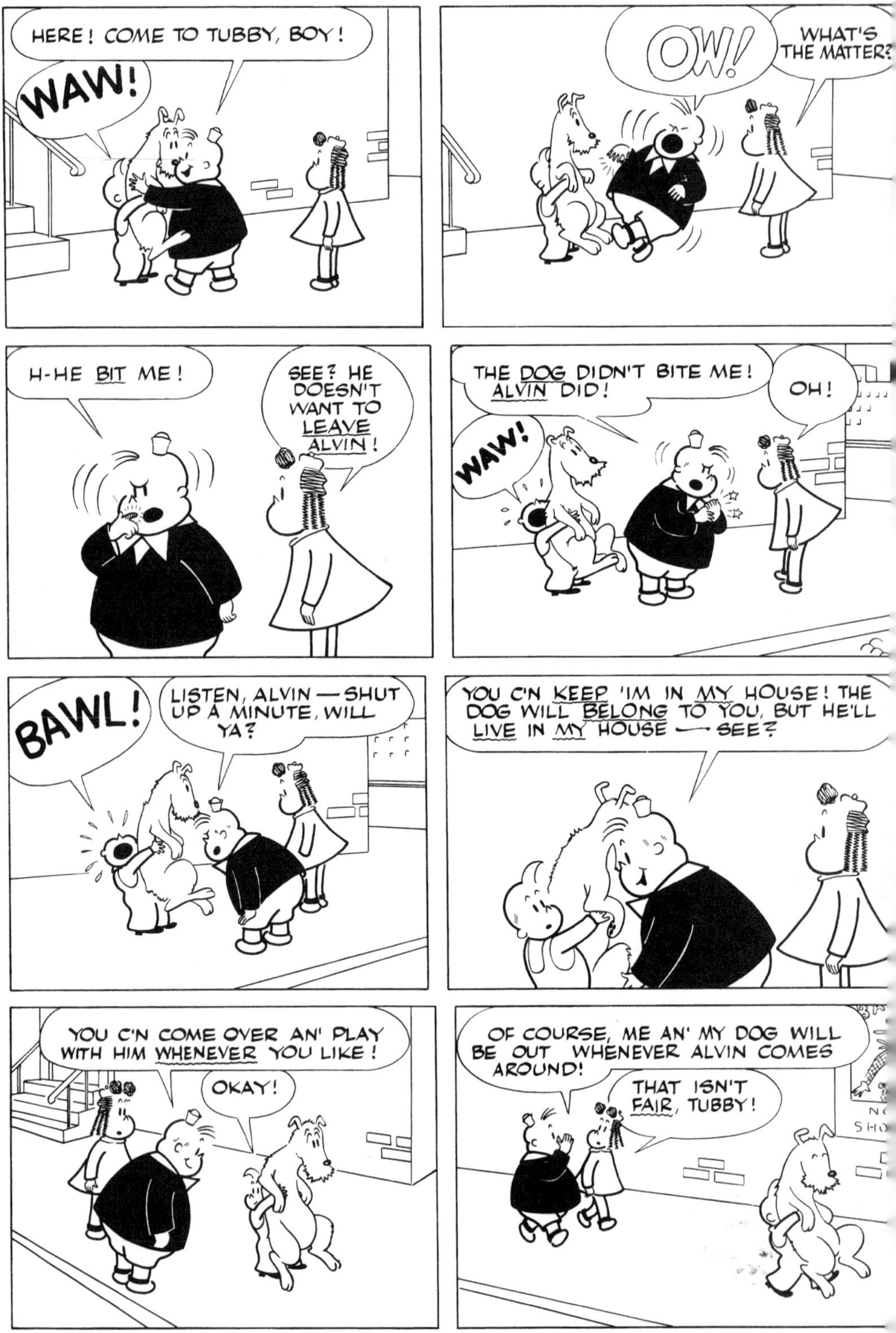
HERE! COME TO TUBBY, BOY!
WAW!
OW!
WHAT'S THE MATTER?
H-HE BIT ME!
SEE? HE DOESN'T WANT TO LEAVE ALVIN!
THE DOG DIDN'T BITE ME! ALVIN DID!
OH!
WAW!
BAWL!
LISTEN, ALVIN — SHUT UP A MINUTE, WILL YA?
YOU C'N KEEP 'IM IN MY HOUSE! THE DOG WILL BELONG TO YOU, BUT HE'LL LIVE IN MY HOUSE — SEE?
YOU C'N COME OVER AN' PLAY WITH HIM WHENEVER YOU LIKE!
OKAY!
OF COURSE, ME AN' MY DOG WILL BE OUT WHENEVER ALVIN COMES AROUND!
THAT ISN'T FAIR, TUBBY!

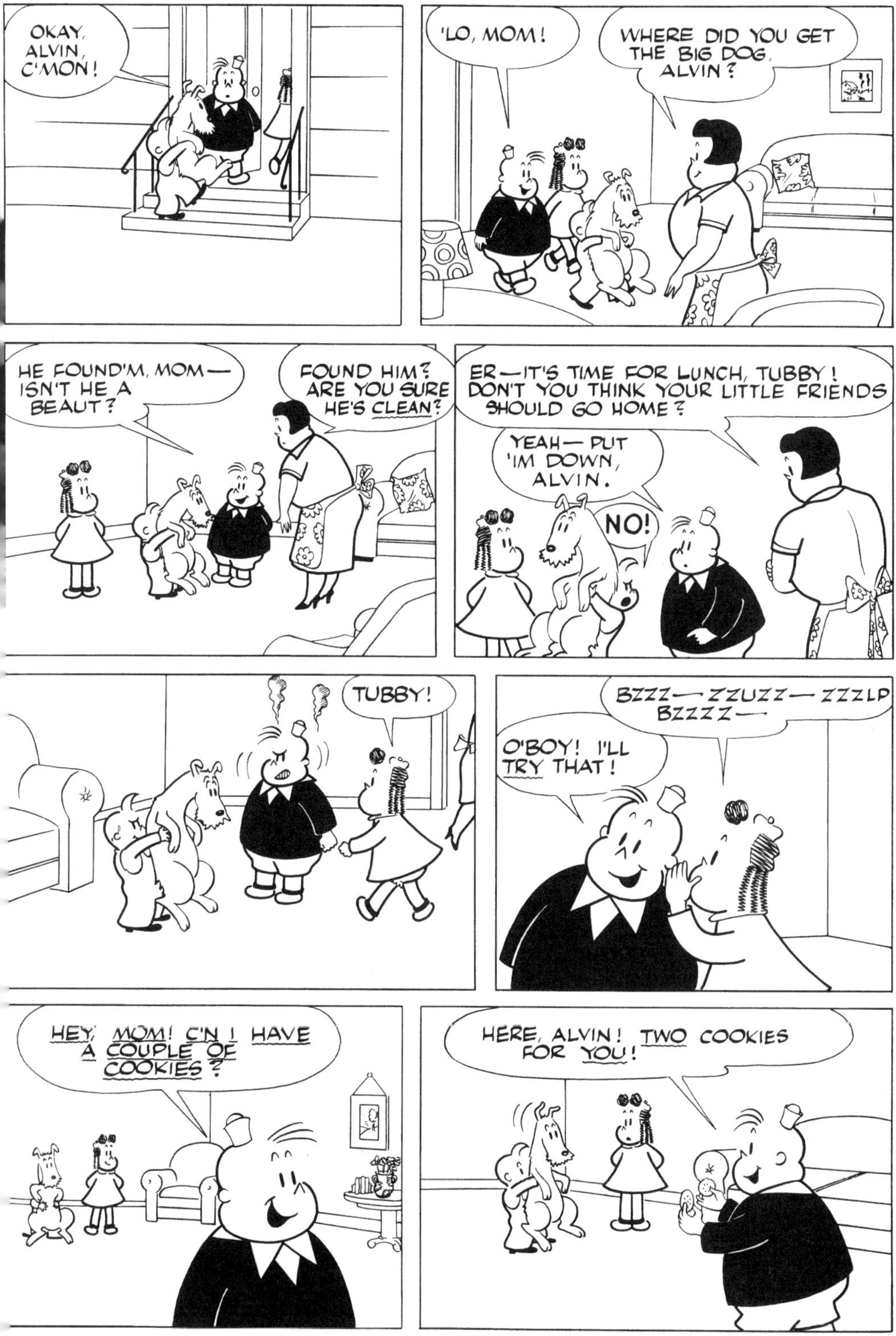
OKAY, ALVIN, C'MON!
'LO, MOM!
WHERE DID YOU GET THE BIG DOG, ALVIN?
HE FOUND'M, MOM— ISN'T HE A BEAUT?
FOUND HIM? ARE YOU SURE HE'S CLEAN?
ER—IT'S TIME FOR LUNCH, TUBBY! DON'T YOU THINK YOUR LITTLE FRIENDS SHOULD GO HOME?
YEAH— PUT 'IM DOWN, ALVIN.
NO!
TUBBY!
BZZZ— ZZUZZ— ZZZLP BZZZZ—
O'BOY! I'LL TRY THAT!
HEY, MOM! C'N I HAVE A COUPLE OF COOKIES?
HERE, ALVIN! TWO COOKIES FOR YOU!

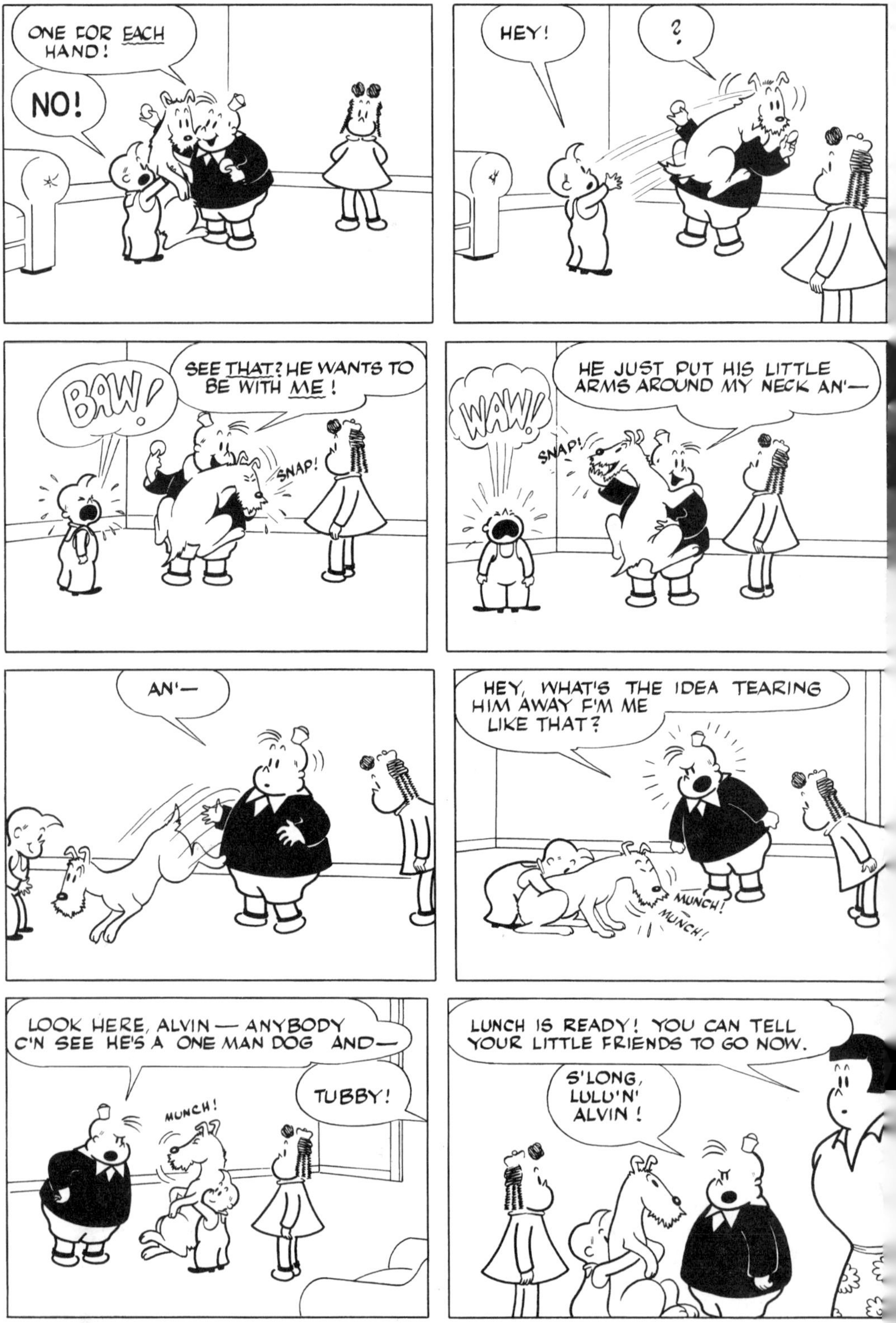
ONE FOR EACH HAND!
NO!
HEY!
?
BAW!
SEE THAT? HE WANTS TO BE WITH ME!
SNAP!
WAW!
SNAP!
HE JUST PUT HIS LITTLE ARMS AROUND MY NECK AN'—
AN'—
HEY, WHAT'S THE IDEA TEARING HIM AWAY F'M ME LIKE THAT?
MUNCH!
MUNCH!
LOOK HERE, ALVIN — ANYBODY C'N SEE HE'S A ONE MAN DOG AND—
TUBBY!
MUNCH!
LUNCH IS READY! YOU CAN TELL YOUR LITTLE FRIENDS TO GO NOW.
S'LONG, LULU'N' ALVIN!

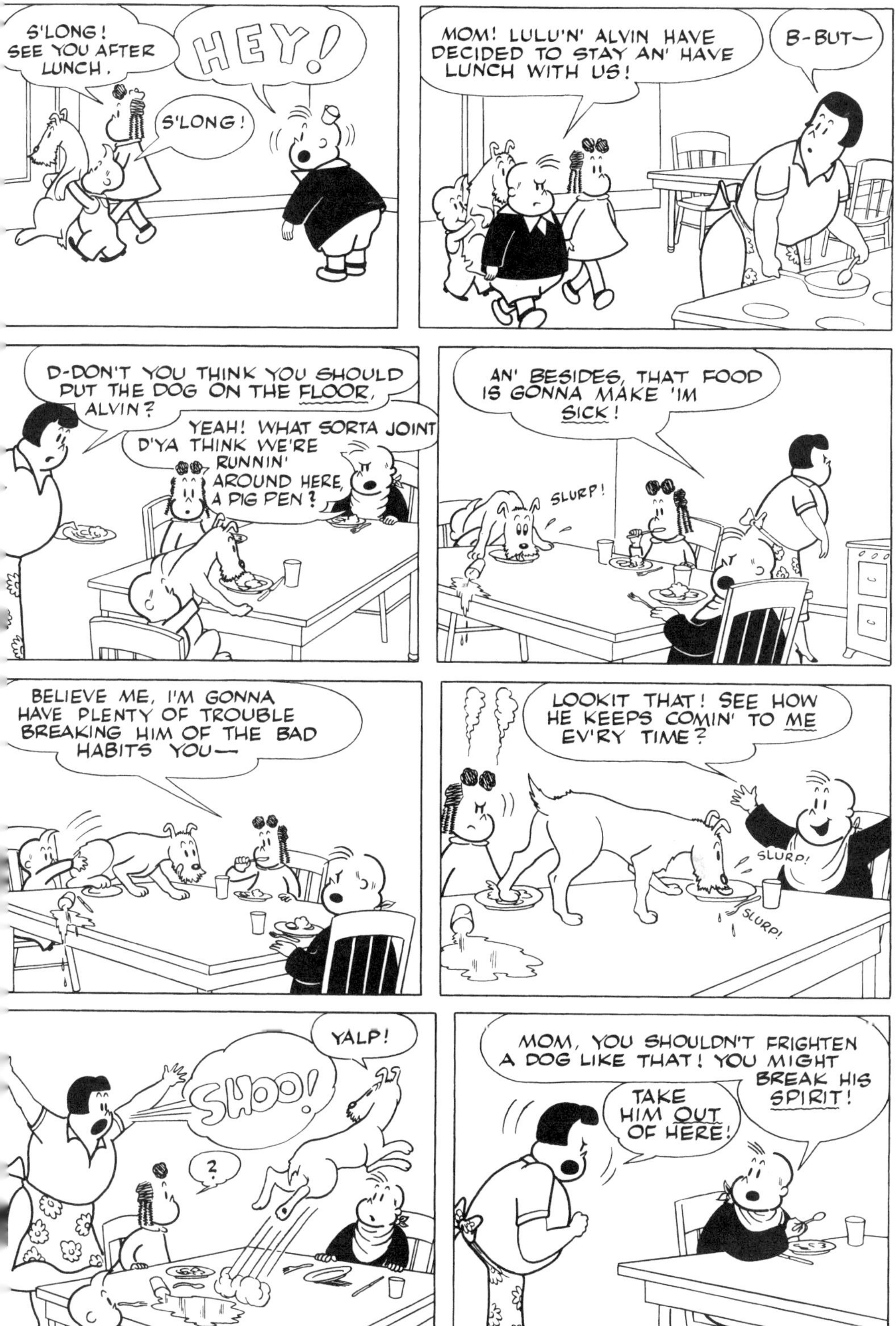
S'LONG! SEE YOU AFTER LUNCH.
HEY!
S'LONG!
MOM! LULU'N' ALVIN HAVE DECIDED TO STAY AN' HAVE LUNCH WITH US!
B-BUT—
D-DON'T YOU THINK YOU SHOULD PUT THE DOG ON THE FLOOR, ALVIN?
YEAH! WHAT SORTA JOINT D'YA THINK WE'RE RUNNIN' AROUND HERE, A PIG PEN?
AN' BESIDES, THAT FOOD IS GONNA MAKE 'IM SICK!
SLURP!
BELIEVE ME, I'M GONNA HAVE PLENTY OF TROUBLE BREAKING HIM OF THE BAD HABITS YOU—
LOOKIT THAT! SEE HOW HE KEEPS COMIN' TO ME EV'RY TIME?
SLURP!
SLURP!
YALP!
SHOO!
?
MOM, YOU SHOULDN'T FRIGHTEN A DOG LIKE THAT! YOU MIGHT BREAK HIS SPIRIT!
TAKE HIM OUT OF HERE!

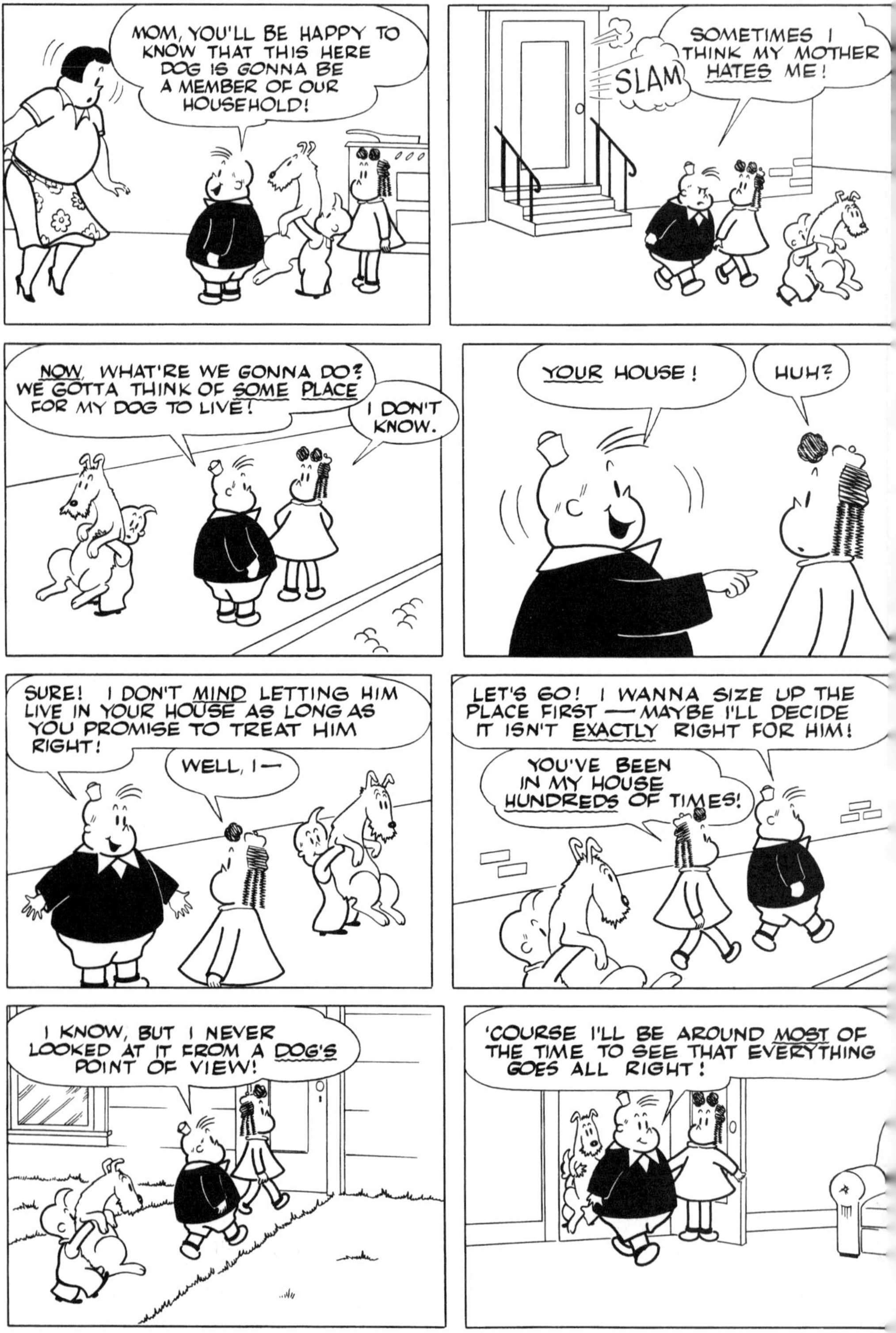

MOM, YOU'LL BE HAPPY TO KNOW THAT THIS HERE DOG IS GONNA BE A MEMBER OF OUR HOUSEHOLD!
SLAM
SOMETIMES I THINK MY MOTHER HATES ME!
NOW, WHAT'RE WE GONNA DO? WE GOTTA THINK OF SOME PLACE FOR MY DOG TO LIVE!
I DON'T KNOW.
YOUR HOUSE!
HUH?
SURE! I DON'T MIND LETTING HIM LIVE IN YOUR HOUSE AS LONG AS YOU PROMISE TO TREAT HIM RIGHT!
WELL, I—
LET'S GO! I WANNA SIZE UP THE PLACE FIRST — MAYBE I'LL DECIDE IT ISN'T EXACTLY RIGHT FOR HIM!
YOU'VE BEEN IN MY HOUSE HUNDREDS OF TIMES!
I KNOW, BUT I NEVER LOOKED AT IT FROM A DOG'S POINT OF VIEW!
'COURSE I'LL BE AROUND MOST OF THE TIME TO SEE THAT EVERYTHING GOES ALL RIGHT!

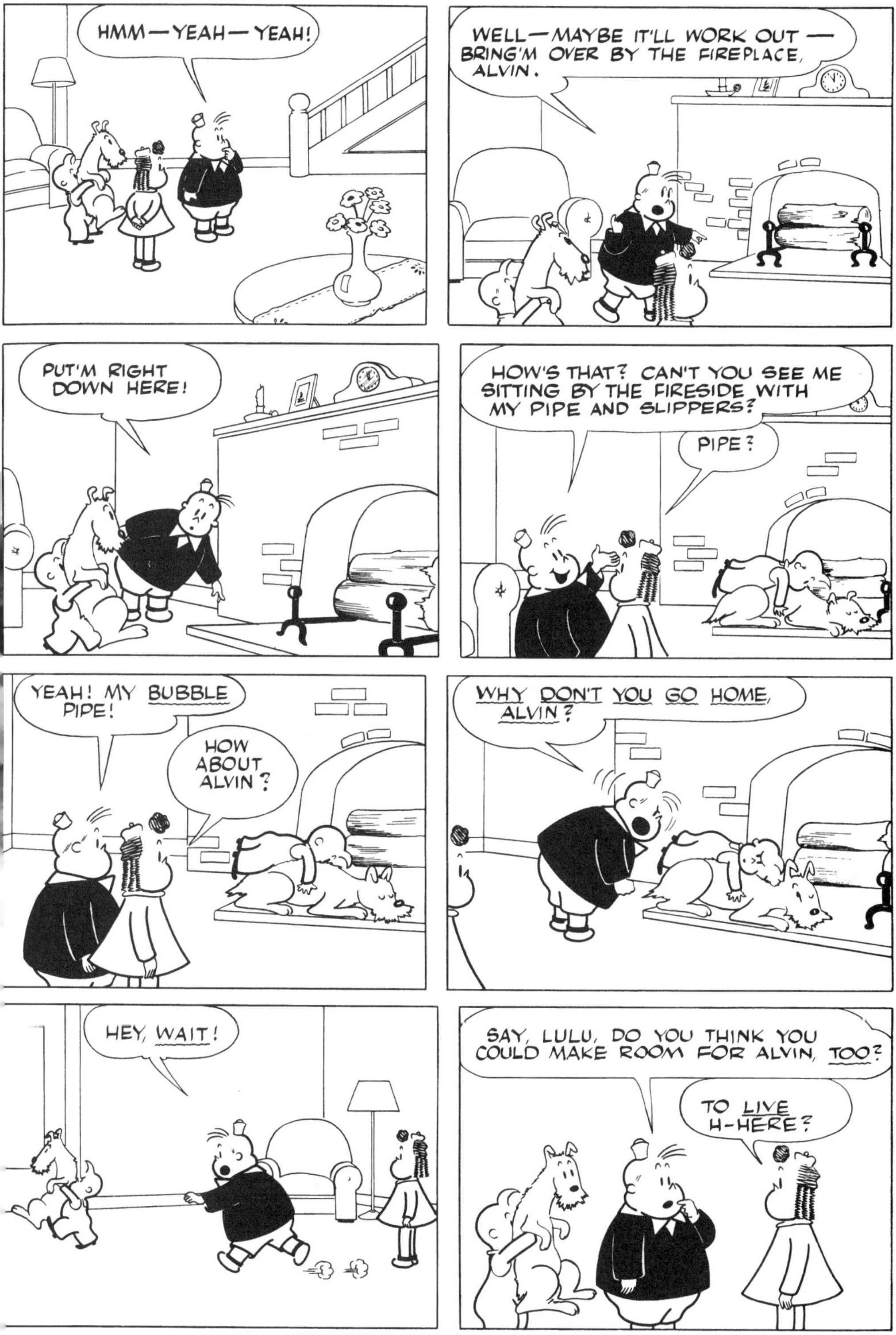
HMM—YEAH—YEAH!
WELL—MAYBE IT'LL WORK OUT—BRING'M OVER BY THE FIREPLACE, ALVIN.
PUT'M RIGHT DOWN HERE!
HOW'S THAT? CAN'T YOU SEE ME SITTING BY THE FIRESIDE WITH MY PIPE AND SLIPPERS?
PIPE?
YEAH! MY BUBBLE PIPE!
HOW ABOUT ALVIN?
WHY DON'T YOU GO HOME, ALVIN?
HEY, WAIT!
SAY, LULU, DO YOU THINK YOU COULD MAKE ROOM FOR ALVIN, TOO?
TO LIVE H-HERE?

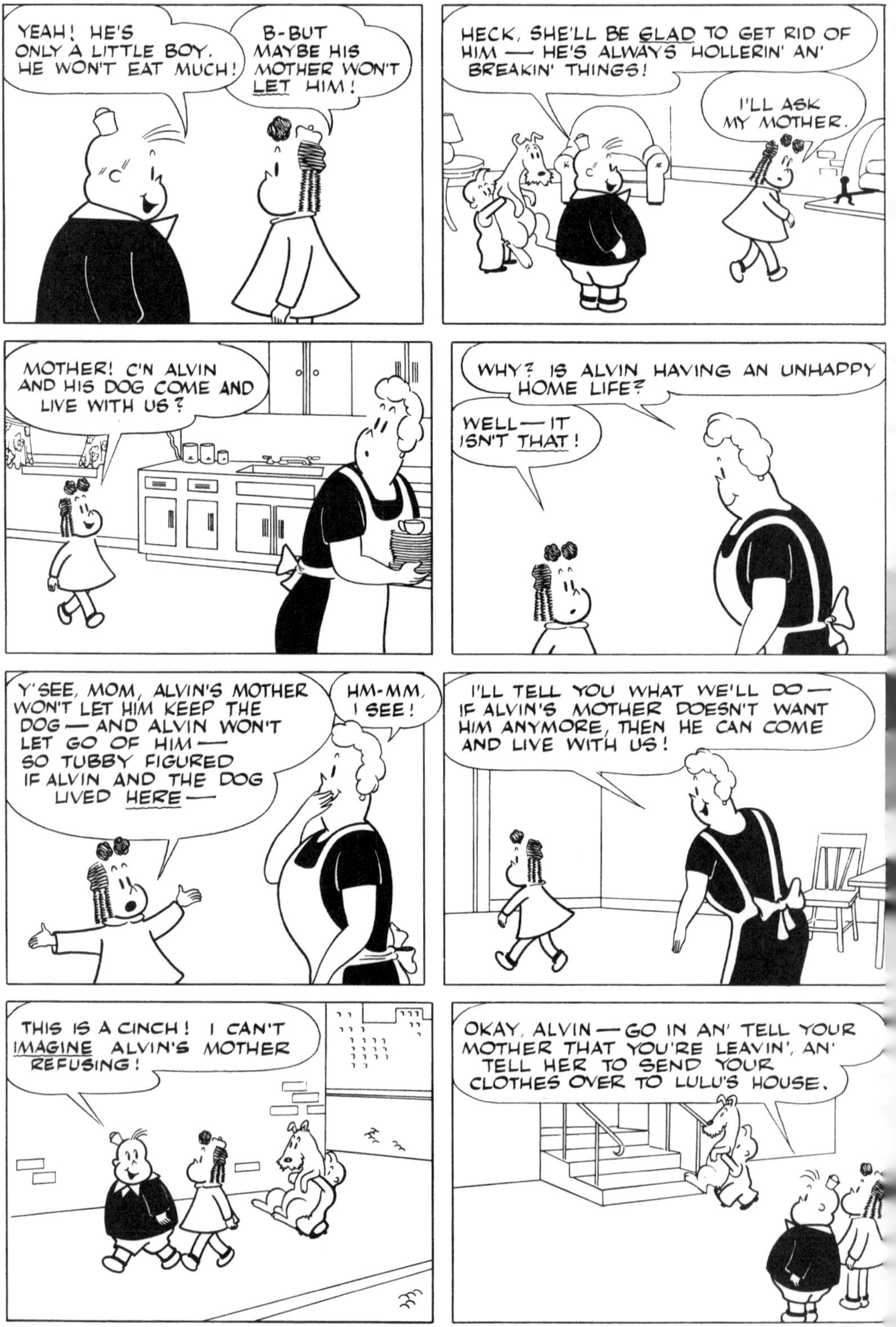
YEAH! HE'S ONLY A LITTLE BOY. HE WON'T EAT MUCH!
B-BUT MAYBE HIS MOTHER WON'T LET HIM!
HECK, SHE'LL BE GLAD TO GET RID OF HIM — HE'S ALWAYS HOLLERIN' AN' BREAKIN' THINGS!
I'LL ASK MY MOTHER.
MOTHER! C'N ALVIN AND HIS DOG COME AND LIVE WITH US?
WHY? IS ALVIN HAVING AN UNHAPPY HOME LIFE?
WELL — IT ISN'T THAT!
Y'SEE, MOM, ALVIN'S MOTHER WON'T LET HIM KEEP THE DOG — AND ALVIN WON'T LET GO OF HIM — SO TUBBY FIGURED IF ALVIN AND THE DOG LIVED HERE —
HM-MM, I SEE!
I'LL TELL YOU WHAT WE'LL DO — IF ALVIN'S MOTHER DOESN'T WANT HIM ANYMORE, THEN HE CAN COME AND LIVE WITH US!
THIS IS A CINCH! I CAN'T IMAGINE ALVIN'S MOTHER REFUSING!
OKAY, ALVIN — GO IN AN' TELL YOUR MOTHER THAT YOU'RE LEAVIN', AN' TELL HER TO SEND YOUR CLOTHES OVER TO LULU'S HOUSE.

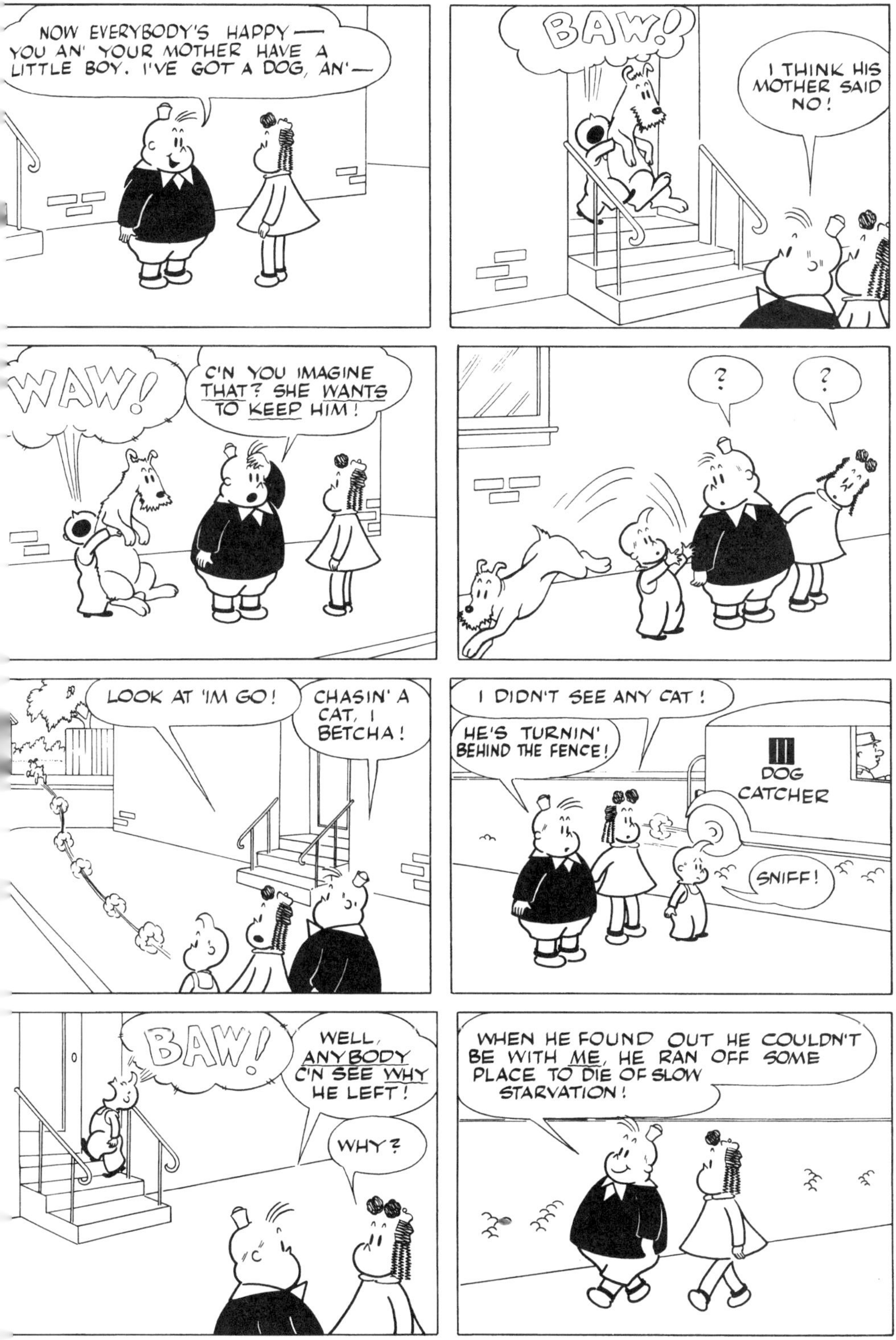
NOW EVERYBODY'S HAPPY— YOU AN' YOUR MOTHER HAVE A LITTLE BOY. I'VE GOT A DOG, AN'—
BAW!
I THINK HIS MOTHER SAID NO!
WAW!
C'N YOU IMAGINE THAT? SHE WANTS TO KEEP HIM!
?
?
LOOK AT 'IM GO!
CHASIN' A CAT, I BETCHA!
I DIDN'T SEE ANY CAT!
HE'S TURNIN' BEHIND THE FENCE!
DOG CATCHER
SNIFF!
BAW!
WELL, ANYBODY C'N SEE WHY HE LEFT!
WHY?
WHEN HE FOUND OUT HE COULDN'T BE WITH ME, HE RAN OFF SOME PLACE TO DIE OF SLOW STARVATION!

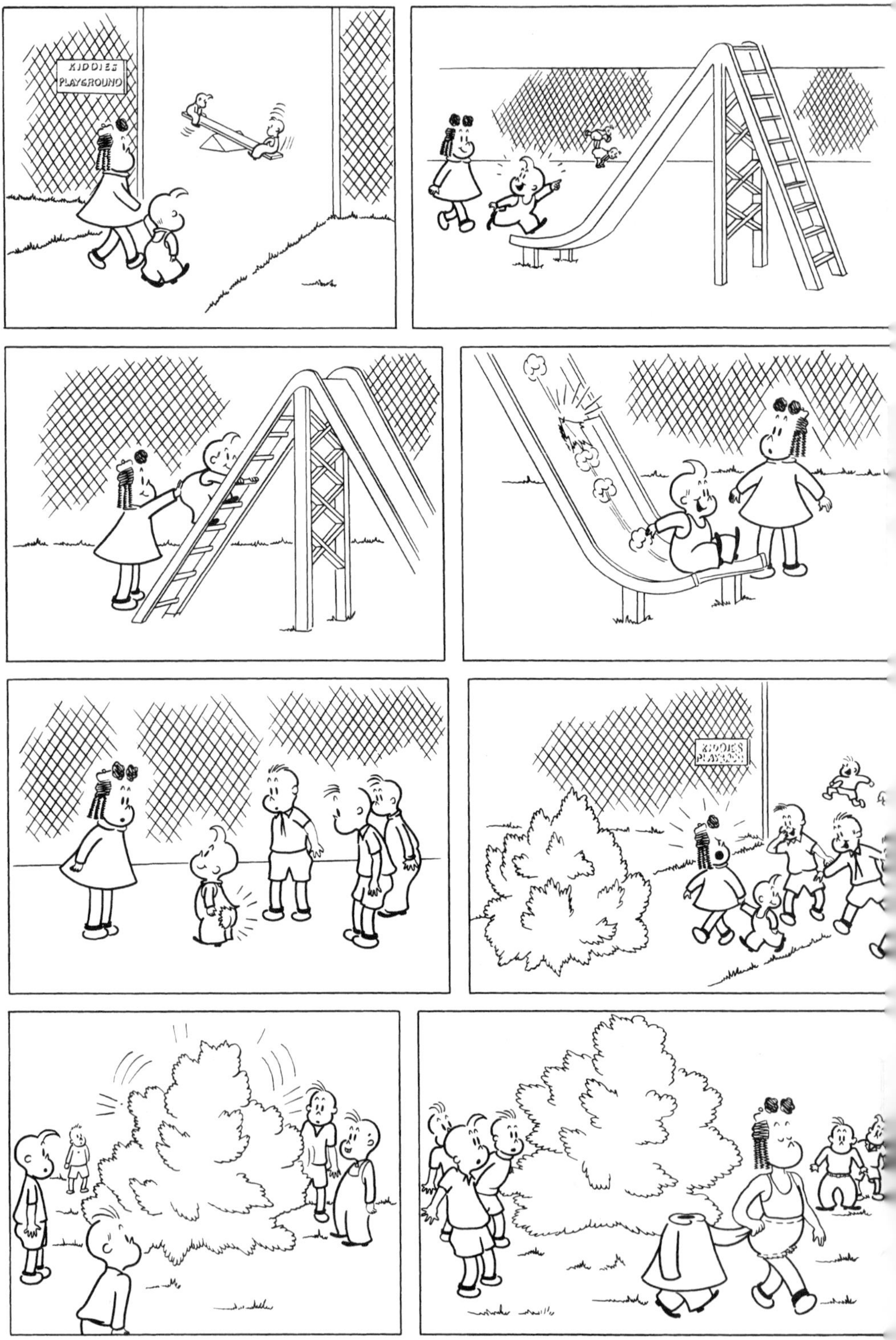
KIDDIES
PLAYGROUND

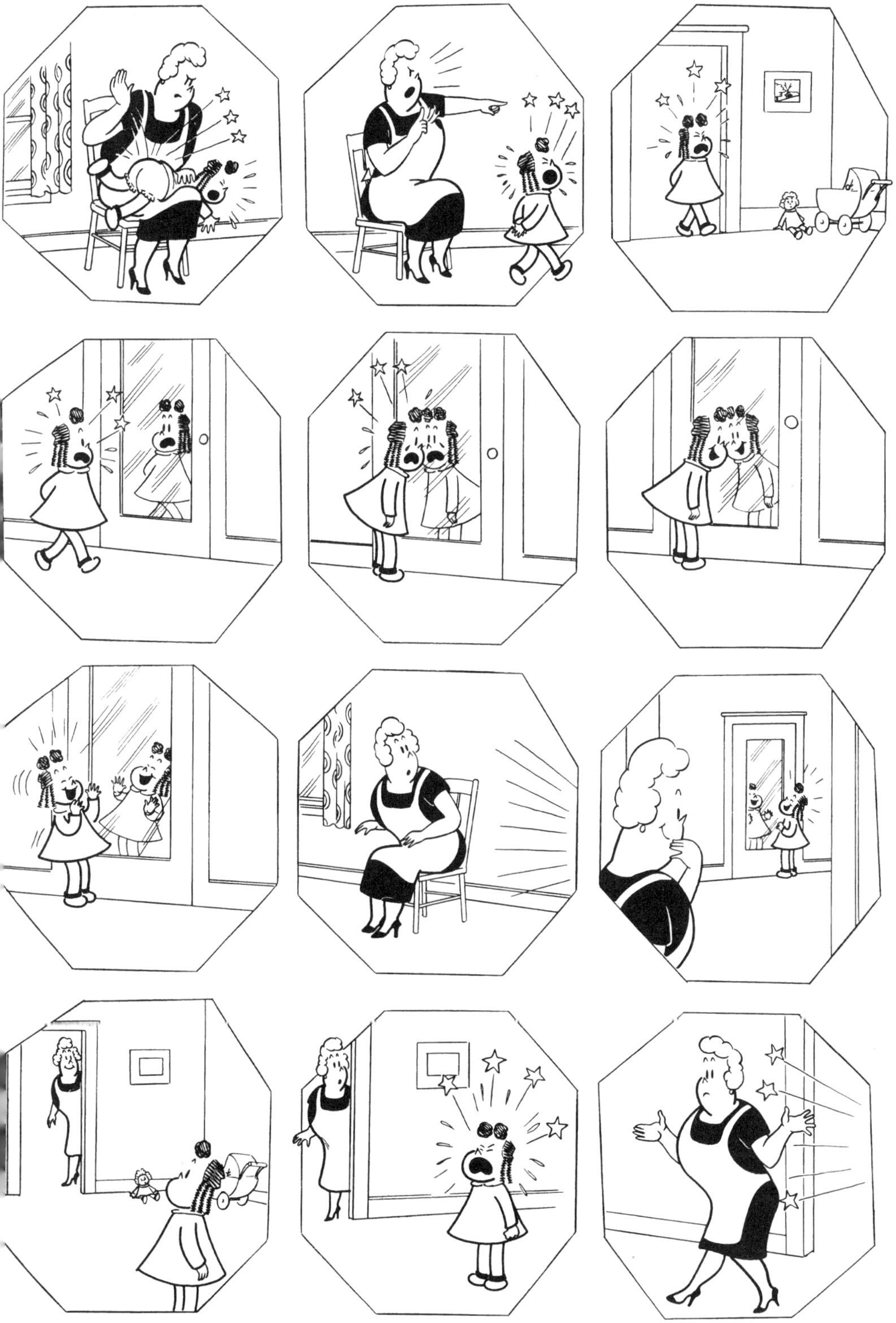

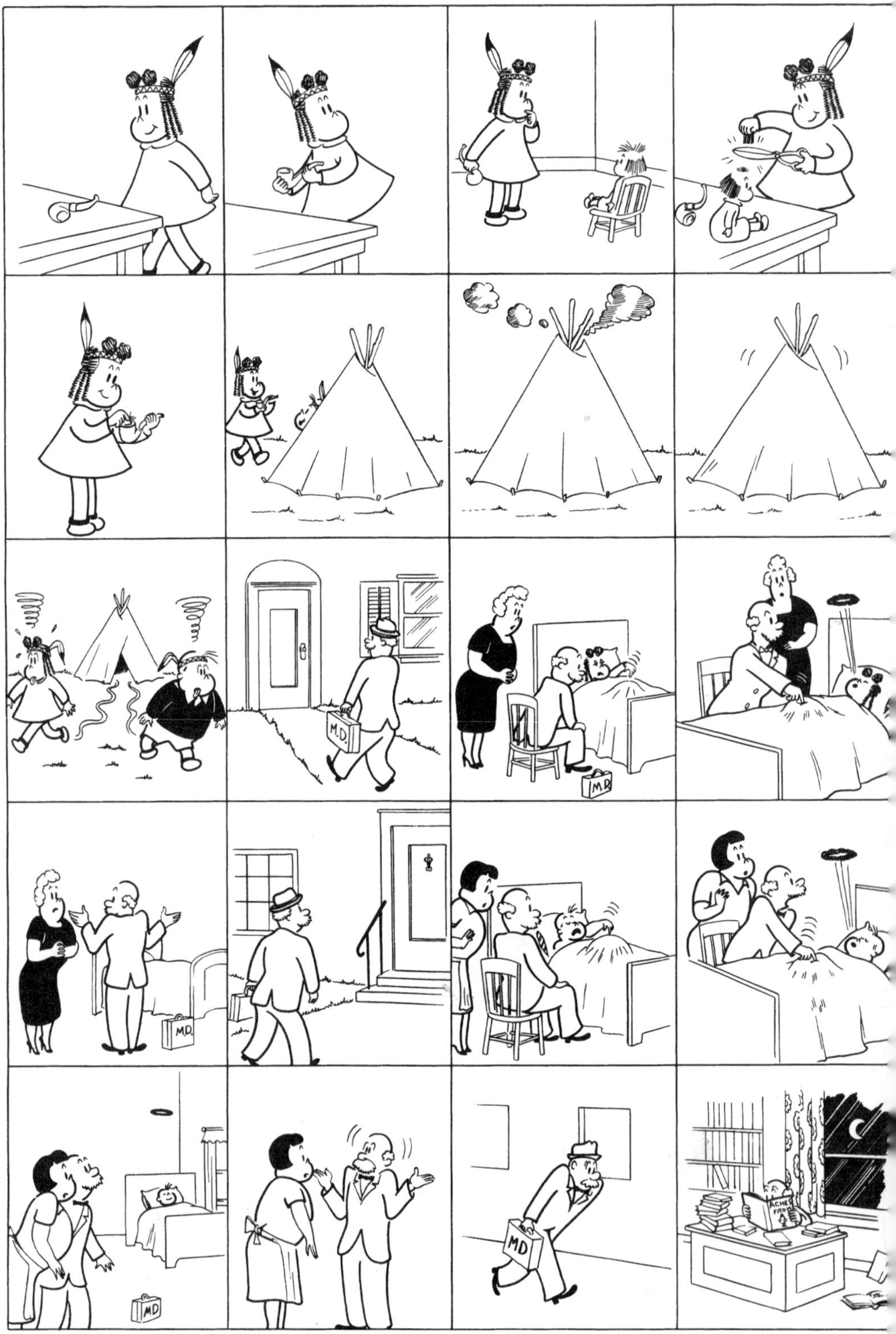
M.D.
M.D.
MD.
MD
MD

marge's

LITTLE LULU

AND THE THREE BEARS

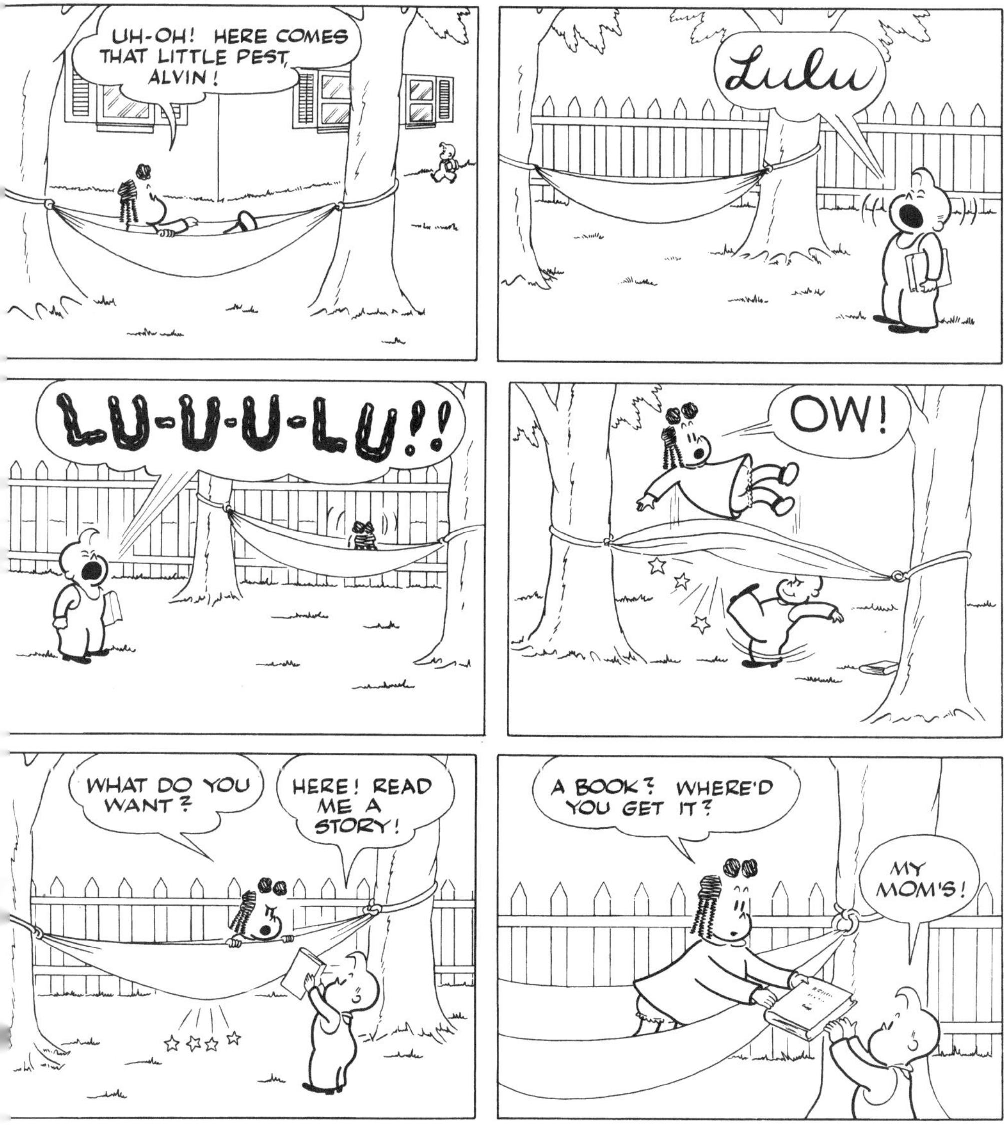

UH-OH! HERE COMES THAT LITTLE PEST, ALVIN!
Lulu
LU-U-U-LU!!
OW!
WHAT DO YOU WANT?
HERE! READ ME A STORY!
A BOOK? WHERE'D YOU GET IT?
MY MOM'S!

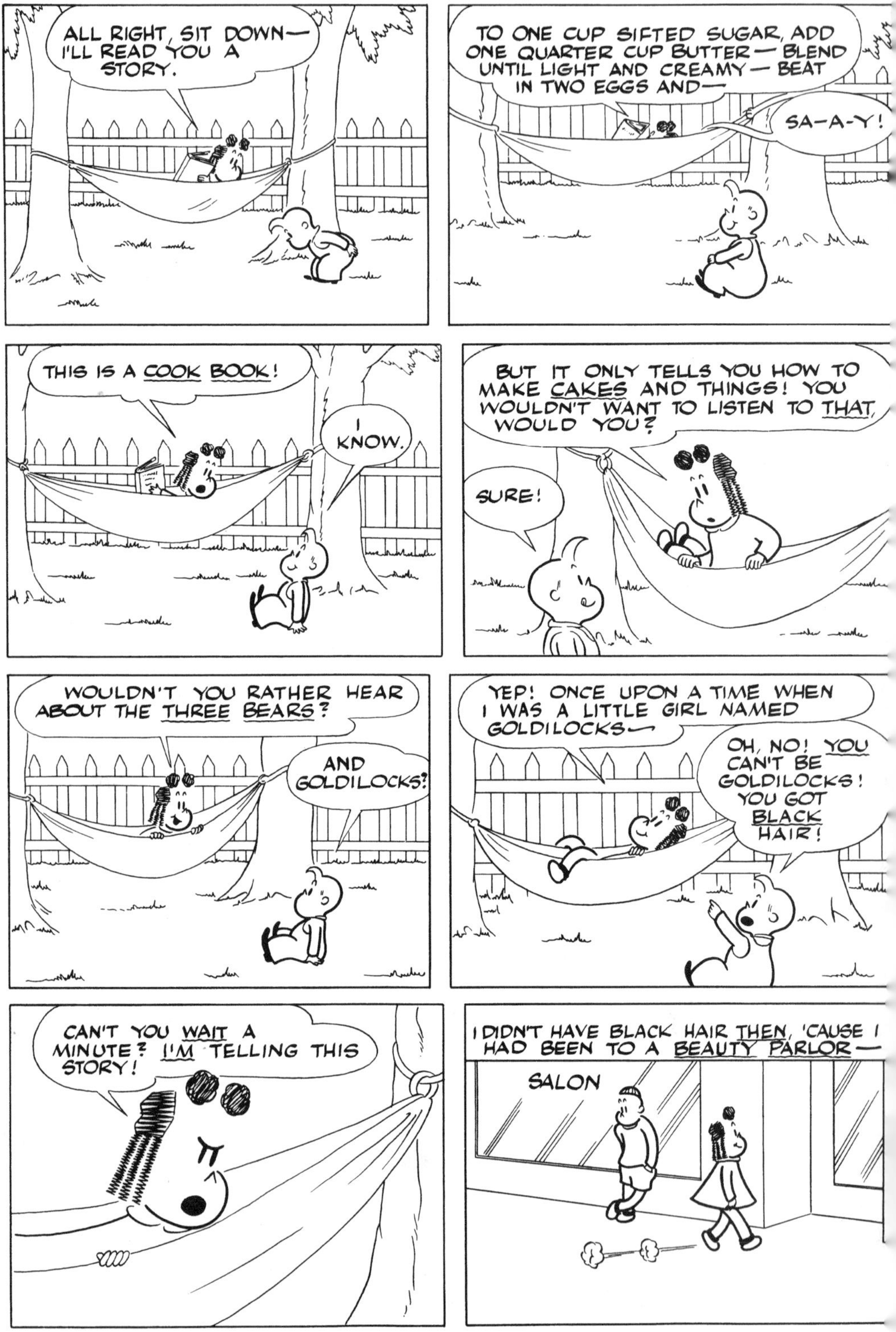

ALL RIGHT, SIT DOWN— I'LL READ YOU A STORY.
TO ONE CUP SIFTED SUGAR, ADD ONE QUARTER CUP BUTTER— BLEND UNTIL LIGHT AND CREAMY— BEAT IN TWO EGGS AND—
SA-A-Y!
THIS IS A COOK BOOK!
I KNOW.
BUT IT ONLY TELLS YOU HOW TO MAKE CAKES AND THINGS! YOU WOULDN'T WANT TO LISTEN TO THAT, WOULD YOU?
SURE!
WOULDN'T YOU RATHER HEAR ABOUT THE THREE BEARS?
AND GOLDILOCKS?
YEP! ONCE UPON A TIME WHEN I WAS A LITTLE GIRL NAMED GOLDILOCKS—
OH, NO! YOU CAN'T BE GOLDILOCKS! YOU GOT BLACK HAIR!
CAN'T YOU WAIT A MINUTE? I'M TELLING THIS STORY!
I DIDN'T HAVE BLACK HAIR THEN, 'CAUSE I HAD BEEN TO A BEAUTY PARLOR—
SALON

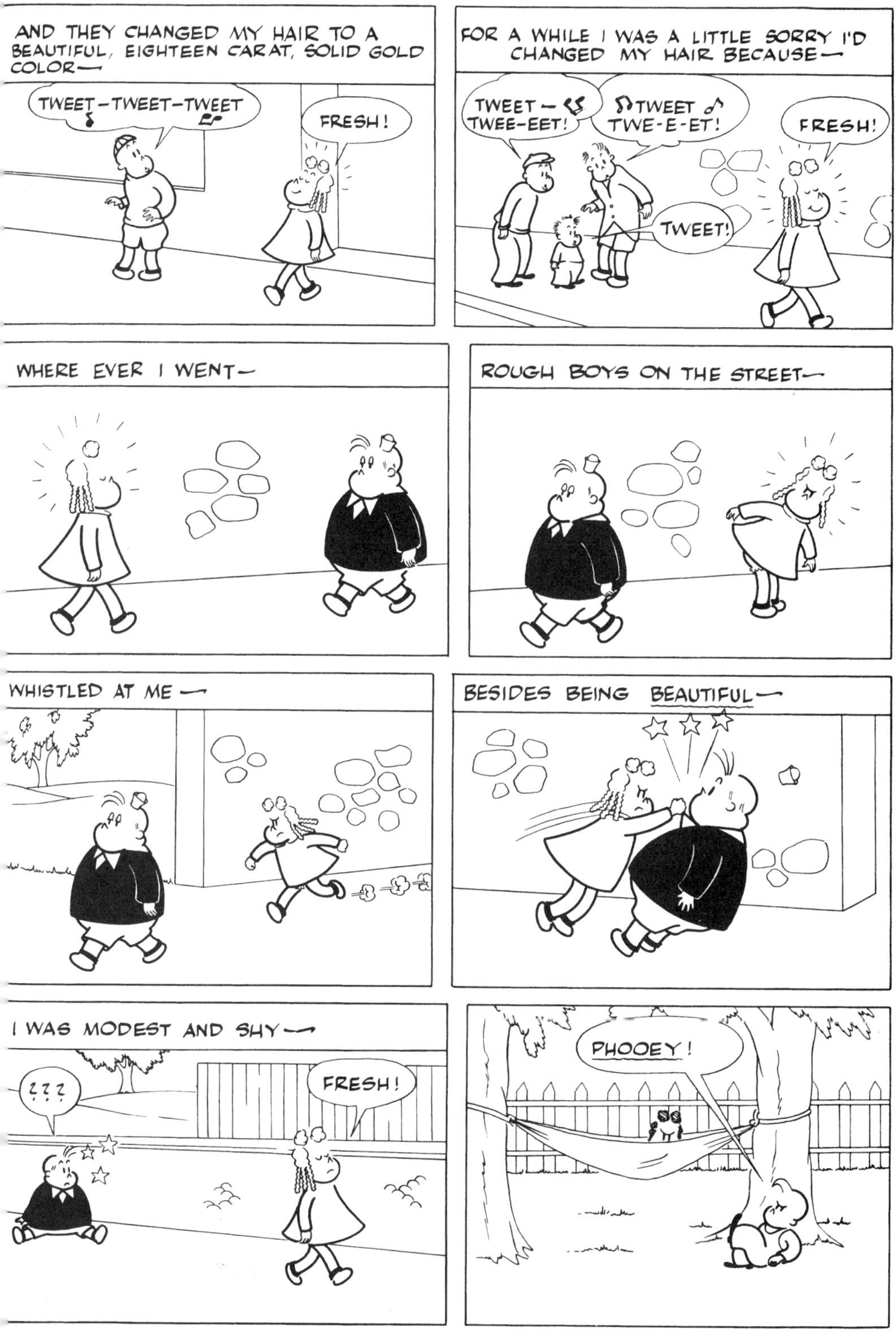
AND THEY CHANGED MY HAIR TO A BEAUTIFUL, EIGHTEEN CARAT, SOLID GOLD COLOR—
TWEET—TWEET—TWEET
FRESH!
FOR A WHILE I WAS A LITTLE SORRY I'D CHANGED MY HAIR BECAUSE—
TWEET— TWEE-EET!
TWEET TWE-E-ET!
FRESH!
TWEET!
WHERE EVER I WENT—
ROUGH BOYS ON THE STREET—
WHISTLED AT ME—
BESIDES BEING BEAUTIFUL—
I WAS MODEST AND SHY—
???
FRESH!
PHOOEY!

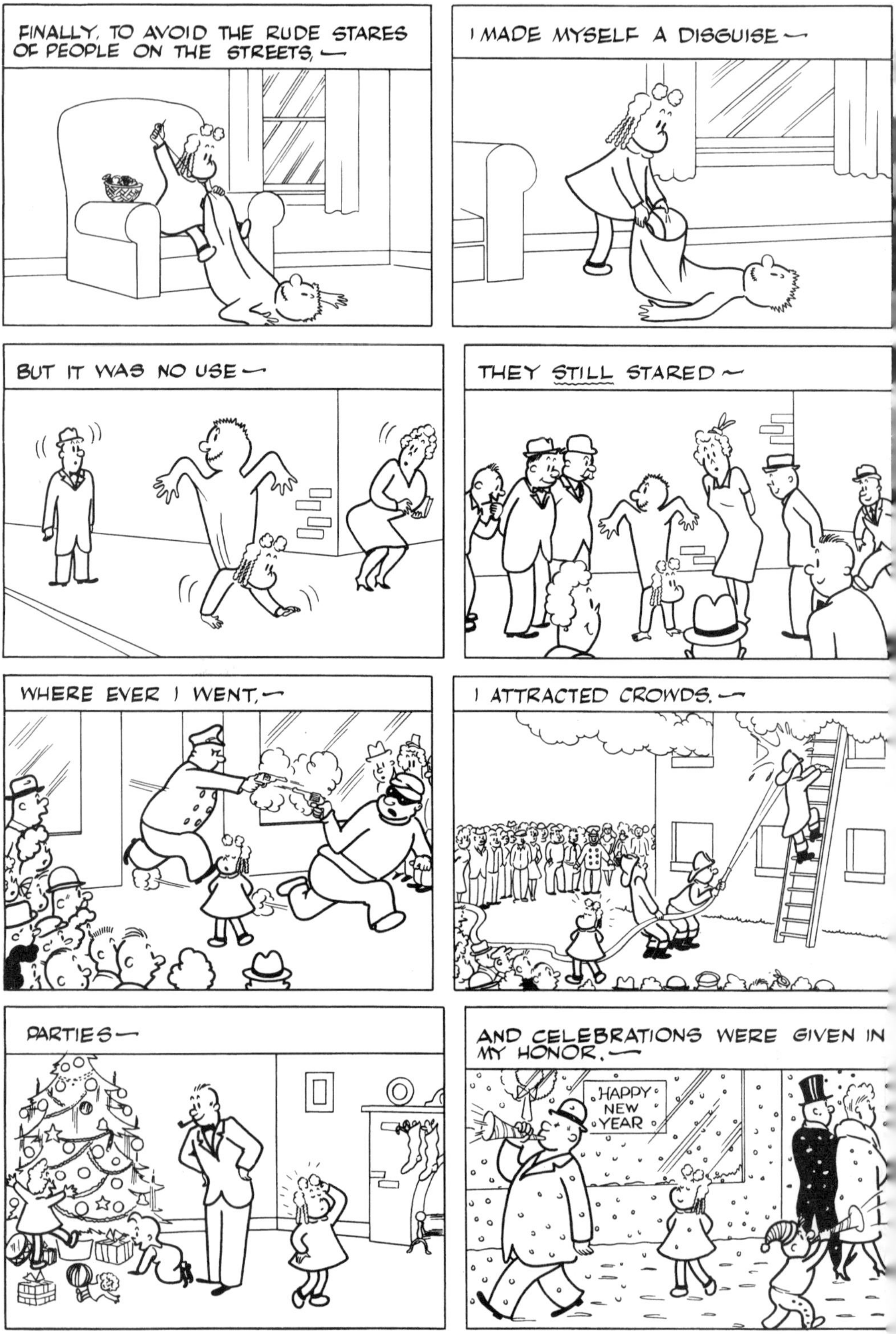
FINALLY, TO AVOID THE RUDE STARES OF PEOPLE ON THE STREETS, —
I MADE MYSELF A DISGUISE —
BUT IT WAS NO USE —
THEY STILL STARED —
WHERE EVER I WENT, —
I ATTRACTED CROWDS. —
PARTIES —
AND CELEBRATIONS WERE GIVEN IN MY HONOR. —
HAPPY NEW YEAR

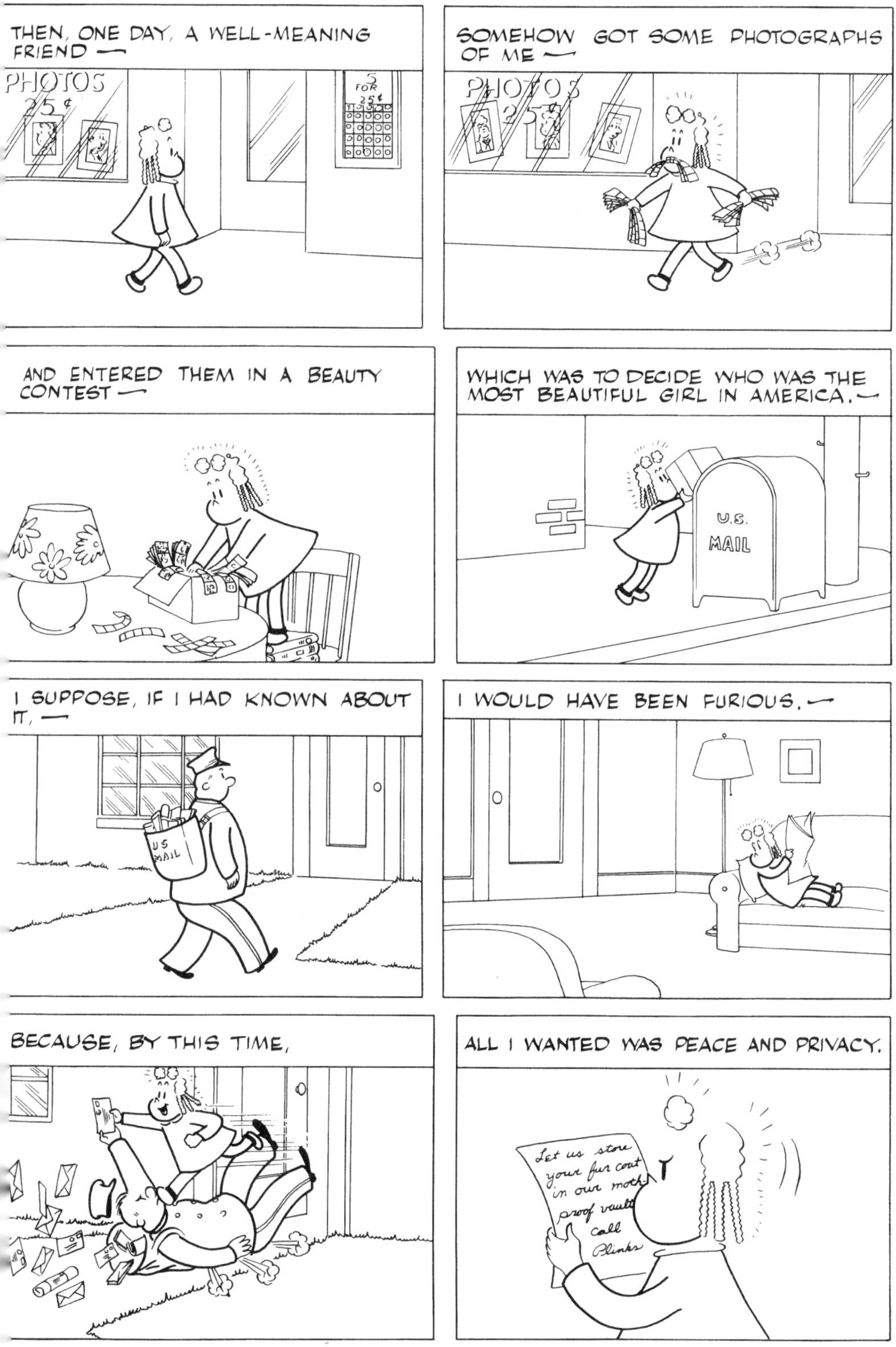
THEN, ONE DAY, A WELL-MEANING FRIEND —
PHOTOS 25¢
5 FOR 25¢
SOMEHOW GOT SOME PHOTOGRAPHS OF ME —
PHOTOS 25¢
AND ENTERED THEM IN A BEAUTY CONTEST —
WHICH WAS TO DECIDE WHO WAS THE MOST BEAUTIFUL GIRL IN AMERICA. —
U.S. MAIL
I SUPPOSE, IF I HAD KNOWN ABOUT IT, —
U.S. MAIL
I WOULD HAVE BEEN FURIOUS. —
BECAUSE, BY THIS TIME,
ALL I WANTED WAS PEACE AND PRIVACY.
Let us store your fur coat in our moth-proof vault Call Blinks

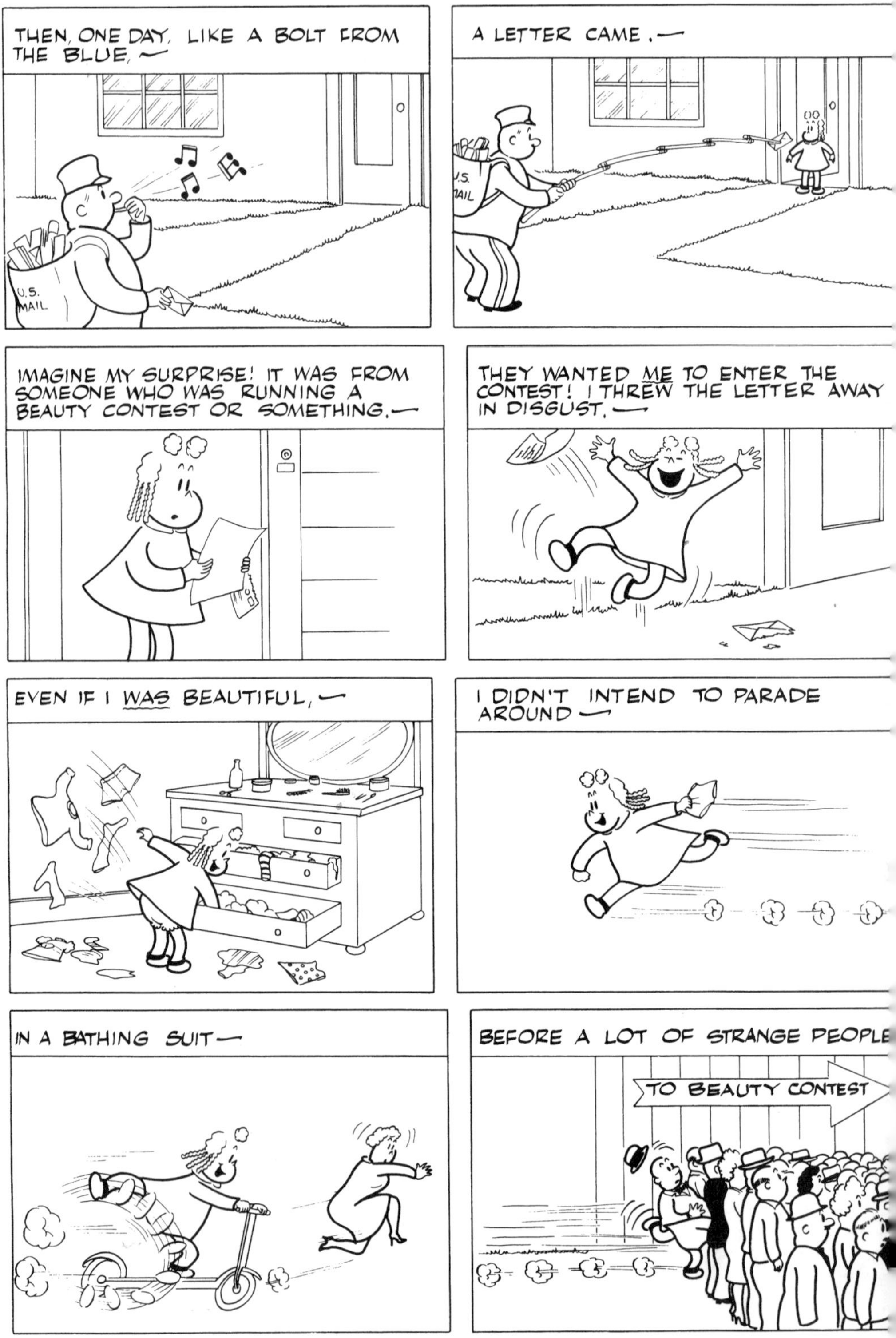
THEN, ONE DAY, LIKE A BOLT FROM THE BLUE, —
U.S. MAIL
A LETTER CAME. —
U.S. MAIL
IMAGINE MY SURPRISE! IT WAS FROM SOMEONE WHO WAS RUNNING A BEAUTY CONTEST OR SOMETHING. —
THEY WANTED ME TO ENTER THE CONTEST! I THREW THE LETTER AWAY IN DISGUST. —
EVEN IF I WAS BEAUTIFUL, —
I DIDN'T INTEND TO PARADE AROUND —
IN A BATHING SUIT —
BEFORE A LOT OF STRANGE PEOPLE
TO BEAUTY CONTEST

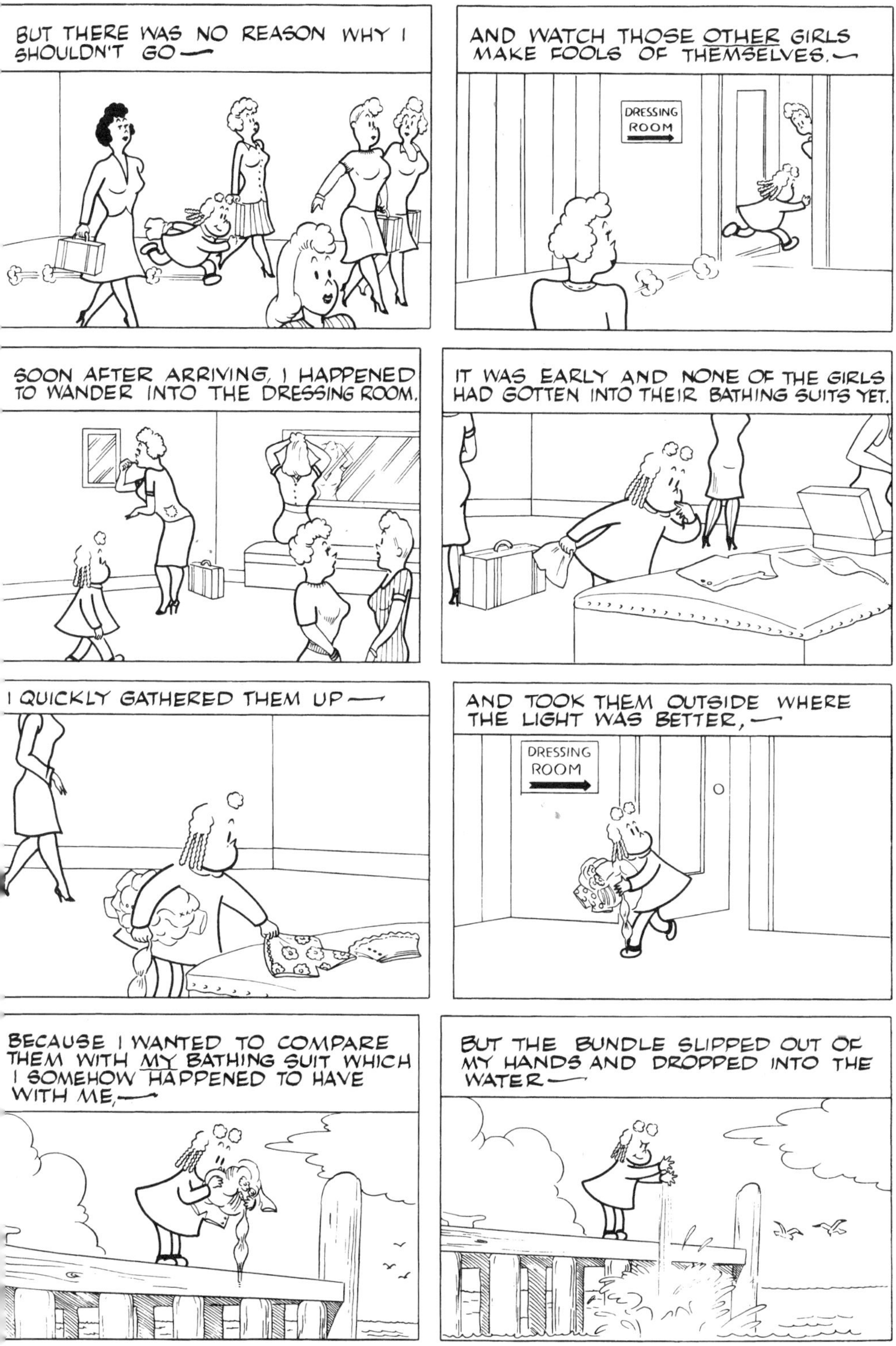
BUT THERE WAS NO REASON WHY I SHOULDN'T GO—
AND WATCH THOSE OTHER GIRLS MAKE FOOLS OF THEMSELVES.—
DRESSING ROOM
SOON AFTER ARRIVING, I HAPPENED TO WANDER INTO THE DRESSING ROOM.
IT WAS EARLY AND NONE OF THE GIRLS HAD GOTTEN INTO THEIR BATHING SUITS YET.
I QUICKLY GATHERED THEM UP—
AND TOOK THEM OUTSIDE WHERE THE LIGHT WAS BETTER,—
DRESSING ROOM
BECAUSE I WANTED TO COMPARE THEM WITH MY BATHING SUIT WHICH I SOMEHOW HAPPENED TO HAVE WITH ME,—
BUT THE BUNDLE SLIPPED OUT OF MY HANDS AND DROPPED INTO THE WATER—

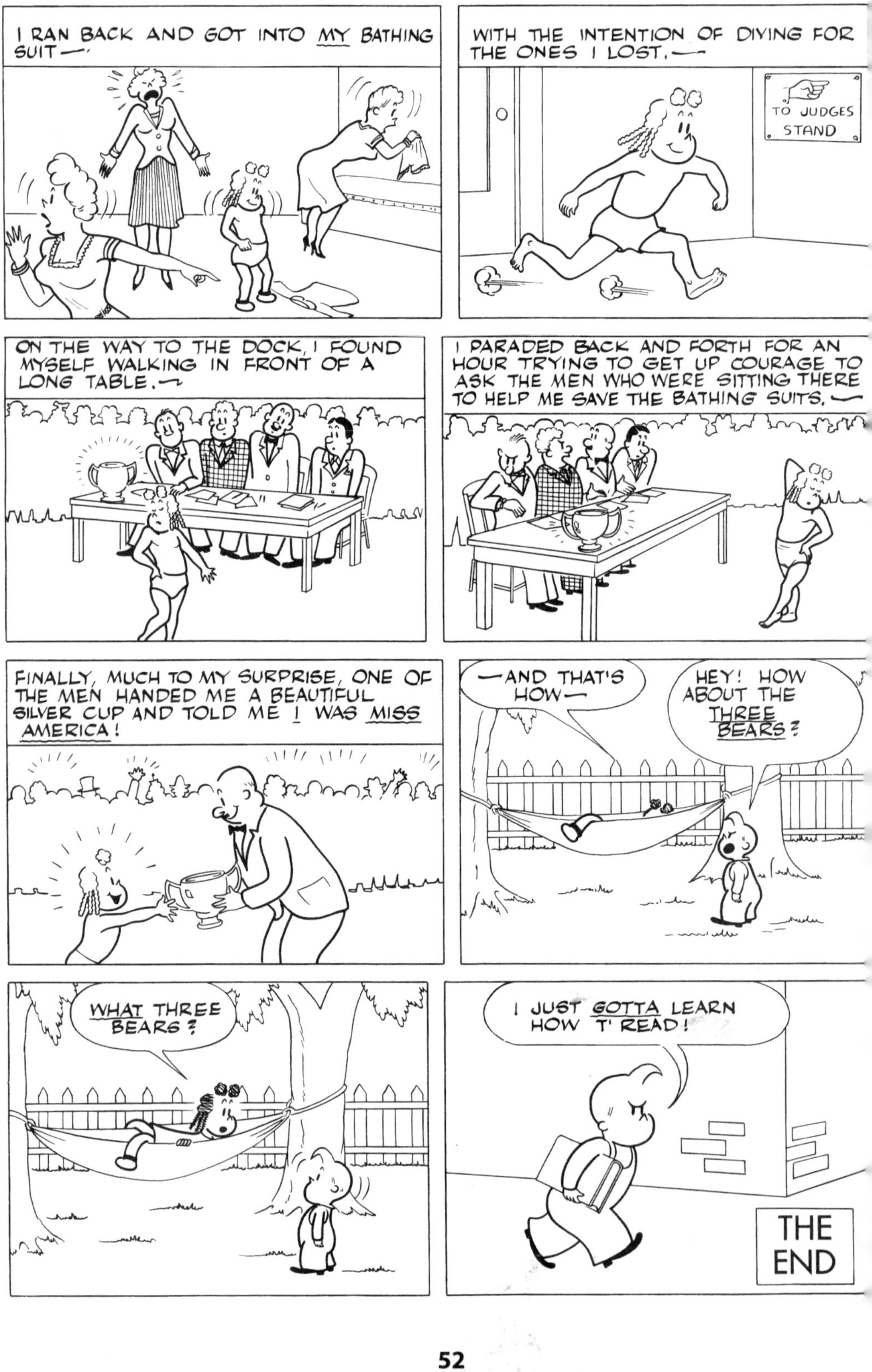
I RAN BACK AND GOT INTO MY BATHING SUIT—
WITH THE INTENTION OF DIVING FOR THE ONES I LOST.—
TO JUDGES STAND
ON THE WAY TO THE DOCK, I FOUND MYSELF WALKING IN FRONT OF A LONG TABLE.—
I PARADED BACK AND FORTH FOR AN HOUR TRYING TO GET UP COURAGE TO ASK THE MEN WHO WERE SITTING THERE TO HELP ME SAVE THE BATHING SUITS.—
FINALLY, MUCH TO MY SURPRISE, ONE OF THE MEN HANDED ME A BEAUTIFUL SILVER CUP AND TOLD ME I WAS MISS AMERICA!
—AND THAT'S HOW—
HEY! HOW ABOUT THE THREE BEARS?
WHAT THREE BEARS?
I JUST GOTTA LEARN HOW T' READ!
THE END

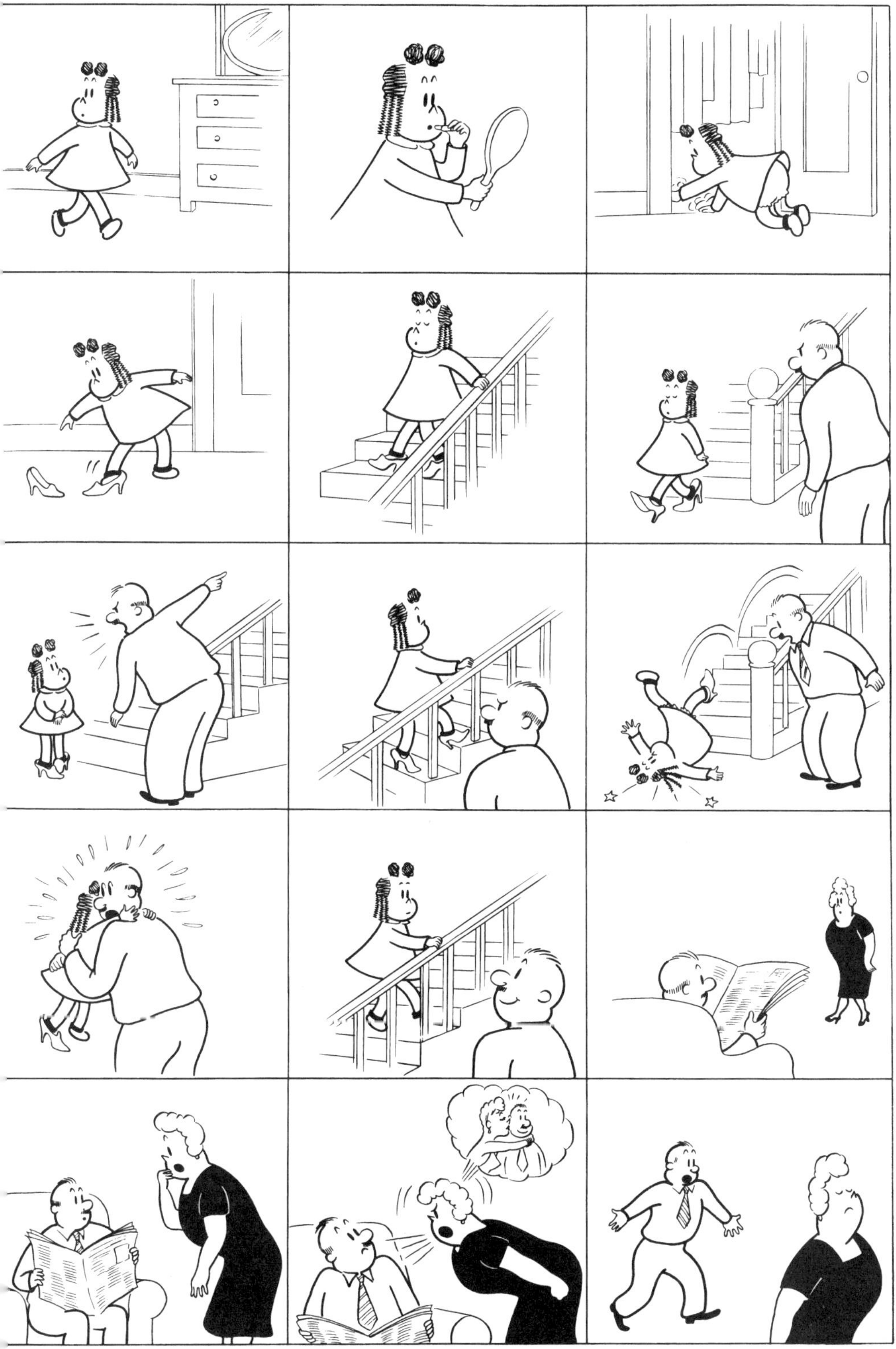

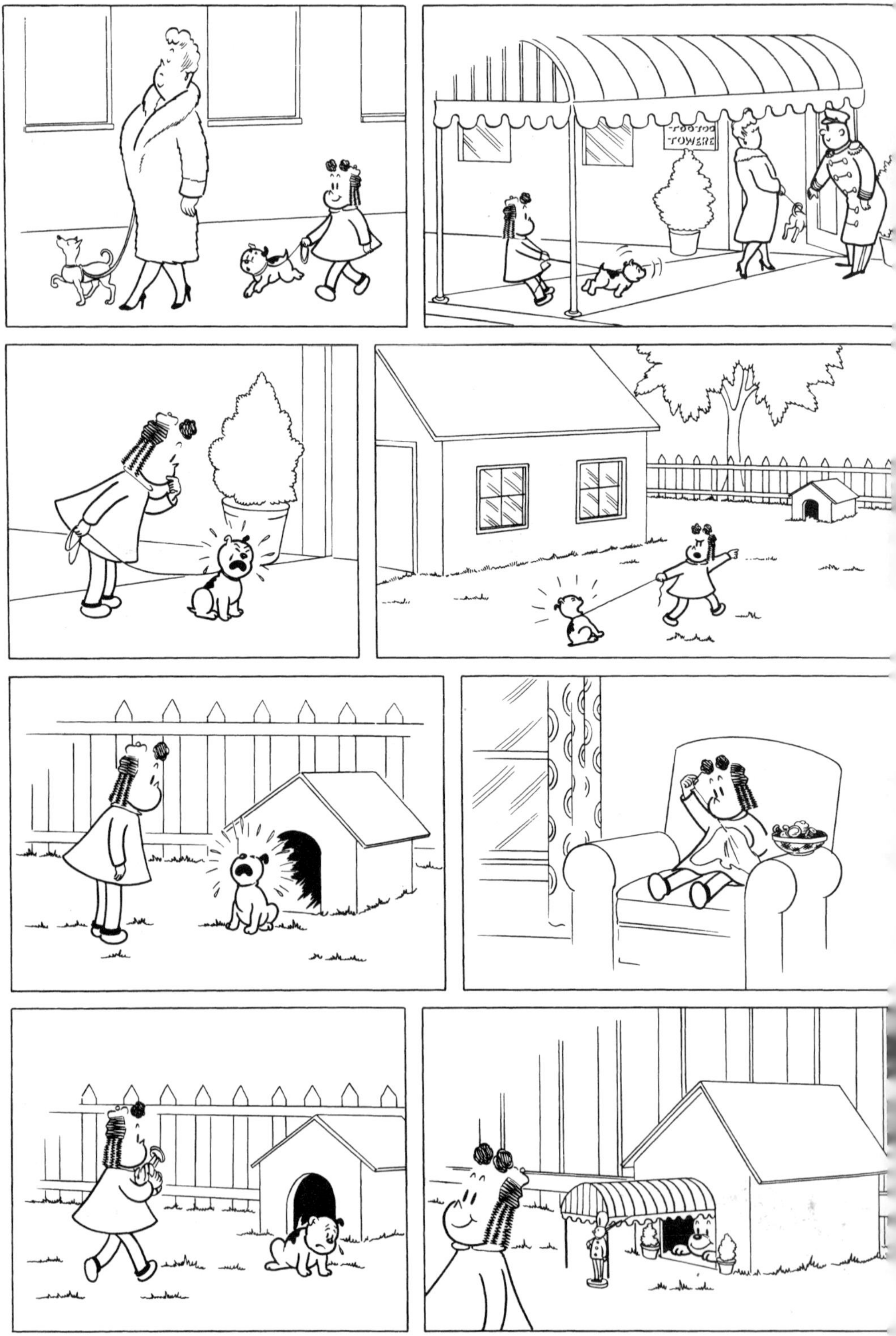
TOO-TOO
TOWERS

MAY I CUT IN?

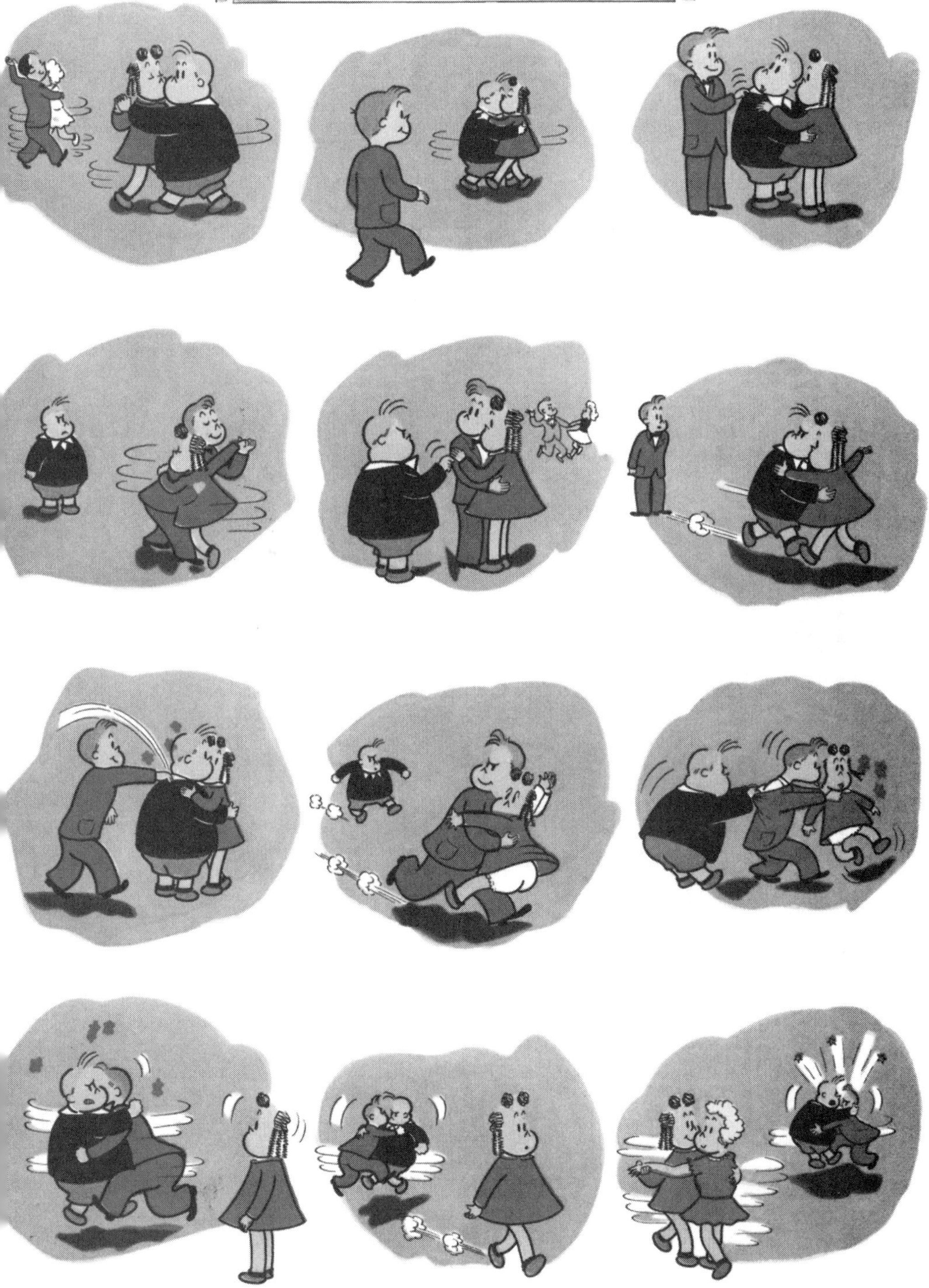

marge's

little lulu

THE HOOKY TEAM

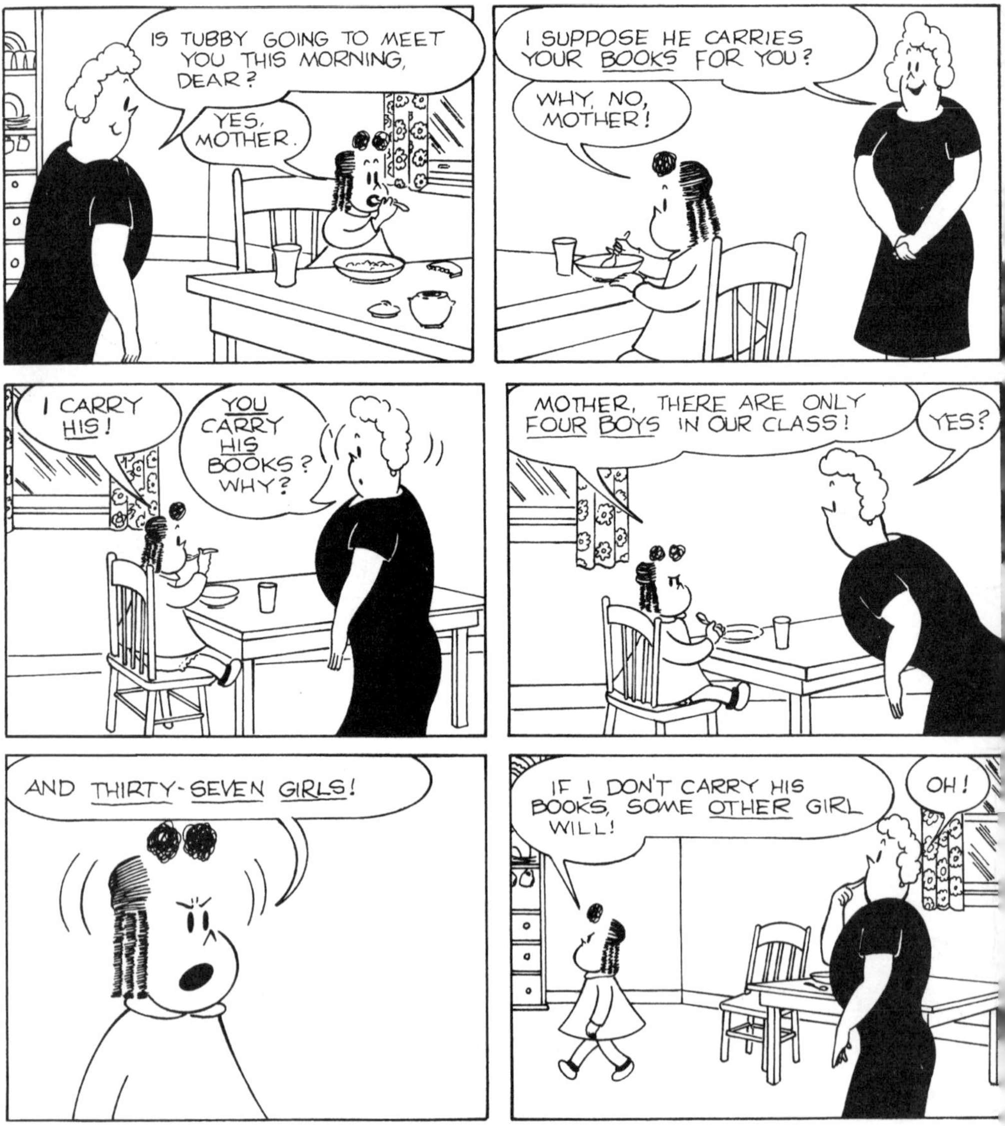

IS TUBBY GOING TO MEET YOU THIS MORNING, DEAR?
YES, MOTHER.
I SUPPOSE HE CARRIES YOUR BOOKS FOR YOU?
WHY, NO, MOTHER!
I CARRY HIS!
YOU CARRY HIS BOOKS? WHY?
MOTHER, THERE ARE ONLY FOUR BOYS IN OUR CLASS!
YES?
AND THIRTY-SEVEN GIRLS!
IF I DON'T CARRY HIS BOOKS, SOME OTHER GIRL WILL!
OH!

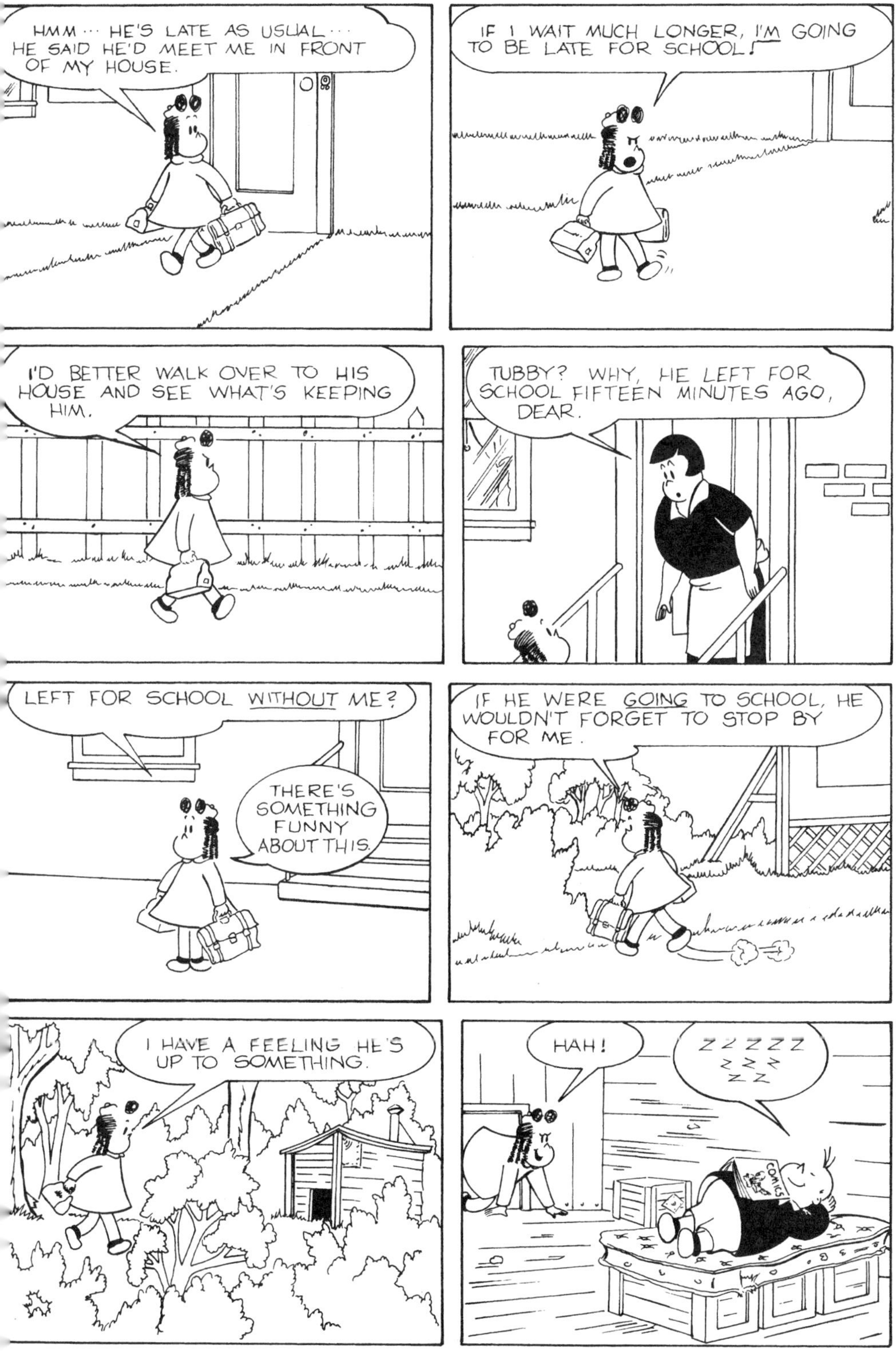
HMM ··· HE'S LATE AS USUAL ··· HE SAID HE'D MEET ME IN FRONT OF MY HOUSE.
IF I WAIT MUCH LONGER, I'M GOING TO BE LATE FOR SCHOOL!
I'D BETTER WALK OVER TO HIS HOUSE AND SEE WHAT'S KEEPING HIM.
TUBBY? WHY, HE LEFT FOR SCHOOL FIFTEEN MINUTES AGO, DEAR.
LEFT FOR SCHOOL WITHOUT ME?
THERE'S SOMETHING FUNNY ABOUT THIS.
IF HE WERE GOING TO SCHOOL, HE WOULDN'T FORGET TO STOP BY FOR ME.
I HAVE A FEELING HE'S UP TO SOMETHING.
HAH!
Z Z Z Z Z
Z Z Z
Z Z
COMICS

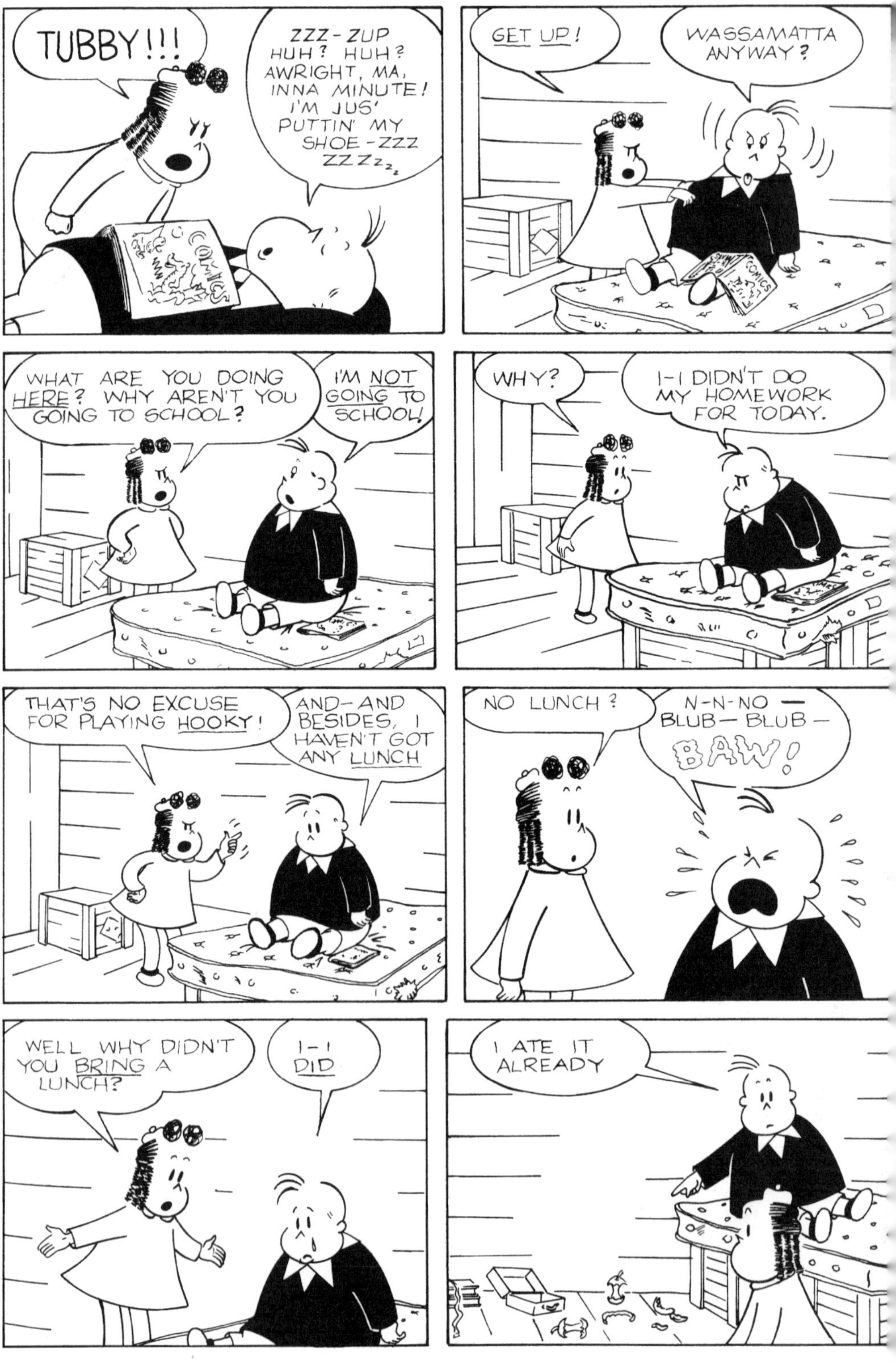
TUBBY!!!
ZZZ-ZUP HUH? HUH? AWRIGHT, MA, INNA MINUTE! I'M JUS' PUTTIN' MY SHOE-ZZZ ZZZzzz
COMICS
GET UP!
WASSAMATTA ANYWAY?
COMICS
WHAT ARE YOU DOING HERE? WHY AREN'T YOU GOING TO SCHOOL?
I'M NOT GOING TO SCHOOL!
WHY?
I-I DIDN'T DO MY HOMEWORK FOR TODAY.
THAT'S NO EXCUSE FOR PLAYING HOOKY!
AND-AND BESIDES, I HAVEN'T GOT ANY LUNCH
NO LUNCH?
N-N-NO — BLUB—BLUB—
BAW!
WELL WHY DIDN'T YOU BRING A LUNCH?
I-I DID
I ATE IT ALREADY

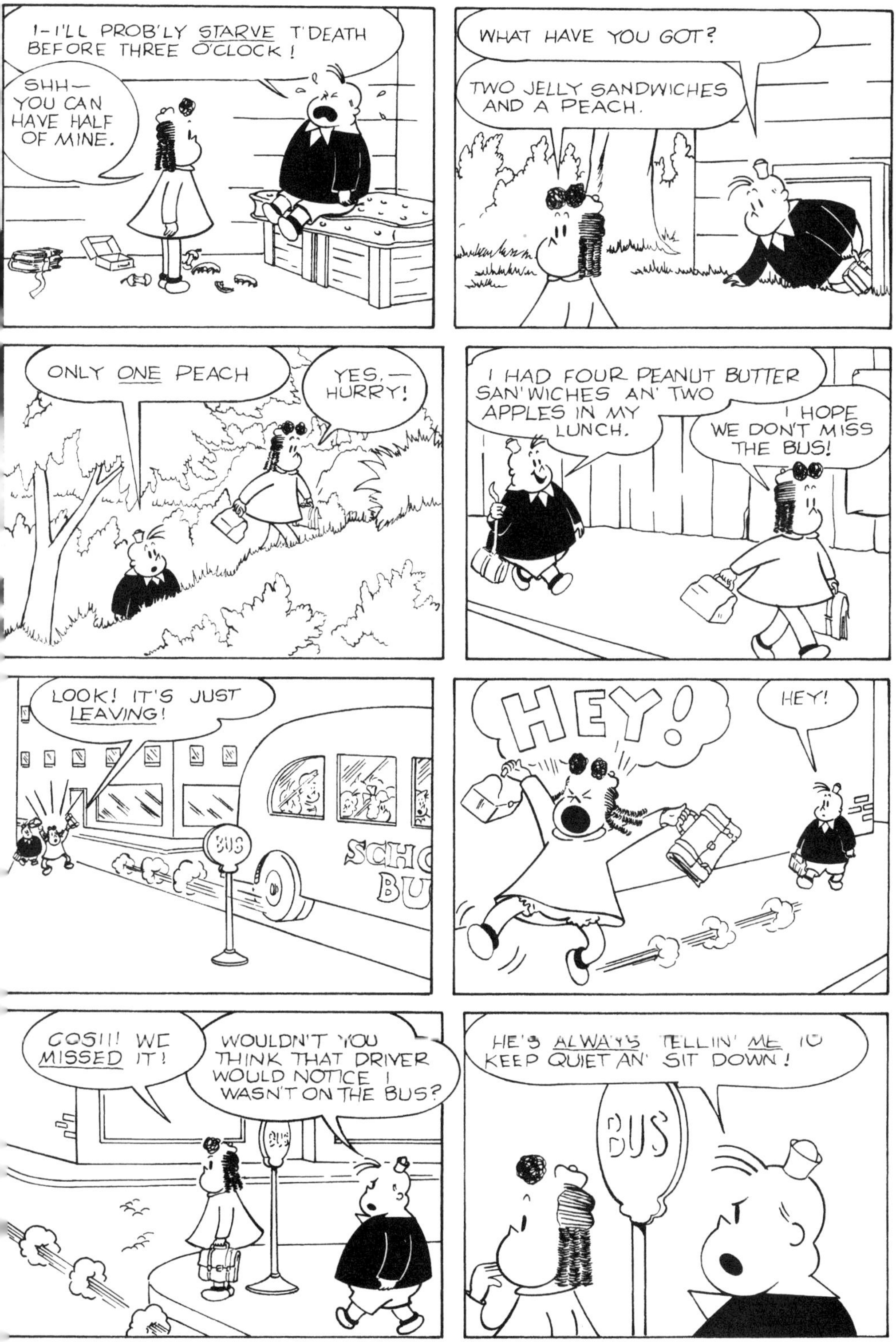
I-I'LL PROB'LY STARVE T'DEATH BEFORE THREE O'CLOCK!
SHH— YOU CAN HAVE HALF OF MINE.
WHAT HAVE YOU GOT?
TWO JELLY SANDWICHES AND A PEACH.
ONLY ONE PEACH
YES,— HURRY!
I HAD FOUR PEANUT BUTTER SAN'WICHES AN' TWO APPLES IN MY LUNCH.
I HOPE WE DON'T MISS THE BUS!
LOOK! IT'S JUST LEAVING!
HEY!
HEY!
GOSH! WE MISSED IT!
WOULDN'T YOU THINK THAT DRIVER WOULD NOTICE I WASN'T ON THE BUS?
HE'S ALWAYS TELLIN' ME TO KEEP QUIET AN' SIT DOWN!

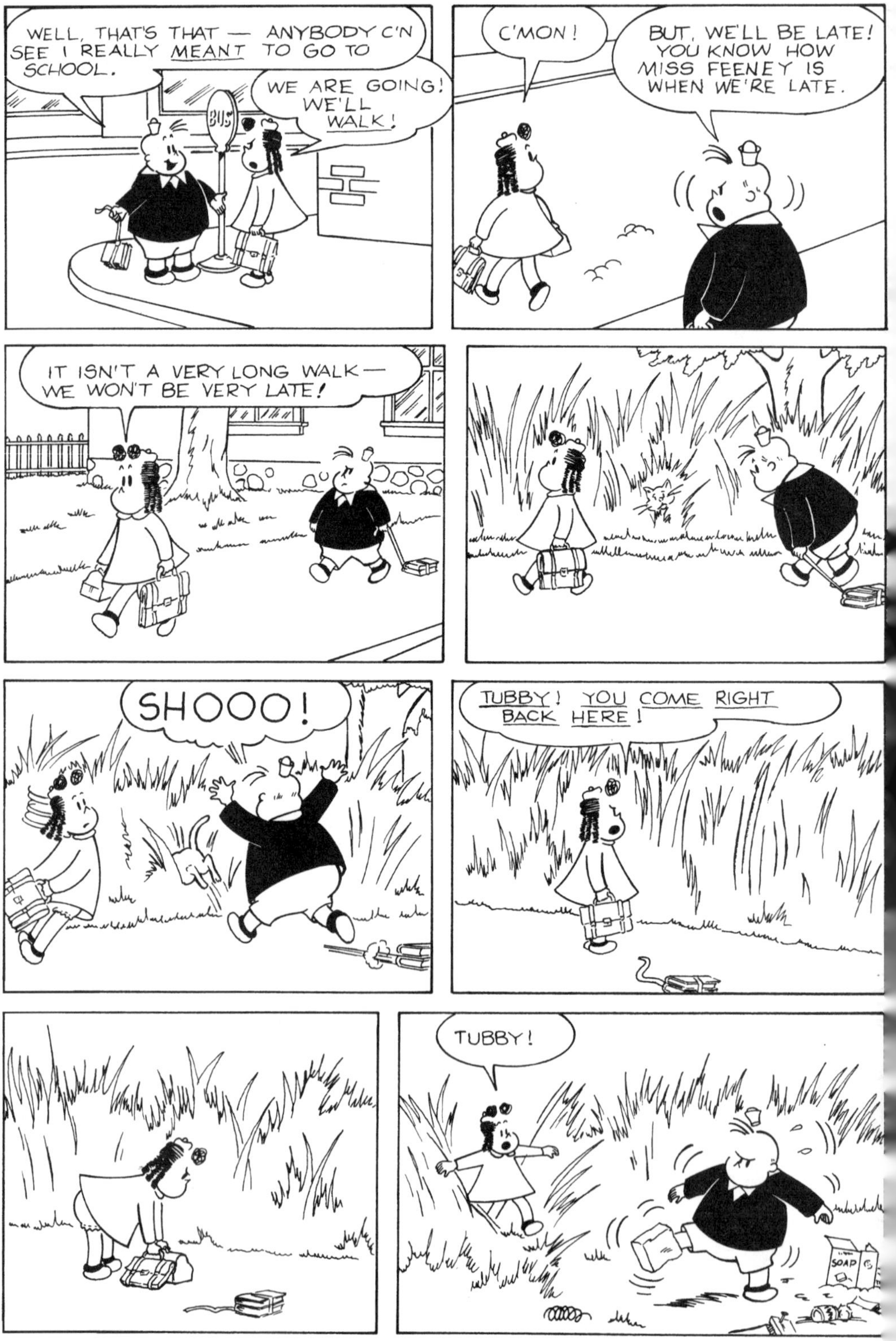
WELL, THAT'S THAT — ANYBODY C'N SEE I REALLY MEANT TO GO TO SCHOOL.
WE ARE GOING! WE'LL WALK!
BUS
C'MON!
BUT, WE'LL BE LATE! YOU KNOW HOW MISS FEENEY IS WHEN WE'RE LATE.
IT ISN'T A VERY LONG WALK— WE WON'T BE VERY LATE!
SHOOO!
TUBBY! YOU COME RIGHT BACK HERE!
TUBBY!
SOAP

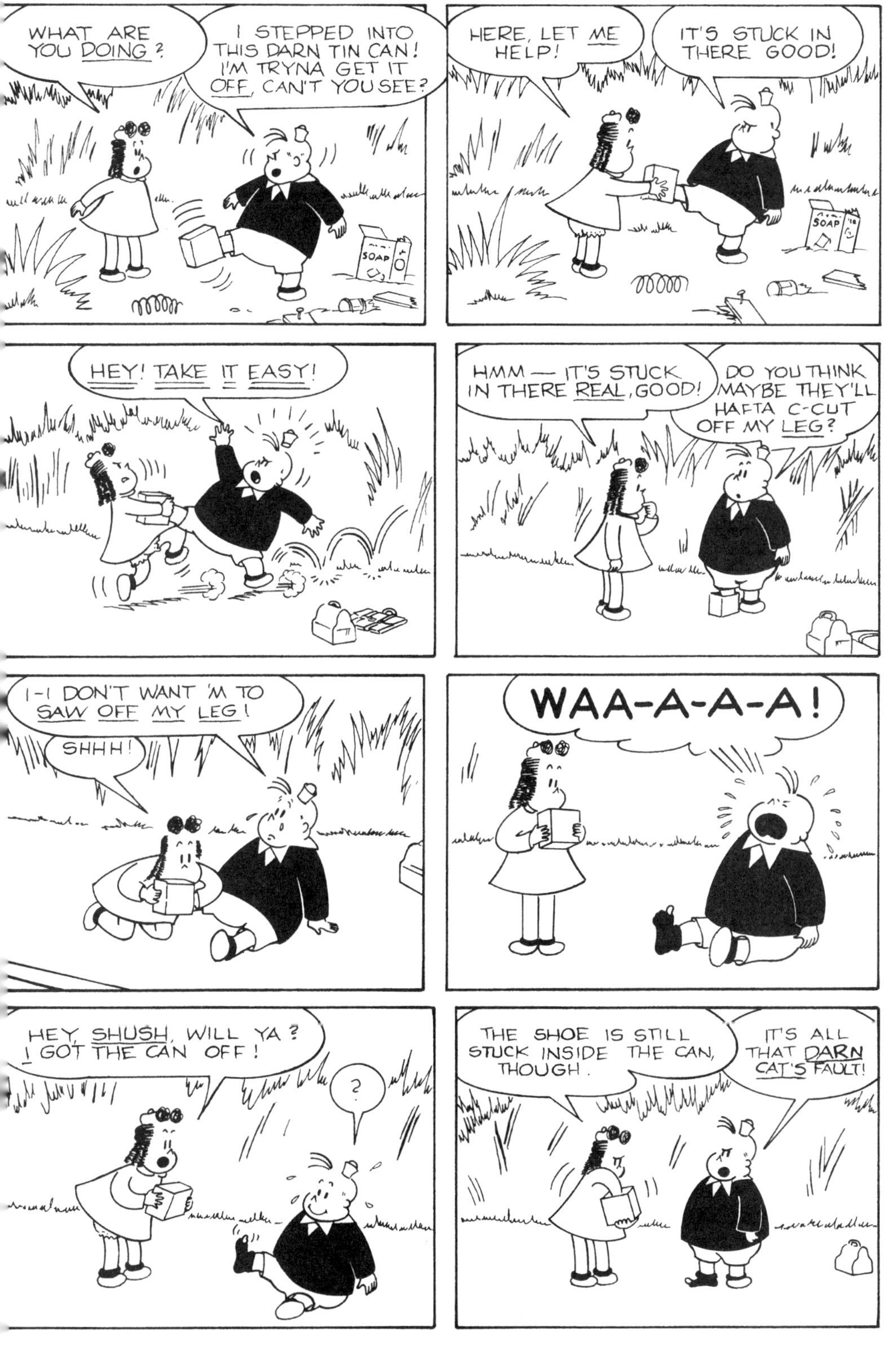
WHAT ARE YOU DOING?
I STEPPED INTO THIS DARN TIN CAN! I'M TRYNA GET IT OFF, CAN'T YOU SEE?
SOAP
HERE, LET ME HELP!
IT'S STUCK IN THERE GOOD!
SOAP
HEY! TAKE IT EASY!
HMM — IT'S STUCK IN THERE REAL, GOOD!
DO YOU THINK MAYBE THEY'LL HAFTA C-CUT OFF MY LEG?
I-I DON'T WANT 'M TO SAW OFF MY LEG!
SHHH!
WAA-A-A-A!
HEY, SHUSH, WILL YA? I GOT THE CAN OFF!
?
THE SHOE IS STILL STUCK INSIDE THE CAN, THOUGH.
IT'S ALL THAT DARN CAT'S FAULT!

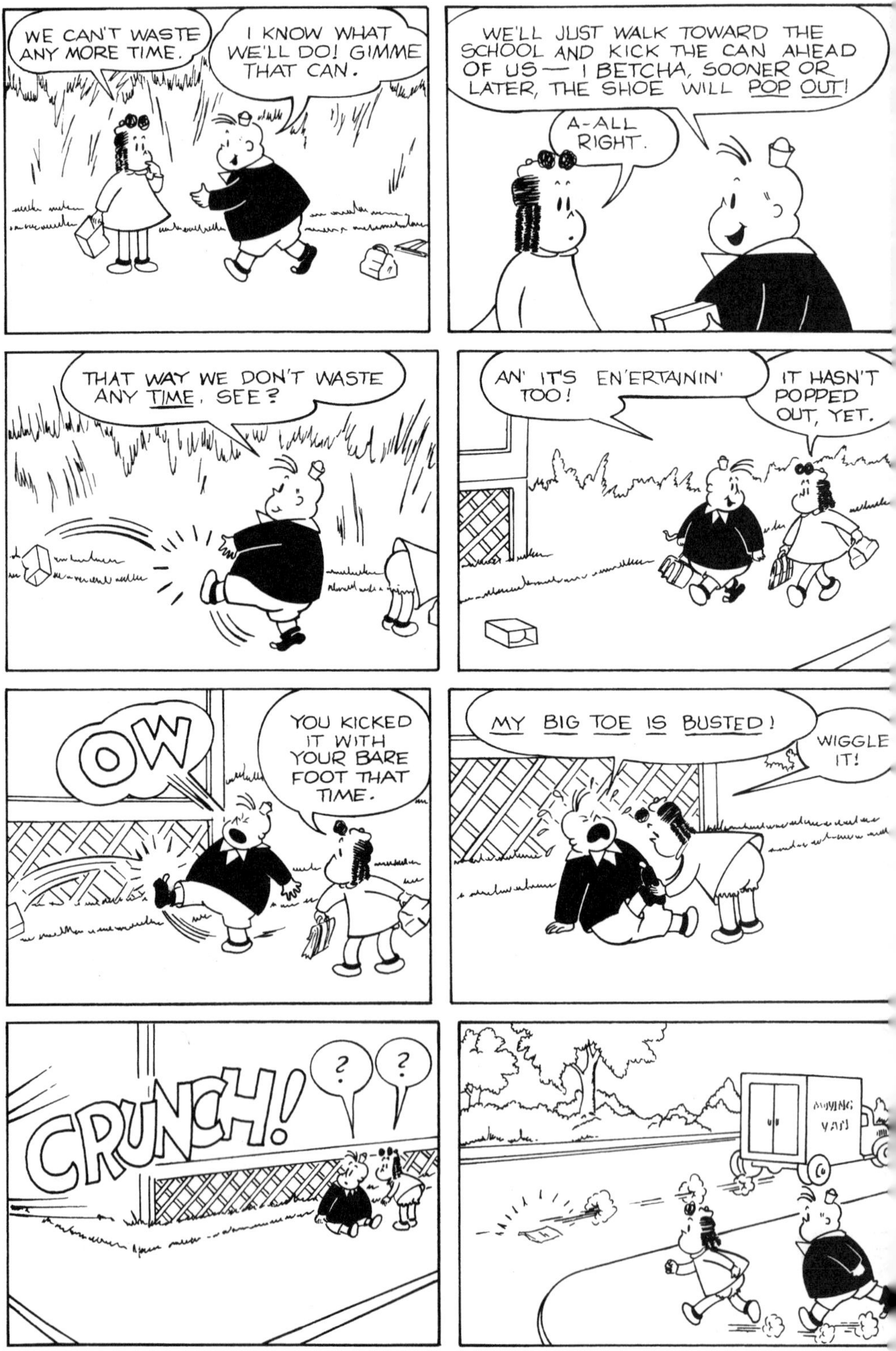
WE CAN'T WASTE ANY MORE TIME.
I KNOW WHAT WE'LL DO! GIMME THAT CAN.
WE'LL JUST WALK TOWARD THE SCHOOL AND KICK THE CAN AHEAD OF US— I BETCHA, SOONER OR LATER, THE SHOE WILL POP OUT!
A-ALL RIGHT.
THAT WAY WE DON'T WASTE ANY TIME, SEE?
AN' IT'S EN'ERTAININ' TOO!
IT HASN'T POPPED OUT, YET.
OW
YOU KICKED IT WITH YOUR BARE FOOT THAT TIME.
MY BIG TOE IS BUSTED!
WIGGLE IT!
CRUNCH!
?
?
MOVING VAN

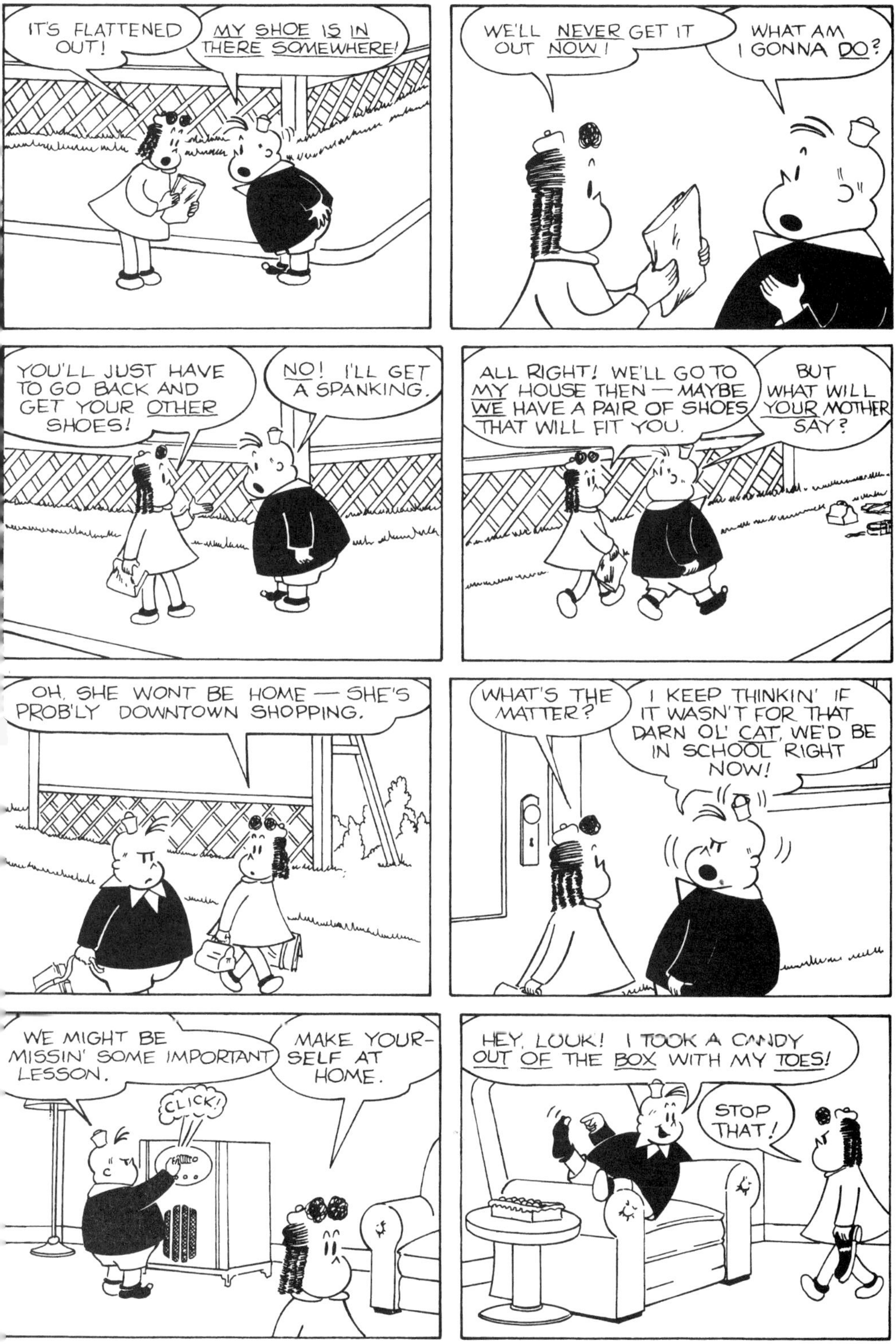
IT'S FLATTENED OUT!
MY SHOE IS IN THERE SOMEWHERE!
WE'LL NEVER GET IT OUT NOW!
WHAT AM I GONNA DO?
YOU'LL JUST HAVE TO GO BACK AND GET YOUR OTHER SHOES!
NO! I'LL GET A SPANKING.
ALL RIGHT! WE'LL GO TO MY HOUSE THEN — MAYBE WE HAVE A PAIR OF SHOES THAT WILL FIT YOU.
BUT WHAT WILL YOUR MOTHER SAY?
OH, SHE WONT BE HOME — SHE'S PROB'LY DOWNTOWN SHOPPING.
WHAT'S THE MATTER?
I KEEP THINKIN' IF IT WASN'T FOR THAT DARN OL' CAT, WE'D BE IN SCHOOL RIGHT NOW!
WE MIGHT BE MISSIN' SOME IMPORTANT LESSON.
CLICK!
MAKE YOURSELF AT HOME.
HEY, LOOK! I TOOK A CANDY OUT OF THE BOX WITH MY TOES!
STOP THAT!

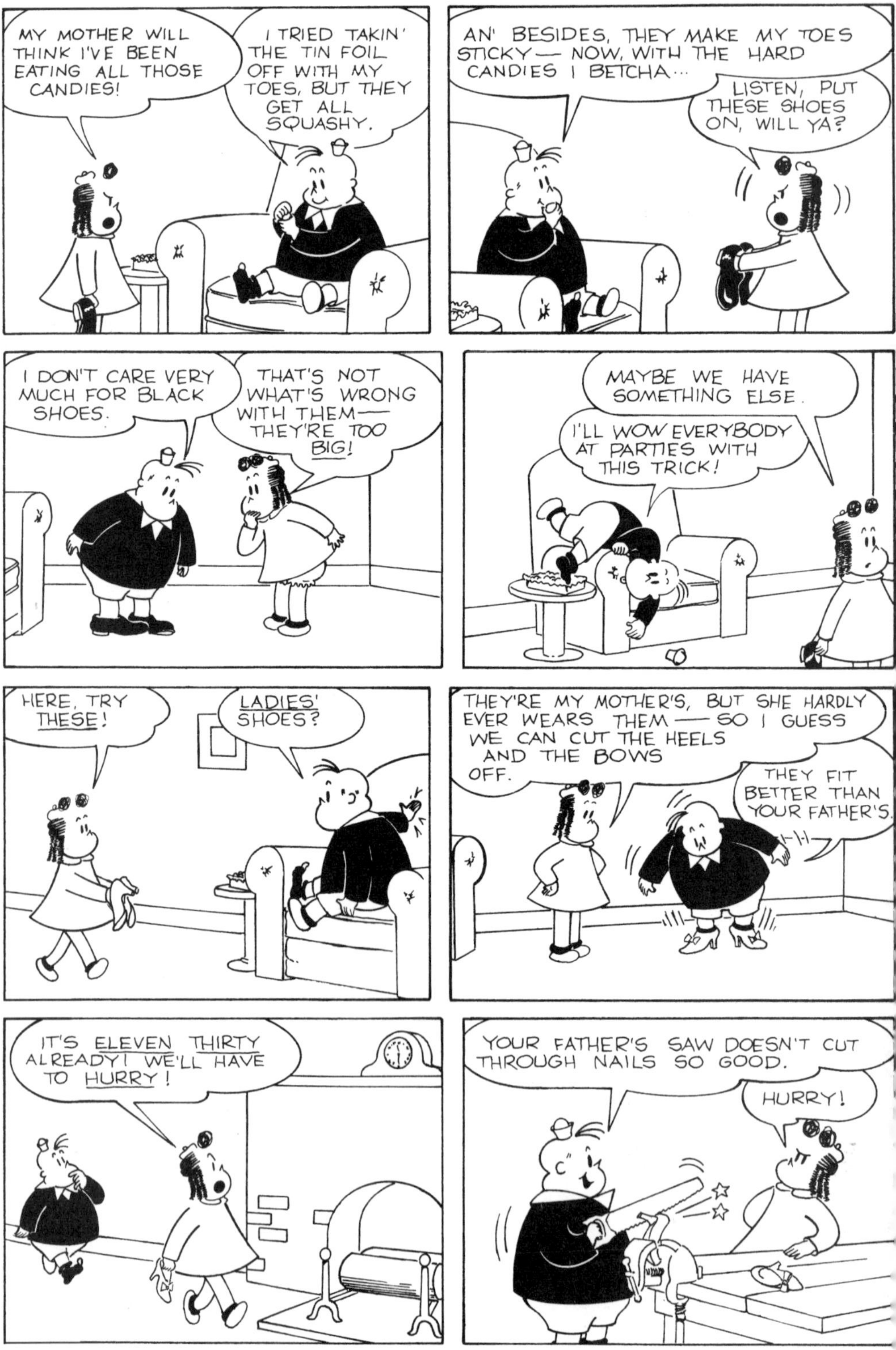
MY MOTHER WILL THINK I'VE BEEN EATING ALL THOSE CANDIES!
I TRIED TAKIN' THE TIN FOIL OFF WITH MY TOES, BUT THEY GET ALL SQUASHY.
AN' BESIDES, THEY MAKE MY TOES STICKY— NOW, WITH THE HARD CANDIES I BETCHA...
LISTEN, PUT THESE SHOES ON, WILL YA?
I DON'T CARE VERY MUCH FOR BLACK SHOES.
THAT'S NOT WHAT'S WRONG WITH THEM— THEY'RE TOO BIG!
MAYBE WE HAVE SOMETHING ELSE.
I'LL WOW EVERYBODY AT PARTIES WITH THIS TRICK!
HERE, TRY THESE!
LADIES' SHOES?
THEY'RE MY MOTHER'S, BUT SHE HARDLY EVER WEARS THEM — SO I GUESS WE CAN CUT THE HEELS AND THE BOWS OFF.
THEY FIT BETTER THAN YOUR FATHER'S.
IT'S ELEVEN THIRTY ALREADY! WE'LL HAVE TO HURRY!
YOUR FATHER'S SAW DOESN'T CUT THROUGH NAILS SO GOOD.
HURRY!

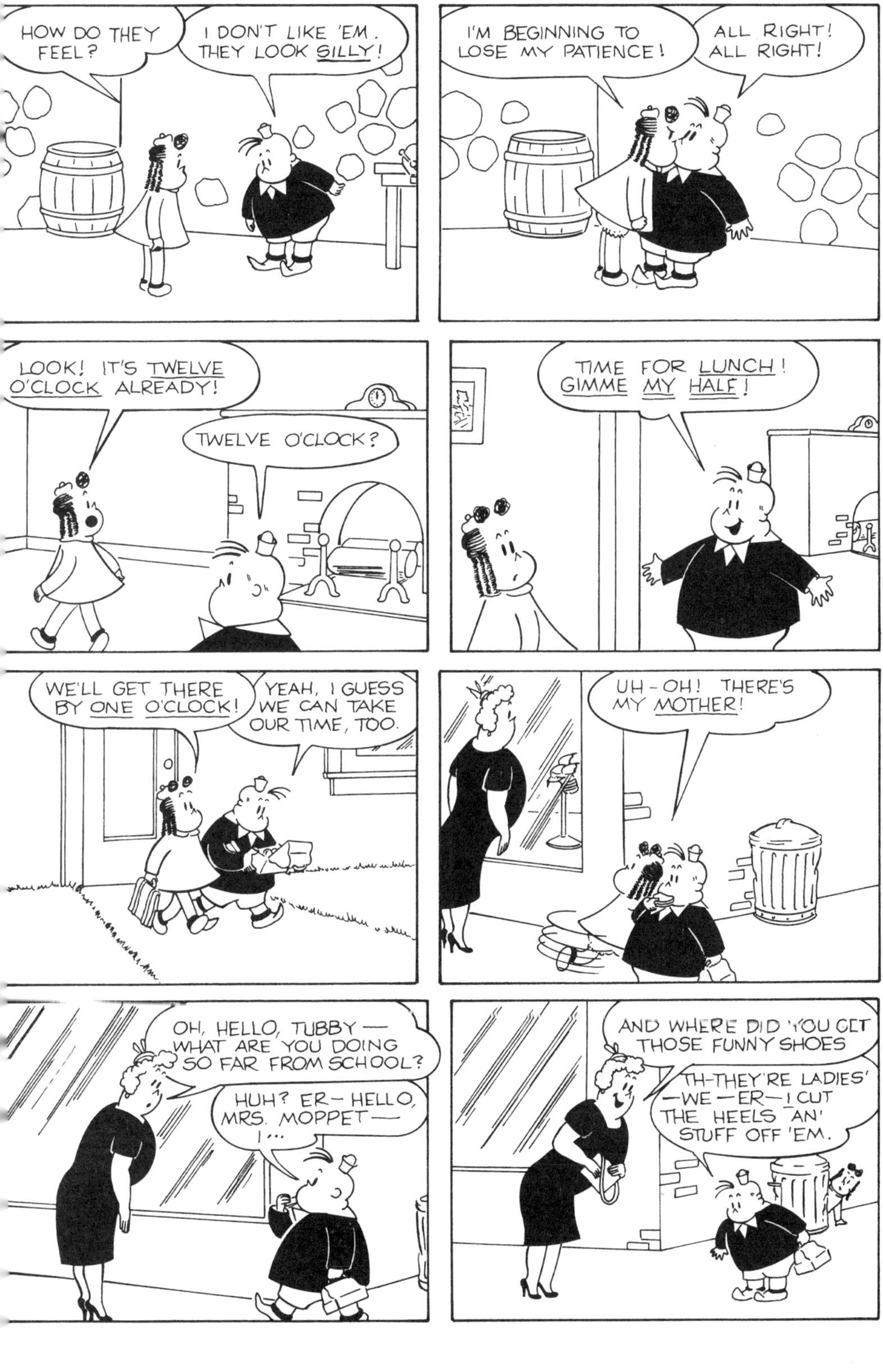
HOW DO THEY FEEL?
I DON'T LIKE 'EM. THEY LOOK SILLY!
I'M BEGINNING TO LOSE MY PATIENCE!
ALL RIGHT! ALL RIGHT!
LOOK! IT'S TWELVE O'CLOCK ALREADY!
TWELVE O'CLOCK?
TIME FOR LUNCH! GIMME MY HALF!
WE'LL GET THERE BY ONE O'CLOCK!
YEAH, I GUESS WE CAN TAKE OUR TIME, TOO.
UH-OH! THERE'S MY MOTHER!
OH, HELLO, TUBBY— WHAT ARE YOU DOING SO FAR FROM SCHOOL?
HUH? ER—HELLO, MRS. MOPPET— I...
AND WHERE DID YOU GET THOSE FUNNY SHOES
TH-THEY'RE LADIES' —WE—ER—I CUT THE HEELS AN' STUFF OFF 'EM.

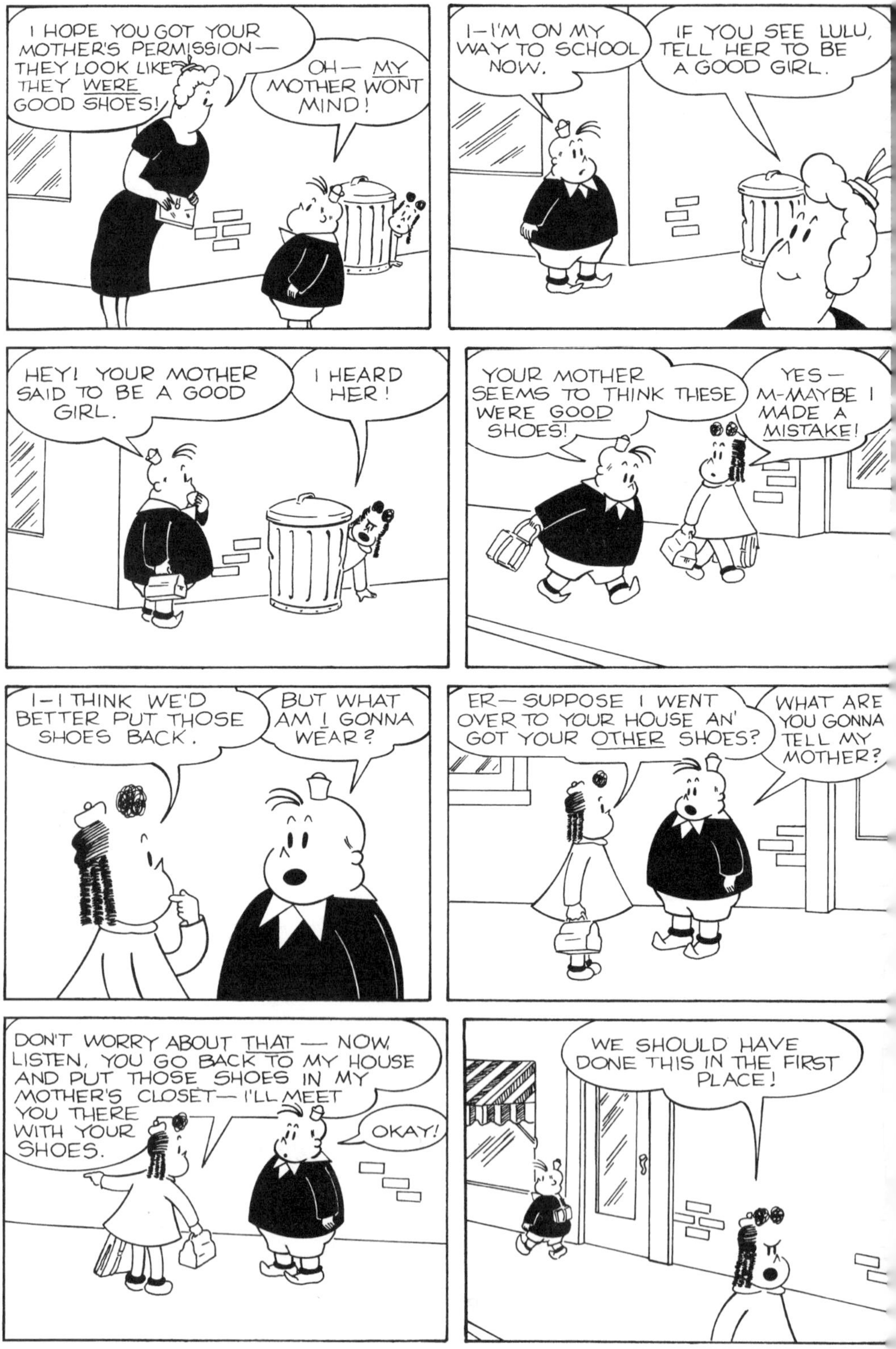
I HOPE YOU GOT YOUR MOTHER'S PERMISSION— THEY LOOK LIKE THEY WERE GOOD SHOES!
OH— MY MOTHER WONT MIND!
I—I'M ON MY WAY TO SCHOOL NOW.
IF YOU SEE LULU, TELL HER TO BE A GOOD GIRL.
HEY! YOUR MOTHER SAID TO BE A GOOD GIRL.
I HEARD HER!
YOUR MOTHER SEEMS TO THINK THESE WERE GOOD SHOES!
YES— M-MAYBE I MADE A MISTAKE!
I—I THINK WE'D BETTER PUT THOSE SHOES BACK.
BUT WHAT AM I GONNA WEAR?
ER— SUPPOSE I WENT OVER TO YOUR HOUSE AN' GOT YOUR OTHER SHOES?
WHAT ARE YOU GONNA TELL MY MOTHER?
DON'T WORRY ABOUT THAT— NOW, LISTEN, YOU GO BACK TO MY HOUSE AND PUT THOSE SHOES IN MY MOTHER'S CLOSET— I'LL MEET YOU THERE WITH YOUR SHOES.
OKAY!
WE SHOULD HAVE DONE THIS IN THE FIRST PLACE!

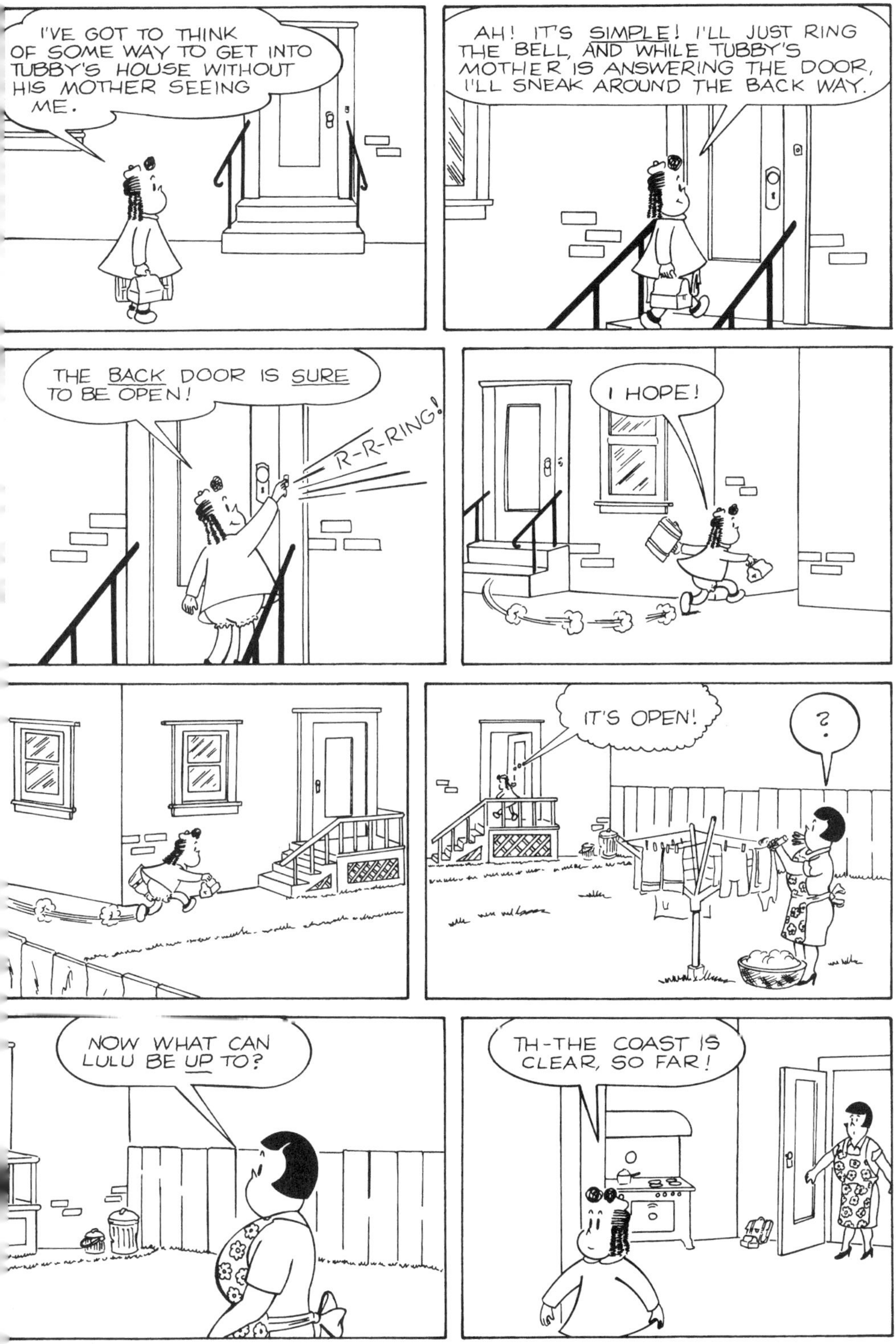
I'VE GOT TO THINK OF SOME WAY TO GET INTO TUBBY'S HOUSE WITHOUT HIS MOTHER SEEING ME.
AH! IT'S SIMPLE! I'LL JUST RING THE BELL, AND WHILE TUBBY'S MOTHER IS ANSWERING THE DOOR, I'LL SNEAK AROUND THE BACK WAY.
THE BACK DOOR IS SURE TO BE OPEN!
R-R-RING!
I HOPE!
IT'S OPEN!
?
NOW WHAT CAN LULU BE UP TO?
TH-THE COAST IS CLEAR, SO FAR!

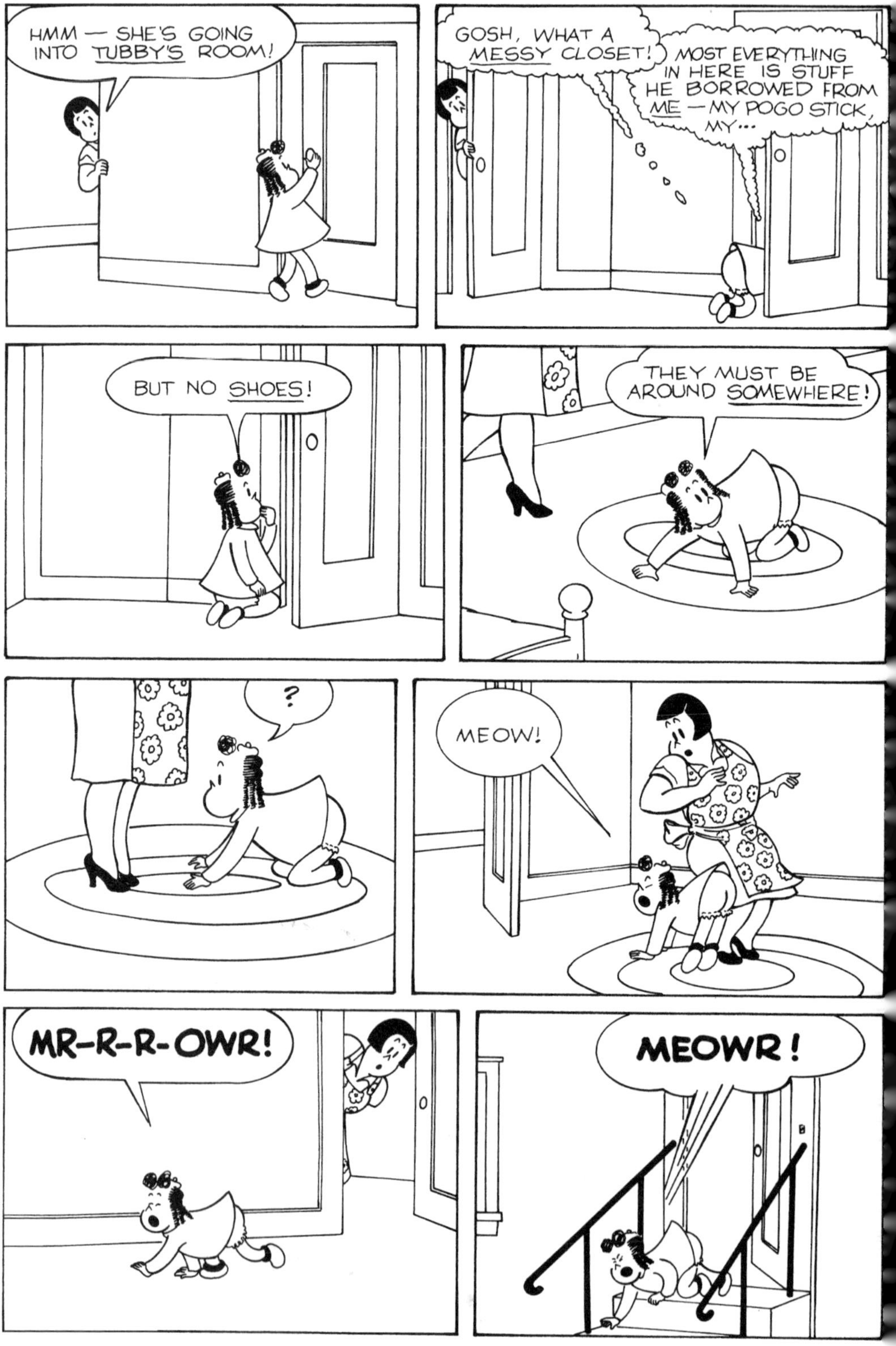
HMM — SHE'S GOING INTO TUBBY'S ROOM!
GOSH, WHAT A MESSY CLOSET!
MOST EVERYTHING IN HERE IS STUFF HE BORROWED FROM ME — MY POGO STICK, MY...
BUT NO SHOES!
THEY MUST BE AROUND SOMEWHERE!
?
MEOW!
MR-R-R-OWR!
MEOWR!

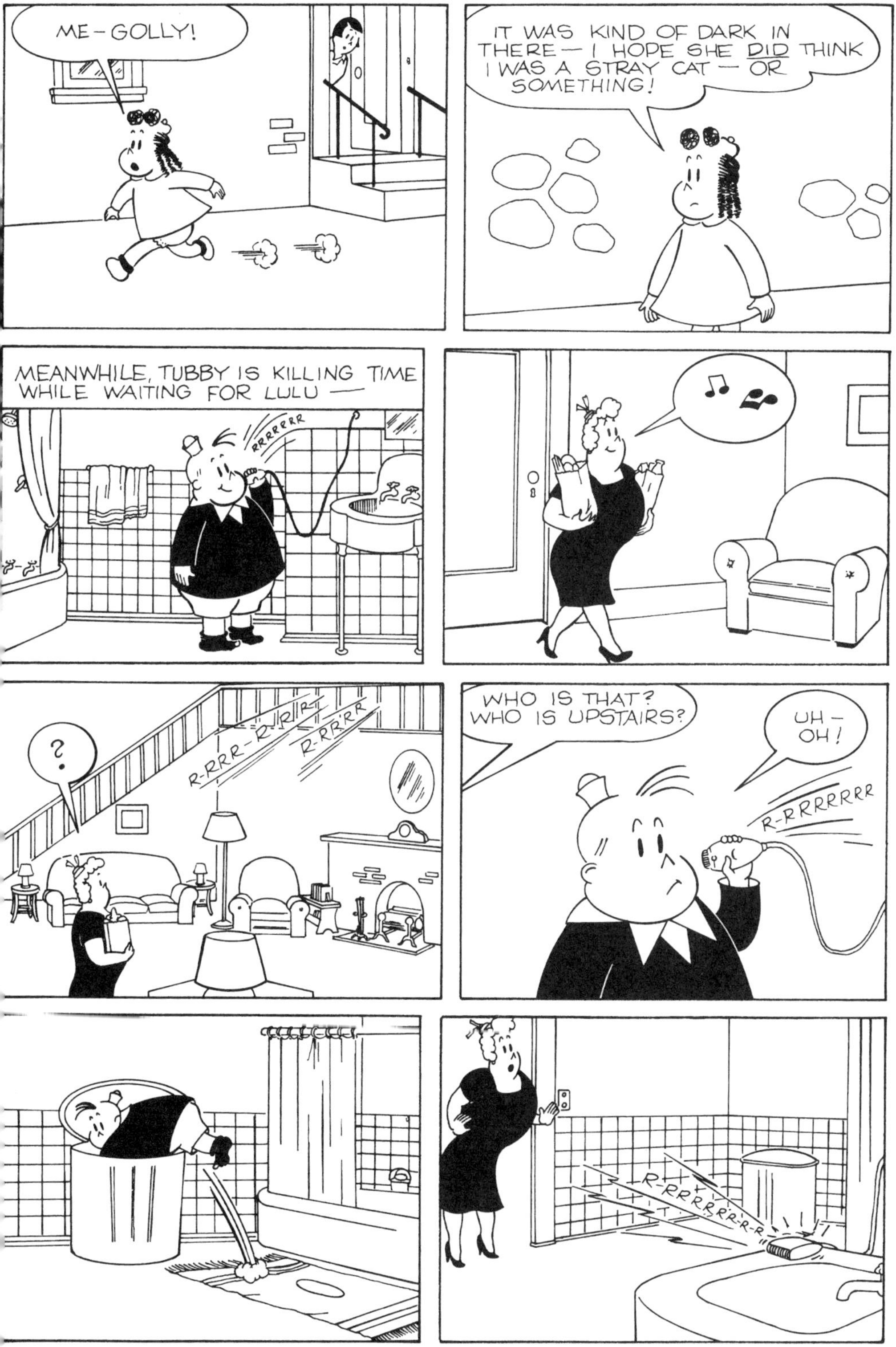
ME-GOLLY!
IT WAS KIND OF DARK IN THERE—I HOPE SHE DID THINK I WAS A STRAY CAT—OR SOMETHING!
MEANWHILE, TUBBY IS KILLING TIME WHILE WAITING FOR LULU—
RRRRRRRR
?
R-RRR-R-R-R-R-RR-R-RR
WHO IS THAT? WHO IS UPSTAIRS?
UH-OH!
R-RRRRRRR
R-RRRRRR-R-R

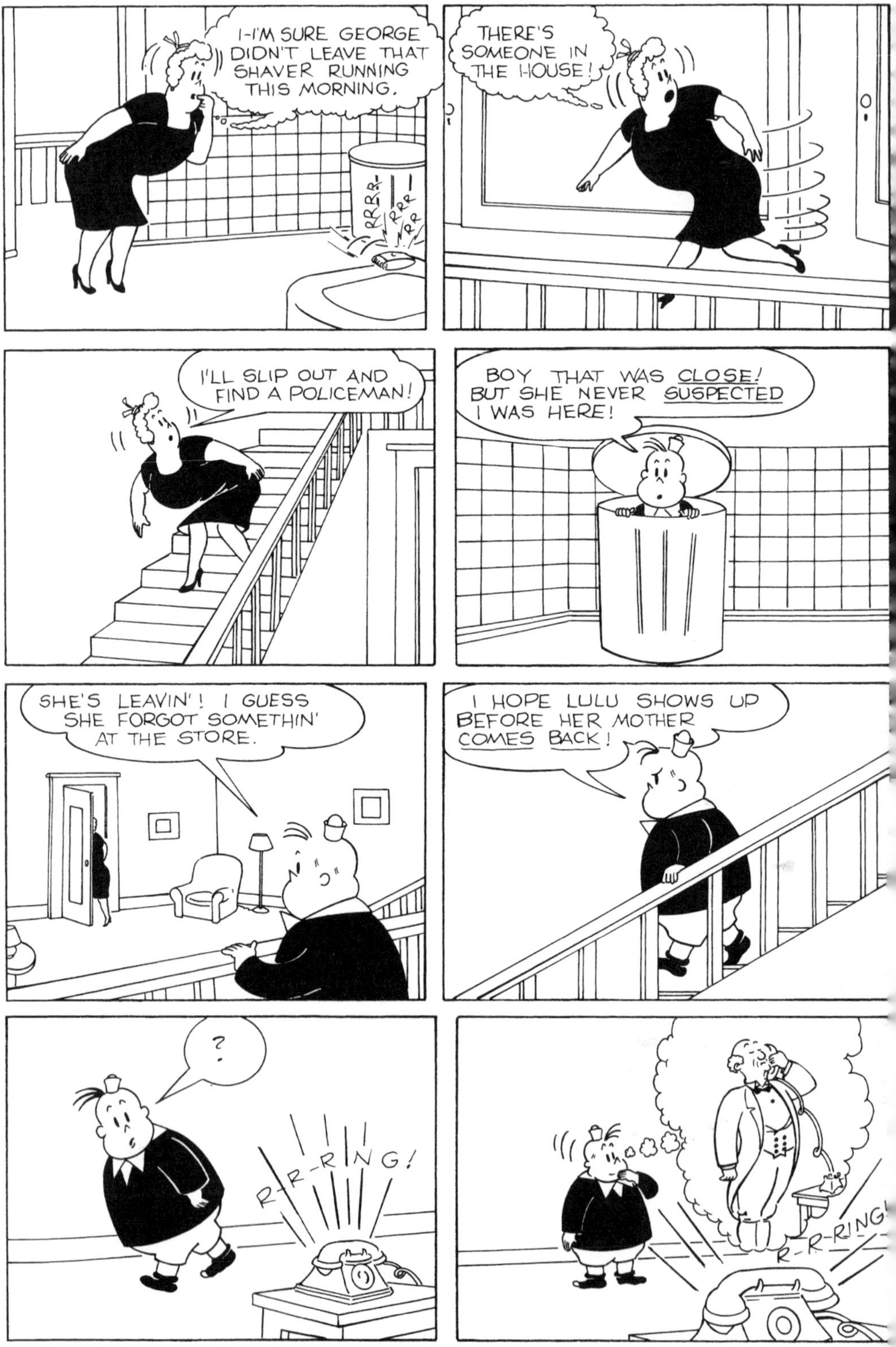
I-I'M SURE GEORGE DIDN'T LEAVE THAT SHAVER RUNNING THIS MORNING.
RRRR
RRR
RR
THERE'S SOMEONE IN THE HOUSE!
I'LL SLIP OUT AND FIND A POLICEMAN!
BOY THAT WAS CLOSE! BUT SHE NEVER SUSPECTED I WAS HERE!
SHE'S LEAVIN'! I GUESS SHE FORGOT SOMETHIN' AT THE STORE.
I HOPE LULU SHOWS UP BEFORE HER MOTHER COMES BACK!
?
R-R-RING!
R-R-RING!

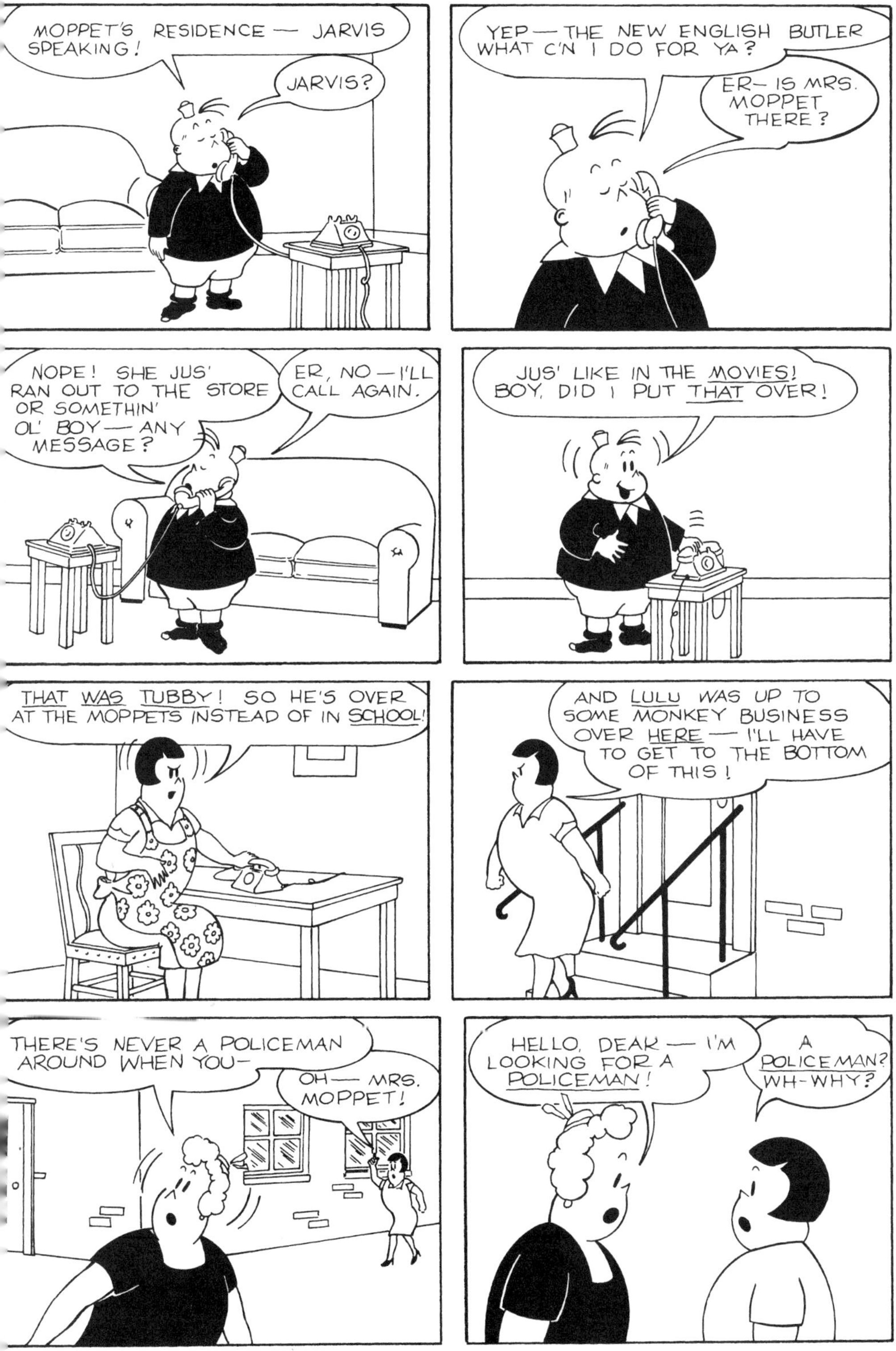
MOPPET'S RESIDENCE — JARVIS SPEAKING!
JARVIS?
YEP — THE NEW ENGLISH BUTLER WHAT C'N I DO FOR YA?
ER— IS MRS. MOPPET THERE?
NOPE! SHE JUS' RAN OUT TO THE STORE OR SOMETHIN' OL' BOY — ANY MESSAGE?
ER, NO — I'LL CALL AGAIN.
JUS' LIKE IN THE MOVIES! BOY, DID I PUT THAT OVER!
THAT WAS TUBBY! SO HE'S OVER AT THE MOPPETS INSTEAD OF IN SCHOOL!
AND LULU WAS UP TO SOME MONKEY BUSINESS OVER HERE — I'LL HAVE TO GET TO THE BOTTOM OF THIS!
THERE'S NEVER A POLICEMAN AROUND WHEN YOU-
OH — MRS. MOPPET!
HELLO, DEAR — I'M LOOKING FOR A POLICEMAN!
A POLICEMAN? WH-WHY?

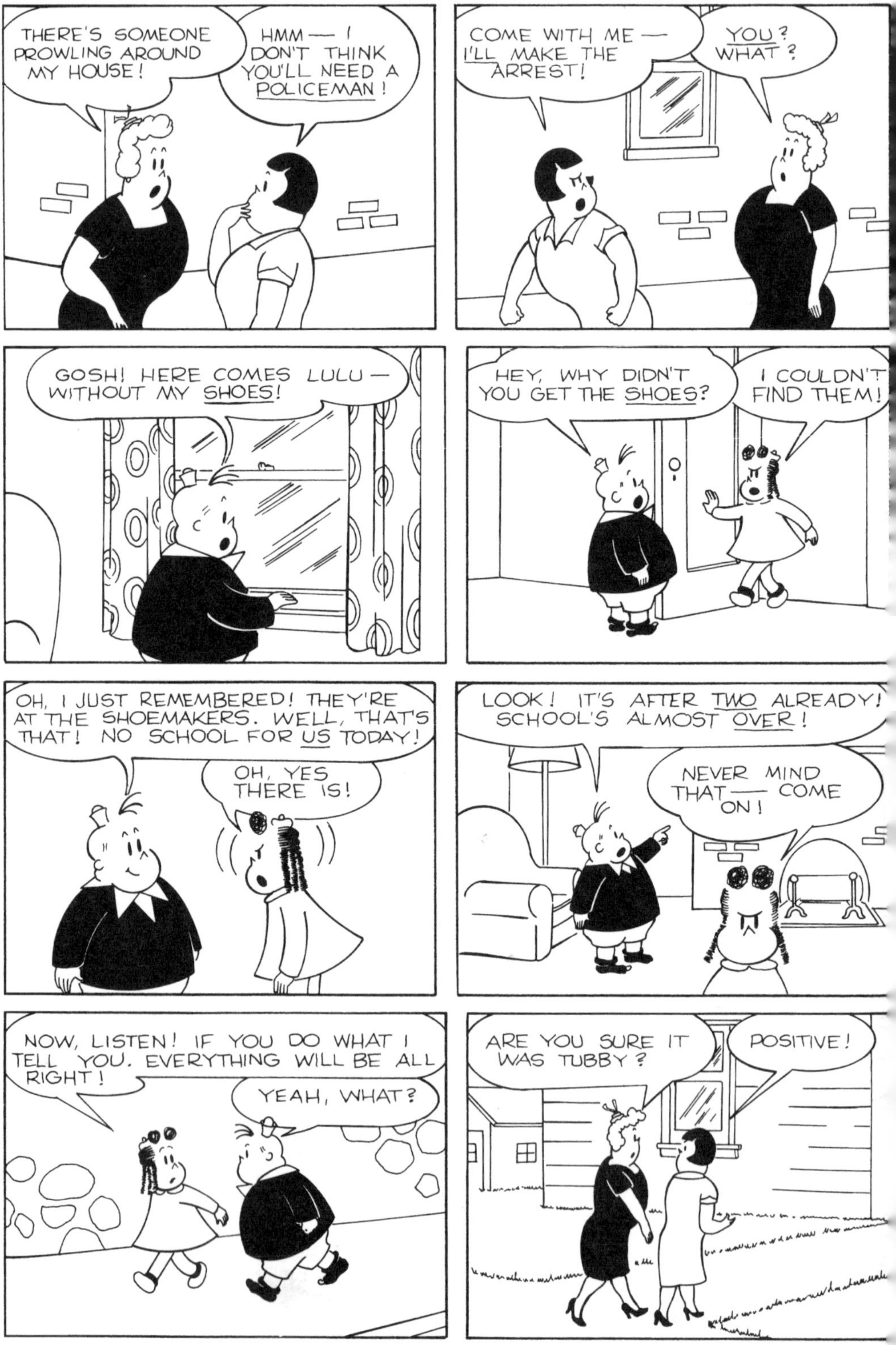
THERE'S SOMEONE PROWLING AROUND MY HOUSE!
HMM — I DON'T THINK YOU'LL NEED A POLICEMAN!
COME WITH ME — I'LL MAKE THE ARREST!
YOU? WHAT?
GOSH! HERE COMES LULU — WITHOUT MY SHOES!
HEY, WHY DIDN'T YOU GET THE SHOES?
I COULDN'T FIND THEM!
OH, I JUST REMEMBERED! THEY'RE AT THE SHOEMAKERS. WELL, THAT'S THAT! NO SCHOOL FOR US TODAY!
OH, YES THERE IS!
LOOK! IT'S AFTER TWO ALREADY! SCHOOL'S ALMOST OVER!
NEVER MIND THAT — COME ON!
NOW, LISTEN! IF YOU DO WHAT I TELL YOU. EVERYTHING WILL BE ALL RIGHT!
YEAH, WHAT?
ARE YOU SURE IT WAS TUBBY?
POSITIVE!

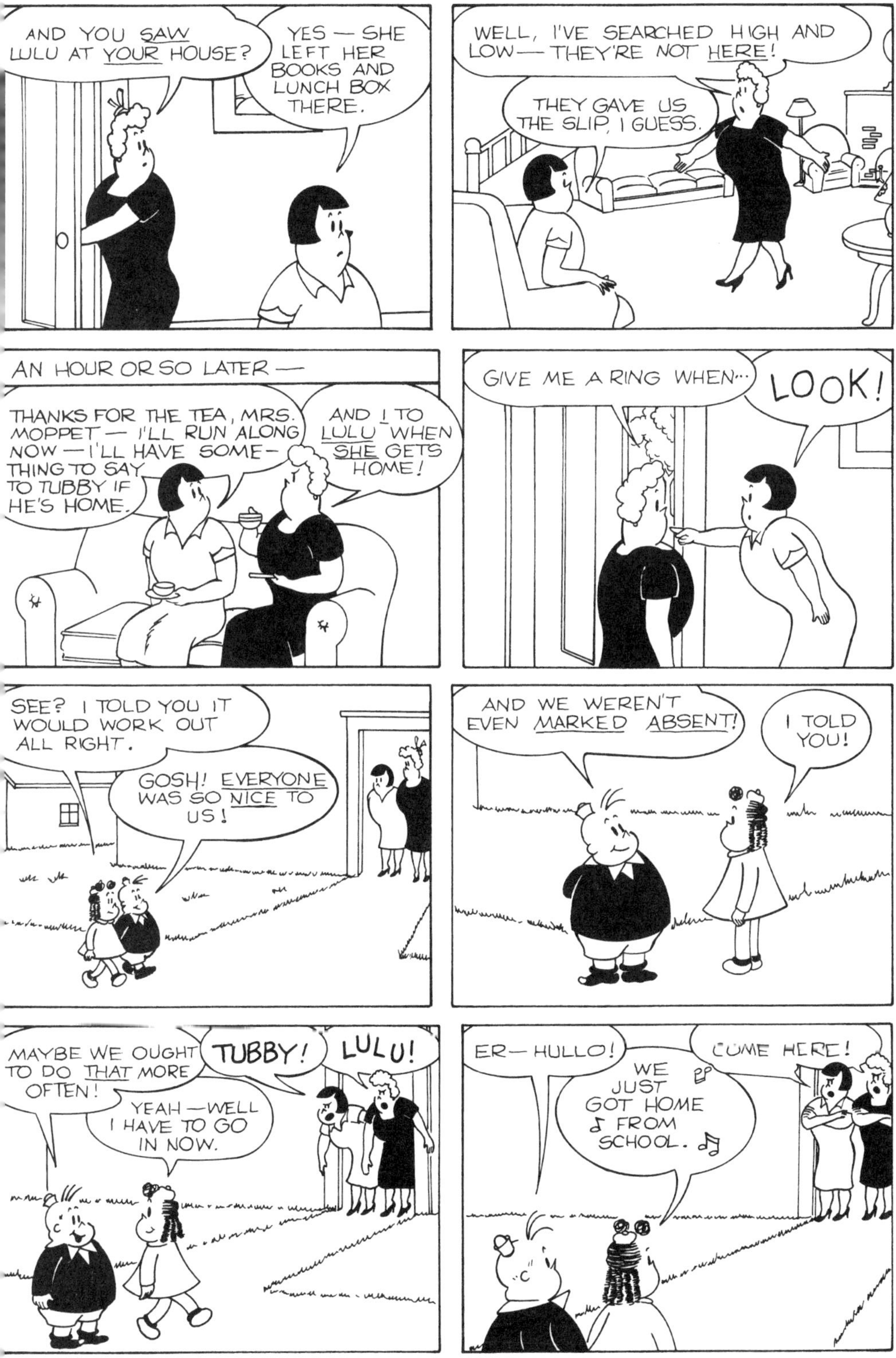
AND YOU SAW LULU AT YOUR HOUSE?
YES — SHE LEFT HER BOOKS AND LUNCH BOX THERE.
WELL, I'VE SEARCHED HIGH AND LOW— THEY'RE NOT HERE!
THEY GAVE US THE SLIP, I GUESS.
AN HOUR OR SO LATER —
THANKS FOR THE TEA, MRS. MOPPET — I'LL RUN ALONG NOW — I'LL HAVE SOMETHING TO SAY TO TUBBY IF HE'S HOME.
AND I TO LULU WHEN SHE GETS HOME!
GIVE ME A RING WHEN...
LOOK!
SEE? I TOLD YOU IT WOULD WORK OUT ALL RIGHT.
GOSH! EVERYONE WAS SO NICE TO US!
AND WE WEREN'T EVEN MARKED ABSENT!
I TOLD YOU!
MAYBE WE OUGHT TO DO THAT MORE OFTEN!
YEAH — WELL I HAVE TO GO IN NOW.
TUBBY!
LULU!
ER— HULLO!
WE JUST GOT HOME FROM SCHOOL.
COME HERE!

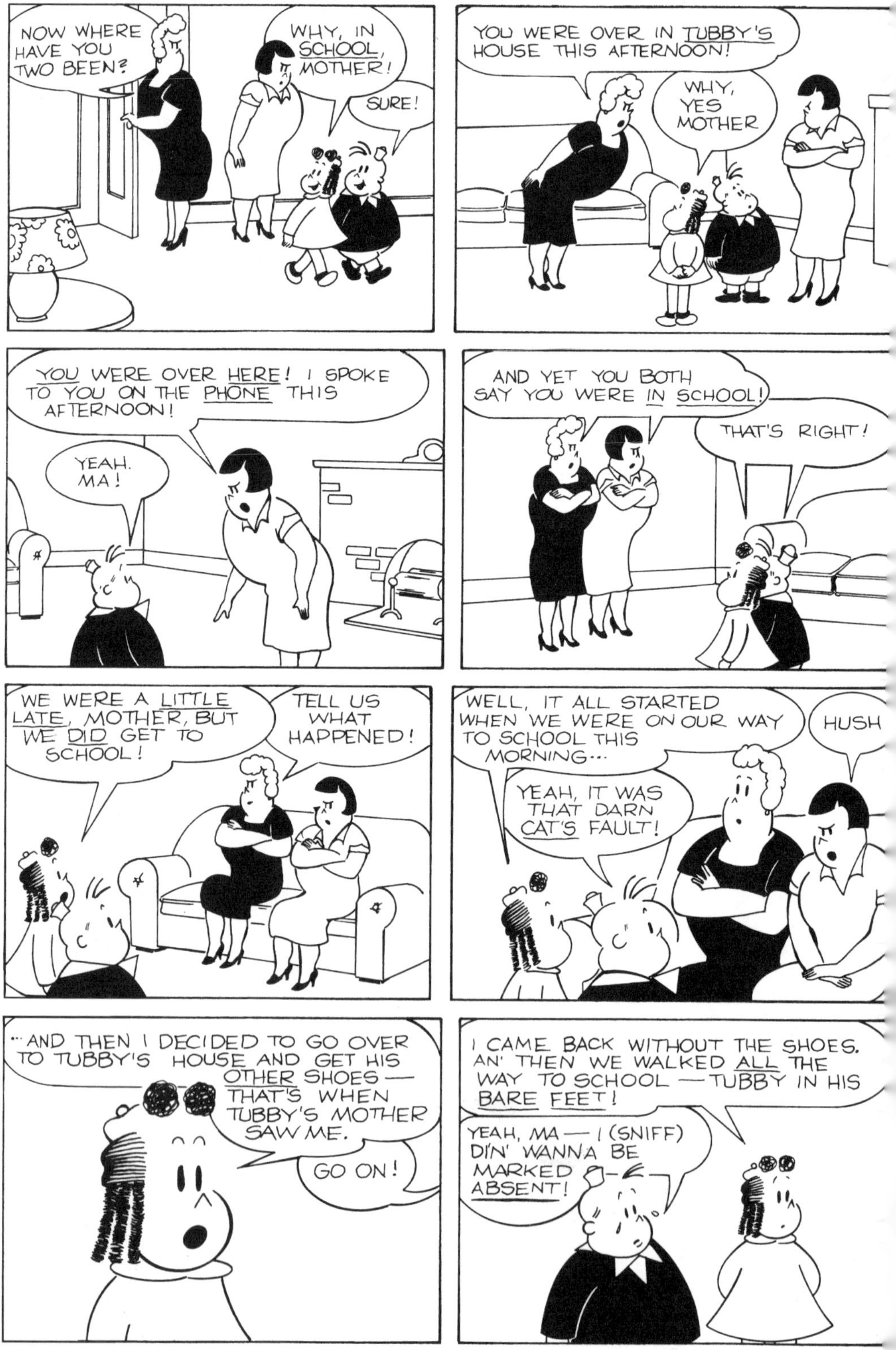
NOW WHERE HAVE YOU TWO BEEN?
WHY, IN SCHOOL, MOTHER!
SURE!
YOU WERE OVER IN TUBBY'S HOUSE THIS AFTERNOON!
WHY, YES MOTHER
YOU WERE OVER HERE! I SPOKE TO YOU ON THE PHONE THIS AFTERNOON!
YEAH. MA!
AND YET YOU BOTH SAY YOU WERE IN SCHOOL!
THAT'S RIGHT!
WE WERE A LITTLE LATE, MOTHER, BUT WE DID GET TO SCHOOL!
TELL US WHAT HAPPENED!
WELL, IT ALL STARTED WHEN WE WERE ON OUR WAY TO SCHOOL THIS MORNING...
HUSH
YEAH, IT WAS THAT DARN CAT'S FAULT!
...AND THEN I DECIDED TO GO OVER TO TUBBY'S HOUSE AND GET HIS OTHER SHOES — THAT'S WHEN TUBBY'S MOTHER SAW ME.
GO ON!
I CAME BACK WITHOUT THE SHOES. AN' THEN WE WALKED ALL THE WAY TO SCHOOL — TUBBY IN HIS BARE FEET!
YEAH, MA — I (SNIFF) DIN' WANNA BE MARKED ABSENT!

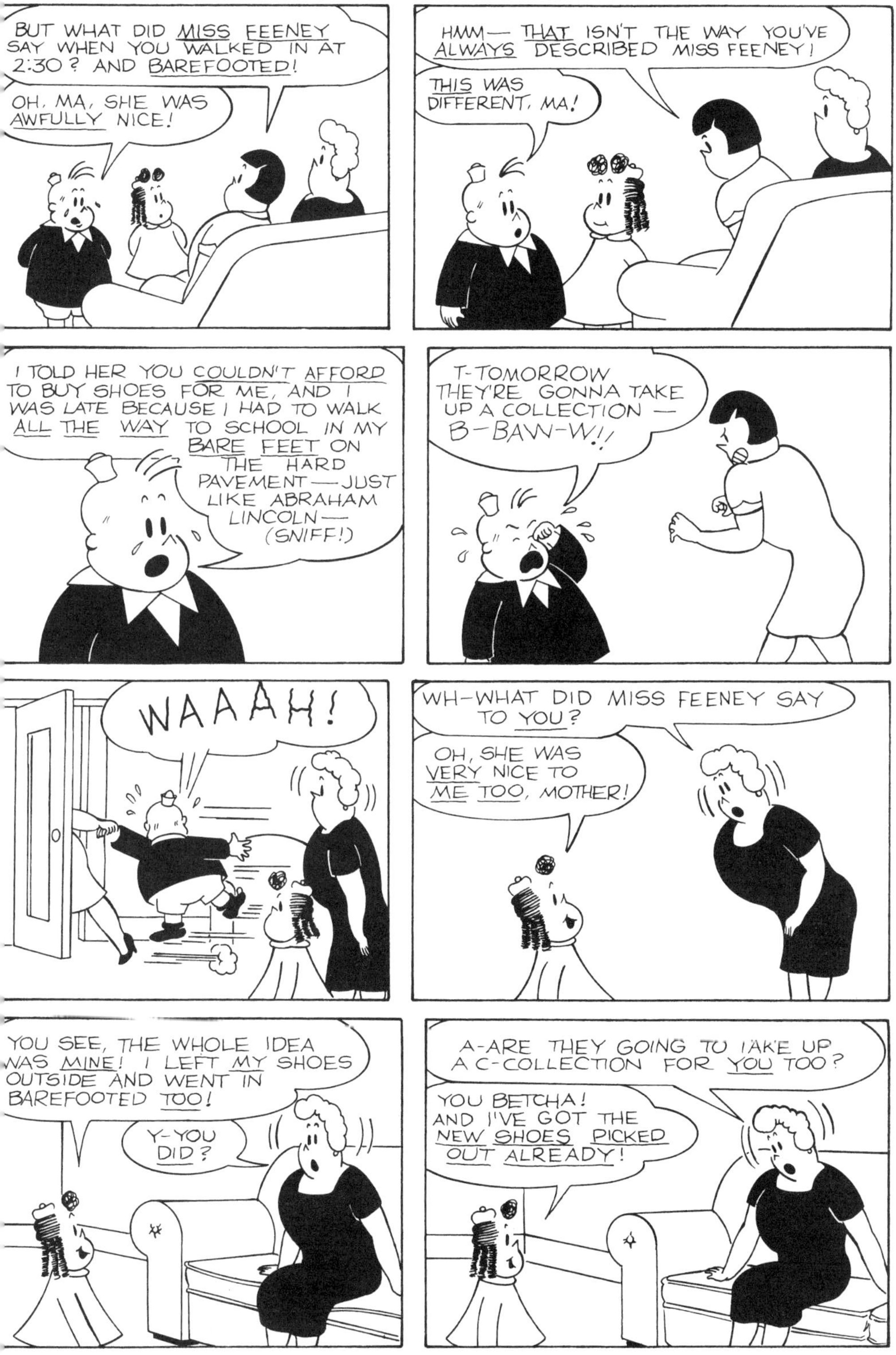

BUT WHAT DID MISS FEENEY SAY WHEN YOU WALKED IN AT 2:30? AND BAREFOOTED!
OH, MA, SHE WAS AWFULLY NICE!
HMM— THAT ISN'T THE WAY YOU'VE ALWAYS DESCRIBED MISS FEENEY!
THIS WAS DIFFERENT, MA!
I TOLD HER YOU COULDN'T AFFORD TO BUY SHOES FOR ME, AND I WAS LATE BECAUSE I HAD TO WALK ALL THE WAY TO SCHOOL IN MY BARE FEET ON THE HARD PAVEMENT—JUST LIKE ABRAHAM LINCOLN— (SNIFF!)
T-TOMORROW THEY'RE GONNA TAKE UP A COLLECTION — B-BAW-W!!
WAAAH!
WH-WHAT DID MISS FEENEY SAY TO YOU?
OH, SHE WAS VERY NICE TO ME TOO, MOTHER!
YOU SEE, THE WHOLE IDEA WAS MINE! I LEFT MY SHOES OUTSIDE AND WENT IN BAREFOOTED TOO!
Y-YOU DID?
A-ARE THEY GOING TO TAKE UP A C-COLLECTION FOR YOU TOO?
YOU BETCHA! AND I'VE GOT THE NEW SHOES PICKED OUT ALREADY!

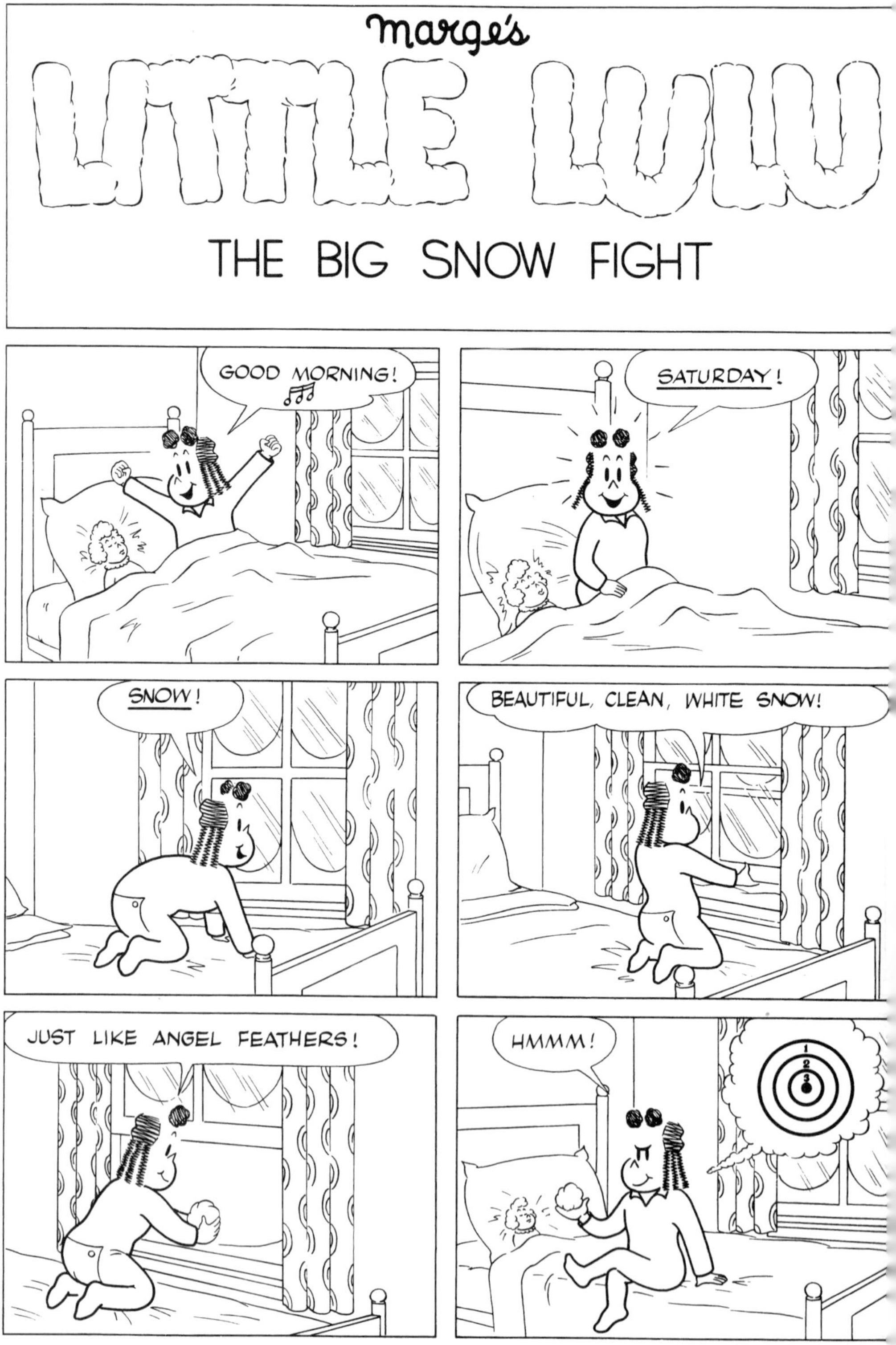
marge's
LITTLE LULU
THE BIG SNOW FIGHT
GOOD MORNING!
SATURDAY!
SNOW!
BEAUTIFUL, CLEAN, WHITE SNOW!
JUST LIKE ANGEL FEATHERS!
HMMM!
1
2
3

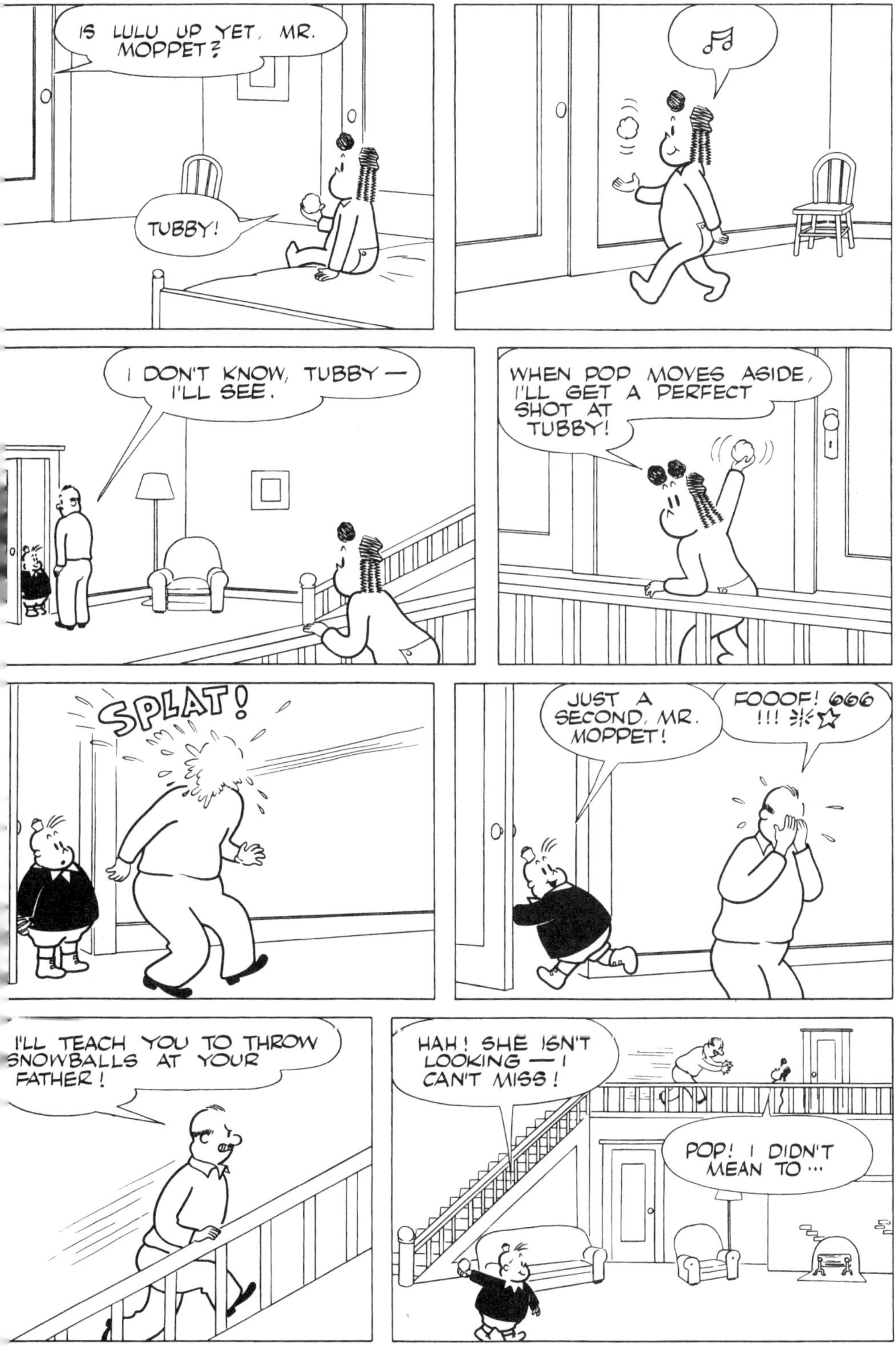
IS LULU UP YET, MR. MOPPET?
TUBBY!
I DON'T KNOW, TUBBY — I'LL SEE.
WHEN POP MOVES ASIDE, I'LL GET A PERFECT SHOT AT TUBBY!
SPLAT!
JUST A SECOND, MR. MOPPET!
FOOOF! !!!
I'LL TEACH YOU TO THROW SNOWBALLS AT YOUR FATHER!
HAH! SHE ISN'T LOOKING — I CAN'T MISS!
POP! I DIDN'T MEAN TO ...

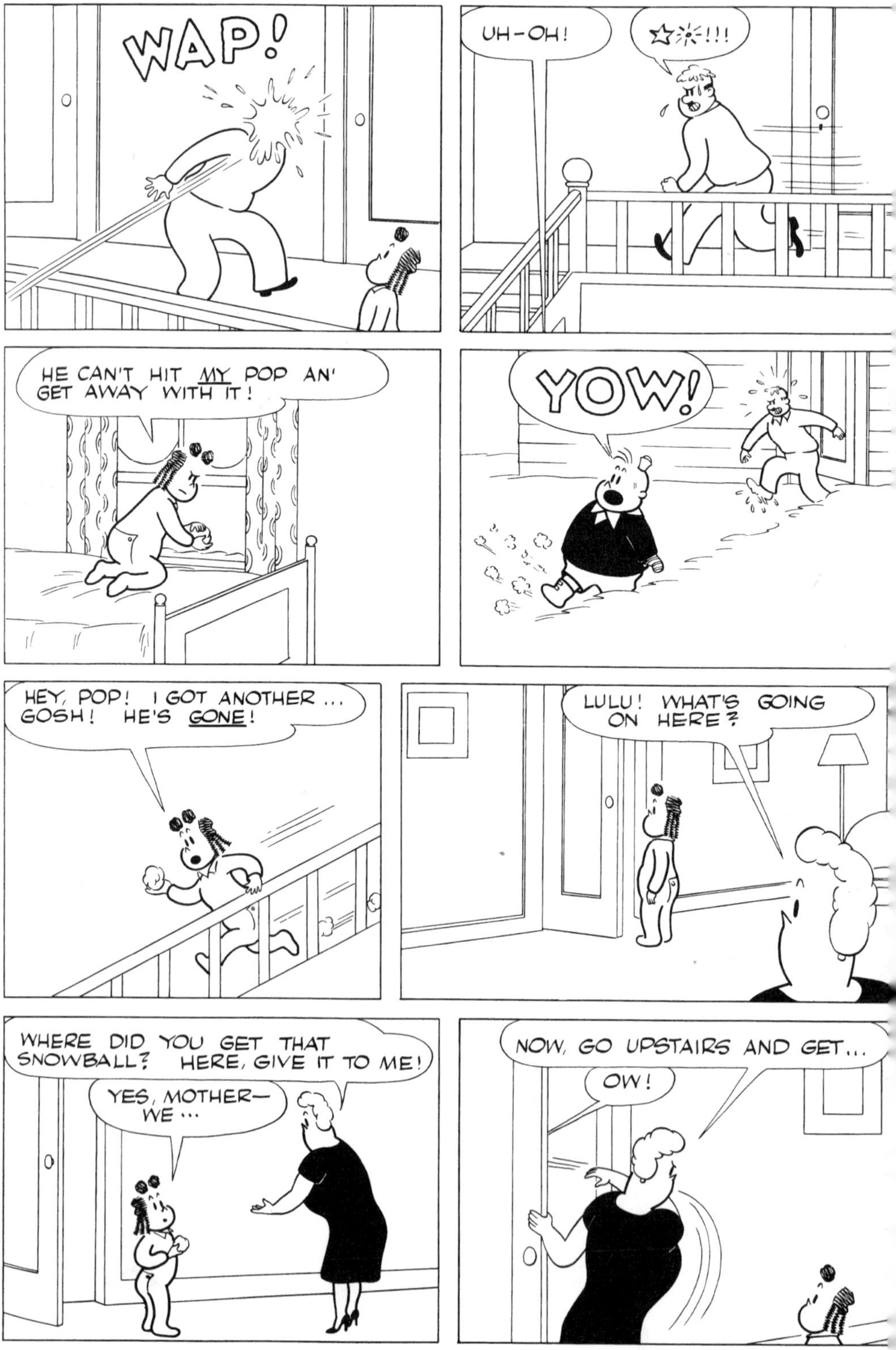
WAP!
UH-OH!
HE CAN'T HIT MY POP AN' GET AWAY WITH IT!
YOW!
HEY, POP! I GOT ANOTHER ... GOSH! HE'S GONE!
LULU! WHAT'S GOING ON HERE?
WHERE DID YOU GET THAT SNOWBALL? HERE, GIVE IT TO ME!
YES, MOTHER— WE ...
NOW, GO UPSTAIRS AND GET...
OW!

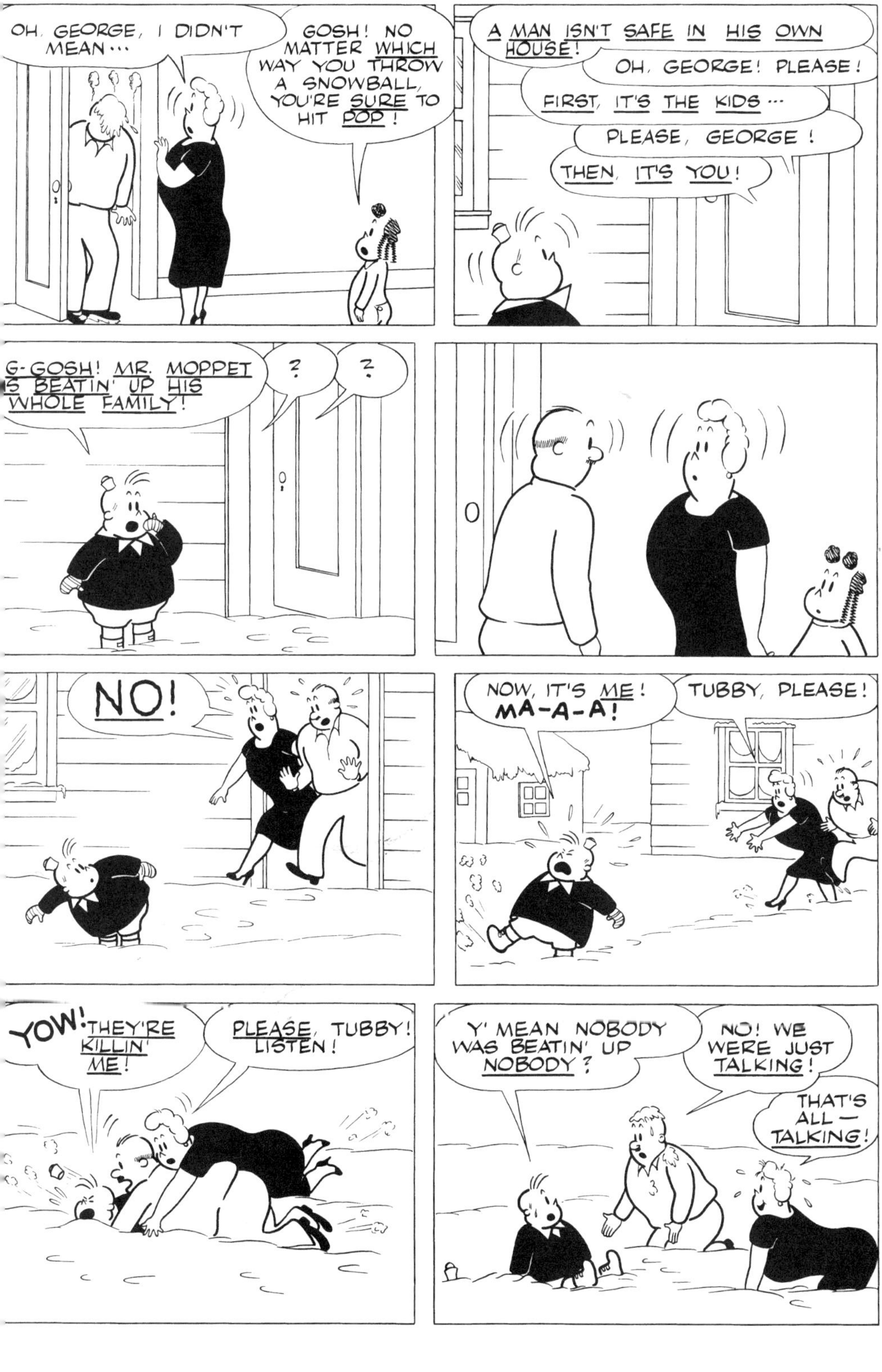
OH, GEORGE, I DIDN'T MEAN...
GOSH! NO MATTER WHICH WAY YOU THROW A SNOWBALL, YOU'RE SURE TO HIT POP!
A MAN ISN'T SAFE IN HIS OWN HOUSE!
OH, GEORGE! PLEASE!
FIRST, IT'S THE KIDS...
PLEASE, GEORGE!
THEN, IT'S YOU!
G-GOSH! MR. MOPPET IS BEATIN' UP HIS WHOLE FAMILY!
?
?
NO!
NOW, IT'S ME! MA-A-A!
TUBBY, PLEASE!
YOW! THEY'RE KILLIN' ME!
PLEASE, TUBBY! LISTEN!
Y' MEAN NOBODY WAS BEATIN' UP NOBODY?
NO! WE WERE JUST TALKING!
THAT'S ALL — TALKING!

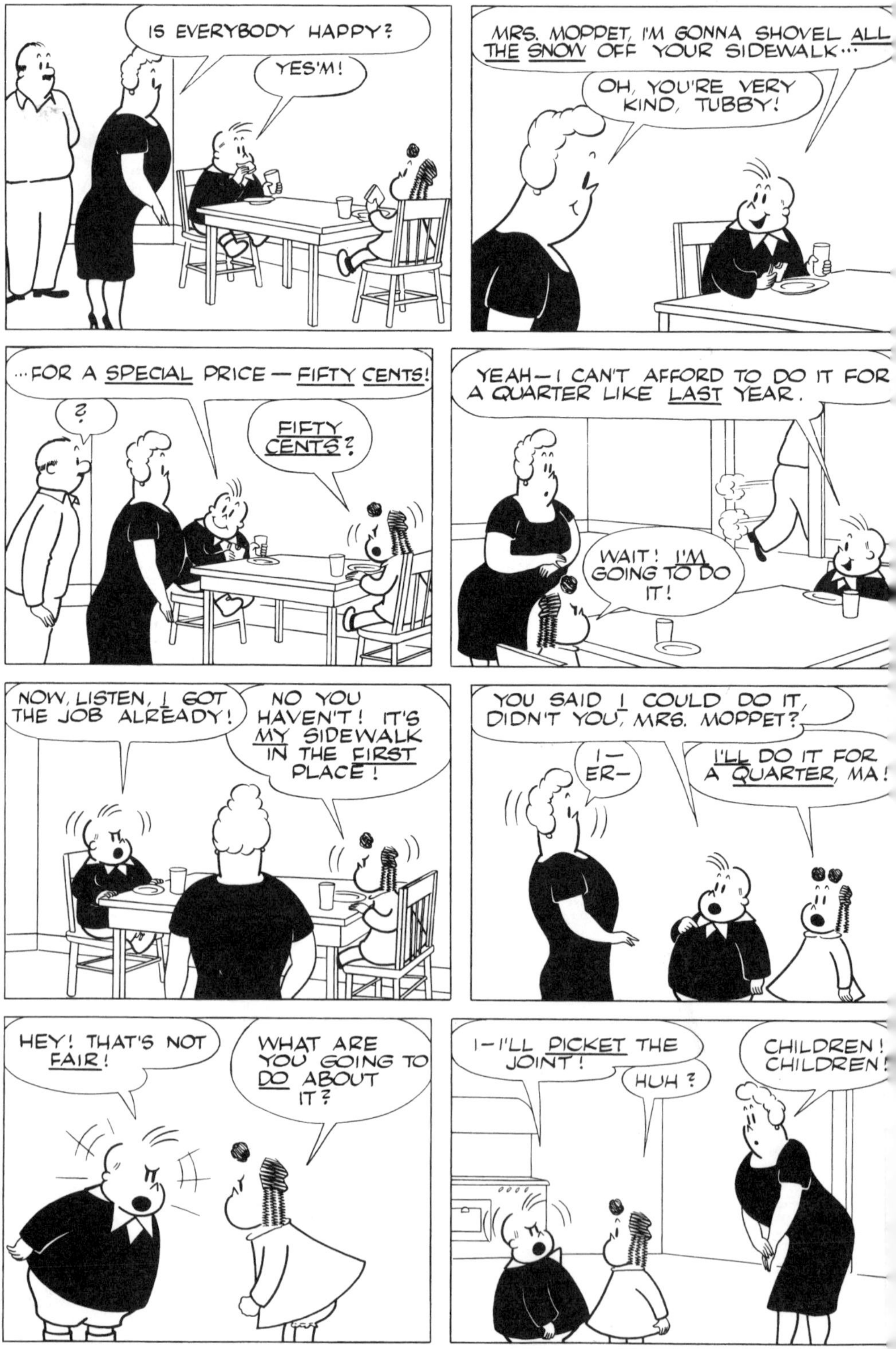
IS EVERYBODY HAPPY?
YES'M!
MRS. MOPPET, I'M GONNA SHOVEL ALL THE SNOW OFF YOUR SIDEWALK...
OH, YOU'RE VERY KIND, TUBBY!
...FOR A SPECIAL PRICE — FIFTY CENTS!
?
FIFTY CENTS?
YEAH — I CAN'T AFFORD TO DO IT FOR A QUARTER LIKE LAST YEAR.
WAIT! I'M GOING TO DO IT!
NOW, LISTEN, I GOT THE JOB ALREADY!
NO YOU HAVEN'T! IT'S MY SIDEWALK IN THE FIRST PLACE!
YOU SAID I COULD DO IT, DIDN'T YOU, MRS. MOPPET?
I— ER—
I'LL DO IT FOR A QUARTER, MA!
HEY! THAT'S NOT FAIR!
WHAT ARE YOU GOING TO DO ABOUT IT?
I—I'LL PICKET THE JOINT!
HUH?
CHILDREN! CHILDREN!

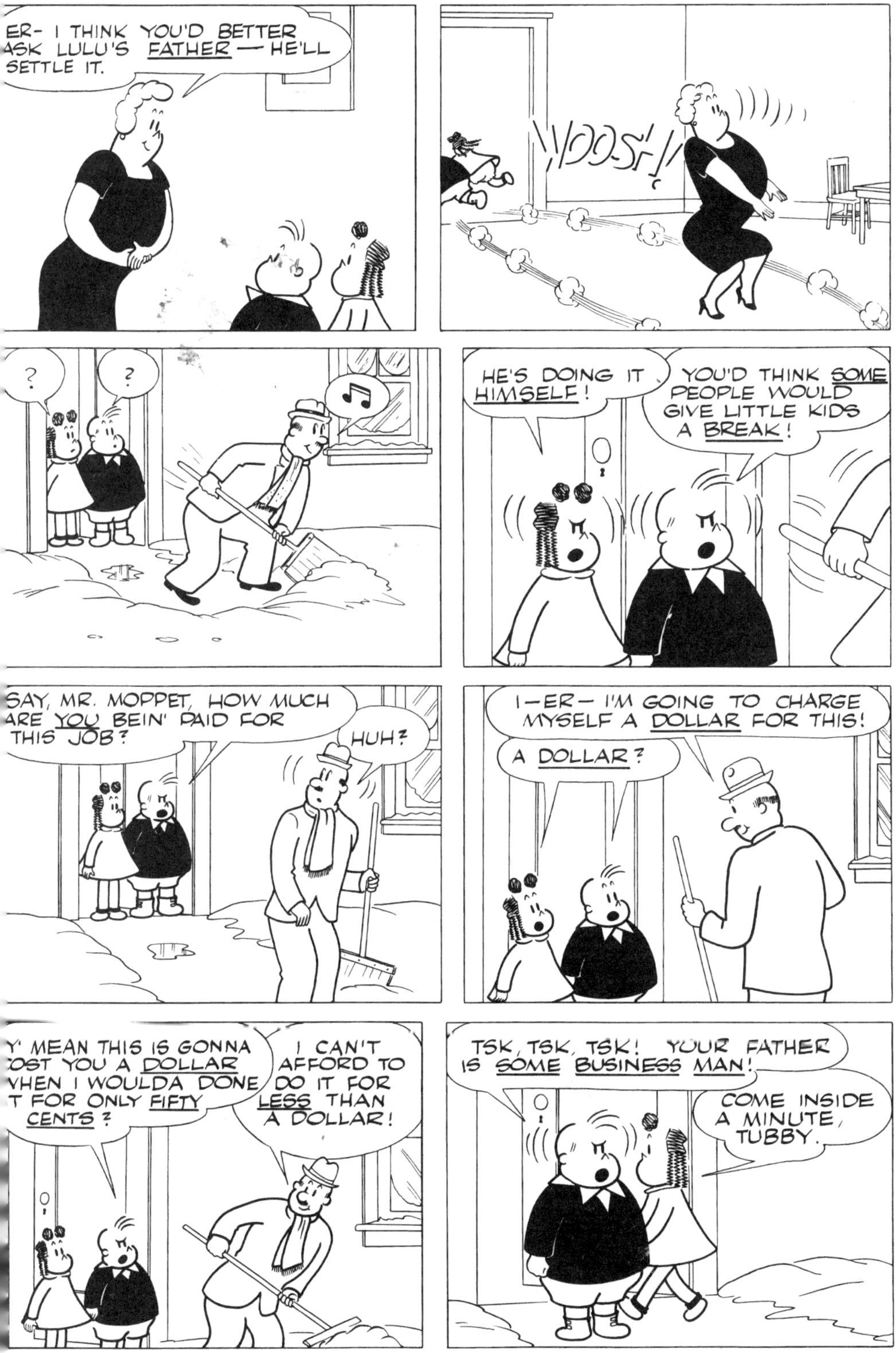
ER- I THINK YOU'D BETTER ASK LULU'S FATHER — HE'LL SETTLE IT.
WOOSH!
?
?
HE'S DOING IT HIMSELF!
YOU'D THINK SOME PEOPLE WOULD GIVE LITTLE KIDS A BREAK!
SAY, MR. MOPPET, HOW MUCH ARE YOU BEIN' PAID FOR THIS JOB?
HUH?
I-ER- I'M GOING TO CHARGE MYSELF A DOLLAR FOR THIS!
A DOLLAR?
Y' MEAN THIS IS GONNA COST YOU A DOLLAR WHEN I WOULDA DONE IT FOR ONLY FIFTY CENTS?
I CAN'T AFFORD TO DO IT FOR LESS THAN A DOLLAR!
TSK, TSK, TSK! YOUR FATHER IS SOME BUSINESS MAN!
COME INSIDE A MINUTE, TUBBY.

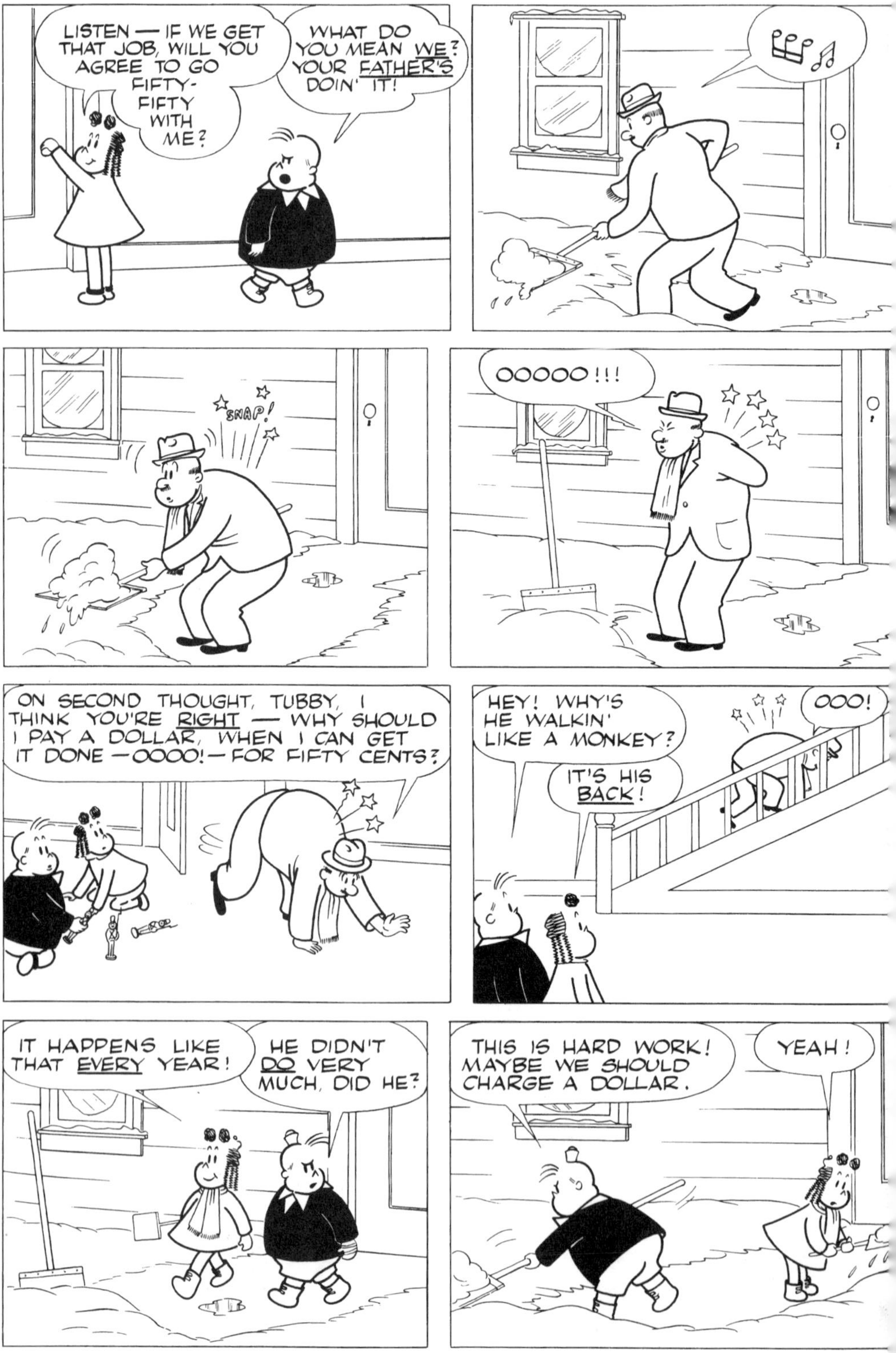
LISTEN — IF WE GET THAT JOB, WILL YOU AGREE TO GO FIFTY-FIFTY WITH ME?
WHAT DO YOU MEAN WE? YOUR FATHER'S DOIN' IT!
SNAP!
OOOOO!!!
ON SECOND THOUGHT, TUBBY, I THINK YOU'RE RIGHT — WHY SHOULD I PAY A DOLLAR, WHEN I CAN GET IT DONE —OOOO!— FOR FIFTY CENTS?
HEY! WHY'S HE WALKIN' LIKE A MONKEY?
OOO!
IT'S HIS BACK!
IT HAPPENS LIKE THAT EVERY YEAR!
HE DIDN'T DO VERY MUCH, DID HE?
THIS IS HARD WORK! MAYBE WE SHOULD CHARGE A DOLLAR.
YEAH!

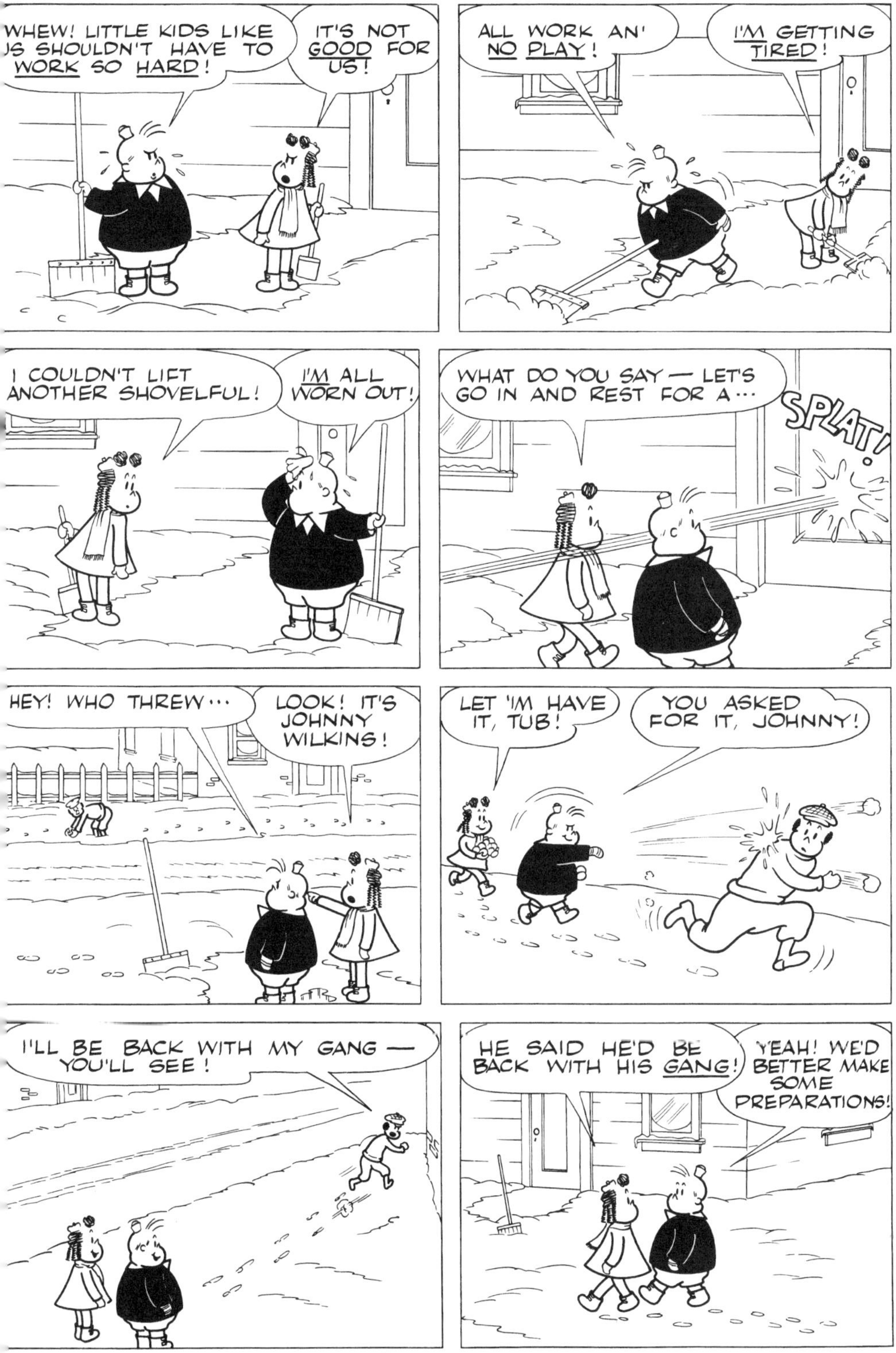
WHEW! LITTLE KIDS LIKE US SHOULDN'T HAVE TO WORK SO HARD!
IT'S NOT GOOD FOR US!
ALL WORK AN' NO PLAY!
I'M GETTING TIRED!
I COULDN'T LIFT ANOTHER SHOVELFUL!
I'M ALL WORN OUT!
WHAT DO YOU SAY — LET'S GO IN AND REST FOR A···
SPLAT!
HEY! WHO THREW···
LOOK! IT'S JOHNNY WILKINS!
LET 'IM HAVE IT, TUB!
YOU ASKED FOR IT, JOHNNY!
I'LL BE BACK WITH MY GANG — YOU'LL SEE!
HE SAID HE'D BE BACK WITH HIS GANG!
YEAH! WE'D BETTER MAKE SOME PREPARATIONS!

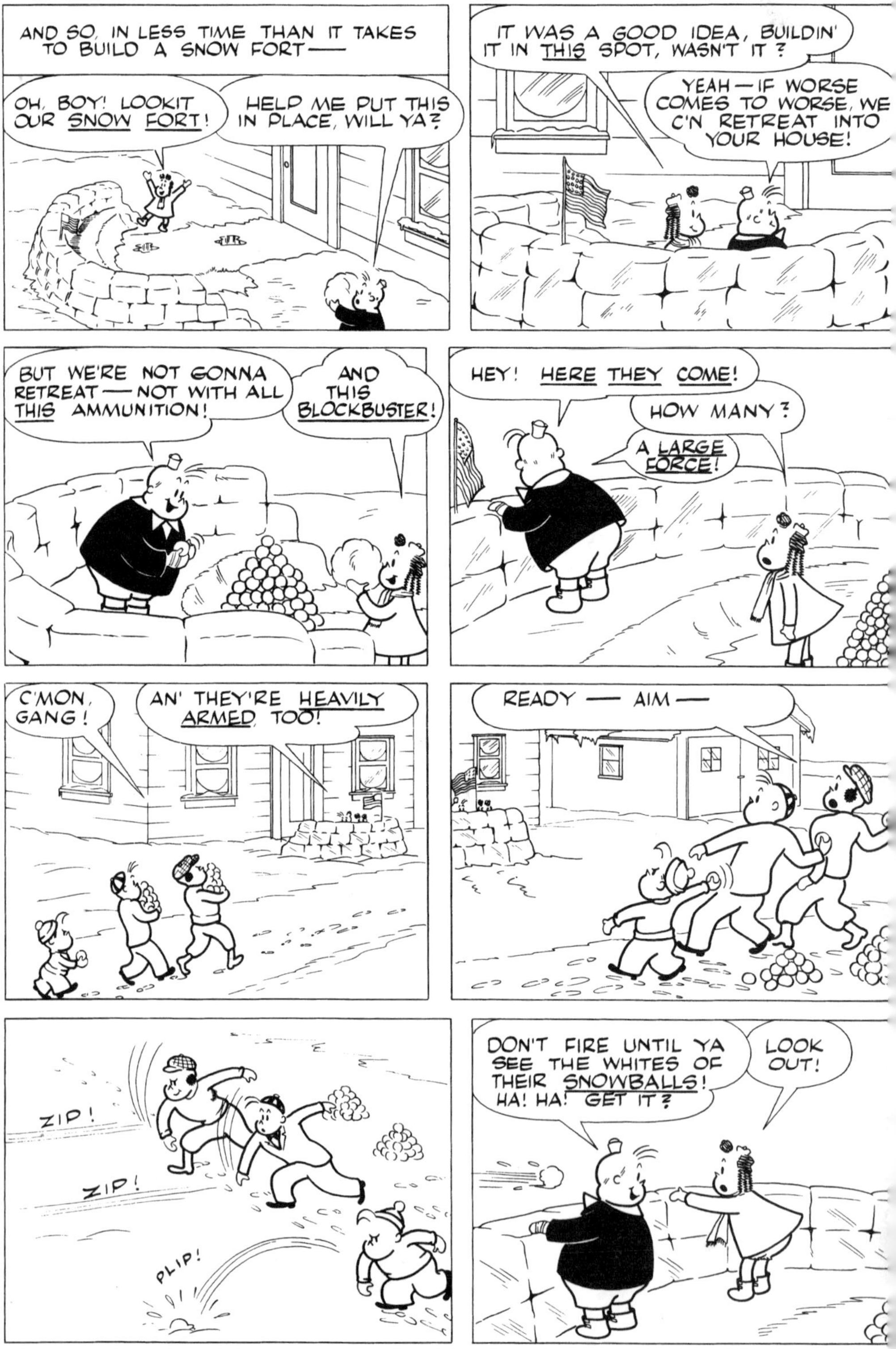

AND SO, IN LESS TIME THAN IT TAKES TO BUILD A SNOW FORT—
OH, BOY! LOOKIT OUR SNOW FORT!
HELP ME PUT THIS IN PLACE, WILL YA?
IT WAS A GOOD IDEA, BUILDIN' IT IN THIS SPOT, WASN'T IT?
YEAH — IF WORSE COMES TO WORSE, WE C'N RETREAT INTO YOUR HOUSE!
BUT WE'RE NOT GONNA RETREAT — NOT WITH ALL THIS AMMUNITION!
AND THIS BLOCKBUSTER!
HEY! HERE THEY COME!
HOW MANY?
A LARGE FORCE!
C'MON, GANG!
AN' THEY'RE HEAVILY ARMED, TOO!
READY — AIM —
ZIP!
ZIP!
PLIP!
DON'T FIRE UNTIL YA SEE THE WHITES OF THEIR SNOWBALLS! HA! HA! GET IT?
LOOK OUT!

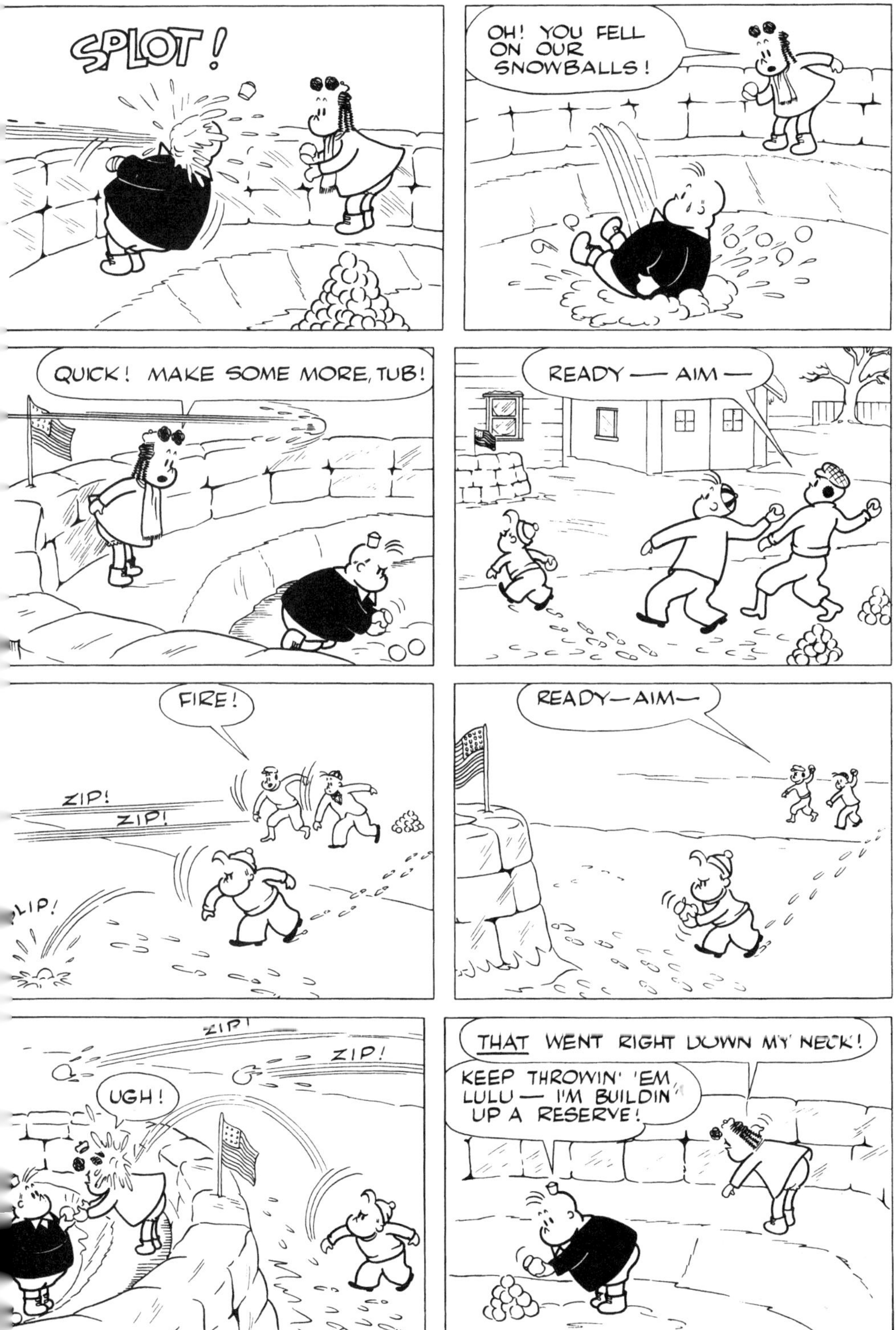
SPLOT!
OH! YOU FELL ON OUR SNOWBALLS!
QUICK! MAKE SOME MORE, TUB!
READY — AIM —
FIRE!
ZIP!
ZIP!
READY—AIM—
ZIP!
ZIP!
UGH!
THAT WENT RIGHT DOWN MY NECK!
KEEP THROWIN' 'EM LULU — I'M BUILDIN UP A RESERVE!

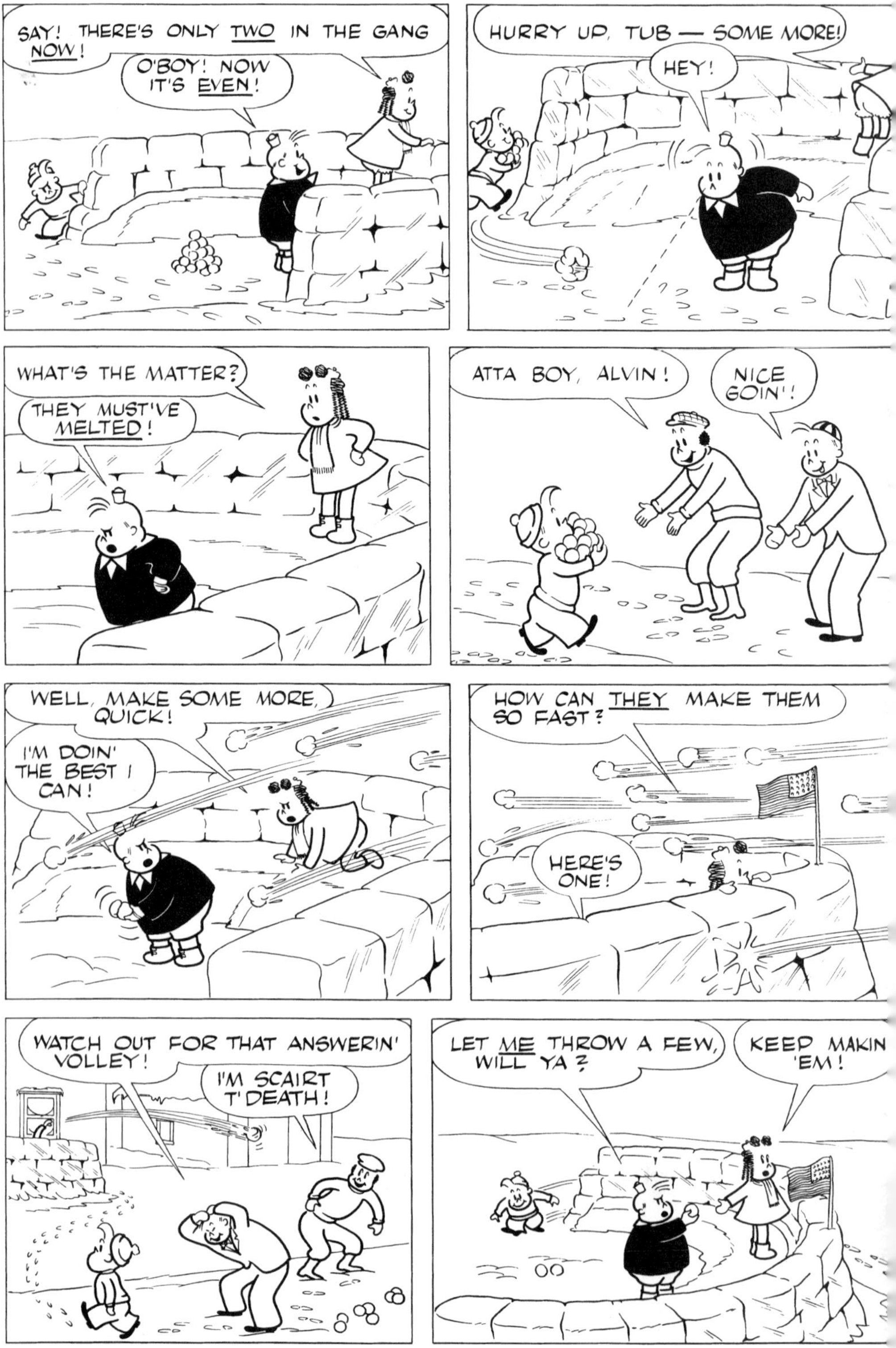
SAY! THERE'S ONLY TWO IN THE GANG NOW!
O'BOY! NOW IT'S EVEN!
HURRY UP, TUB — SOME MORE!
HEY!
WHAT'S THE MATTER?
THEY MUST'VE MELTED!
ATTA BOY, ALVIN!
NICE GOIN'!
WELL, MAKE SOME MORE, QUICK!
I'M DOIN' THE BEST I CAN!
HOW CAN THEY MAKE THEM SO FAST?
HERE'S ONE!
WATCH OUT FOR THAT ANSWERIN' VOLLEY!
I'M SCAIRT T'DEATH!
LET ME THROW A FEW, WILL YA?
KEEP MAKIN 'EM!

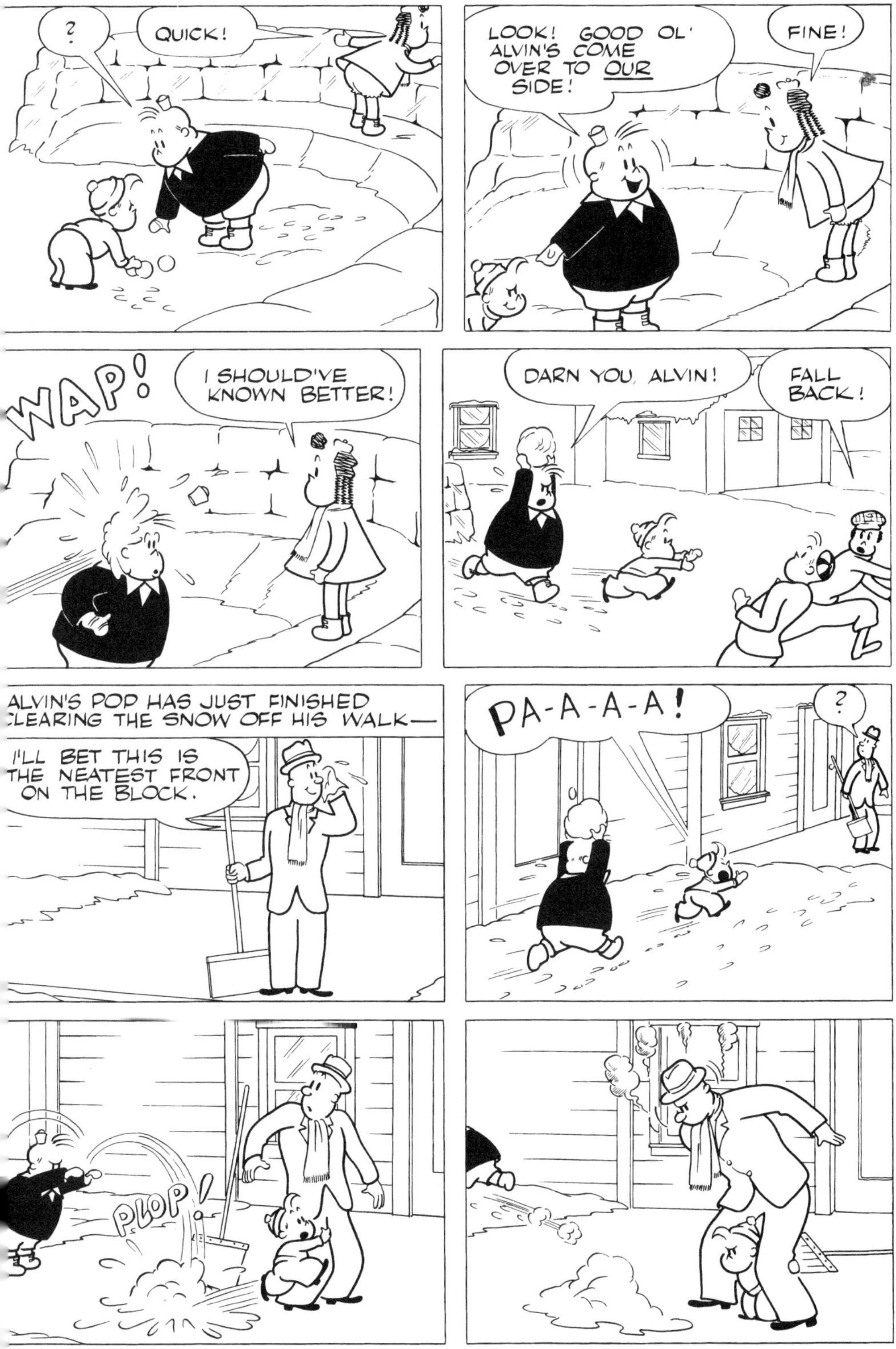
?
QUICK!
LOOK! GOOD OL' ALVIN'S COME OVER TO OUR SIDE!
FINE!
WAP!
I SHOULD'VE KNOWN BETTER!
DARN YOU, ALVIN!
FALL BACK!
ALVIN'S POP HAS JUST FINISHED CLEARING THE SNOW OFF HIS WALK—
I'LL BET THIS IS THE NEATEST FRONT ON THE BLOCK.
PA-A-A-A!
?
PLOP!

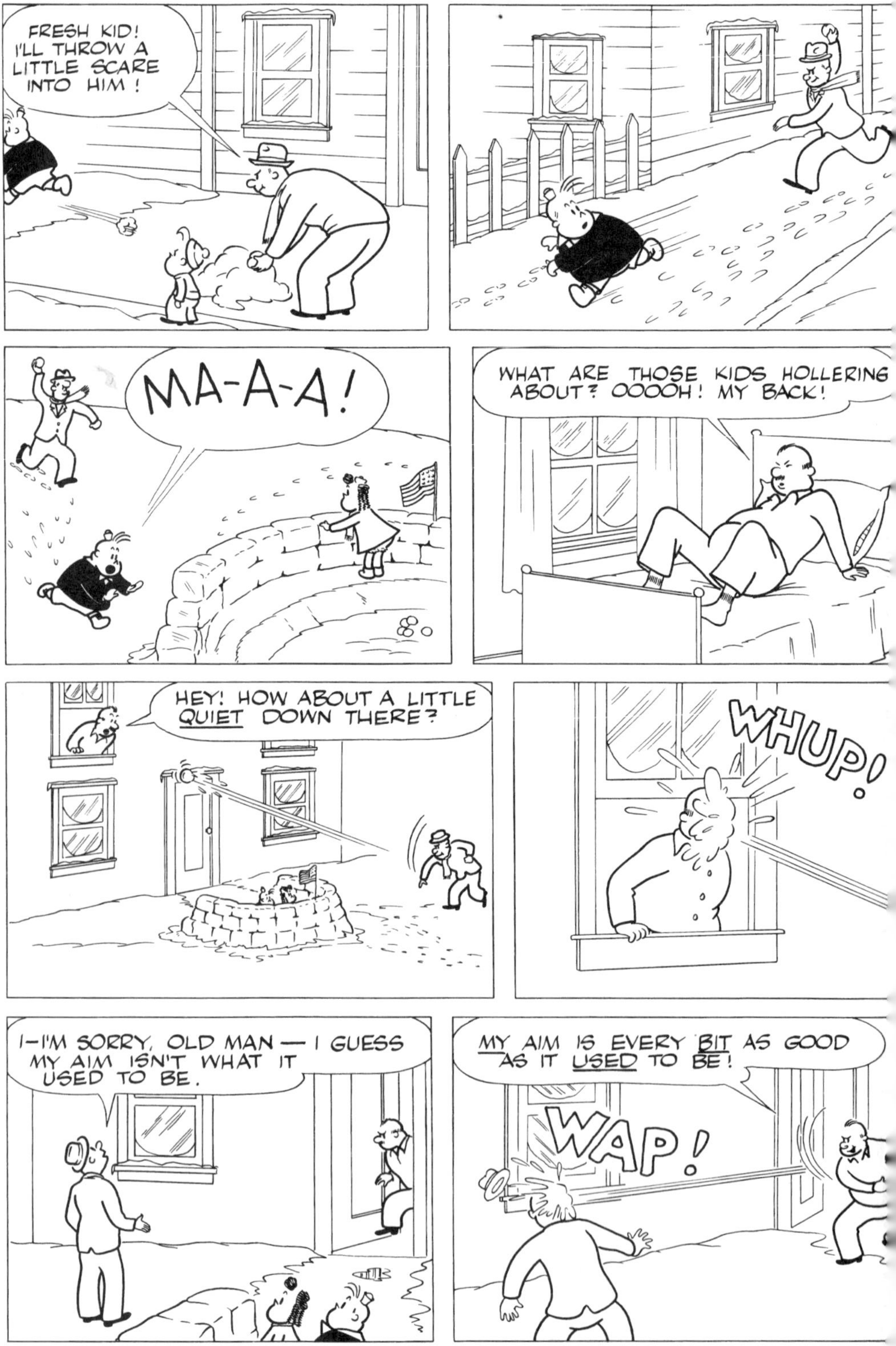
FRESH KID! I'LL THROW A LITTLE SCARE INTO HIM!
MA-A-A!
WHAT ARE THOSE KIDS HOLLERING ABOUT? OOOOH! MY BACK!
HEY! HOW ABOUT A LITTLE QUIET DOWN THERE?
WHUP!
I-I'M SORRY, OLD MAN — I GUESS MY AIM ISN'T WHAT IT USED TO BE.
MY AIM IS EVERY BIT AS GOOD AS IT USED TO BE!
WAP!

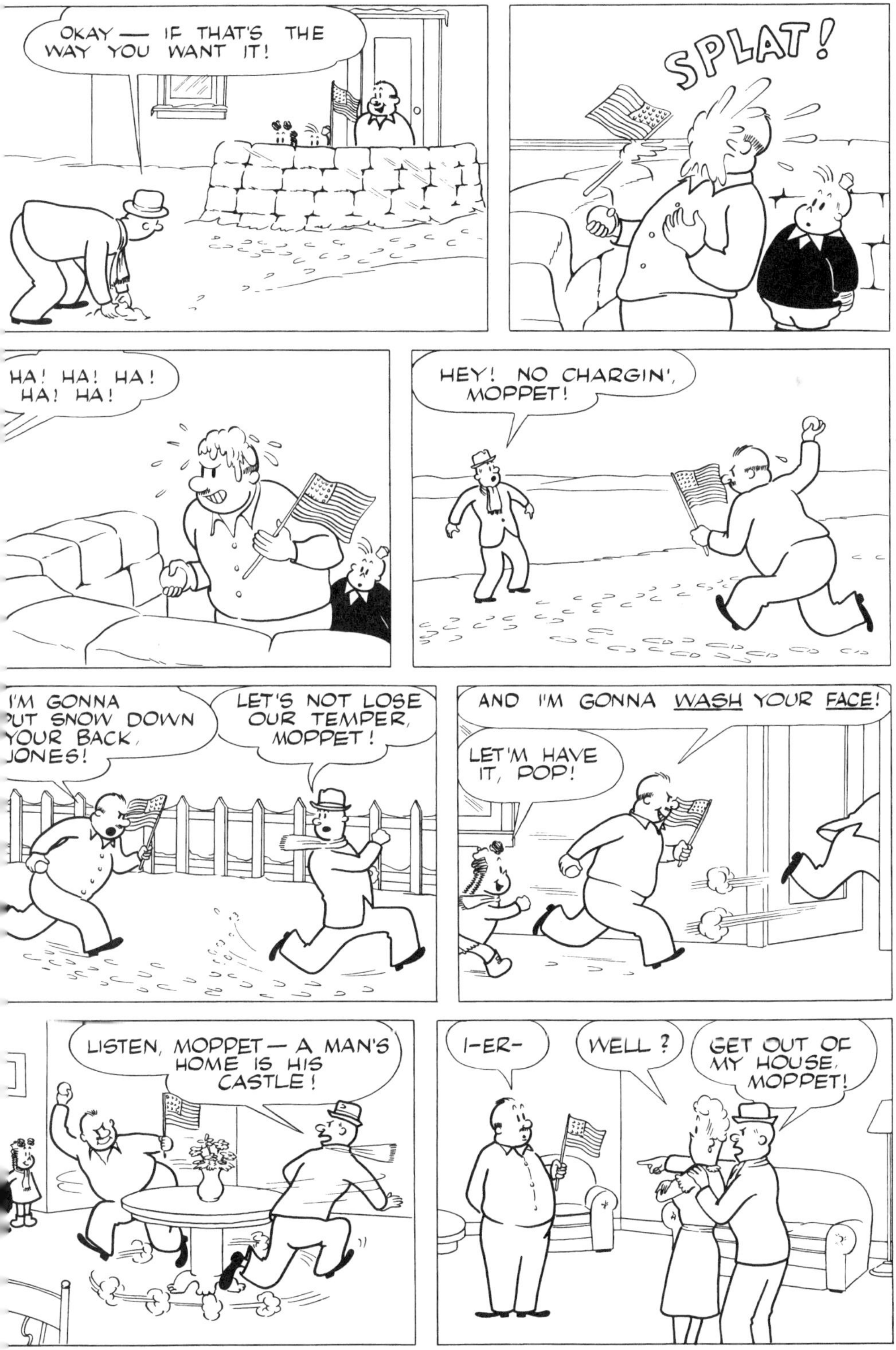
OKAY — IF THAT'S THE WAY YOU WANT IT!
SPLAT!
HA! HA! HA! HA! HA!
HEY! NO CHARGIN', MOPPET!
I'M GONNA PUT SNOW DOWN YOUR BACK, JONES!
LET'S NOT LOSE OUR TEMPER, MOPPET!
AND I'M GONNA WASH YOUR FACE!
LET'M HAVE IT, POP!
LISTEN, MOPPET — A MAN'S HOME IS HIS CASTLE!
I-ER-
WELL ?
GET OUT OF MY HOUSE, MOPPET!

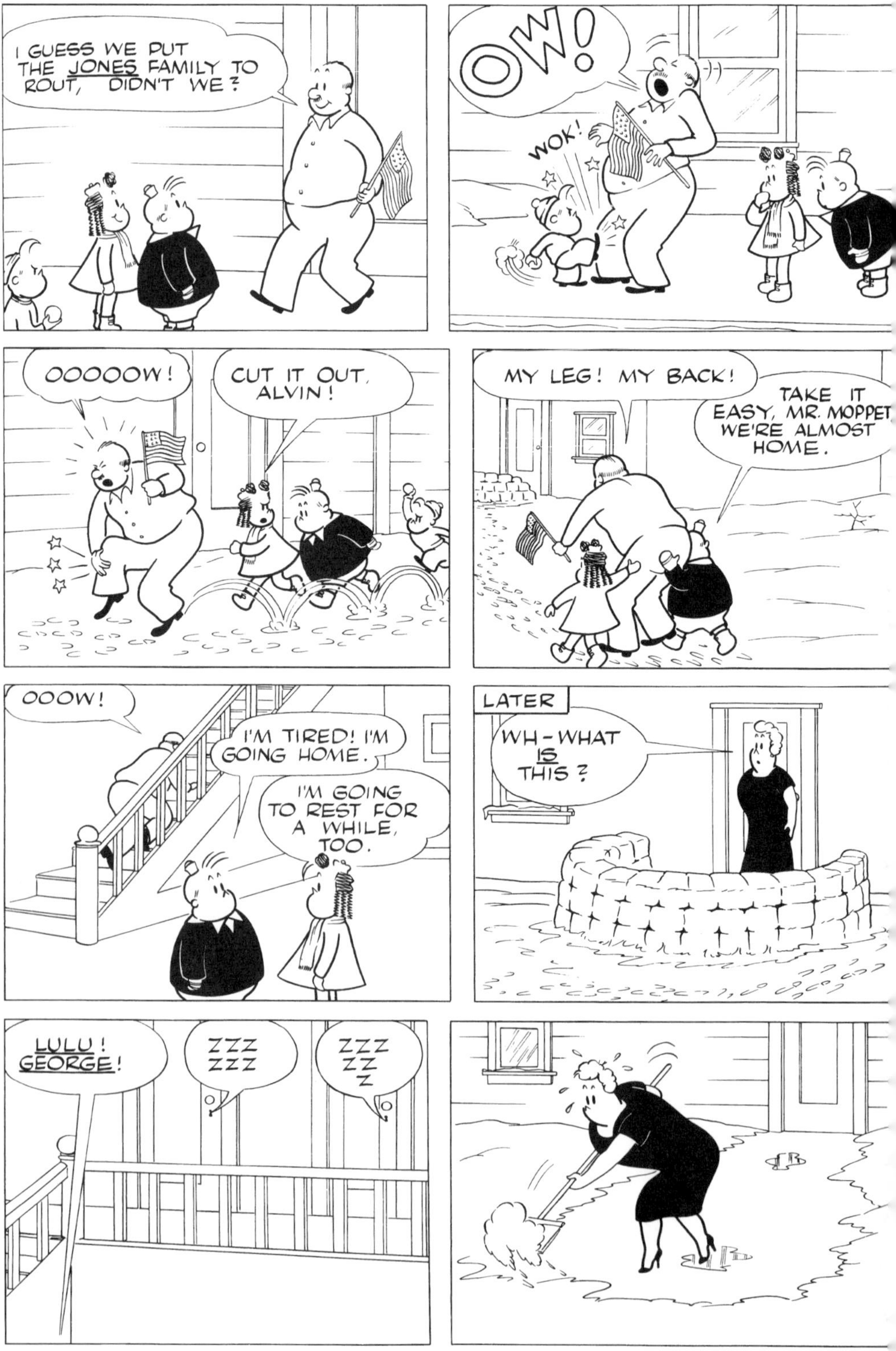
I GUESS WE PUT THE JONES FAMILY TO ROUT, DIDN'T WE?
OW!
WOK!
OOOOOW!
CUT IT OUT, ALVIN!
MY LEG! MY BACK!
TAKE IT EASY, MR. MOPPET. WE'RE ALMOST HOME.
OOOW!
I'M TIRED! I'M GOING HOME.
I'M GOING TO REST FOR A WHILE, TOO.
LATER
WH-WHAT IS THIS?
LULU! GEORGE!
ZZZ ZZZ
ZZZ ZZ Z

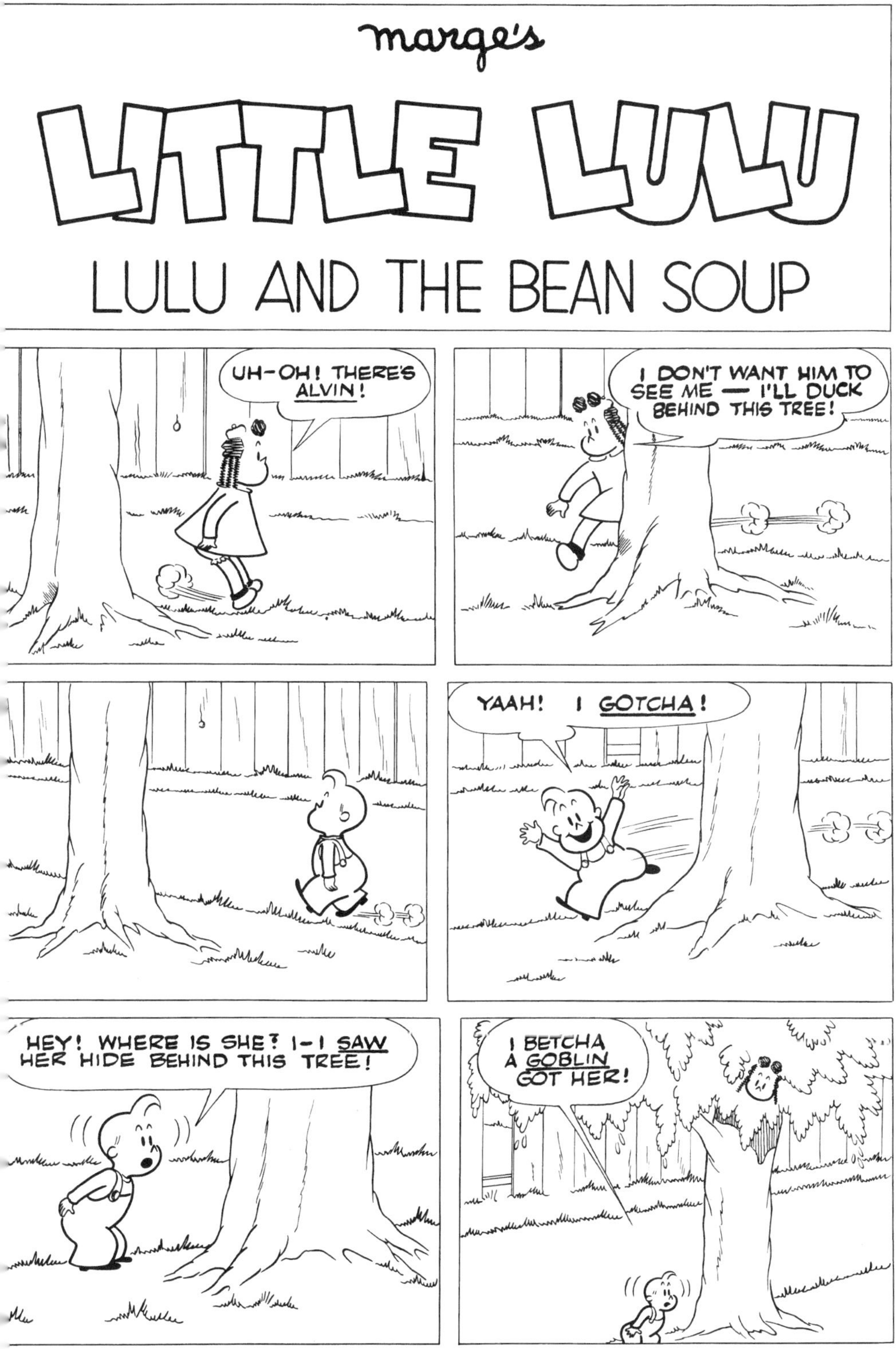
marge's
LITTLE LULU
LULU AND THE BEAN SOUP
UH-OH! THERE'S ALVIN!
I DON'T WANT HIM TO SEE ME — I'LL DUCK BEHIND THIS TREE!
YAAH! I GOTCHA!
HEY! WHERE IS SHE? I-I SAW HER HIDE BEHIND THIS TREE!
I BETCHA A GOBLIN GOT HER!

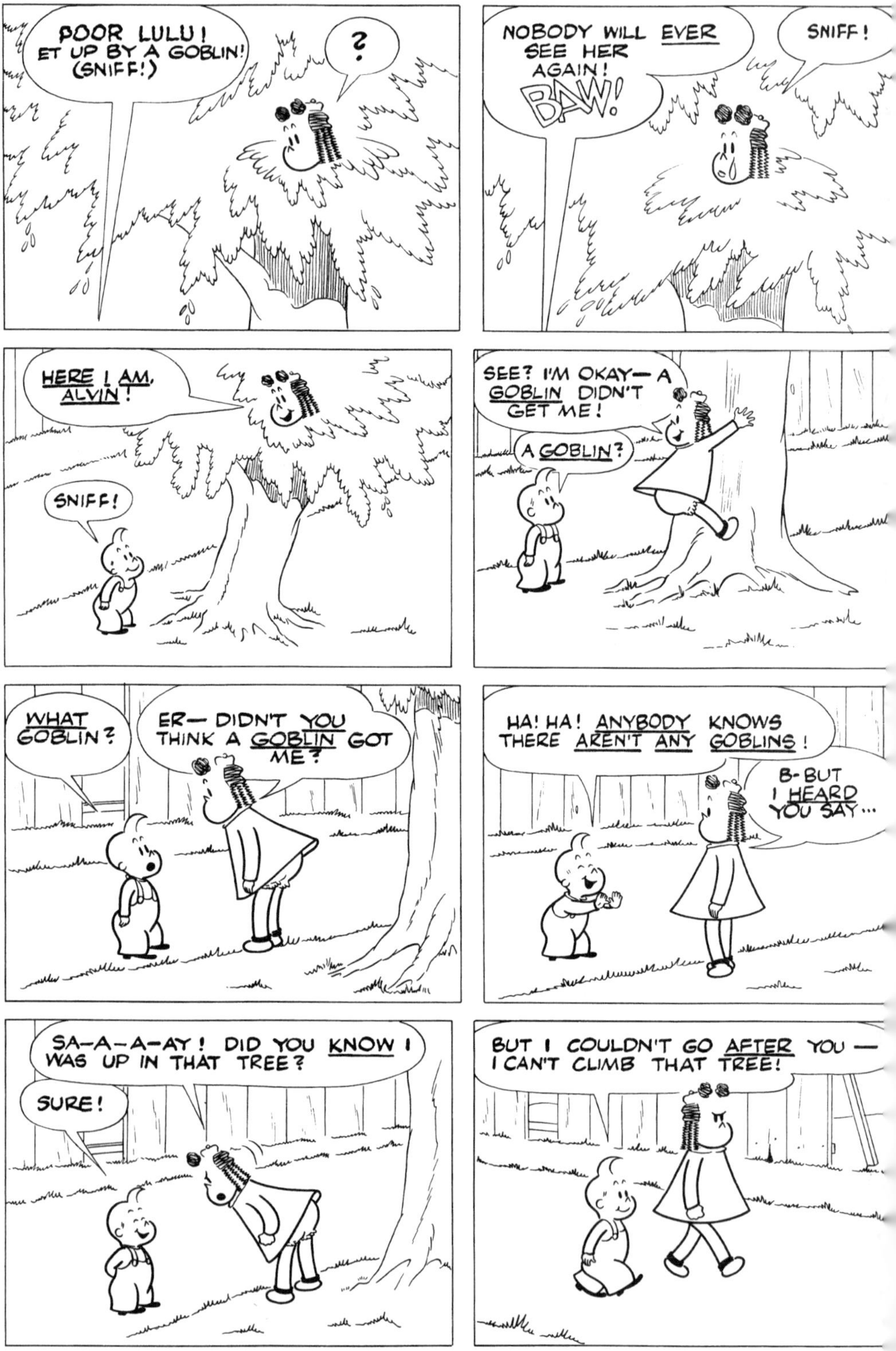
POOR LULU! ET UP BY A GOBLIN! (SNIFF!)
?
NOBODY WILL EVER SEE HER AGAIN! BAW!
SNIFF!
HERE I AM, ALVIN!
SNIFF!
SEE? I'M OKAY— A GOBLIN DIDN'T GET ME!
A GOBLIN?
WHAT GOBLIN?
ER— DIDN'T YOU THINK A GOBLIN GOT ME?
HA! HA! ANYBODY KNOWS THERE AREN'T ANY GOBLINS!
B-BUT I HEARD YOU SAY...
SA-A-A-AY! DID YOU KNOW I WAS UP IN THAT TREE?
SURE!
BUT I COULDN'T GO AFTER YOU — I CAN'T CLIMB THAT TREE!

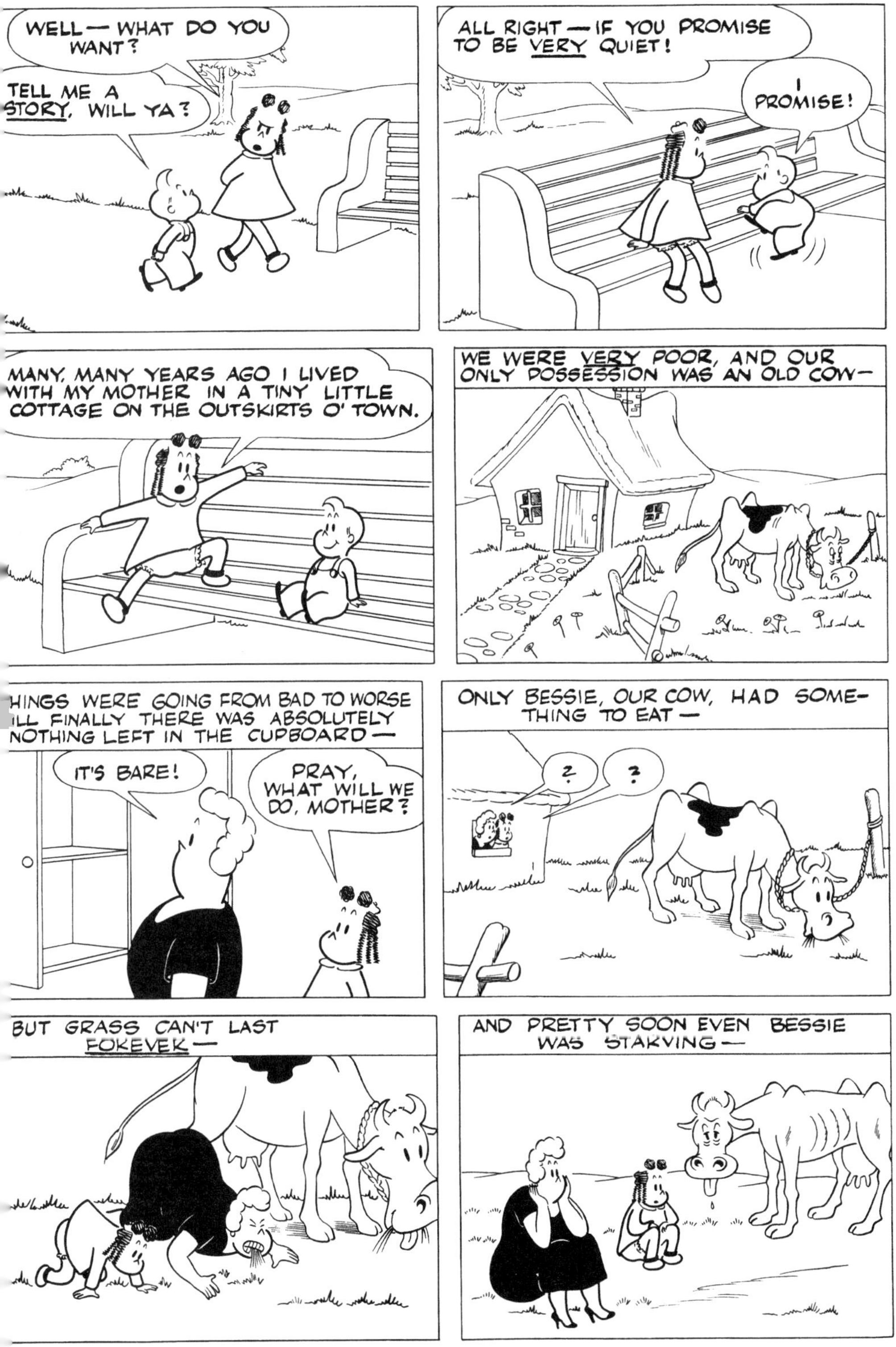

WELL — WHAT DO YOU WANT?
TELL ME A STORY, WILL YA?
ALL RIGHT — IF YOU PROMISE TO BE VERY QUIET!
I PROMISE!
MANY, MANY YEARS AGO I LIVED WITH MY MOTHER IN A TINY LITTLE COTTAGE ON THE OUTSKIRTS O' TOWN.
WE WERE VERY POOR, AND OUR ONLY POSSESSION WAS AN OLD COW —
HINGS WERE GOING FROM BAD TO WORSE ILL FINALLY THERE WAS ABSOLUTELY NOTHING LEFT IN THE CUPBOARD —
IT'S BARE!
PRAY, WHAT WILL WE DO, MOTHER?
ONLY BESSIE, OUR COW, HAD SOMETHING TO EAT —
?
?
BUT GRASS CAN'T LAST FOKEVEK —
AND PRETTY SOON EVEN BESSIE WAS STAKVING —

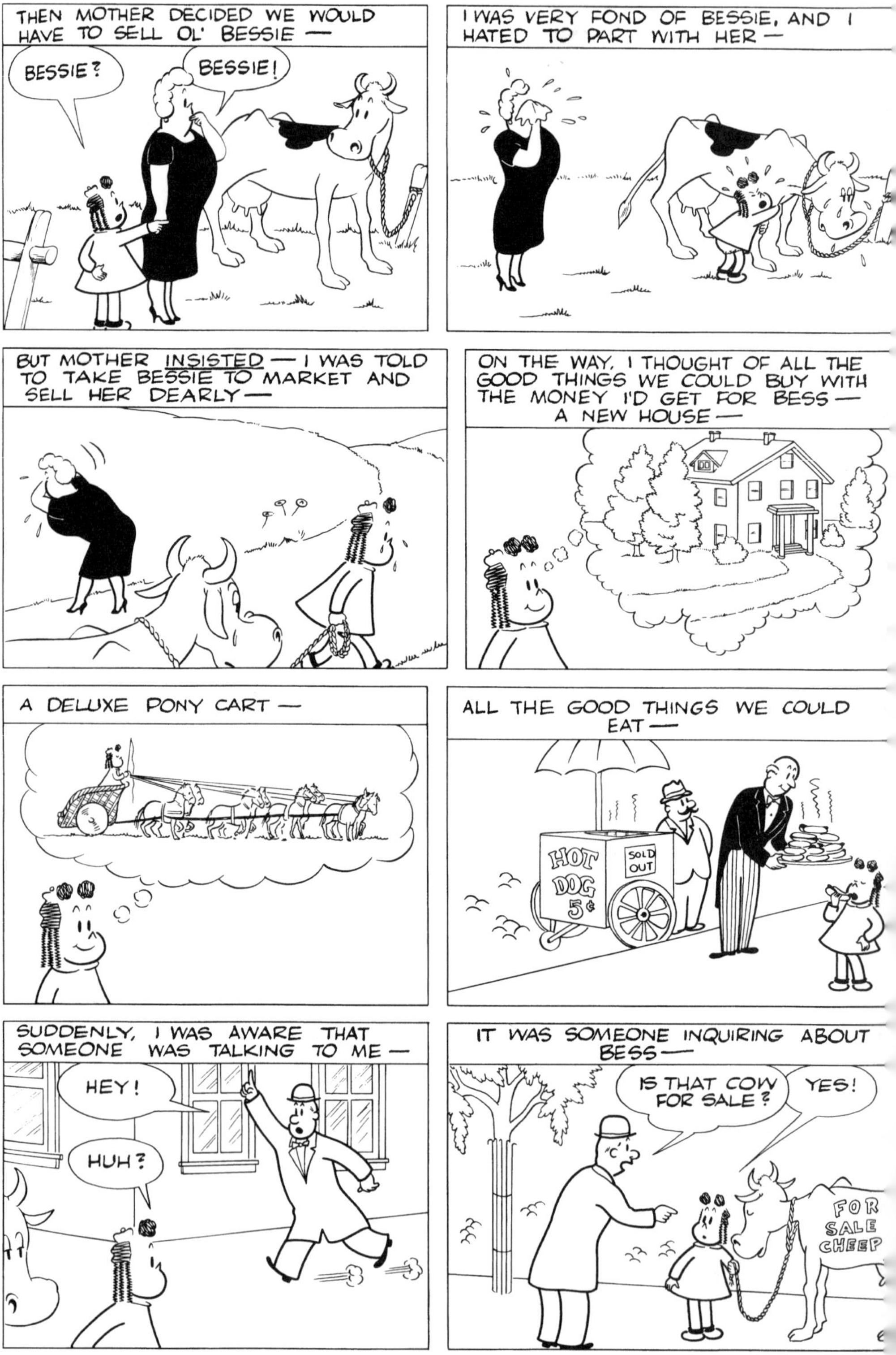
THEN MOTHER DECIDED WE WOULD HAVE TO SELL OL' BESSIE —
BESSIE?
BESSIE!
I WAS VERY FOND OF BESSIE, AND I HATED TO PART WITH HER —
BUT MOTHER INSISTED — I WAS TOLD TO TAKE BESSIE TO MARKET AND SELL HER DEARLY —
ON THE WAY, I THOUGHT OF ALL THE GOOD THINGS WE COULD BUY WITH THE MONEY I'D GET FOR BESS — A NEW HOUSE —
A DELUXE PONY CART —
ALL THE GOOD THINGS WE COULD EAT —
HOT DOG 5¢
SOLD OUT
SUDDENLY, I WAS AWARE THAT SOMEONE WAS TALKING TO ME —
HEY!
HUH?
IT WAS SOMEONE INQUIRING ABOUT BESS —
IS THAT COW FOR SALE?
YES!
FOR SALE CHEEP

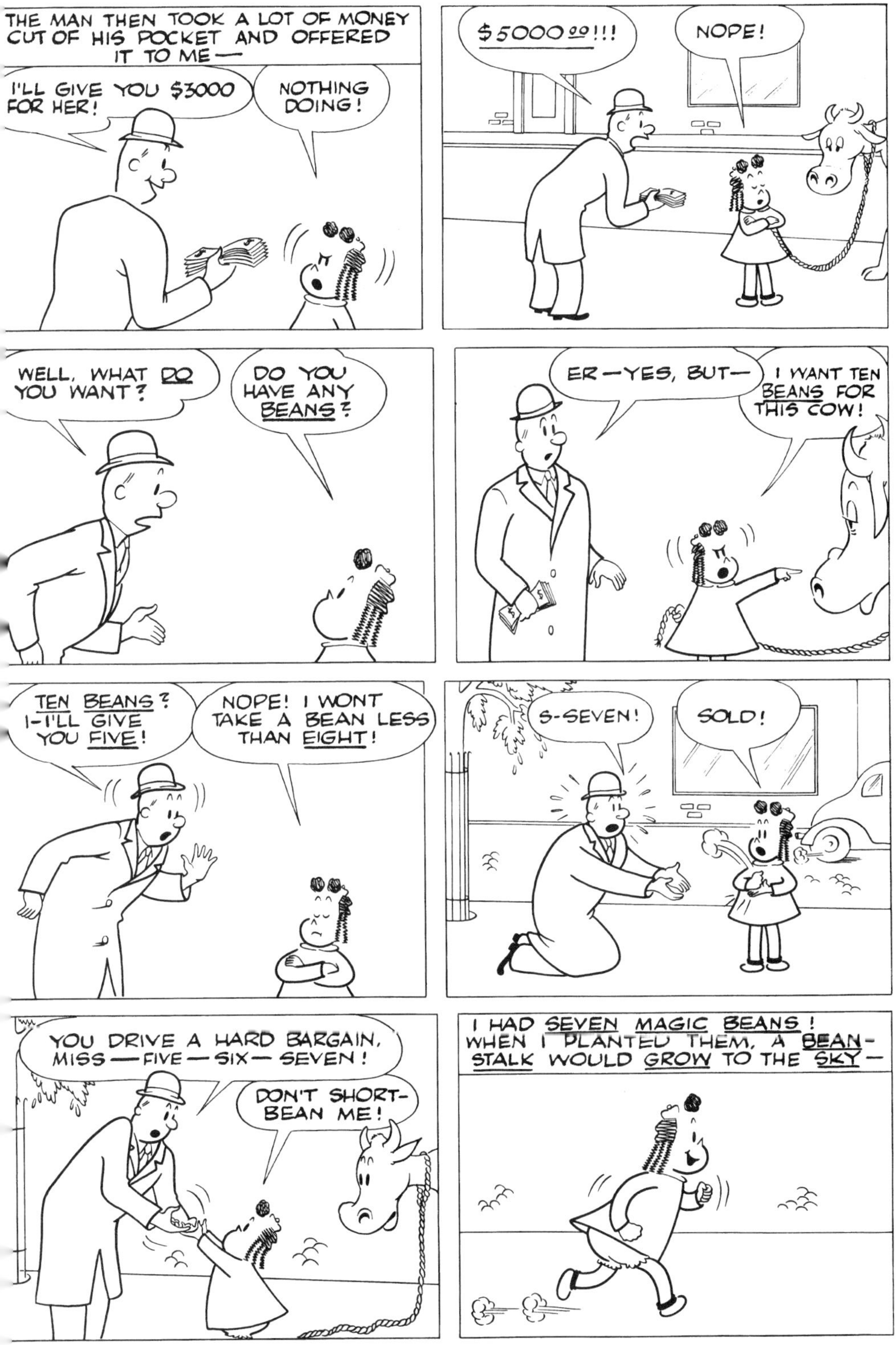
THE MAN THEN TOOK A LOT OF MONEY OUT OF HIS POCKET AND OFFERED IT TO ME—
I'LL GIVE YOU $3000 FOR HER!
NOTHING DOING!
$5000.00!!!
NOPE!
WELL, WHAT DO YOU WANT?
DO YOU HAVE ANY BEANS?
ER—YES, BUT—
I WANT TEN BEANS FOR THIS COW!
TEN BEANS? I-I'LL GIVE YOU FIVE!
NOPE! I WONT TAKE A BEAN LESS THAN EIGHT!
S-SEVEN!
SOLD!
YOU DRIVE A HARD BARGAIN, MISS—FIVE—SIX—SEVEN!
DON'T SHORT-BEAN ME!
I HAD SEVEN MAGIC BEANS! WHEN I PLANTED THEM, A BEAN-STALK WOULD GROW TO THE SKY—

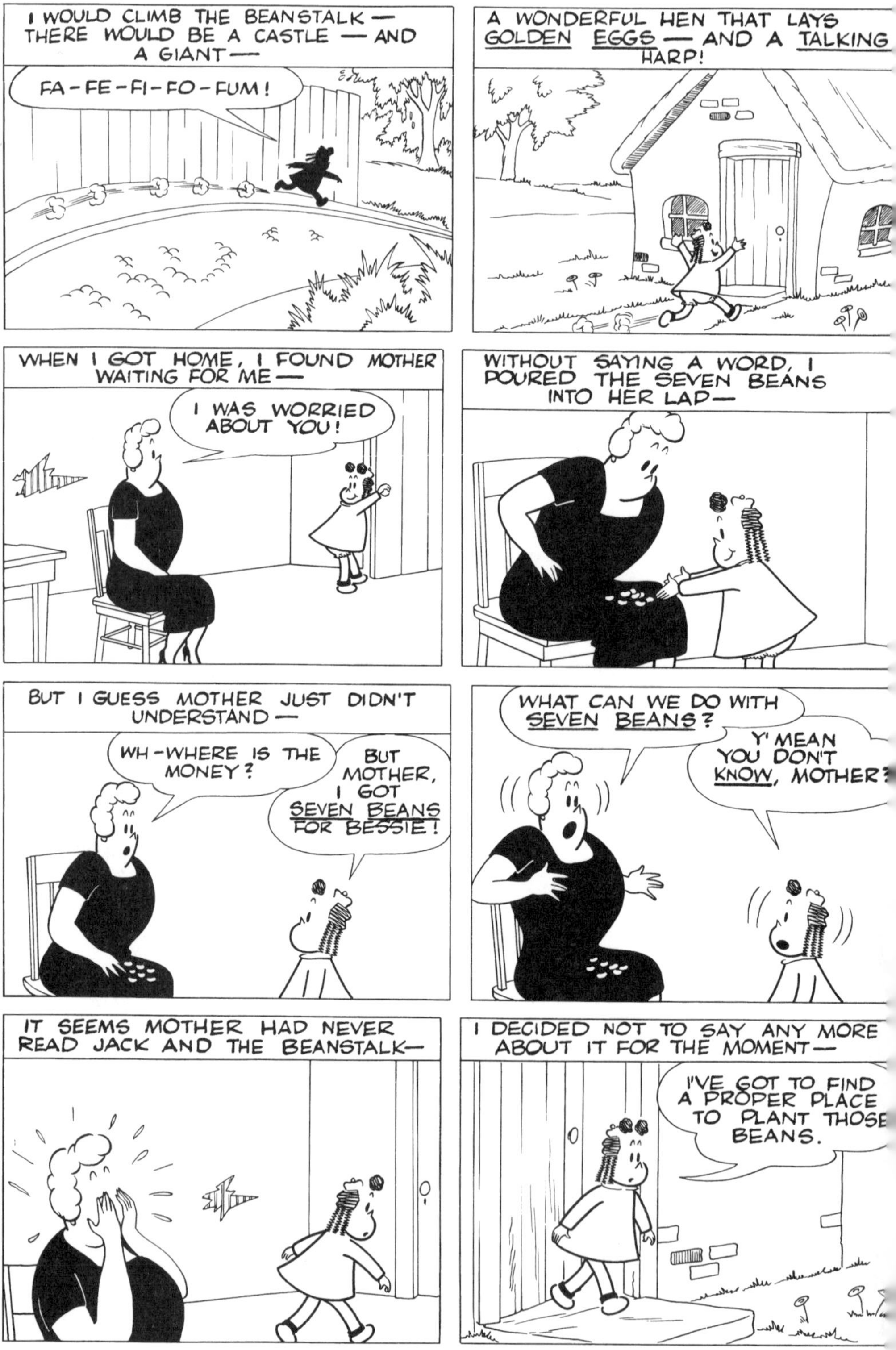
I WOULD CLIMB THE BEANSTALK — THERE WOULD BE A CASTLE — AND A GIANT —
FA-FE-FI-FO-FUM!
A WONDERFUL HEN THAT LAYS GOLDEN EGGS — AND A TALKING HARP!
WHEN I GOT HOME, I FOUND MOTHER WAITING FOR ME —
I WAS WORRIED ABOUT YOU!
WITHOUT SAYING A WORD, I POURED THE SEVEN BEANS INTO HER LAP —
BUT I GUESS MOTHER JUST DIDN'T UNDERSTAND —
WH-WHERE IS THE MONEY?
BUT MOTHER, I GOT SEVEN BEANS FOR BESSIE!
WHAT CAN WE DO WITH SEVEN BEANS?
Y' MEAN YOU DON'T KNOW, MOTHER?
IT SEEMS MOTHER HAD NEVER READ JACK AND THE BEANSTALK —
I DECIDED NOT TO SAY ANY MORE ABOUT IT FOR THE MOMENT —
I'VE GOT TO FIND A PROPER PLACE TO PLANT THOSE BEANS.

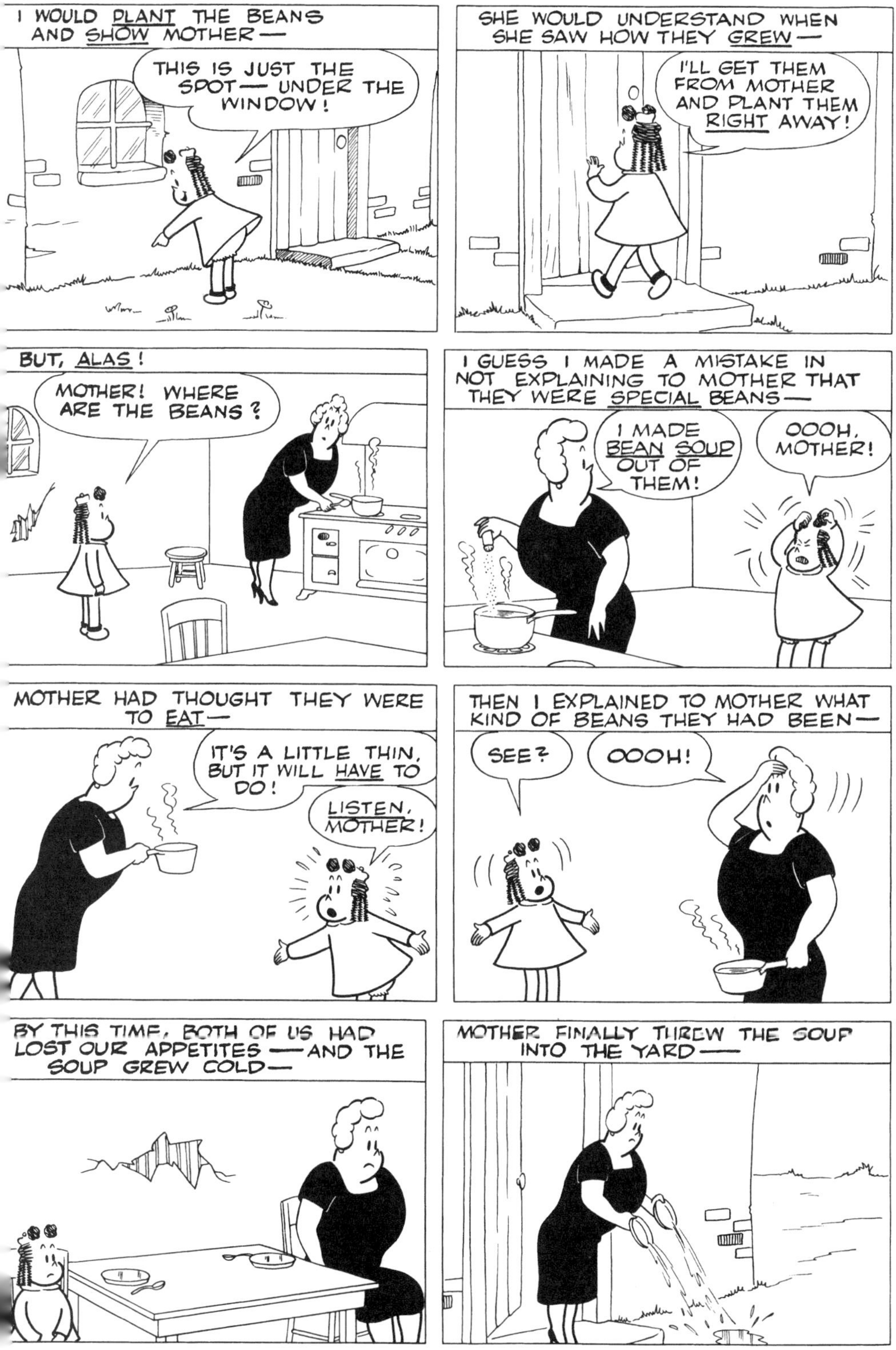
I WOULD PLANT THE BEANS AND SHOW MOTHER—
THIS IS JUST THE SPOT— UNDER THE WINDOW!
SHE WOULD UNDERSTAND WHEN SHE SAW HOW THEY GREW—
I'LL GET THEM FROM MOTHER AND PLANT THEM RIGHT AWAY!
BUT, ALAS!
MOTHER! WHERE ARE THE BEANS?
I GUESS I MADE A MISTAKE IN NOT EXPLAINING TO MOTHER THAT THEY WERE SPECIAL BEANS—
I MADE BEAN SOUP OUT OF THEM!
OOOH, MOTHER!
MOTHER HAD THOUGHT THEY WERE TO EAT—
IT'S A LITTLE THIN, BUT IT WILL HAVE TO DO!
LISTEN, MOTHER!
THEN I EXPLAINED TO MOTHER WHAT KIND OF BEANS THEY HAD BEEN—
SEE?
OOOH!
BY THIS TIME, BOTH OF US HAD LOST OUR APPETITES—AND THE SOUP GREW COLD—
MOTHER FINALLY THREW THE SOUP INTO THE YARD—

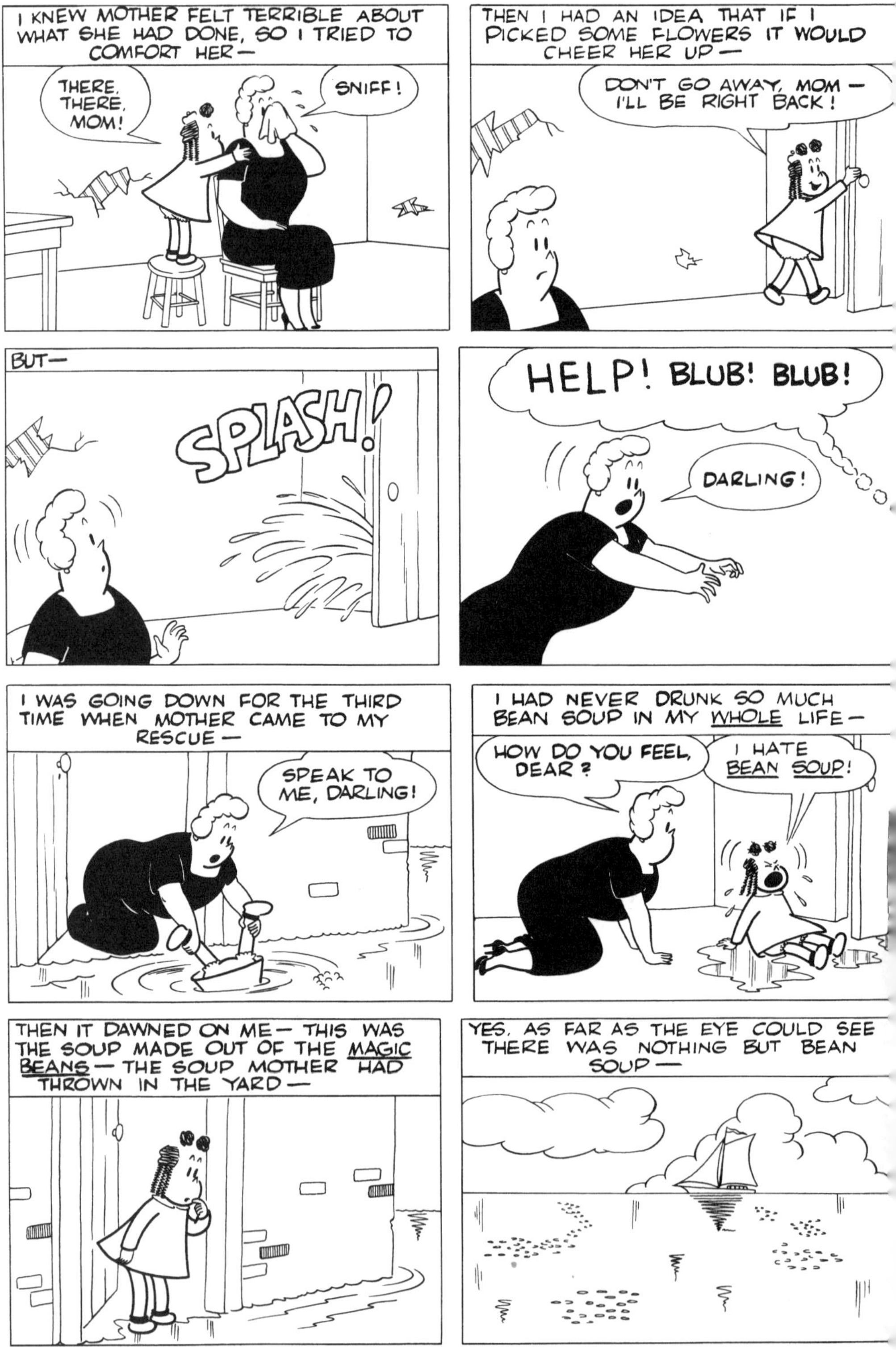

I KNEW MOTHER FELT TERRIBLE ABOUT WHAT SHE HAD DONE, SO I TRIED TO COMFORT HER—
THERE, THERE, MOM!
SNIFF!
THEN I HAD AN IDEA THAT IF I PICKED SOME FLOWERS IT WOULD CHEER HER UP—
DON'T GO AWAY, MOM— I'LL BE RIGHT BACK!
BUT—
SPLASH!
HELP! BLUB! BLUB!
DARLING!
I WAS GOING DOWN FOR THE THIRD TIME WHEN MOTHER CAME TO MY RESCUE—
SPEAK TO ME, DARLING!
I HAD NEVER DRUNK SO MUCH BEAN SOUP IN MY WHOLE LIFE—
HOW DO YOU FEEL, DEAR?
I HATE BEAN SOUP!
THEN IT DAWNED ON ME— THIS WAS THE SOUP MADE OUT OF THE MAGIC BEANS— THE SOUP MOTHER HAD THROWN IN THE YARD—
YES, AS FAR AS THE EYE COULD SEE THERE WAS NOTHING BUT BEAN SOUP—

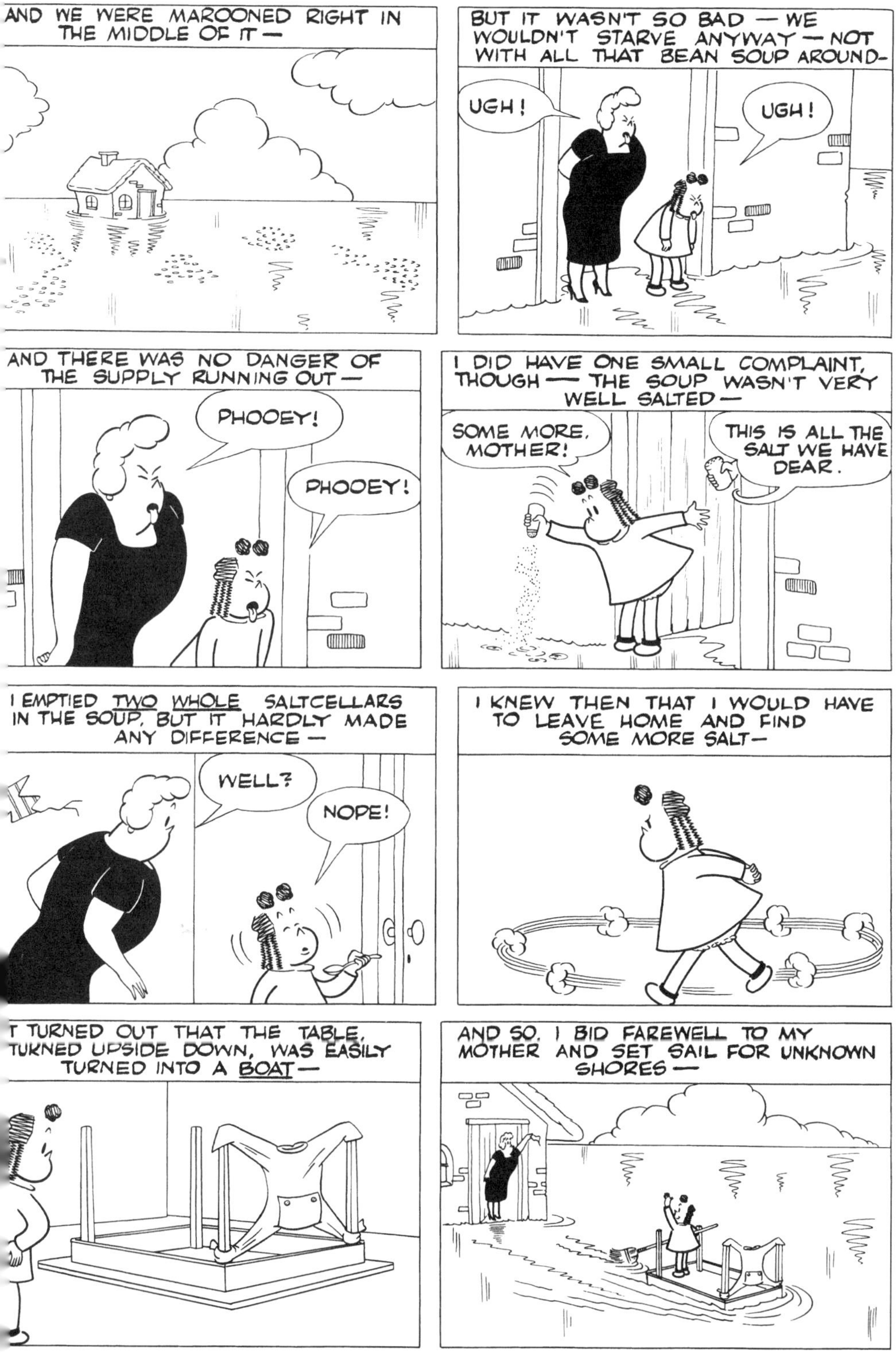
AND WE WERE MAROONED RIGHT IN THE MIDDLE OF IT —
BUT IT WASN'T SO BAD — WE WOULDN'T STARVE ANYWAY — NOT WITH ALL THAT BEAN SOUP AROUND-
UGH!
UGH!
AND THERE WAS NO DANGER OF THE SUPPLY RUNNING OUT —
PHOOEY!
PHOOEY!
I DID HAVE ONE SMALL COMPLAINT, THOUGH — THE SOUP WASN'T VERY WELL SALTED —
SOME MORE, MOTHER!
THIS IS ALL THE SALT WE HAVE DEAR.
I EMPTIED TWO WHOLE SALTCELLARS IN THE SOUP, BUT IT HARDLY MADE ANY DIFFERENCE —
WELL?
NOPE!
I KNEW THEN THAT I WOULD HAVE TO LEAVE HOME AND FIND SOME MORE SALT —
T TURNED OUT THAT THE TABLE, TURNED UPSIDE DOWN, WAS EASILY TURNED INTO A BOAT —
AND SO, I BID FAREWELL TO MY MOTHER AND SET SAIL FOR UNKNOWN SHORES —

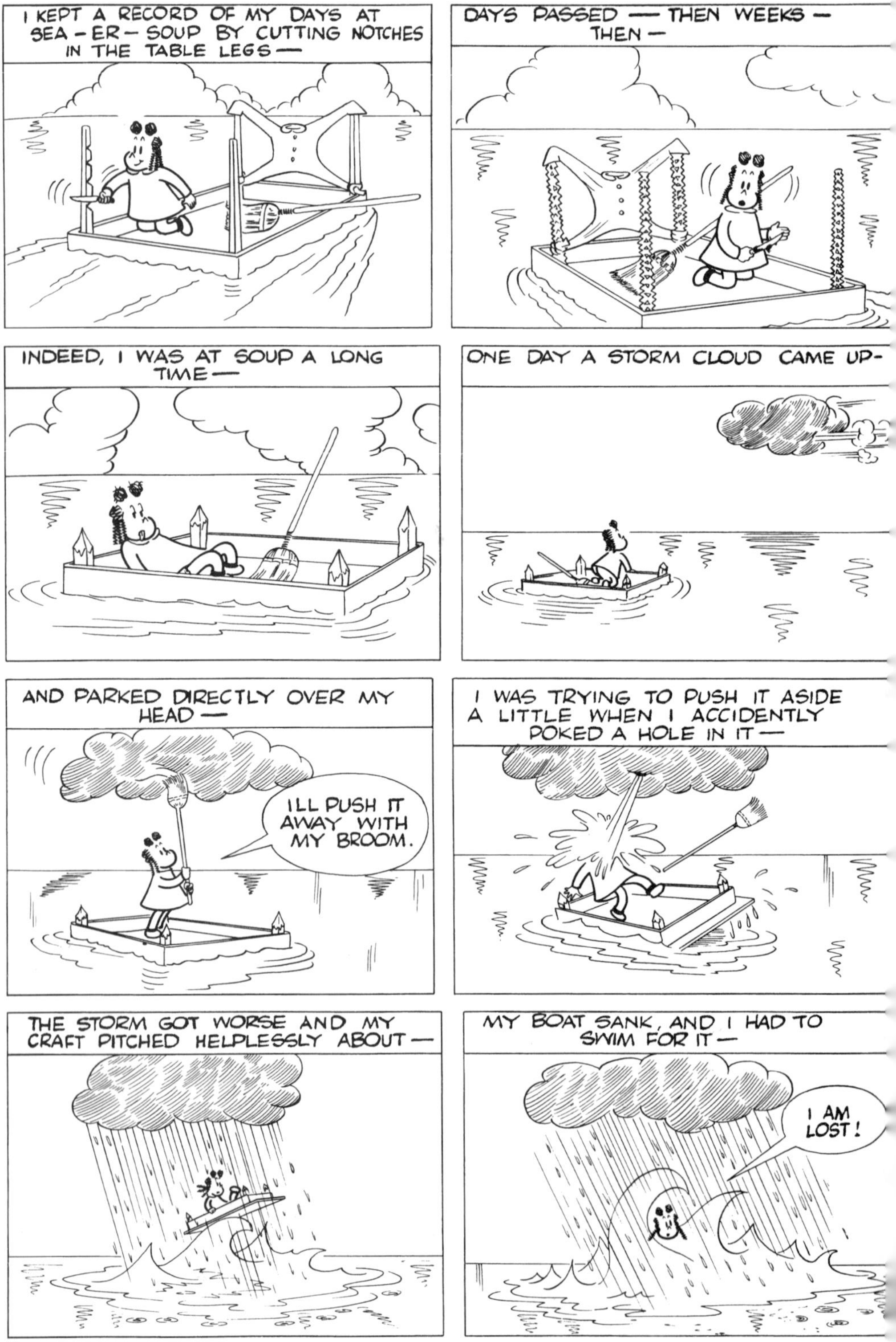
I KEPT A RECORD OF MY DAYS AT SEA - ER - SOUP BY CUTTING NOTCHES IN THE TABLE LEGS —
DAYS PASSED — THEN WEEKS — THEN —
INDEED, I WAS AT SOUP A LONG TIME —
ONE DAY A STORM CLOUD CAME UP-
AND PARKED DIRECTLY OVER MY HEAD —
ILL PUSH IT AWAY WITH MY BROOM.
I WAS TRYING TO PUSH IT ASIDE A LITTLE WHEN I ACCIDENTLY POKED A HOLE IN IT —
THE STORM GOT WORSE AND MY CRAFT PITCHED HELPLESSLY ABOUT —
MY BOAT SANK, AND I HAD TO SWIM FOR IT —
I AM LOST!

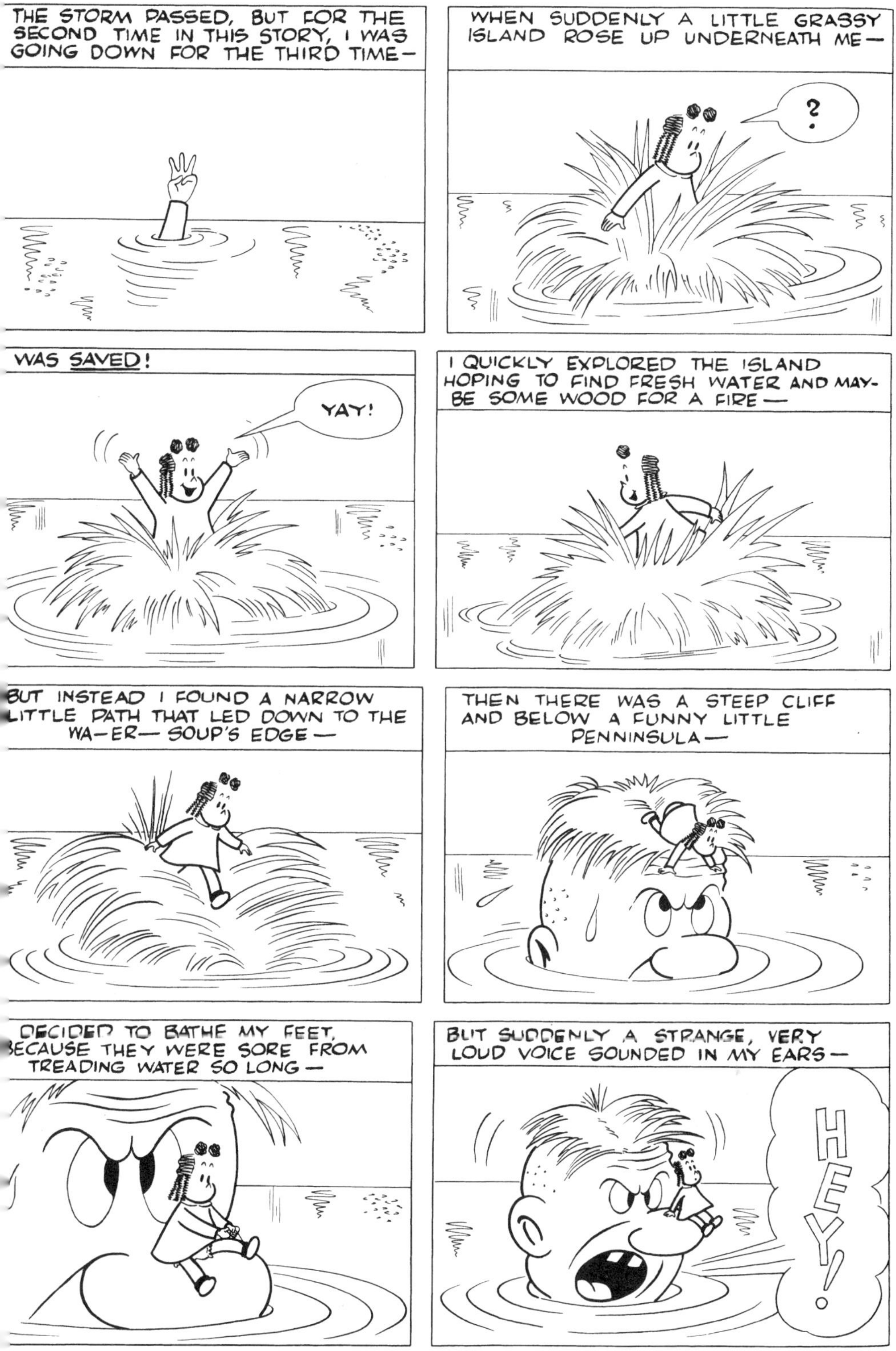
THE STORM PASSED, BUT FOR THE SECOND TIME IN THIS STORY, I WAS GOING DOWN FOR THE THIRD TIME—
WHEN SUDDENLY A LITTLE GRASSY ISLAND ROSE UP UNDERNEATH ME—
?
WAS SAVED!
YAY!
I QUICKLY EXPLORED THE ISLAND HOPING TO FIND FRESH WATER AND MAY-BE SOME WOOD FOR A FIRE—
BUT INSTEAD I FOUND A NARROW LITTLE PATH THAT LED DOWN TO THE WA—ER—SOUP'S EDGE—
THEN THERE WAS A STEEP CLIFF AND BELOW A FUNNY LITTLE PENNINSULA—
DECIDED TO BATHE MY FEET, BECAUSE THEY WERE SORE FROM TREADING WATER SO LONG—
BUT SUDDENLY A STRANGE, VERY LOUD VOICE SOUNDED IN MY EARS—
HEY!

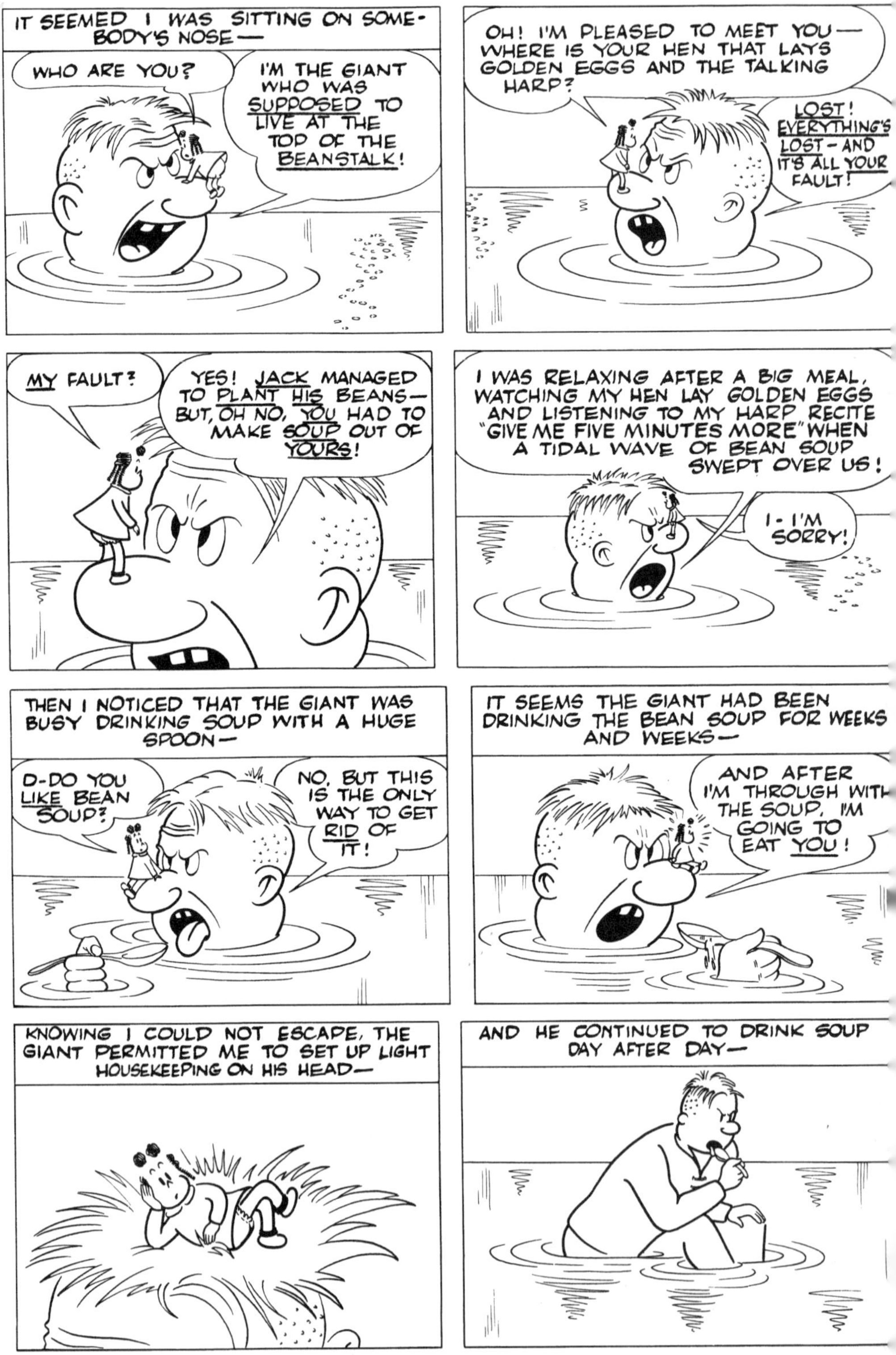
IT SEEMED I WAS SITTING ON SOMEBODY'S NOSE—
WHO ARE YOU?
I'M THE GIANT WHO WAS SUPPOSED TO LIVE AT THE TOP OF THE BEANSTALK!
OH! I'M PLEASED TO MEET YOU— WHERE IS YOUR HEN THAT LAYS GOLDEN EGGS AND THE TALKING HARP?
LOST! EVERYTHING'S LOST—AND IT'S ALL YOUR FAULT!
MY FAULT?
YES! JACK MANAGED TO PLANT HIS BEANS— BUT, OH NO, YOU HAD TO MAKE SOUP OUT OF YOURS!
I WAS RELAXING AFTER A BIG MEAL, WATCHING MY HEN LAY GOLDEN EGGS AND LISTENING TO MY HARP RECITE "GIVE ME FIVE MINUTES MORE" WHEN A TIDAL WAVE OF BEAN SOUP SWEPT OVER US!
I-I'M SORRY!
THEN I NOTICED THAT THE GIANT WAS BUSY DRINKING SOUP WITH A HUGE SPOON—
D-DO YOU LIKE BEAN SOUP?
NO, BUT THIS IS THE ONLY WAY TO GET RID OF IT!
IT SEEMS THE GIANT HAD BEEN DRINKING THE BEAN SOUP FOR WEEKS AND WEEKS—
AND AFTER I'M THROUGH WITH THE SOUP, I'M GOING TO EAT YOU!
KNOWING I COULD NOT ESCAPE, THE GIANT PERMITTED ME TO SET UP LIGHT HOUSEKEEPING ON HIS HEAD—
AND HE CONTINUED TO DRINK SOUP DAY AFTER DAY—

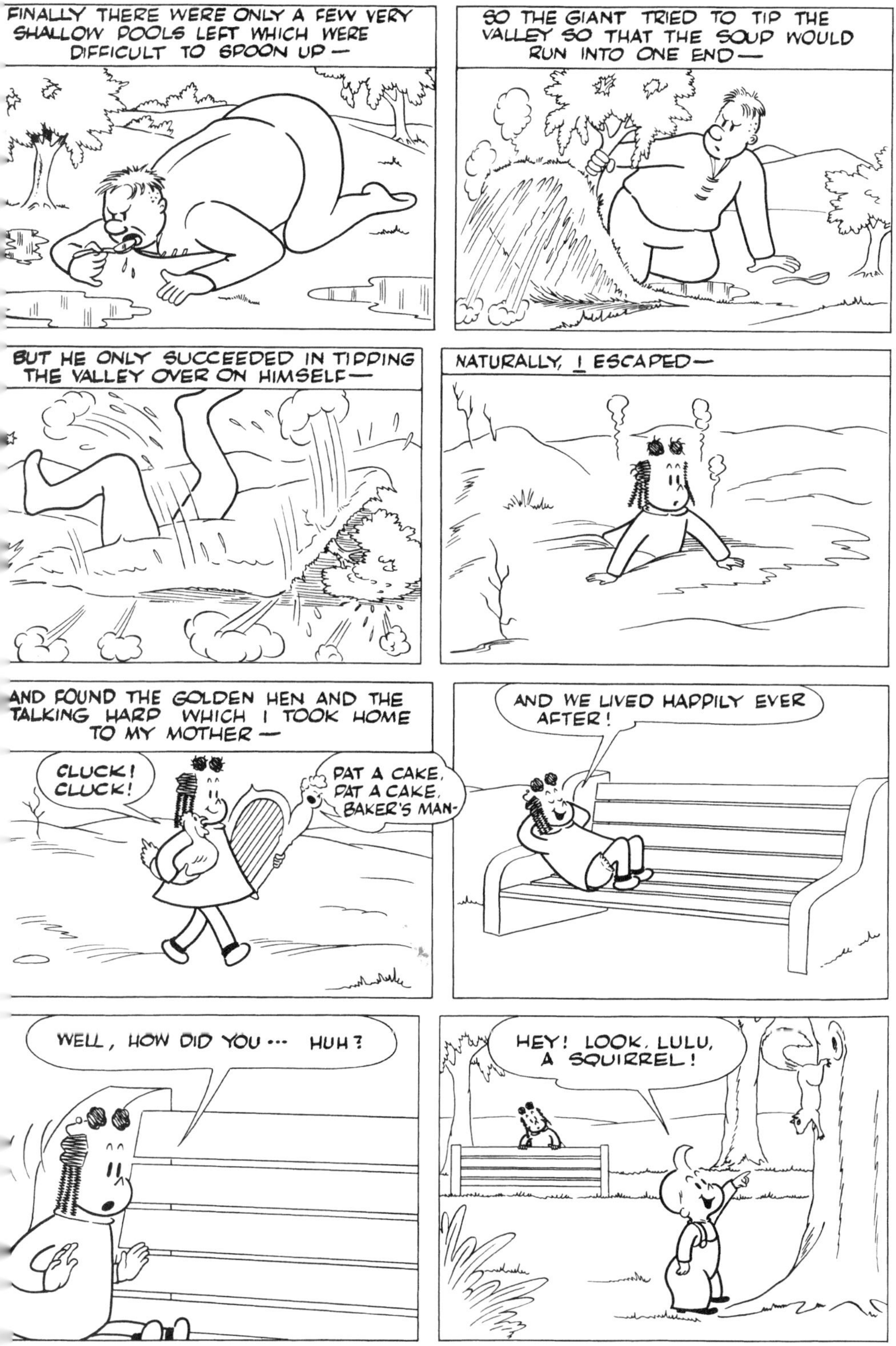
FINALLY THERE WERE ONLY A FEW VERY SHALLOW POOLS LEFT WHICH WERE DIFFICULT TO SPOON UP—
SO THE GIANT TRIED TO TIP THE VALLEY SO THAT THE SOUP WOULD RUN INTO ONE END—
BUT HE ONLY SUCCEEDED IN TIPPING THE VALLEY OVER ON HIMSELF—
NATURALLY, I ESCAPED—
AND FOUND THE GOLDEN HEN AND THE TALKING HARP WHICH I TOOK HOME TO MY MOTHER—
CLUCK! CLUCK!
PAT A CAKE, PAT A CAKE, BAKER'S MAN-
AND WE LIVED HAPPILY EVER AFTER!
WELL, HOW DID YOU ··· HUH?
HEY! LOOK, LULU, A SQUIRREL!

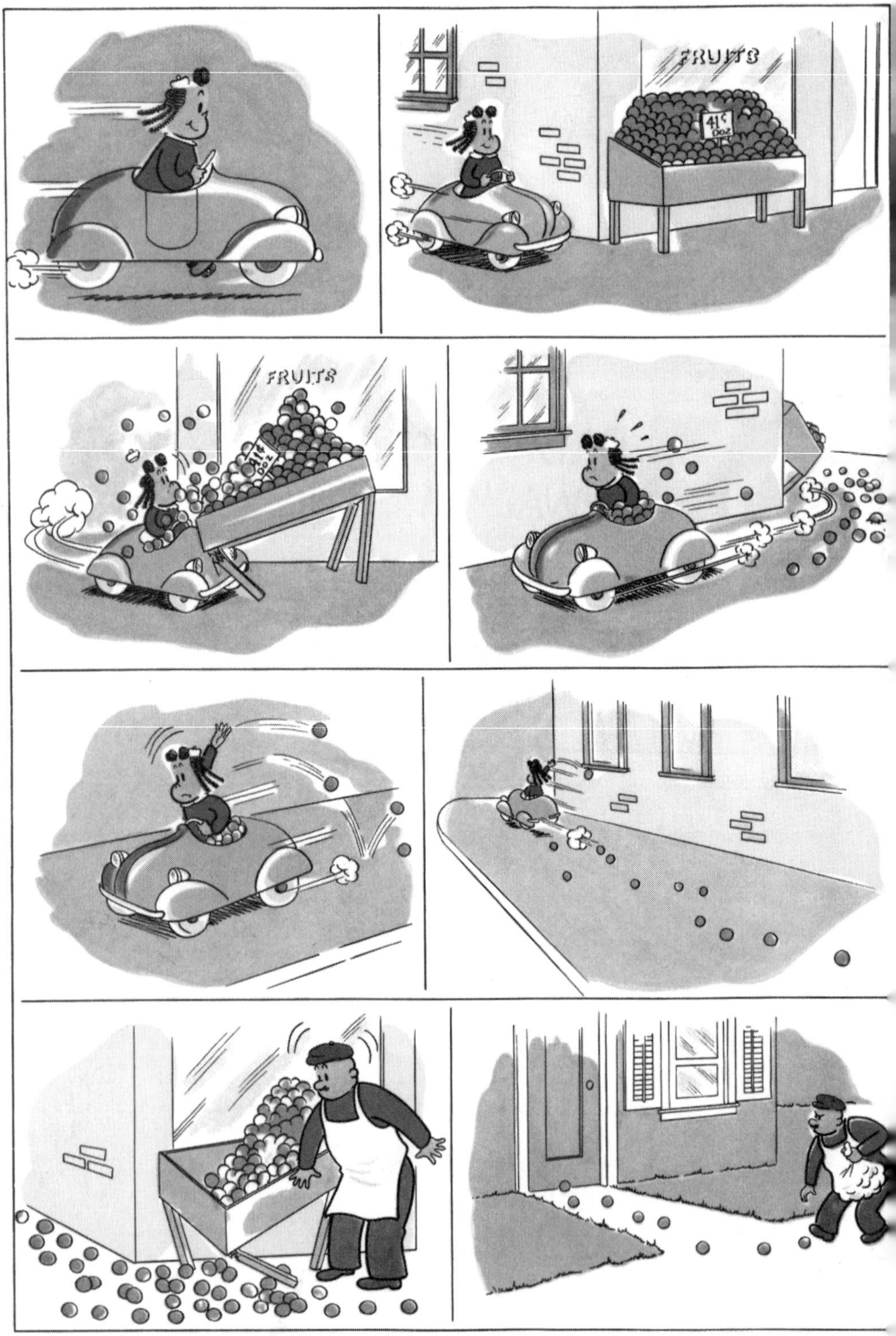
FRUITS
41¢ DOZ
FRUITS
41¢ DOZ

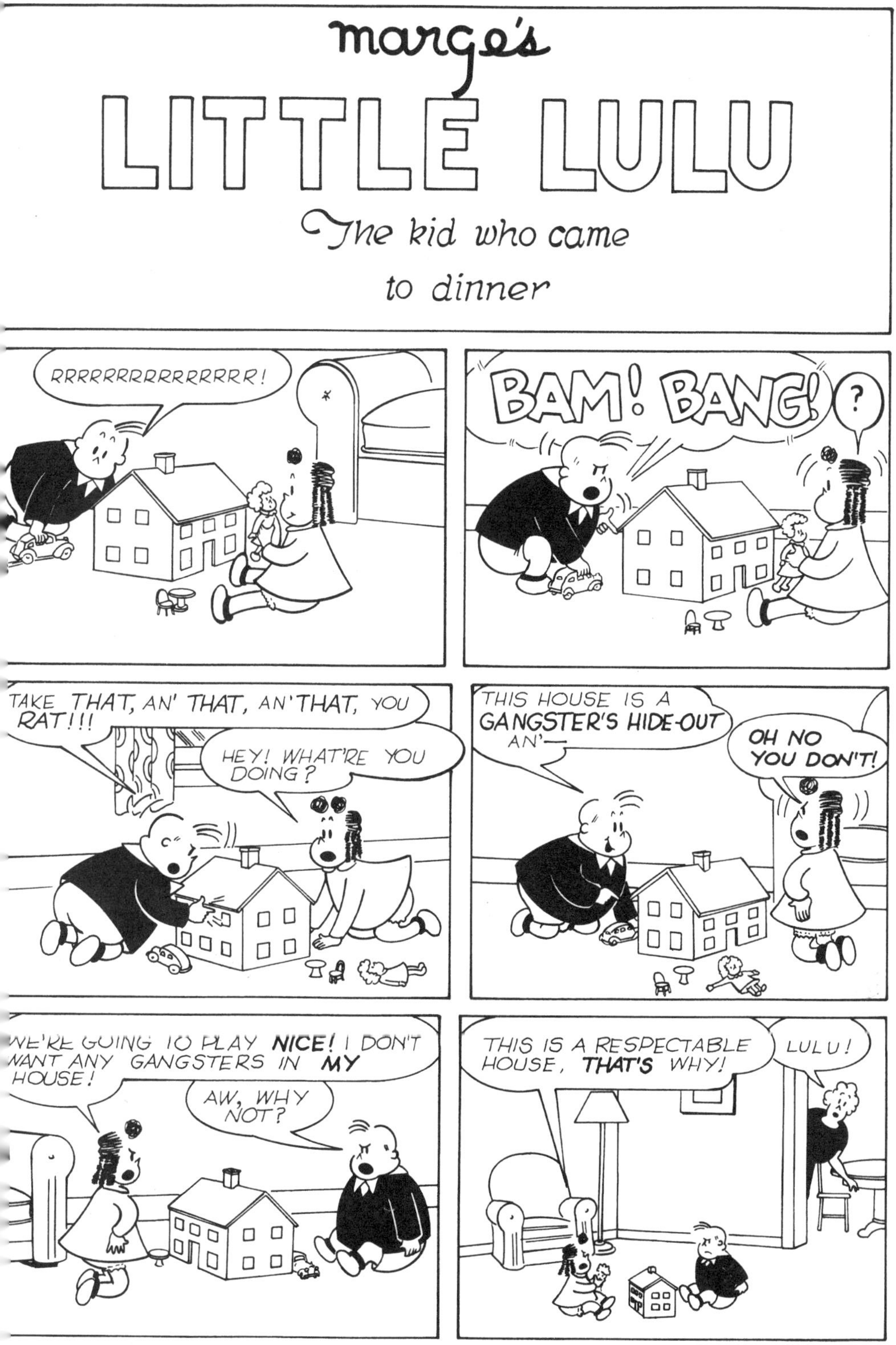
marge's
LITTLE LULU
The kid who came to dinner
RRRRRRRRRRRRRR!
BAM! BANG!
?
TAKE THAT, AN' THAT, AN' THAT, YOU RAT!!!
HEY! WHAT'RE YOU DOING?
THIS HOUSE IS A GANGSTER'S HIDE-OUT AN'—
OH NO YOU DON'T!
WE'RE GOING TO PLAY NICE! I DON'T WANT ANY GANGSTERS IN MY HOUSE!
AW, WHY NOT?
THIS IS A RESPECTABLE HOUSE, THAT'S WHY!
LULU!

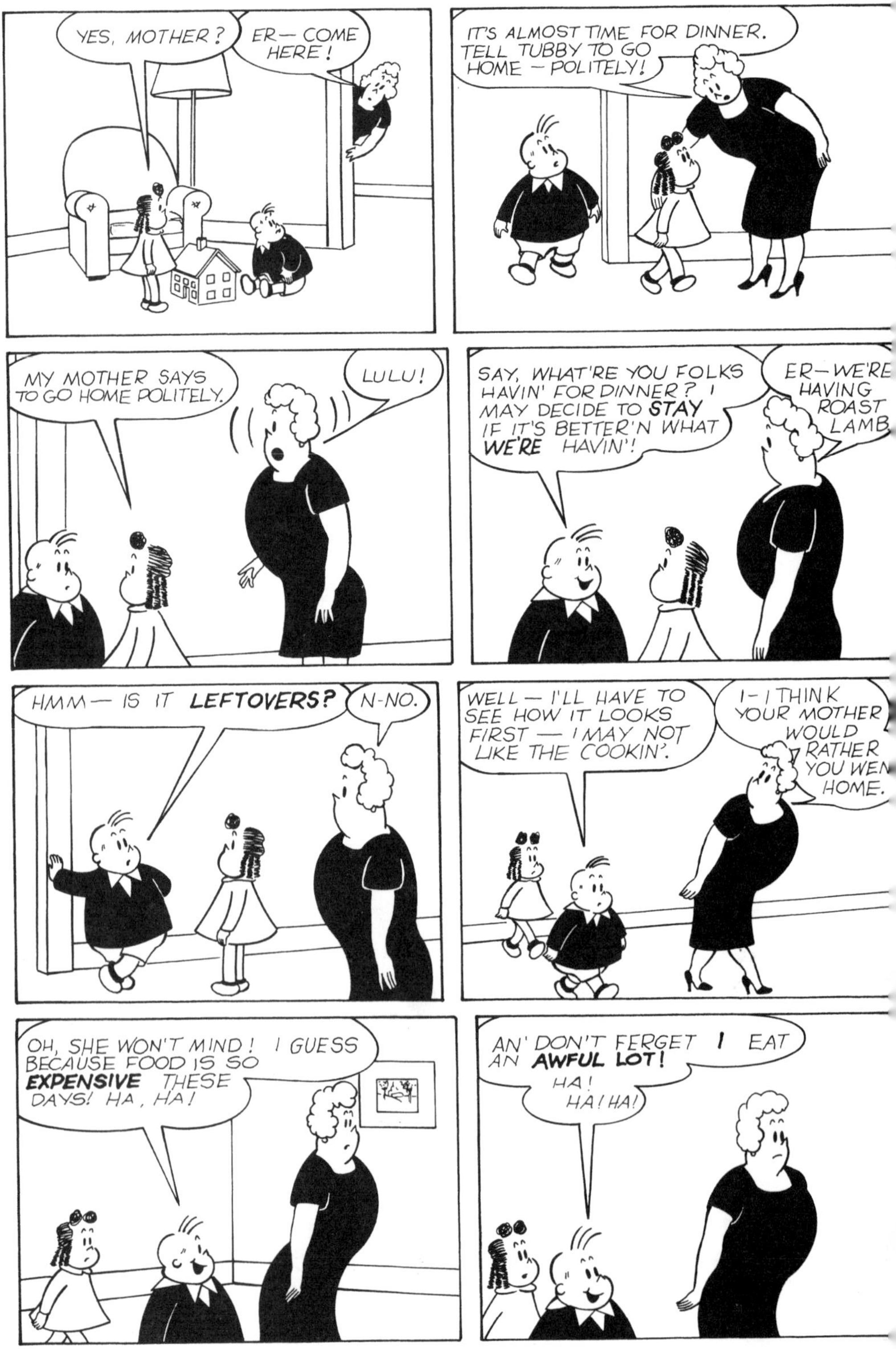
YES, MOTHER?
ER— COME HERE!
IT'S ALMOST TIME FOR DINNER. TELL TUBBY TO GO HOME — POLITELY!
MY MOTHER SAYS TO GO HOME POLITELY.
LULU!
SAY, WHAT'RE YOU FOLKS HAVIN' FOR DINNER? I MAY DECIDE TO STAY IF IT'S BETTER'N WHAT WE'RE HAVIN'!
ER—WE'RE HAVING ROAST LAMB.
HMM— IS IT LEFTOVERS?
N-NO.
WELL— I'LL HAVE TO SEE HOW IT LOOKS FIRST — I MAY NOT LIKE THE COOKIN'.
I-I THINK YOUR MOTHER WOULD RATHER YOU WENT HOME.
OH, SHE WON'T MIND! I GUESS BECAUSE FOOD IS SO EXPENSIVE THESE DAYS! HA, HA!
AN' DON'T FERGET I EAT AN AWFUL LOT!
HA! HA! HA!

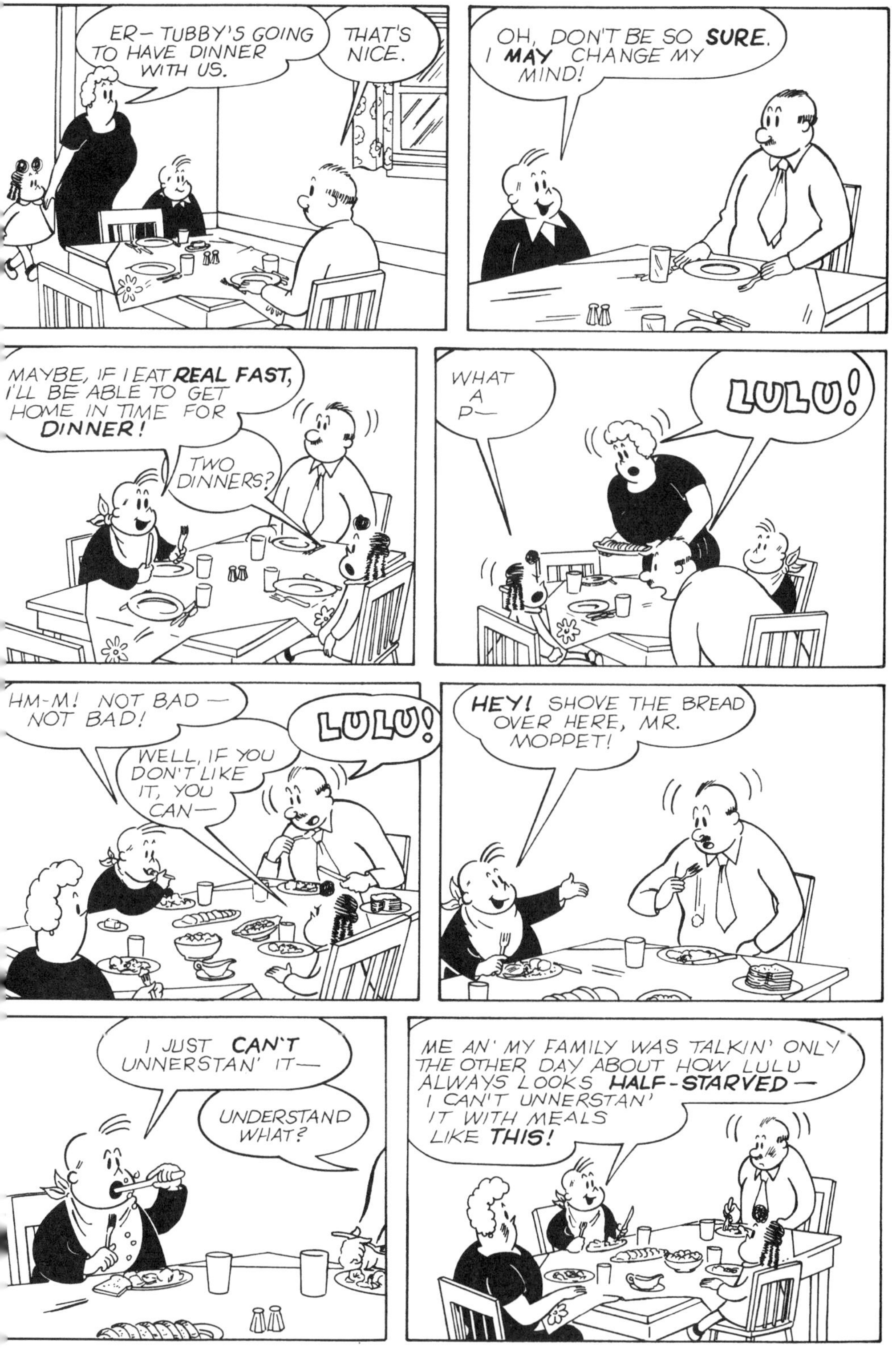
ER— TUBBY'S GOING TO HAVE DINNER WITH US.
THAT'S NICE.
OH, DON'T BE SO SURE. I MAY CHANGE MY MIND!
MAYBE, IF I EAT REAL FAST, I'LL BE ABLE TO GET HOME IN TIME FOR DINNER!
TWO DINNERS?
WHAT A P—
LULU!
HM-M! NOT BAD— NOT BAD!
LULU!
WELL, IF YOU DON'T LIKE IT, YOU CAN—
HEY! SHOVE THE BREAD OVER HERE, MR. MOPPET!
I JUST CAN'T UNNERSTAN' IT—
UNDERSTAND WHAT?
ME AN' MY FAMILY WAS TALKIN' ONLY THE OTHER DAY ABOUT HOW LULU ALWAYS LOOKS HALF-STARVED— I CAN'T UNNERSTAN' IT WITH MEALS LIKE THIS!

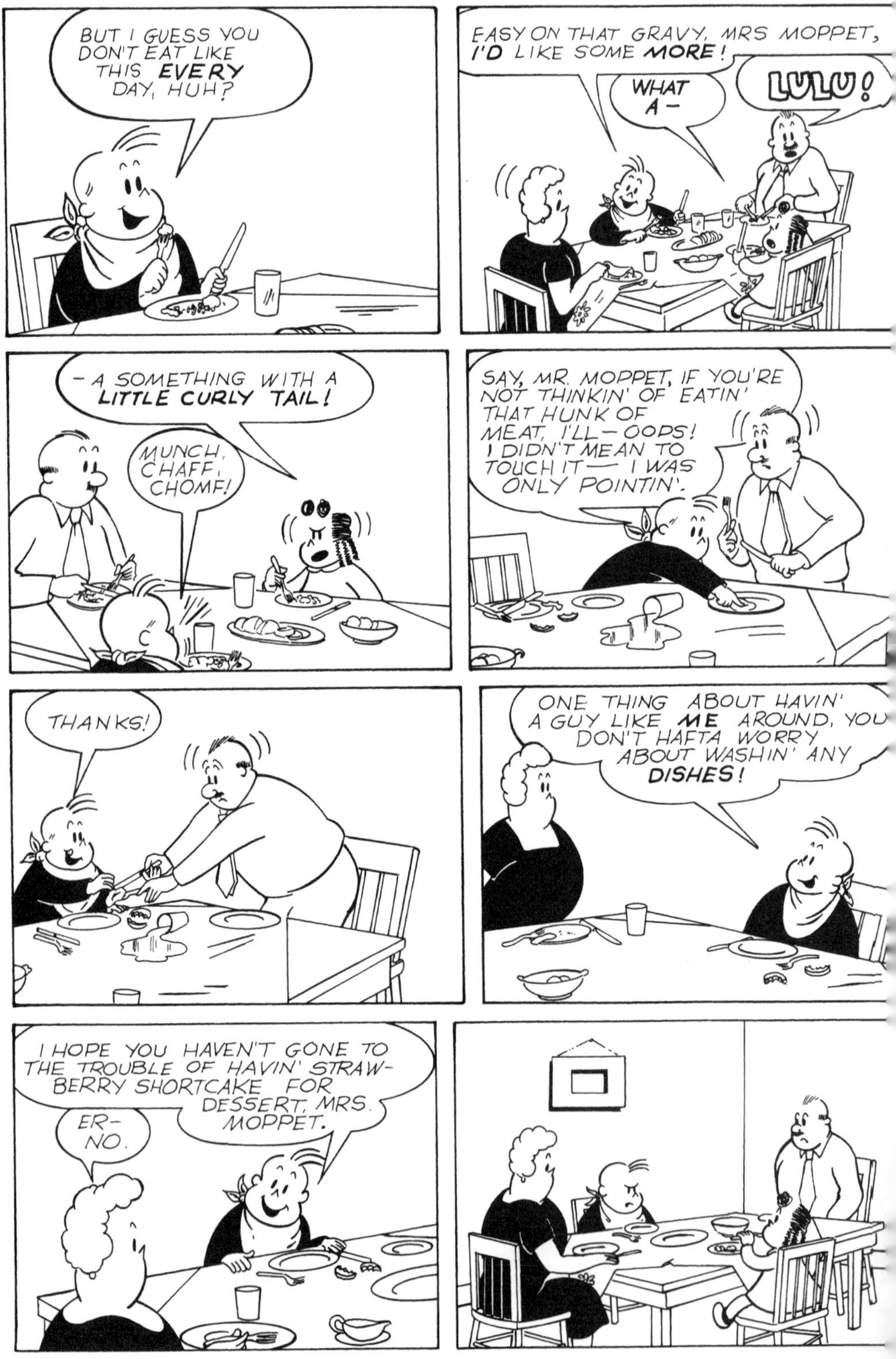
BUT I GUESS YOU DON'T EAT LIKE THIS EVERY DAY, HUH?
EASY ON THAT GRAVY, MRS MOPPET, I'D LIKE SOME MORE!
WHAT A—
LULU!
—A SOMETHING WITH A LITTLE CURLY TAIL!
MUNCH, CHAFF, CHOMF!
SAY, MR. MOPPET, IF YOU'RE NOT THINKIN' OF EATIN' THAT HUNK OF MEAT, I'LL—OOPS! I DIDN'T MEAN TO TOUCH IT— I WAS ONLY POINTIN'.
THANKS!
ONE THING ABOUT HAVIN' A GUY LIKE ME AROUND, YOU DON'T HAFTA WORRY ABOUT WASHIN' ANY DISHES!
I HOPE YOU HAVEN'T GONE TO THE TROUBLE OF HAVIN' STRAWBERRY SHORTCAKE FOR DESSERT, MRS. MOPPET.
ER— NO.

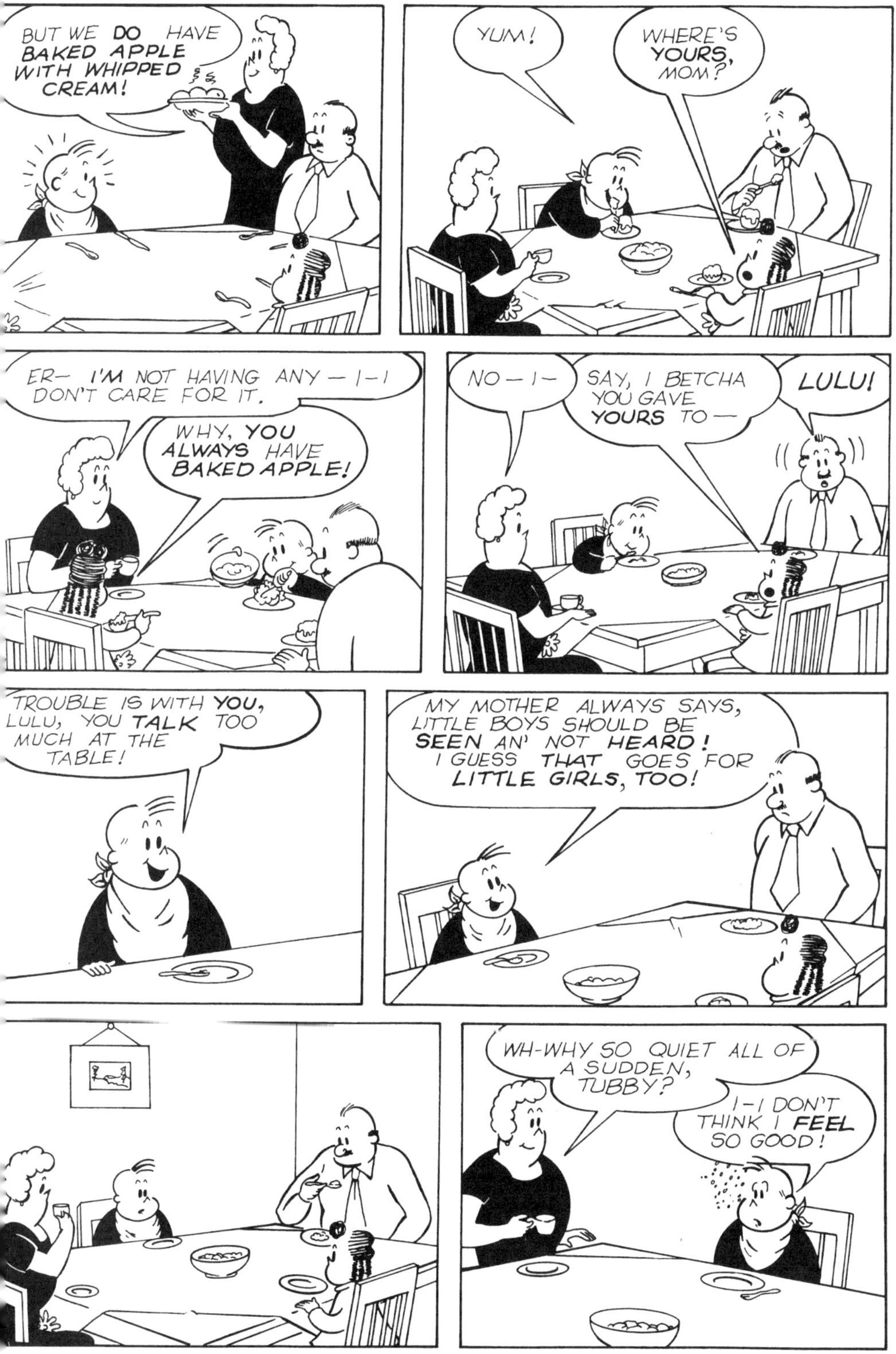

BUT WE DO HAVE BAKED APPLE WITH WHIPPED CREAM!
YUM!
WHERE'S YOURS, MOM?
ER— I'M NOT HAVING ANY — I—I DON'T CARE FOR IT.
WHY, YOU ALWAYS HAVE BAKED APPLE!
NO — I —
SAY, I BETCHA YOU GAVE YOURS TO —
LULU!
TROUBLE IS WITH YOU, LULU, YOU TALK TOO MUCH AT THE TABLE!
MY MOTHER ALWAYS SAYS, LITTLE BOYS SHOULD BE SEEN AN' NOT HEARD! I GUESS THAT GOES FOR LITTLE GIRLS, TOO!
WH-WHY SO QUIET ALL OF A SUDDEN, TUBBY?
I—I DON'T THINK I FEEL SO GOOD!

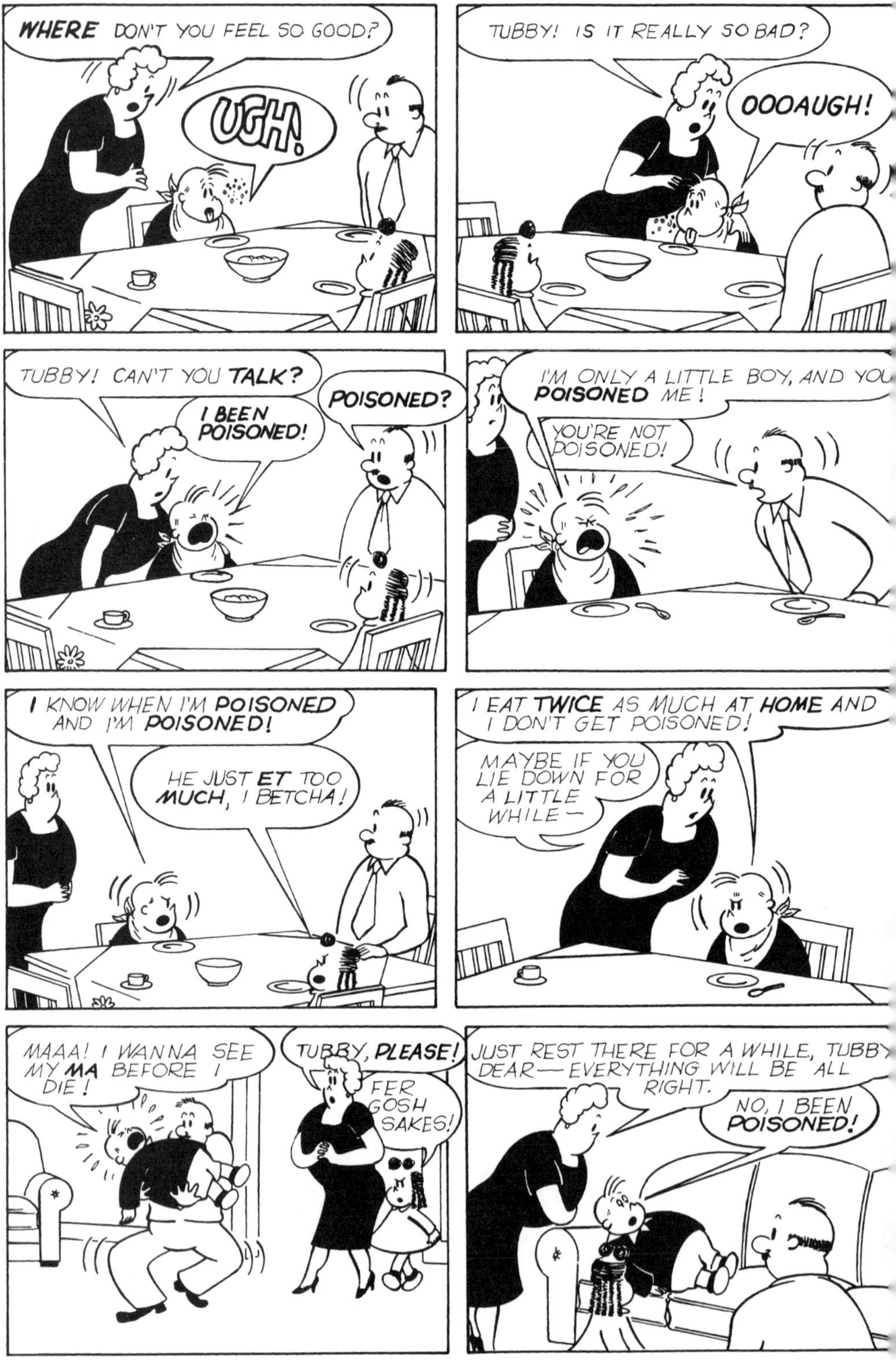
WHERE DON'T YOU FEEL SO GOOD?
UGH!
TUBBY! IS IT REALLY SO BAD?
OOOAUGH!
TUBBY! CAN'T YOU TALK?
I BEEN POISONED!
POISONED?
I'M ONLY A LITTLE BOY, AND YOU POISONED ME!
YOU'RE NOT POISONED!
I KNOW WHEN I'M POISONED AND I'M POISONED!
HE JUST ET TOO MUCH, I BETCHA!
I EAT TWICE AS MUCH AT HOME AND I DON'T GET POISONED!
MAYBE IF YOU LIE DOWN FOR A LITTLE WHILE—
MAAA! I WANNA SEE MY MA BEFORE I DIE!
TUBBY, PLEASE!
FER GOSH SAKES!
JUST REST THERE FOR A WHILE, TUBBY DEAR—EVERYTHING WILL BE ALL RIGHT.
NO, I BEEN POISONED!

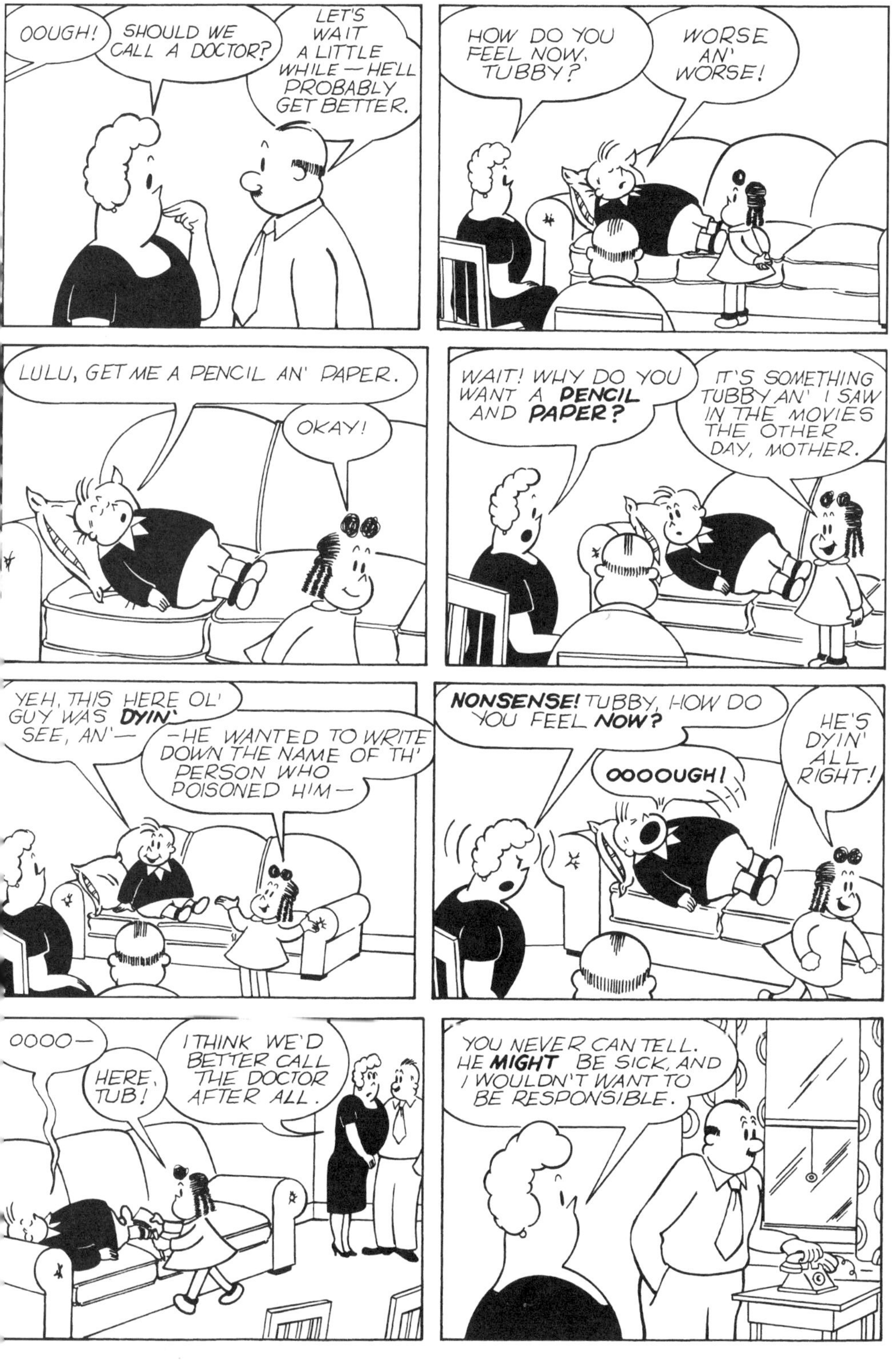
OOUGH!
SHOULD WE CALL A DOCTOR?
LET'S WAIT A LITTLE WHILE — HE'LL PROBABLY GET BETTER.
HOW DO YOU FEEL NOW, TUBBY?
WORSE AN' WORSE!
LULU, GET ME A PENCIL AN' PAPER.
OKAY!
WAIT! WHY DO YOU WANT A PENCIL AND PAPER?
IT'S SOMETHING TUBBY AN' I SAW IN THE MOVIES THE OTHER DAY, MOTHER.
YEH, THIS HERE OL' GUY WAS DYIN' SEE, AN'—
—HE WANTED TO WRITE DOWN THE NAME OF TH' PERSON WHO POISONED HIM—
NONSENSE! TUBBY, HOW DO YOU FEEL NOW?
OOOOUGH!
HE'S DYIN' ALL RIGHT!
OOOO—
HERE, TUB!
I THINK WE'D BETTER CALL THE DOCTOR AFTER ALL.
YOU NEVER CAN TELL. HE MIGHT BE SICK, AND I WOULDN'T WANT TO BE RESPONSIBLE.

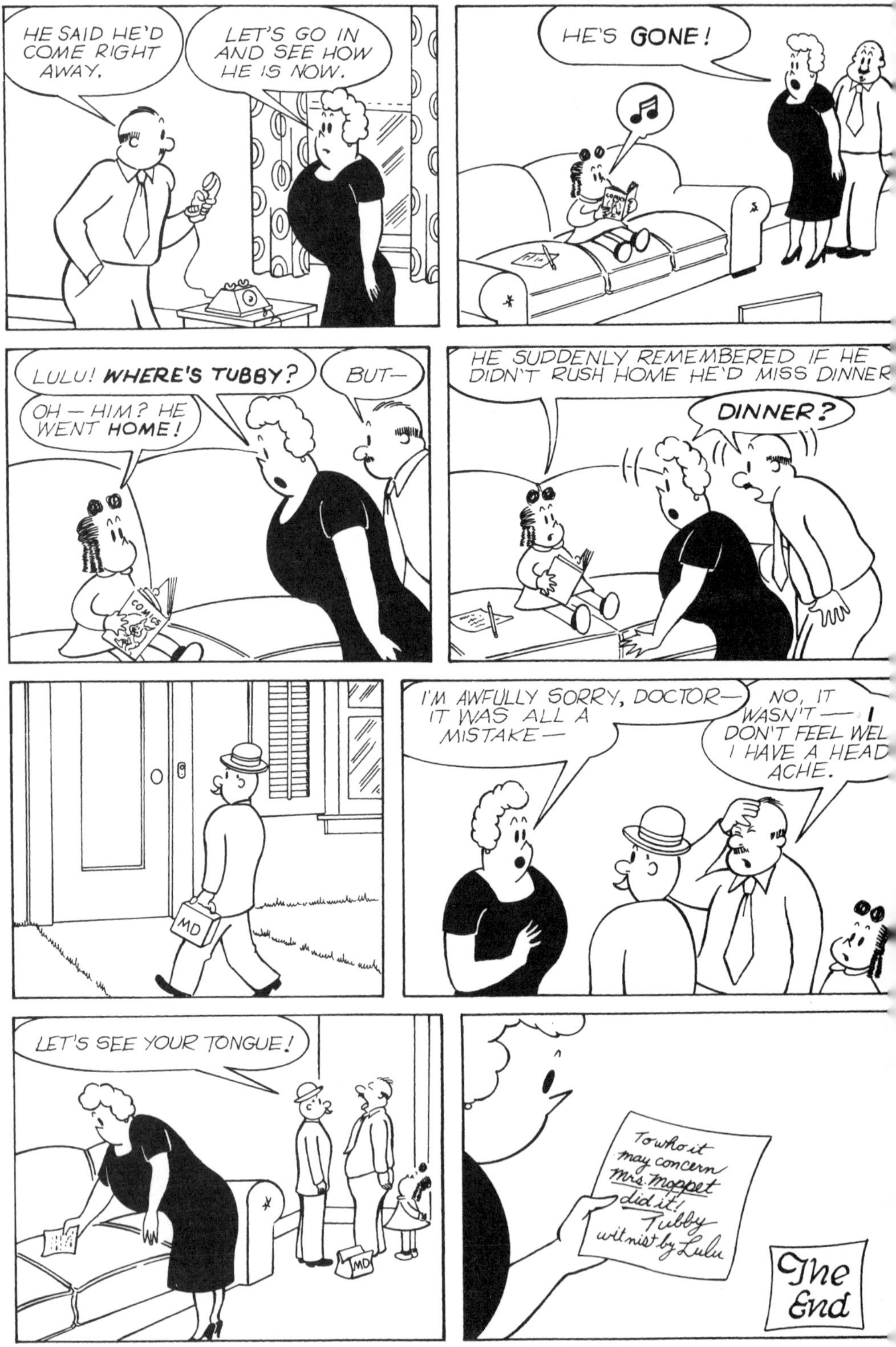
HE SAID HE'D COME RIGHT AWAY.
LET'S GO IN AND SEE HOW HE IS NOW.
HE'S GONE!
LULU! WHERE'S TUBBY?
BUT—
OH — HIM? HE WENT HOME!
HE SUDDENLY REMEMBERED IF HE DIDN'T RUSH HOME HE'D MISS DINNER
DINNER?
MD
I'M AWFULLY SORRY, DOCTOR— IT WAS ALL A MISTAKE—
NO, IT WASN'T — I DON'T FEEL WEL I HAVE A HEAD ACHE.
LET'S SEE YOUR TONGUE!
MD
To who it may concern Mrs. Moppet did it! Tubby witnist by Lulu
The End

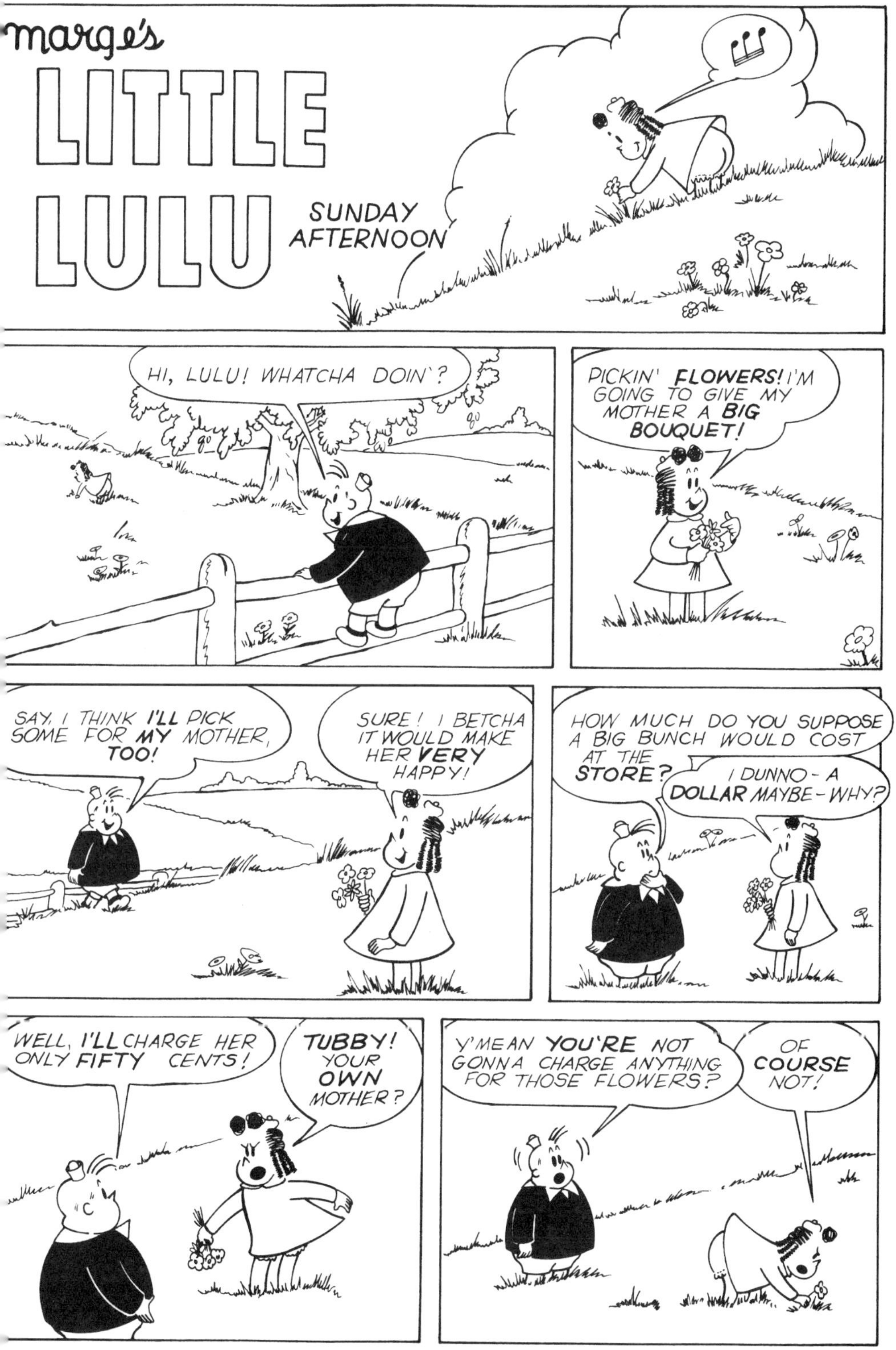
marge's
LITTLE LULU
SUNDAY AFTERNOON
HI, LULU! WHATCHA DOIN'?
PICKIN' FLOWERS! I'M GOING TO GIVE MY MOTHER A BIG BOUQUET!
SAY, I THINK I'LL PICK SOME FOR MY MOTHER, TOO!
SURE! I BETCHA IT WOULD MAKE HER VERY HAPPY!
HOW MUCH DO YOU SUPPOSE A BIG BUNCH WOULD COST AT THE STORE?
I DUNNO - A DOLLAR MAYBE - WHY?
WELL, I'LL CHARGE HER ONLY FIFTY CENTS!
TUBBY! YOUR OWN MOTHER?
Y'MEAN YOU'RE NOT GONNA CHARGE ANYTHING FOR THOSE FLOWERS?
OF COURSE NOT!

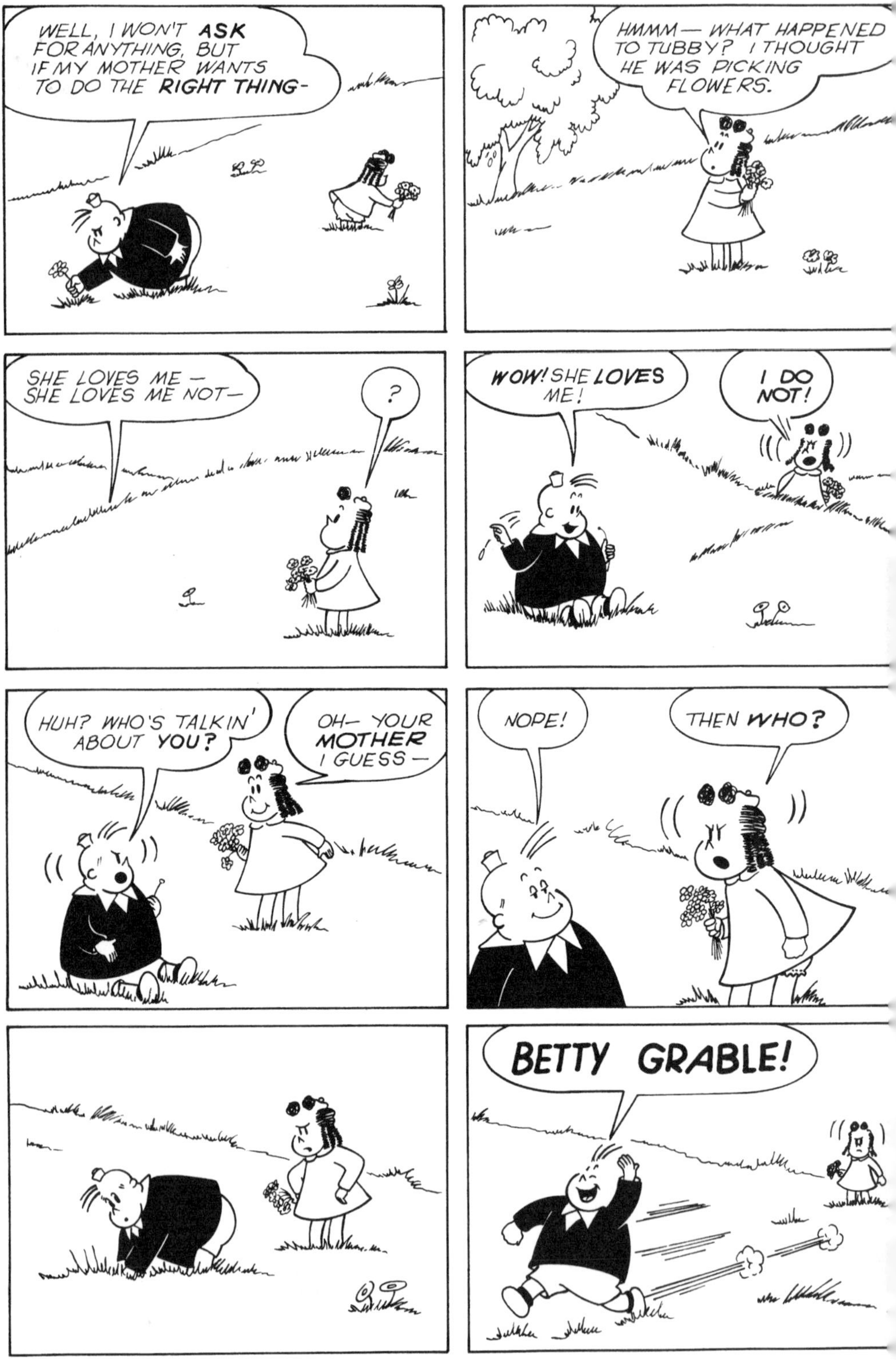
WELL, I WON'T ASK FOR ANYTHING, BUT IF MY MOTHER WANTS TO DO THE RIGHT THING-
HMMM— WHAT HAPPENED TO TUBBY? I THOUGHT HE WAS PICKING FLOWERS.
SHE LOVES ME — SHE LOVES ME NOT—
?
WOW! SHE LOVES ME!
I DO NOT!
HUH? WHO'S TALKIN' ABOUT YOU?
OH— YOUR MOTHER I GUESS —
NOPE!
THEN WHO?
BETTY GRABLE!

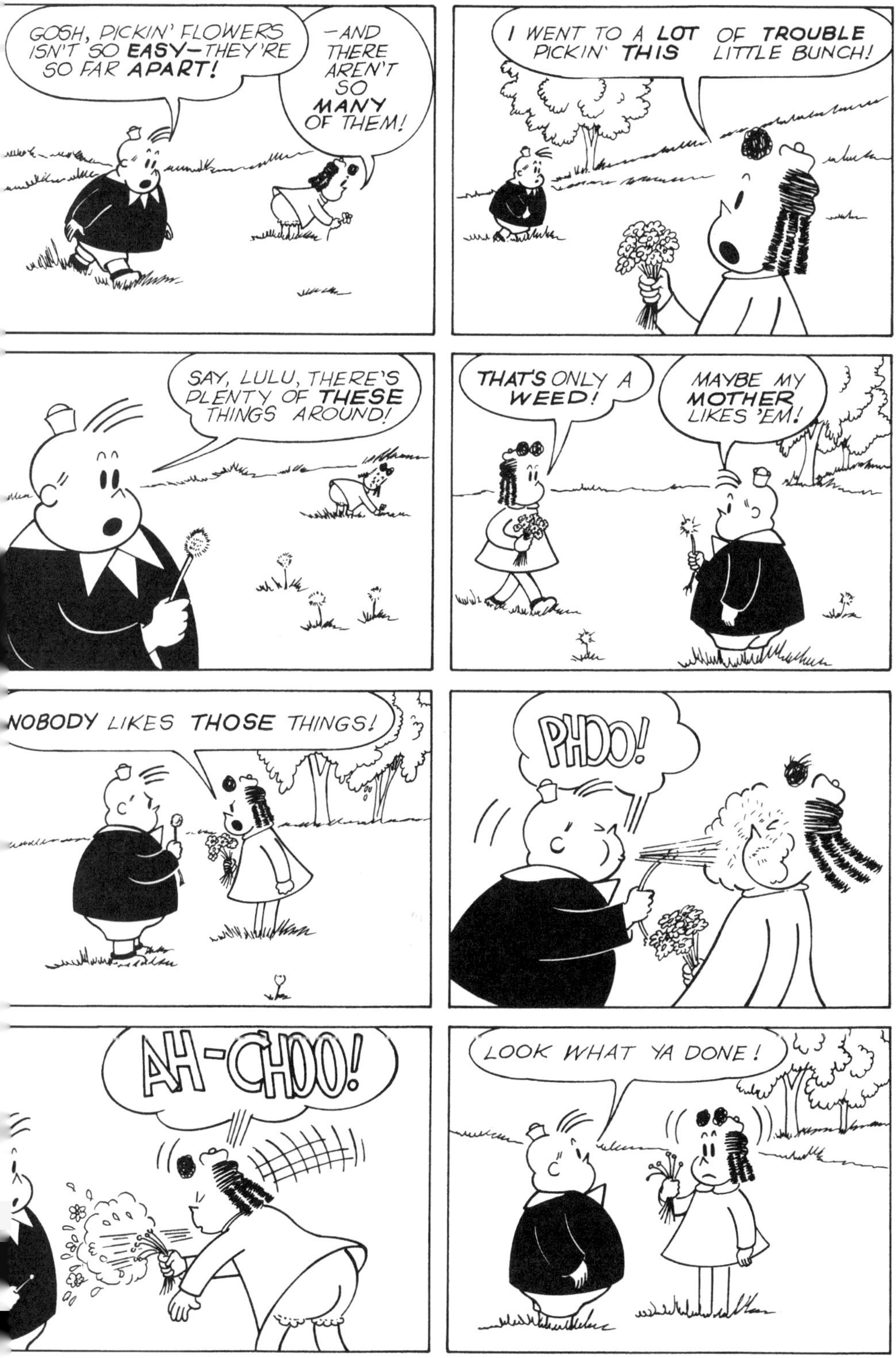
GOSH, PICKIN' FLOWERS ISN'T SO EASY—THEY'RE SO FAR APART!
—AND THERE AREN'T SO MANY OF THEM!
I WENT TO A LOT OF TROUBLE PICKIN' THIS LITTLE BUNCH!
SAY, LULU, THERE'S PLENTY OF THESE THINGS AROUND!
THAT'S ONLY A WEED!
MAYBE MY MOTHER LIKES 'EM!
NOBODY LIKES THOSE THINGS!
PHOO!
AH-CHOO!
LOOK WHAT YA DONE!

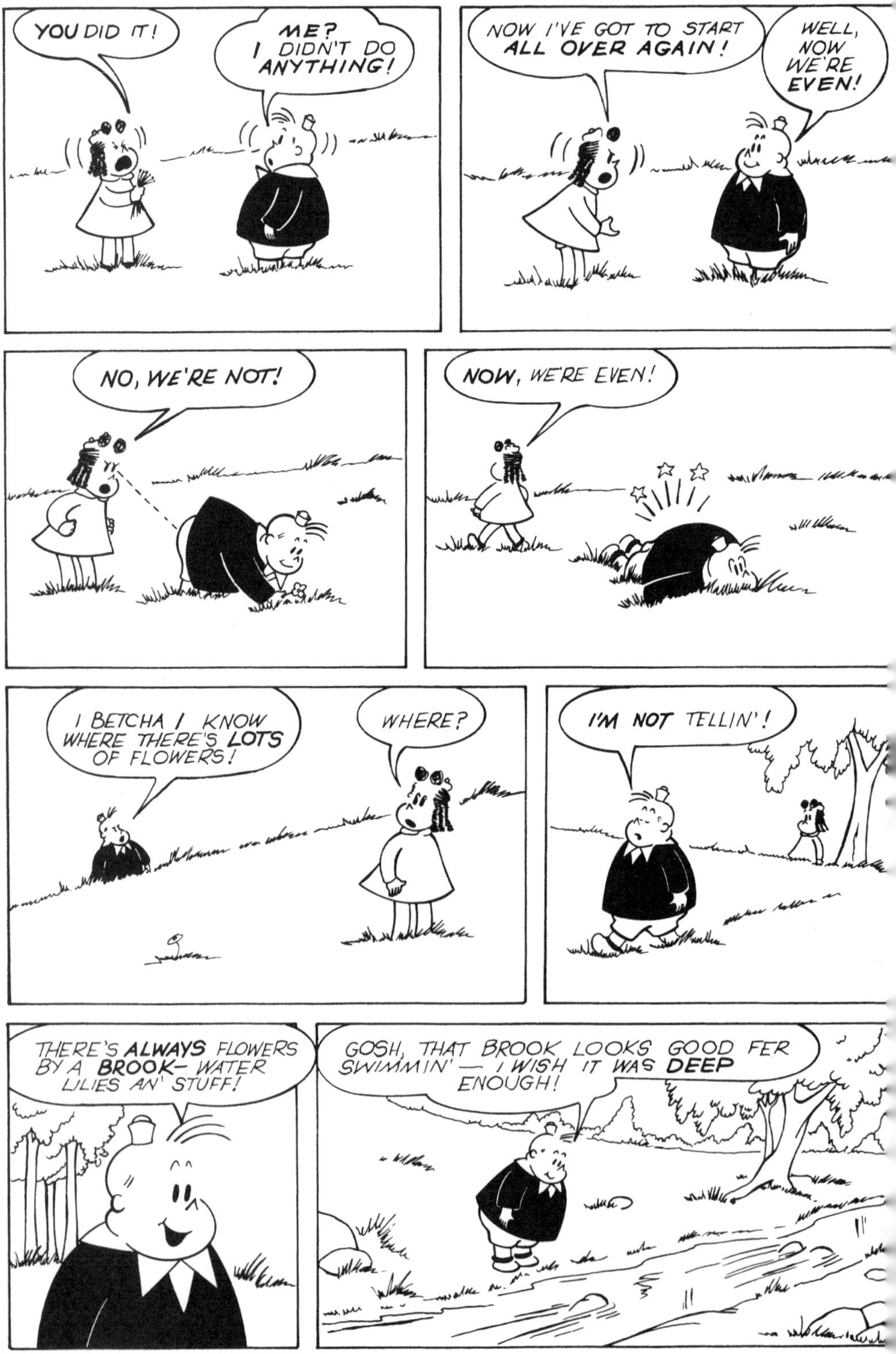
YOU DID IT!
ME? I DIDN'T DO ANYTHING!
NOW I'VE GOT TO START ALL OVER AGAIN!
WELL, NOW WE'RE EVEN!
NO, WE'RE NOT!
NOW, WE'RE EVEN!
I BETCHA I KNOW WHERE THERE'S LOTS OF FLOWERS!
WHERE?
I'M NOT TELLIN'!
THERE'S ALWAYS FLOWERS BY A BROOK— WATER LILIES AN' STUFF!
GOSH, THAT BROOK LOOKS GOOD FER SWIMMIN' — I WISH IT WAS DEEP ENOUGH!

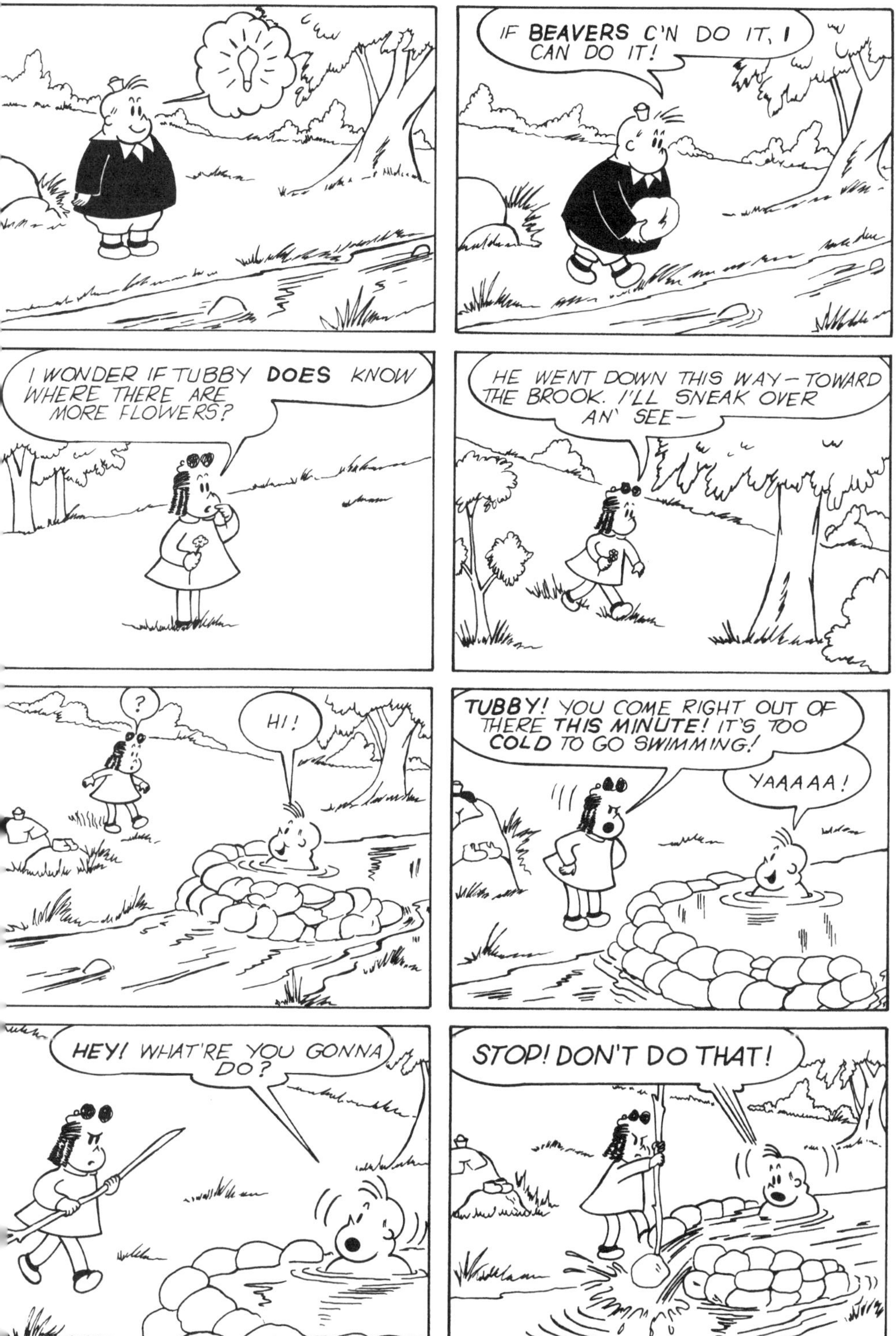
IF BEAVERS C'N DO IT, I CAN DO IT!
I WONDER IF TUBBY DOES KNOW WHERE THERE ARE MORE FLOWERS?
HE WENT DOWN THIS WAY—TOWARD THE BROOK. I'LL SNEAK OVER AN' SEE—
?
HI!
TUBBY! YOU COME RIGHT OUT OF THERE THIS MINUTE! IT'S TOO COLD TO GO SWIMMING!
YAAAAA!
HEY! WHAT'RE YOU GONNA DO?
STOP! DON'T DO THAT!

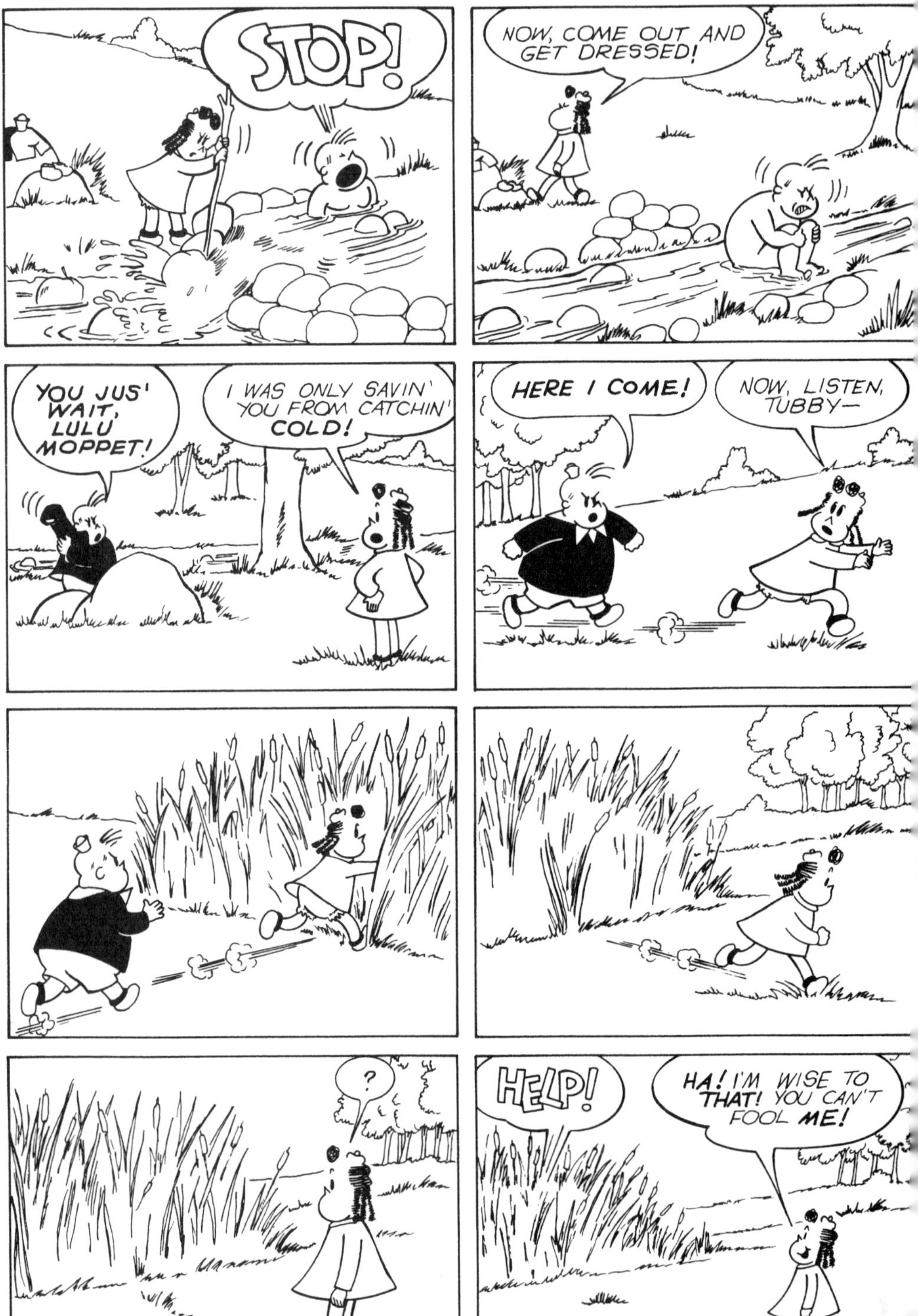
STOP!
NOW, COME OUT AND GET DRESSED!
YOU JUS' WAIT, LULU MOPPET!
I WAS ONLY SAVIN' YOU FROM CATCHIN' COLD!
HERE I COME!
NOW, LISTEN, TUBBY—
?
HELP!
HA! I'M WISE TO THAT! YOU CAN'T FOOL ME!

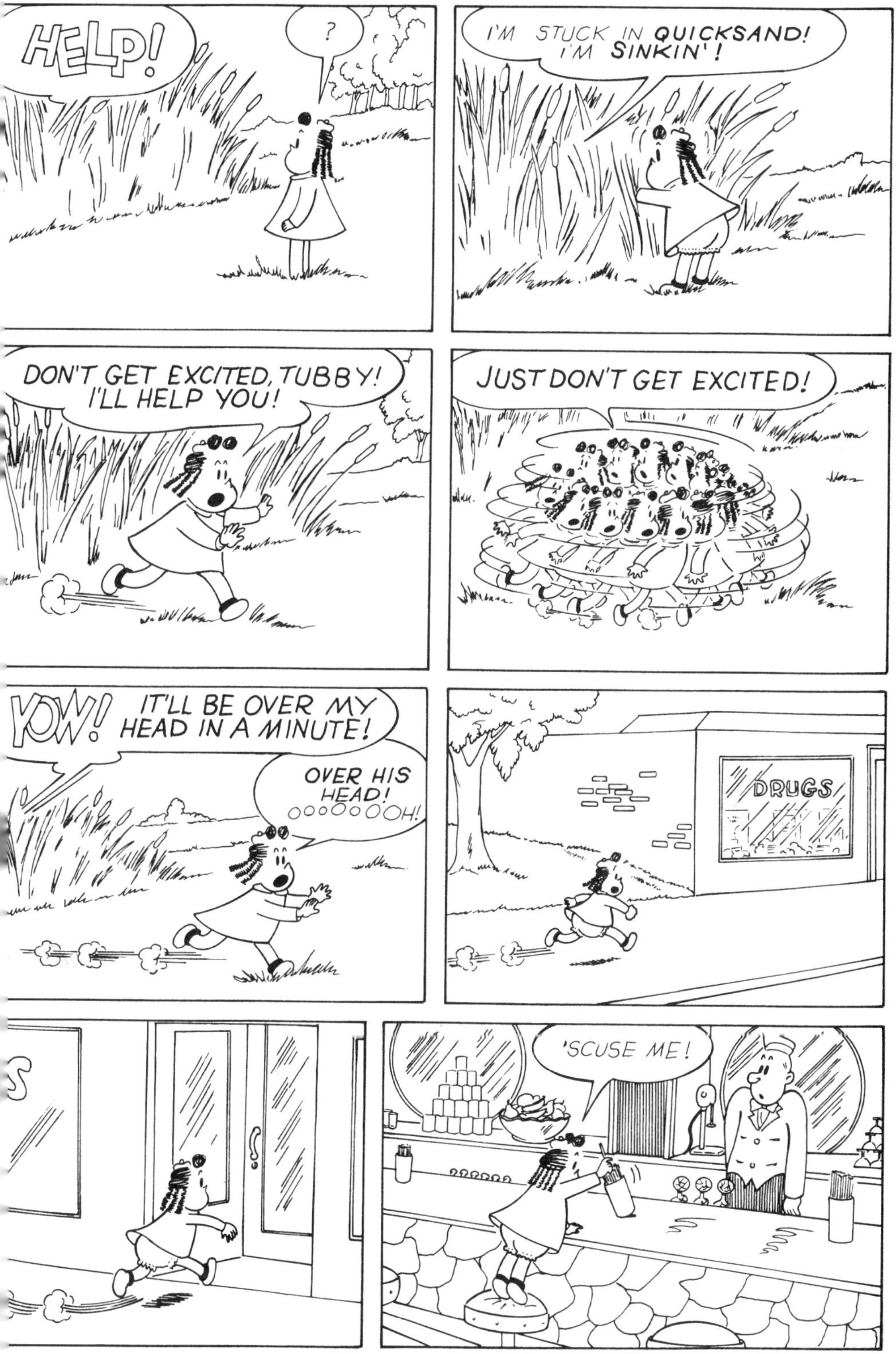
HELP!
?
I'M STUCK IN QUICKSAND! I'M SINKIN'!
DON'T GET EXCITED, TUBBY! I'LL HELP YOU!
JUST DON'T GET EXCITED!
YOW! IT'LL BE OVER MY HEAD IN A MINUTE!
OVER HIS HEAD! OOOOOOOH!
DRUGS
'SCUSE ME!

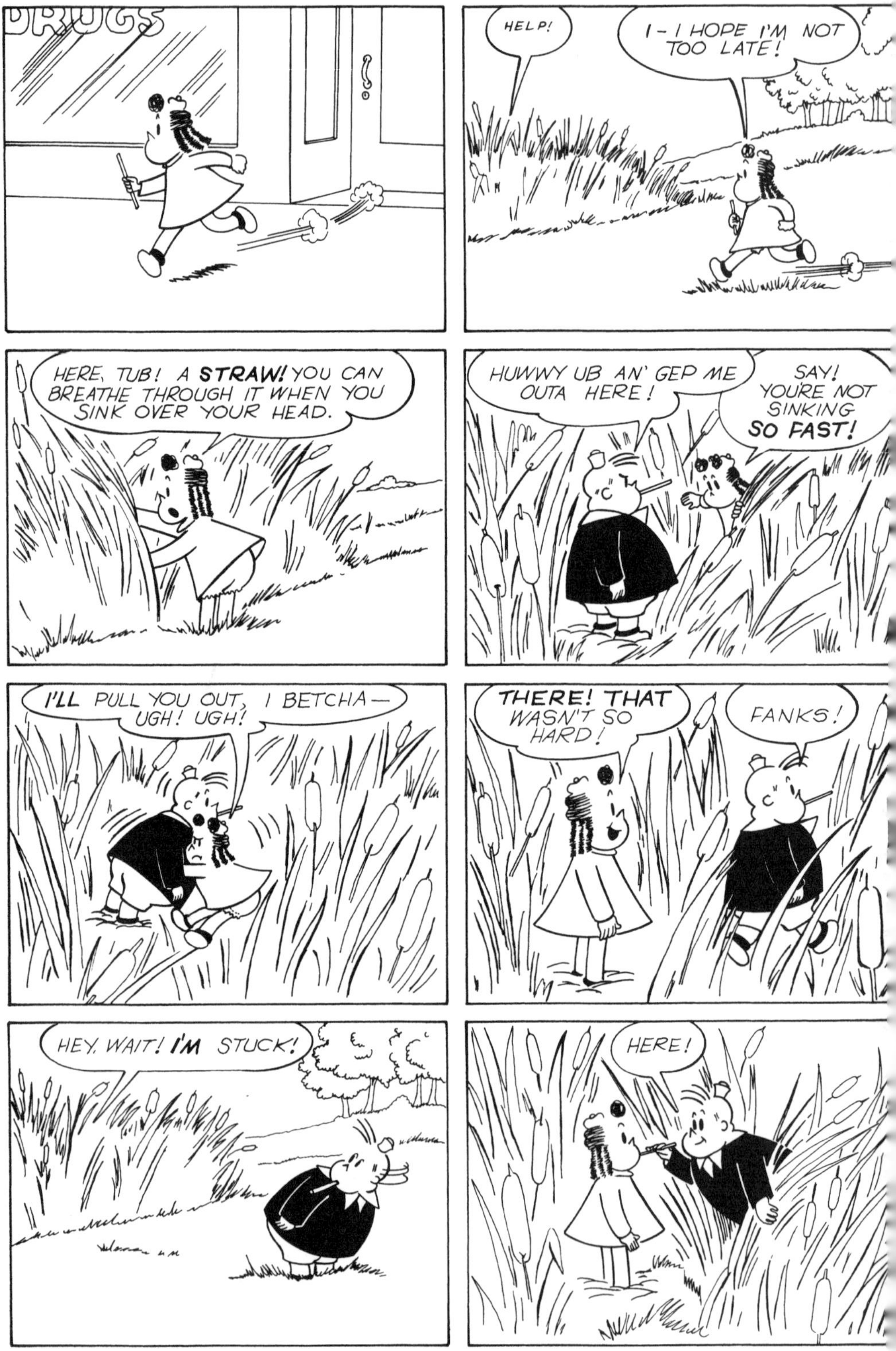
DRUGS
HELP!
I - I HOPE I'M NOT TOO LATE!
HERE, TUB! A STRAW! YOU CAN BREATHE THROUGH IT WHEN YOU SINK OVER YOUR HEAD.
HUWWY UB AN' GEP ME OUTA HERE!
SAY! YOU'RE NOT SINKING SO FAST!
I'LL PULL YOU OUT, I BETCHA— UGH! UGH!
THERE! THAT WASN'T SO HARD!
FANKS!
HEY, WAIT! I'M STUCK!
HERE!

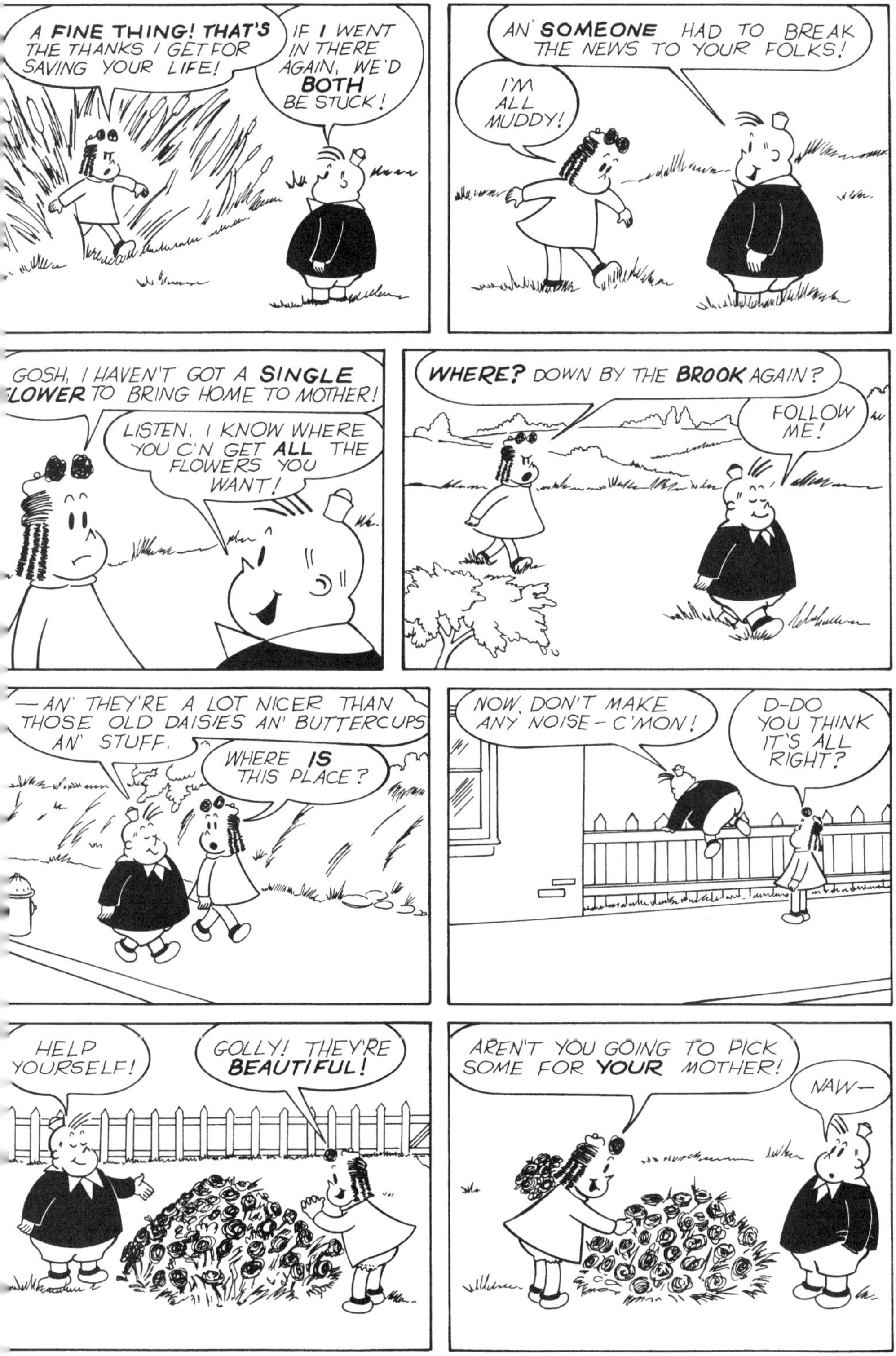
A FINE THING! THAT'S THE THANKS I GET FOR SAVING YOUR LIFE!
IF I WENT IN THERE AGAIN, WE'D BOTH BE STUCK!
AN' SOMEONE HAD TO BREAK THE NEWS TO YOUR FOLKS!
I'M ALL MUDDY!
GOSH, I HAVEN'T GOT A SINGLE FLOWER TO BRING HOME TO MOTHER!
LISTEN, I KNOW WHERE YOU C'N GET ALL THE FLOWERS YOU WANT!
WHERE? DOWN BY THE BROOK AGAIN?
FOLLOW ME!
—AN' THEY'RE A LOT NICER THAN THOSE OLD DAISIES AN' BUTTERCUPS AN' STUFF.
WHERE IS THIS PLACE?
NOW, DON'T MAKE ANY NOISE—C'MON!
D-DO YOU THINK IT'S ALL RIGHT?
HELP YOURSELF!
GOLLY! THEY'RE BEAUTIFUL!
AREN'T YOU GOING TO PICK SOME FOR YOUR MOTHER!
NAW—

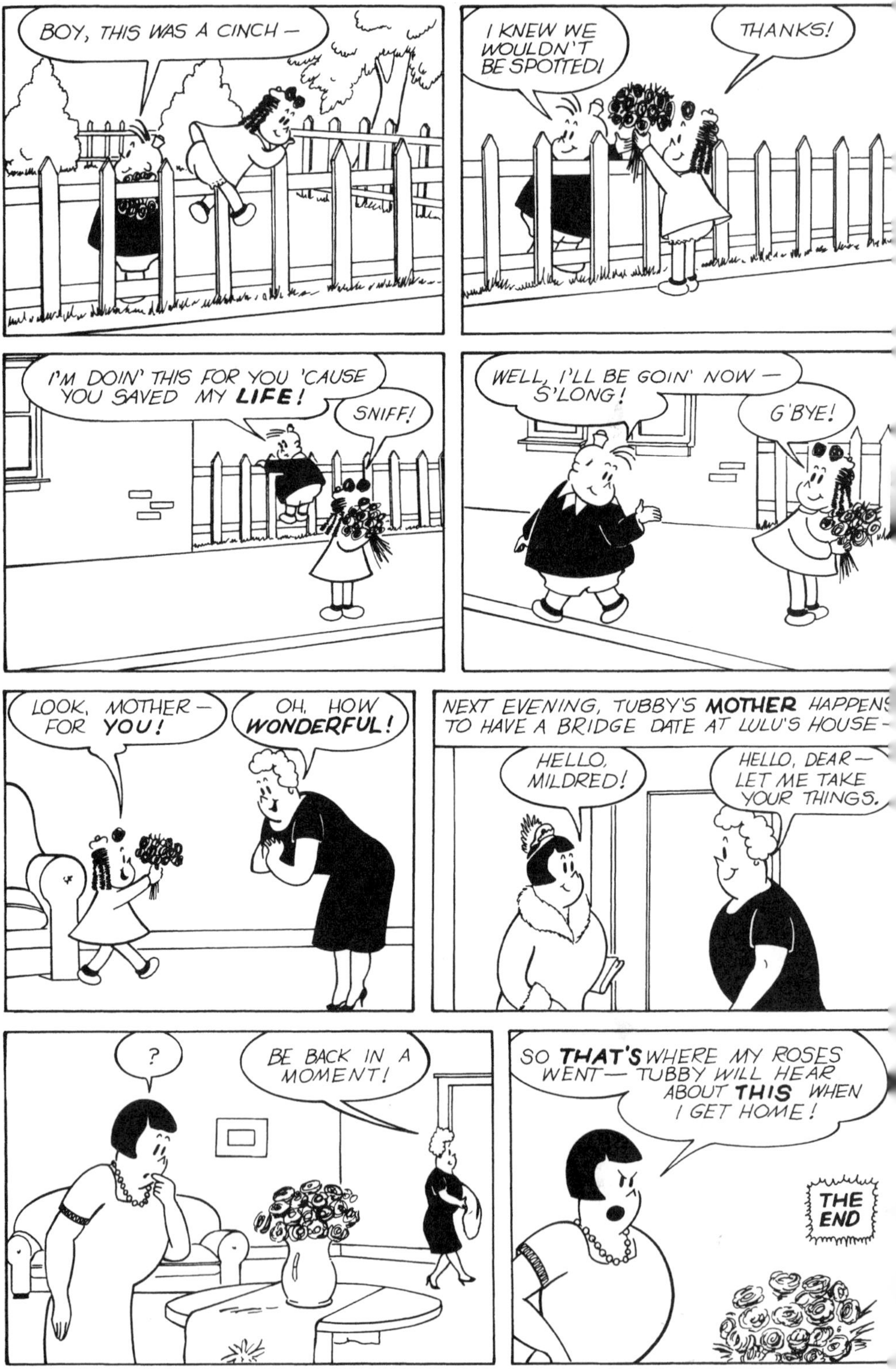
BOY, THIS WAS A CINCH—
I KNEW WE WOULDN'T BE SPOTTED!
THANKS!
I'M DOIN' THIS FOR YOU 'CAUSE YOU SAVED MY LIFE!
SNIFF!
WELL, I'LL BE GOIN' NOW— S'LONG!
G'BYE!
LOOK, MOTHER— FOR YOU!
OH, HOW WONDERFUL!
NEXT EVENING, TUBBY'S MOTHER HAPPENS TO HAVE A BRIDGE DATE AT LULU'S HOUSE—
HELLO, MILDRED!
HELLO, DEAR— LET ME TAKE YOUR THINGS.
?
BE BACK IN A MOMENT!
SO THAT'S WHERE MY ROSES WENT— TUBBY WILL HEAR ABOUT THIS WHEN I GET HOME!
THE END

marge's

Little Lulu

FORBIDDEN FRUIT

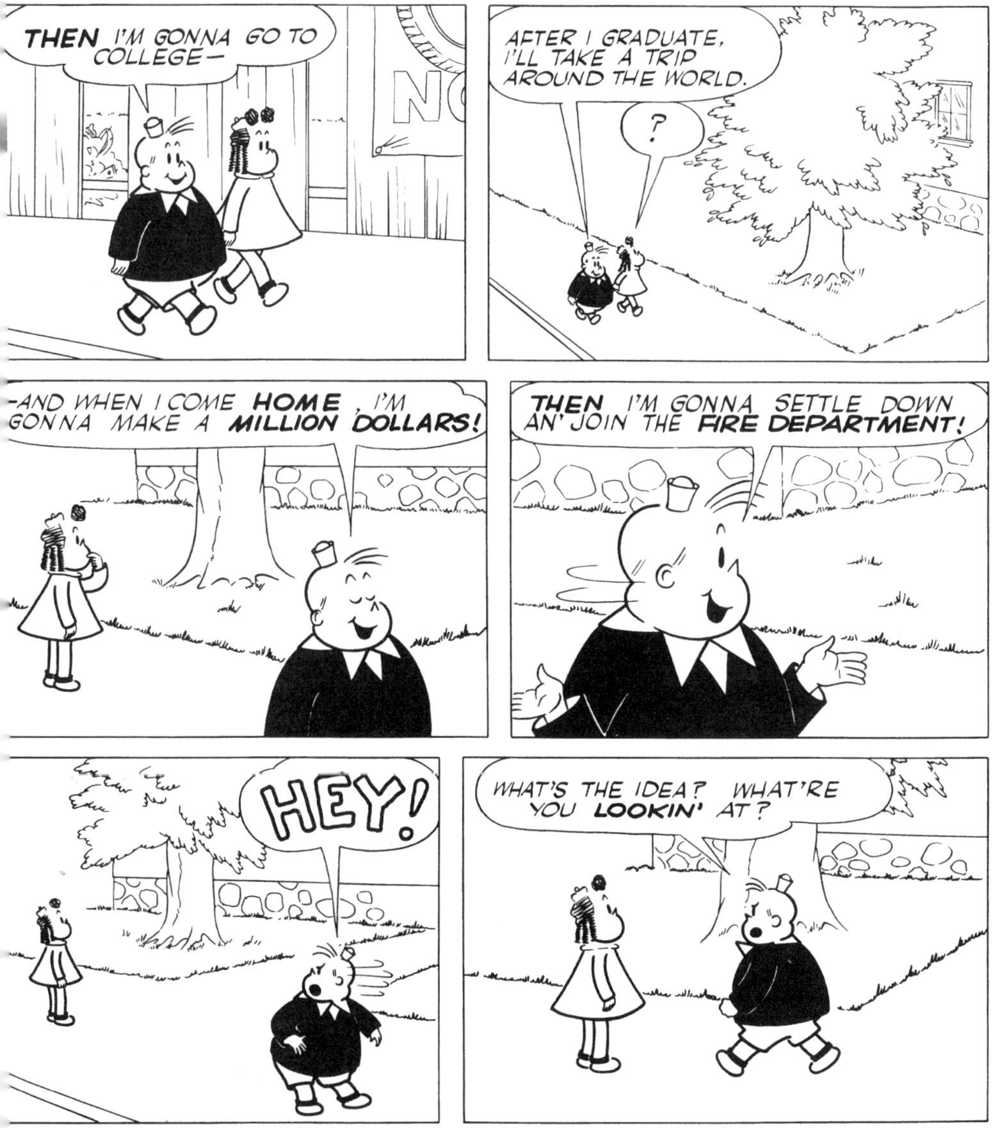
THEN I'M GONNA GO TO COLLEGE—
AFTER I GRADUATE, I'LL TAKE A TRIP AROUND THE WORLD.
?
-AND WHEN I COME HOME, I'M GONNA MAKE A MILLION DOLLARS!
THEN I'M GONNA SETTLE DOWN AN' JOIN THE FIRE DEPARTMENT!
HEY!
WHAT'S THE IDEA? WHAT'RE YOU LOOKIN' AT?

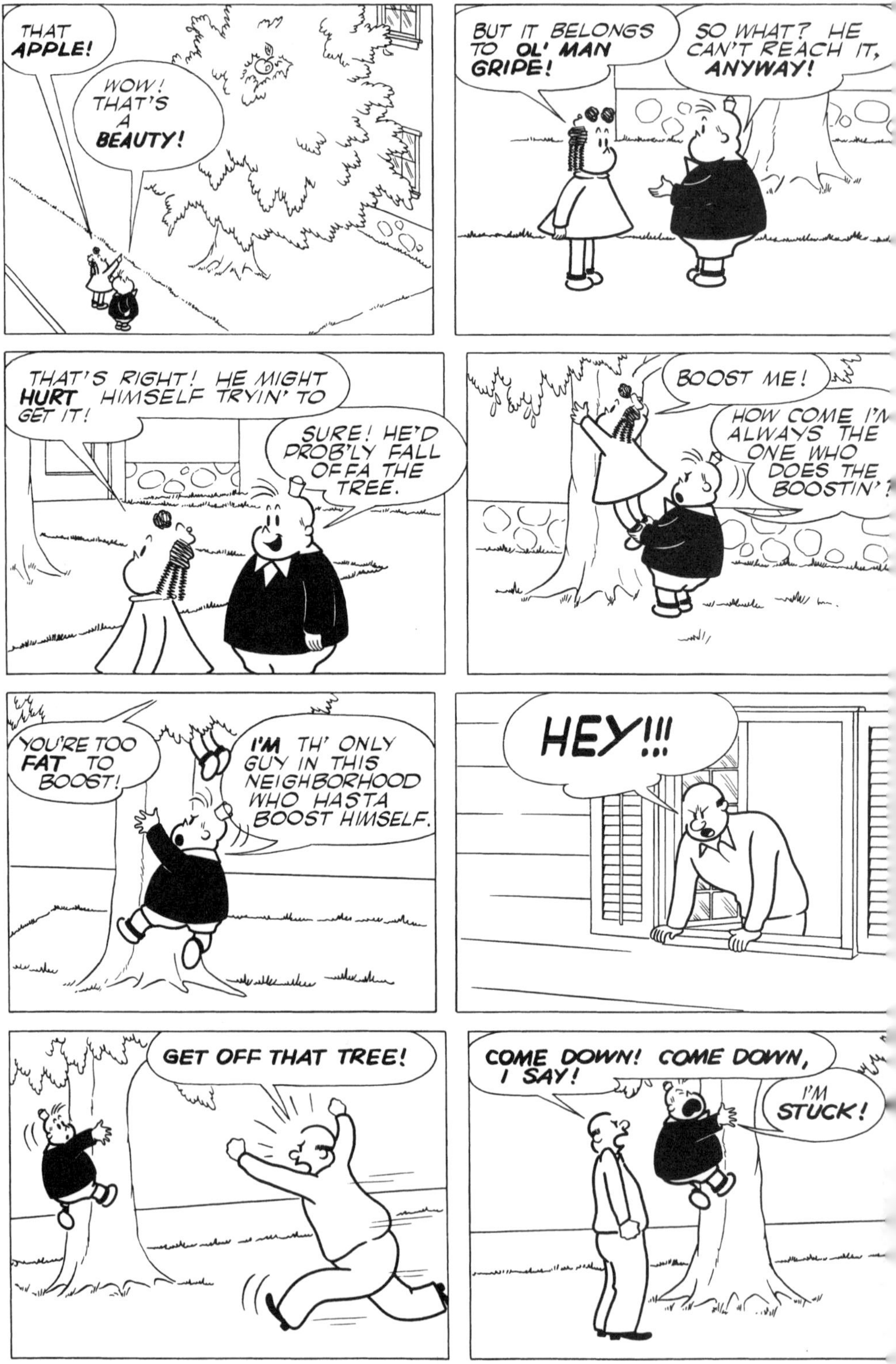
THAT APPLE!
WOW! THAT'S A BEAUTY!
BUT IT BELONGS TO OL' MAN GRIPE!
SO WHAT? HE CAN'T REACH IT, ANYWAY!
THAT'S RIGHT! HE MIGHT HURT HIMSELF TRYIN' TO GET IT!
SURE! HE'D PROB'LY FALL OFFA THE TREE.
BOOST ME!
HOW COME I'M ALWAYS THE ONE WHO DOES THE BOOSTIN'?
YOU'RE TOO FAT TO BOOST!
I'M TH' ONLY GUY IN THIS NEIGHBORHOOD WHO HASTA BOOST HIMSELF.
HEY!!!
GET OFF THAT TREE!
COME DOWN! COME DOWN, I SAY!
I'M STUCK!

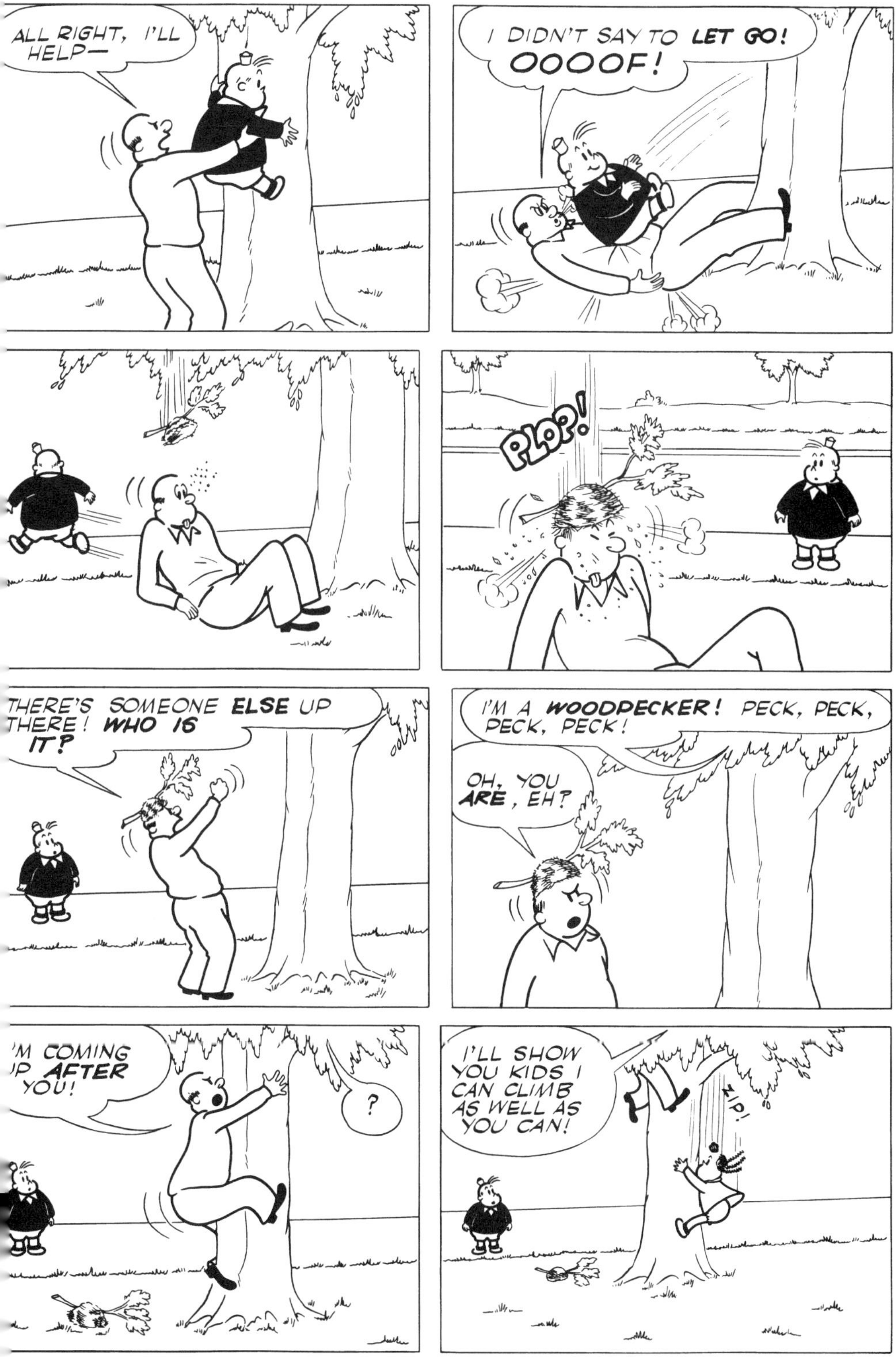
ALL RIGHT, I'LL HELP—
I DIDN'T SAY TO LET GO! OOOOF!
PLOP!
THERE'S SOMEONE ELSE UP THERE! WHO IS IT?
I'M A WOODPECKER! PECK, PECK, PECK, PECK!
OH, YOU ARE, EH?
'M COMING P AFTER YOU!
?
I'LL SHOW YOU KIDS I CAN CLIMB AS WELL AS YOU CAN!
ZIP!

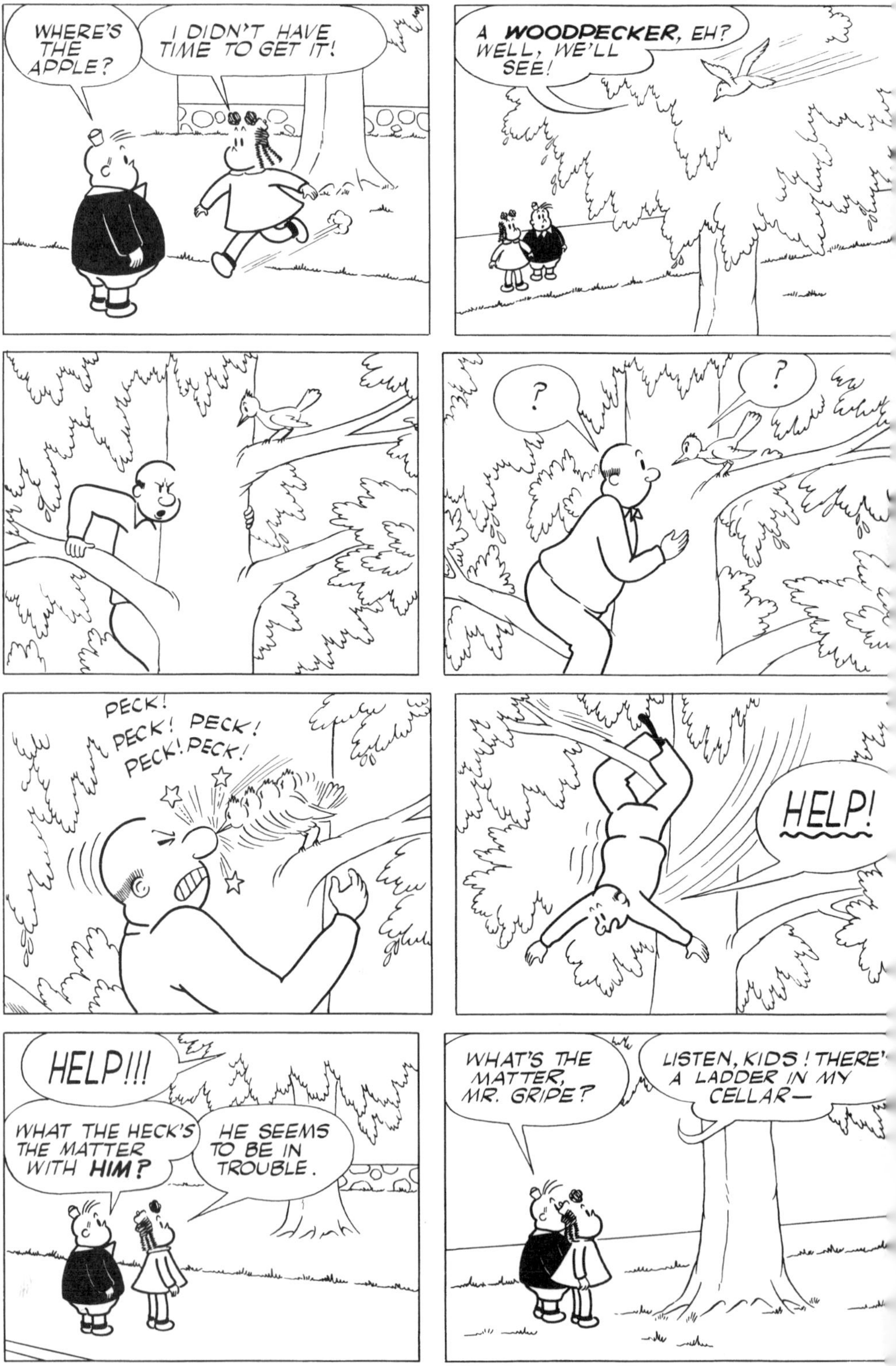
WHERE'S THE APPLE?
I DIDN'T HAVE TIME TO GET IT!
A WOODPECKER, EH? WELL, WE'LL SEE!
?
?
PECK! PECK! PECK! PECK! PECK!
HELP!
HELP!!!
WHAT THE HECK'S THE MATTER WITH HIM?
HE SEEMS TO BE IN TROUBLE.
WHAT'S THE MATTER, MR. GRIPE?
LISTEN, KIDS! THERE'S A LADDER IN MY CELLAR—

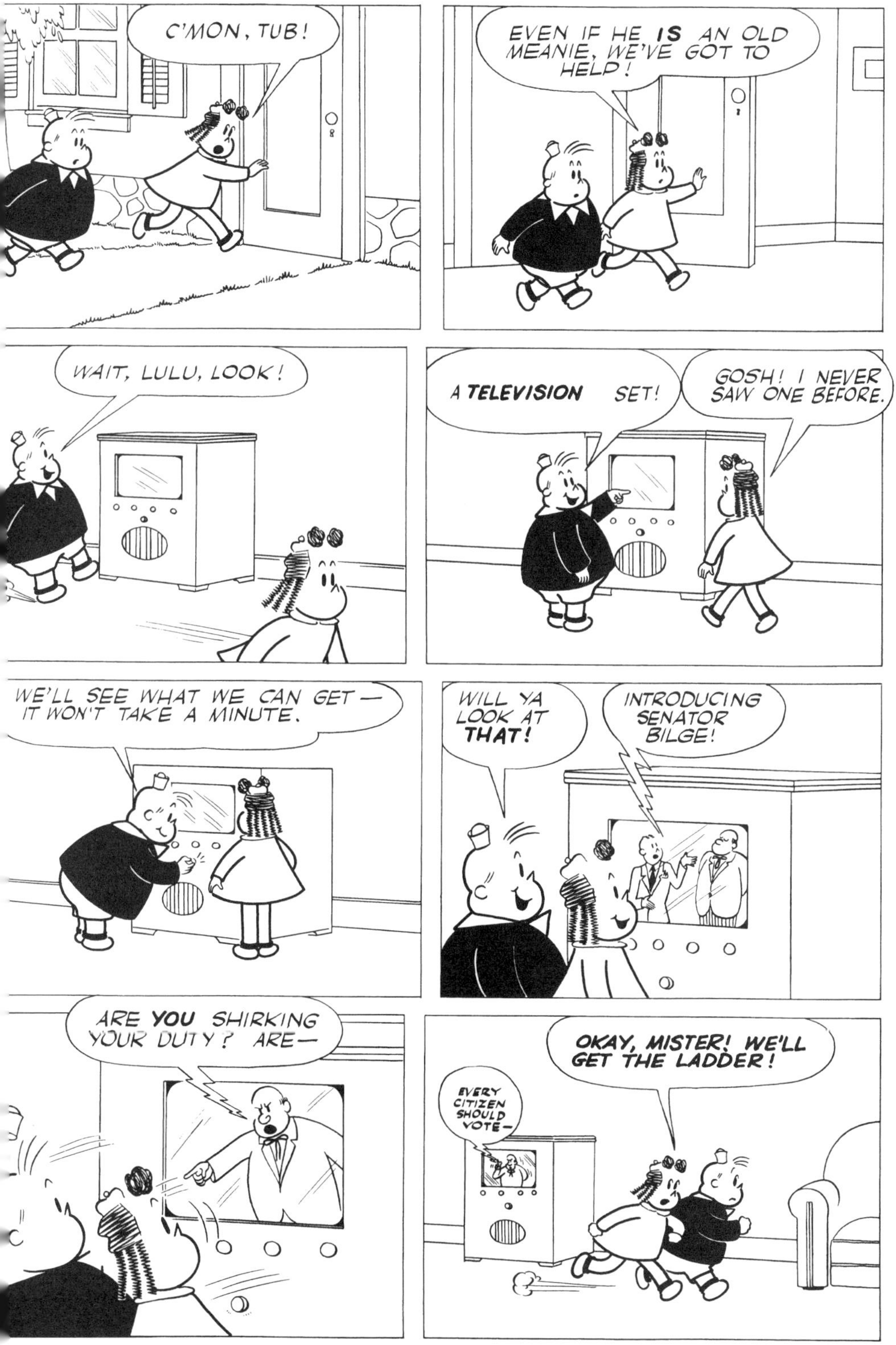
C'MON, TUB!
EVEN IF HE IS AN OLD MEANIE, WE'VE GOT TO HELP!
WAIT, LULU, LOOK!
A TELEVISION SET!
GOSH! I NEVER SAW ONE BEFORE.
WE'LL SEE WHAT WE CAN GET — IT WON'T TAKE A MINUTE.
WILL YA LOOK AT THAT!
INTRODUCING SENATOR BILGE!
ARE YOU SHIRKING YOUR DUTY? ARE—
EVERY CITIZEN SHOULD VOTE—
OKAY, MISTER! WE'LL GET THE LADDER!

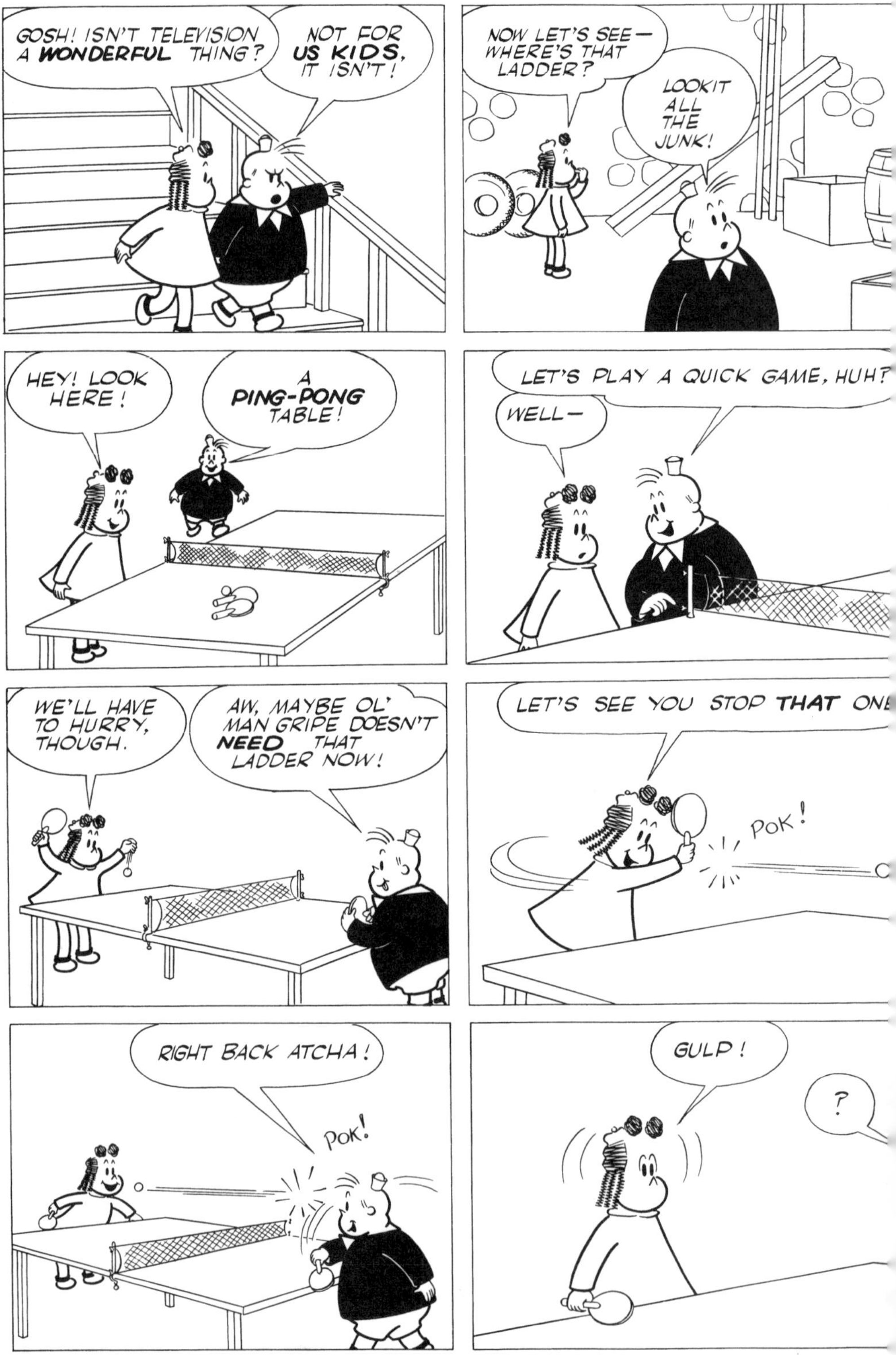
GOSH! ISN'T TELEVISION A WONDERFUL THING?
NOT FOR US KIDS, IT ISN'T!
NOW LET'S SEE— WHERE'S THAT LADDER?
LOOKIT ALL THE JUNK!
HEY! LOOK HERE!
A PING-PONG TABLE!
LET'S PLAY A QUICK GAME, HUH?
WELL—
WE'LL HAVE TO HURRY, THOUGH.
AW, MAYBE OL' MAN GRIPE DOESN'T NEED THAT LADDER NOW!
LET'S SEE YOU STOP THAT ONE
POK!
RIGHT BACK ATCHA!
POK!
GULP!
?

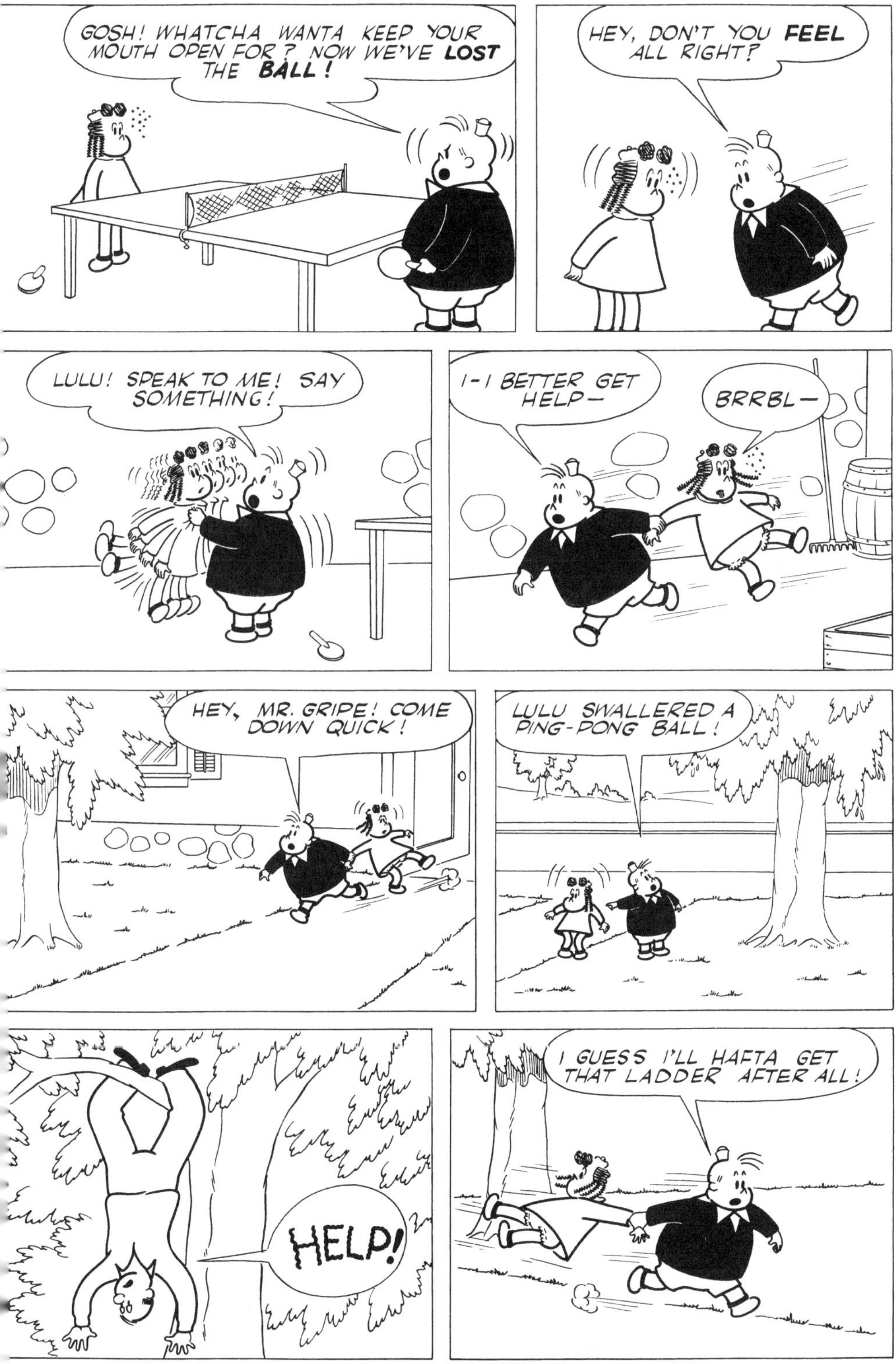
GOSH! WHATCHA WANTA KEEP YOUR MOUTH OPEN FOR? NOW WE'VE LOST THE BALL!
HEY, DON'T YOU FEEL ALL RIGHT?
LULU! SPEAK TO ME! SAY SOMETHING!
I-I BETTER GET HELP—
BRRBL—
HEY, MR. GRIPE! COME DOWN QUICK!
LULU SWALLERED A PING-PONG BALL!
HELP!
I GUESS I'LL HAFTA GET THAT LADDER AFTER ALL!

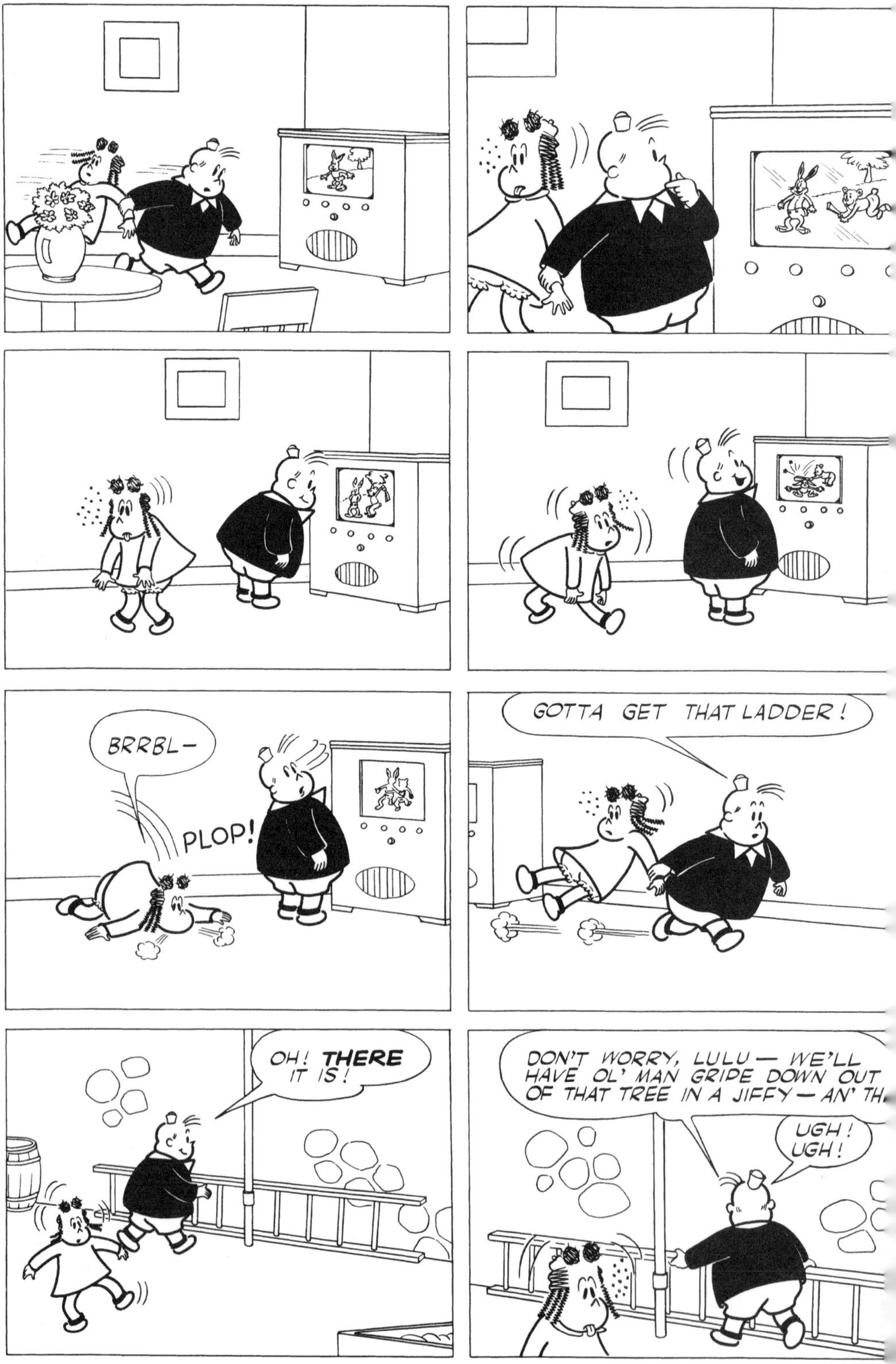
BRRBL-
PLOP!
GOTTA GET THAT LADDER!
OH! THERE IT IS!
DON'T WORRY, LULU — WE'LL HAVE OL' MAN GRIPE DOWN OUT OF THAT TREE IN A JIFFY — AN' TH
UGH! UGH!

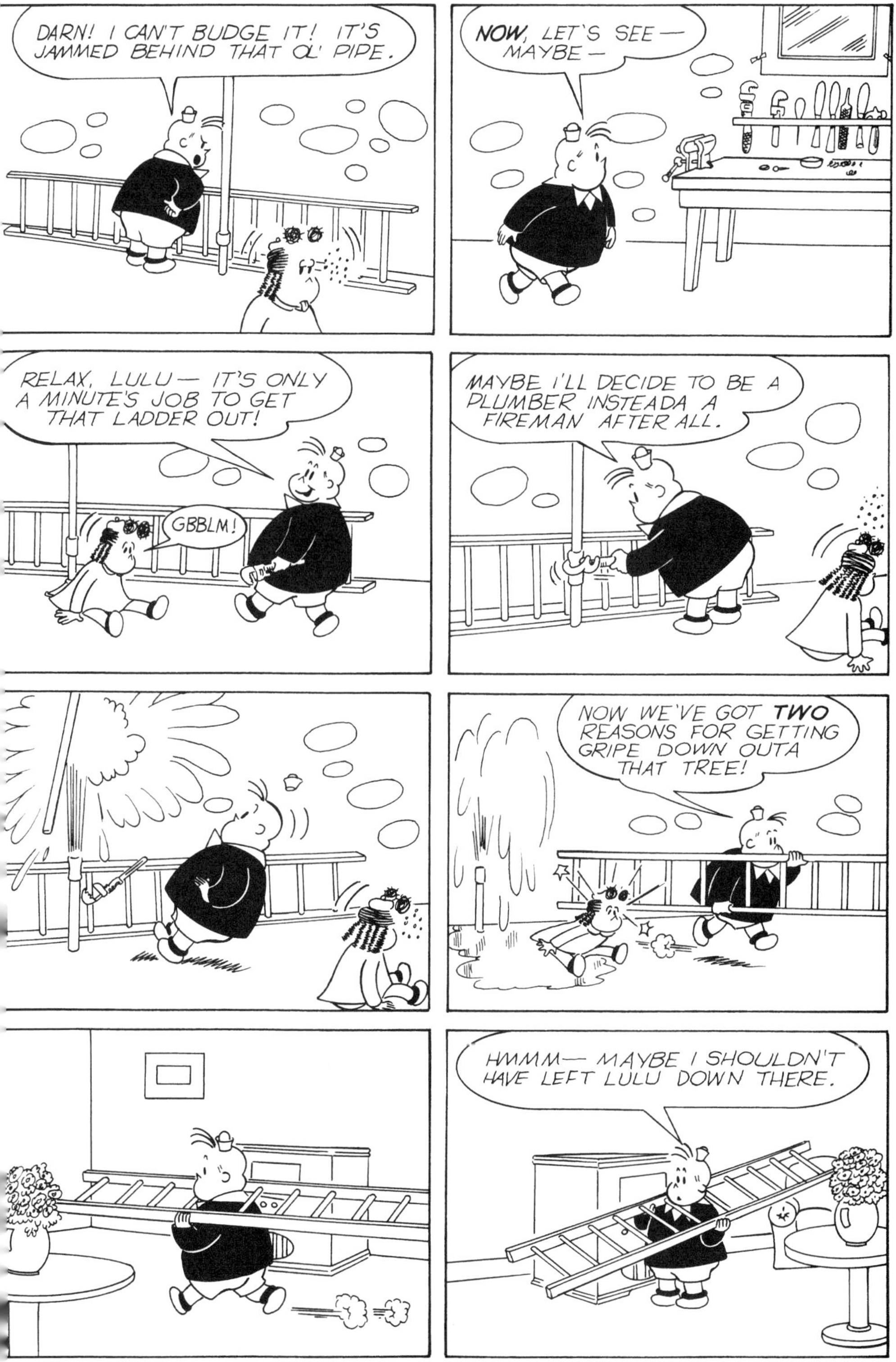
DARN! I CAN'T BUDGE IT! IT'S JAMMED BEHIND THAT OL' PIPE.
NOW, LET'S SEE— MAYBE—
RELAX, LULU— IT'S ONLY A MINUTE'S JOB TO GET THAT LADDER OUT!
GBBLM!
MAYBE I'LL DECIDE TO BE A PLUMBER INSTEADA A FIREMAN AFTER ALL.
NOW WE'VE GOT TWO REASONS FOR GETTING GRIPE DOWN OUTA THAT TREE!
HMMM— MAYBE I SHOULDN'T HAVE LEFT LULU DOWN THERE.

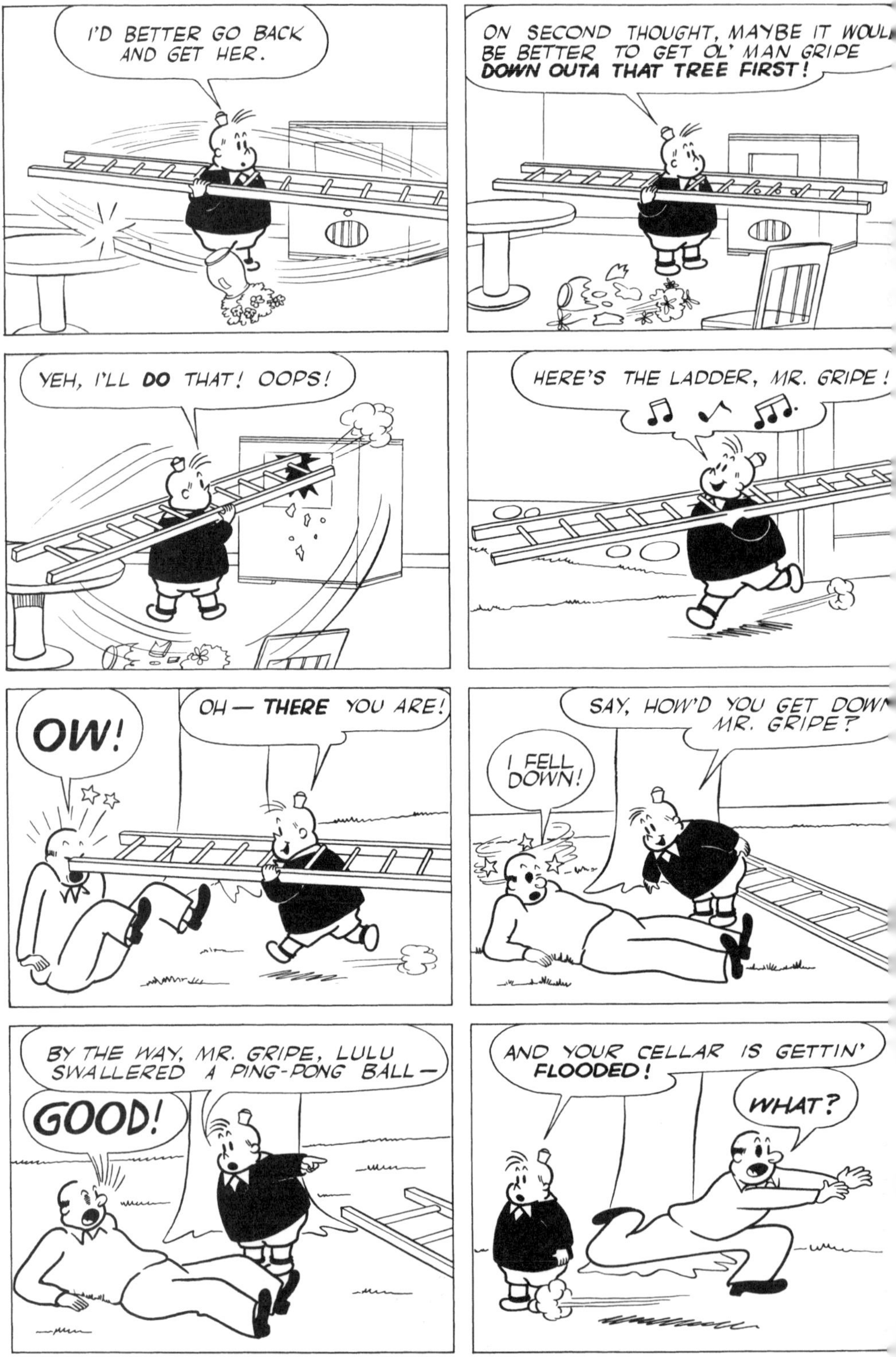
I'D BETTER GO BACK AND GET HER.
ON SECOND THOUGHT, MAYBE IT WOUL BE BETTER TO GET OL' MAN GRIPE DOWN OUTA THAT TREE FIRST!
YEH, I'LL DO THAT! OOPS!
HERE'S THE LADDER, MR. GRIPE!
OW!
OH — THERE YOU ARE!
SAY, HOW'D YOU GET DOWN MR. GRIPE?
I FELL DOWN!
BY THE WAY, MR. GRIPE, LULU SWALLERED A PING-PONG BALL—
GOOD!
AND YOUR CELLAR IS GETTIN' FLOODED!
WHAT?

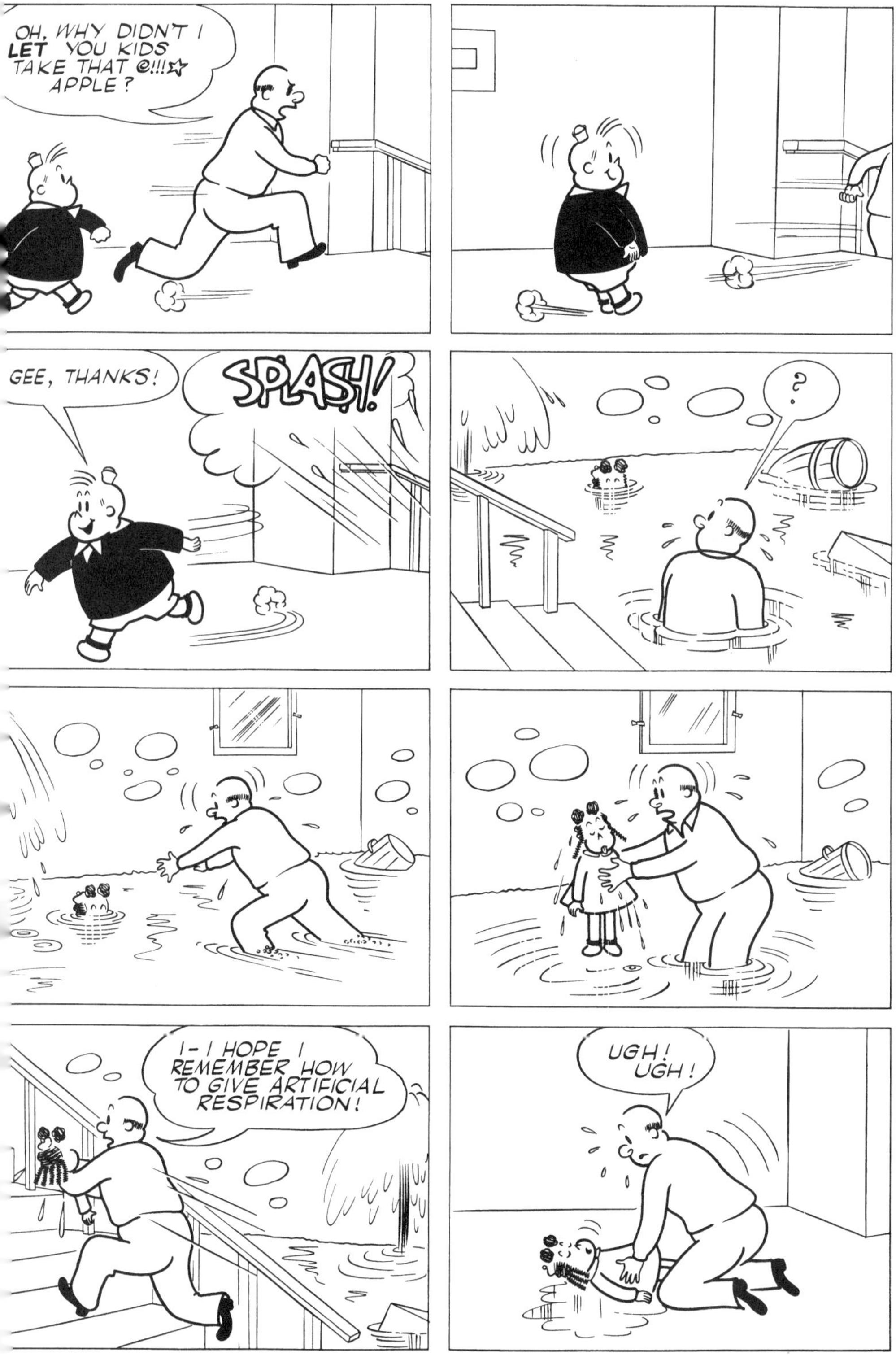
OH, WHY DIDN'T I LET YOU KIDS TAKE THAT @!!!☆ APPLE?
GEE, THANKS!
SPLASH!
?
I- I HOPE I REMEMBER HOW TO GIVE ARTIFICIAL RESPIRATION!
UGH! UGH!

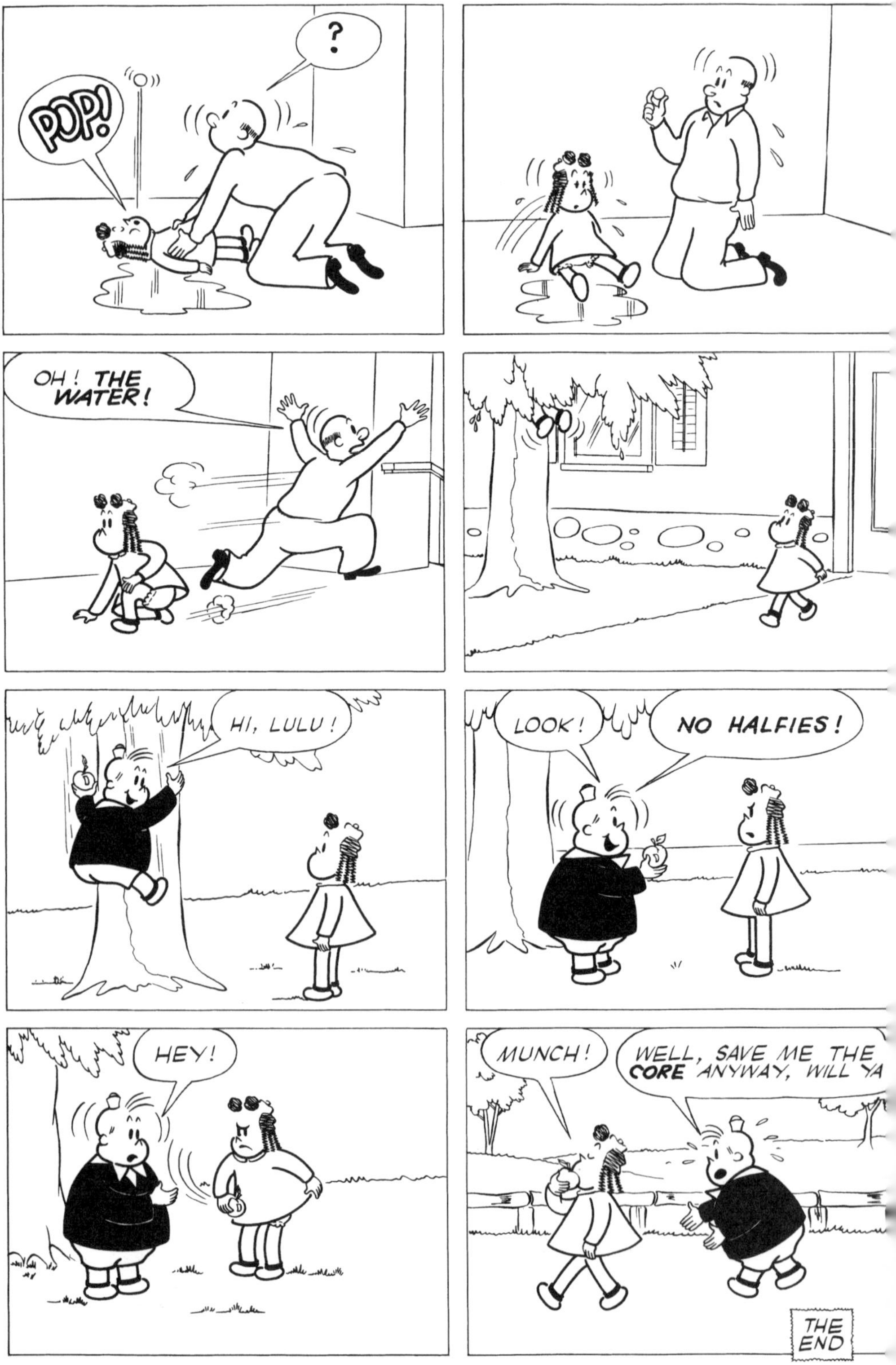
POP!
?
OH! THE WATER!
HI, LULU!
LOOK!
NO HALFIES!
HEY!
MUNCH!
WELL, SAVE ME THE CORE ANYWAY, WILL YA
THE END

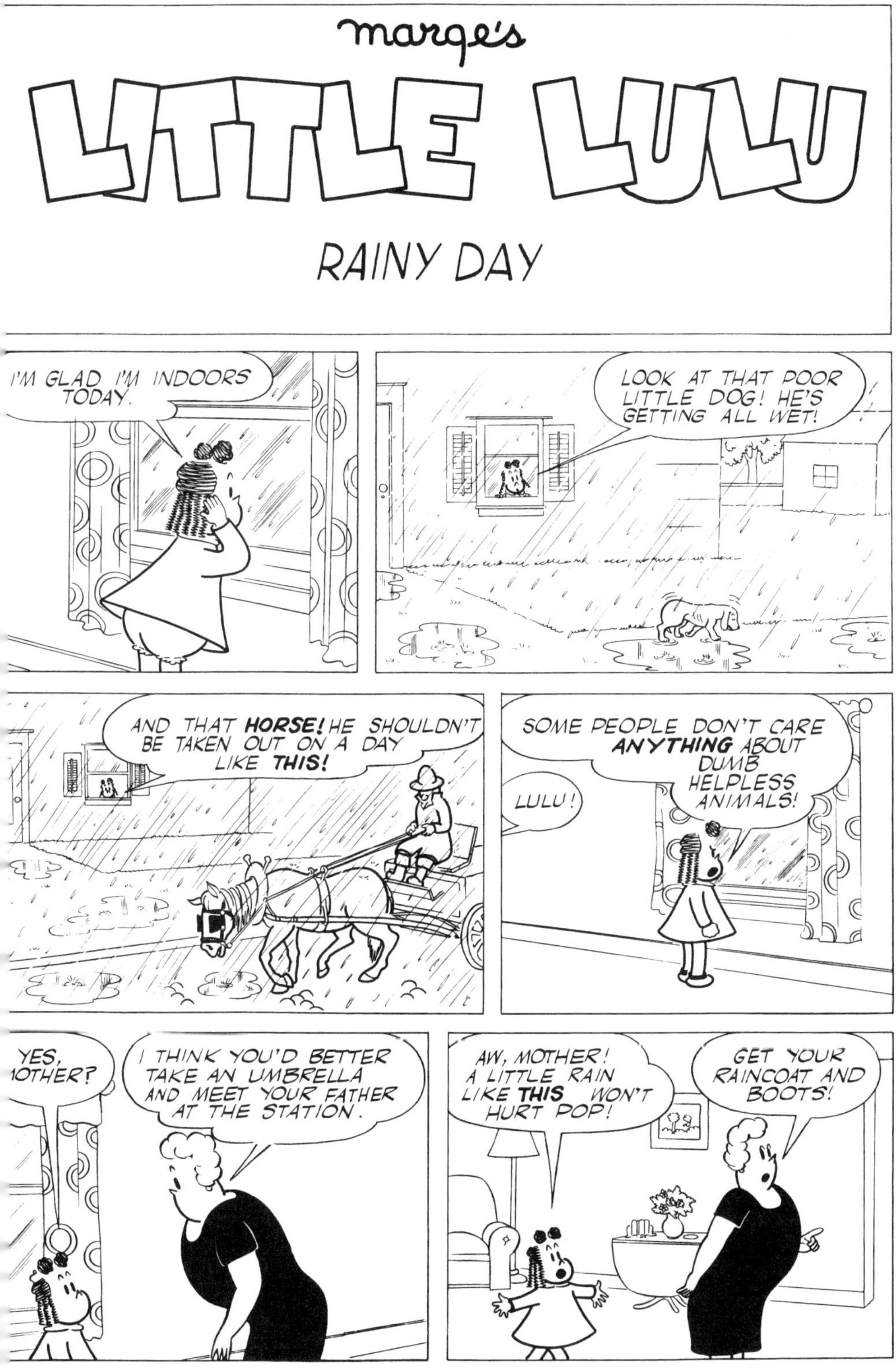
marge's
LITTLE LULU
RAINY DAY
I'M GLAD I'M INDOORS TODAY.
LOOK AT THAT POOR LITTLE DOG! HE'S GETTING ALL WET!
AND THAT HORSE! HE SHOULDN'T BE TAKEN OUT ON A DAY LIKE THIS!
SOME PEOPLE DON'T CARE ANYTHING ABOUT DUMB HELPLESS ANIMALS!
LULU!
YES, MOTHER?
I THINK YOU'D BETTER TAKE AN UMBRELLA AND MEET YOUR FATHER AT THE STATION.
AW, MOTHER! A LITTLE RAIN LIKE THIS WON'T HURT POP!
GET YOUR RAINCOAT AND BOOTS!

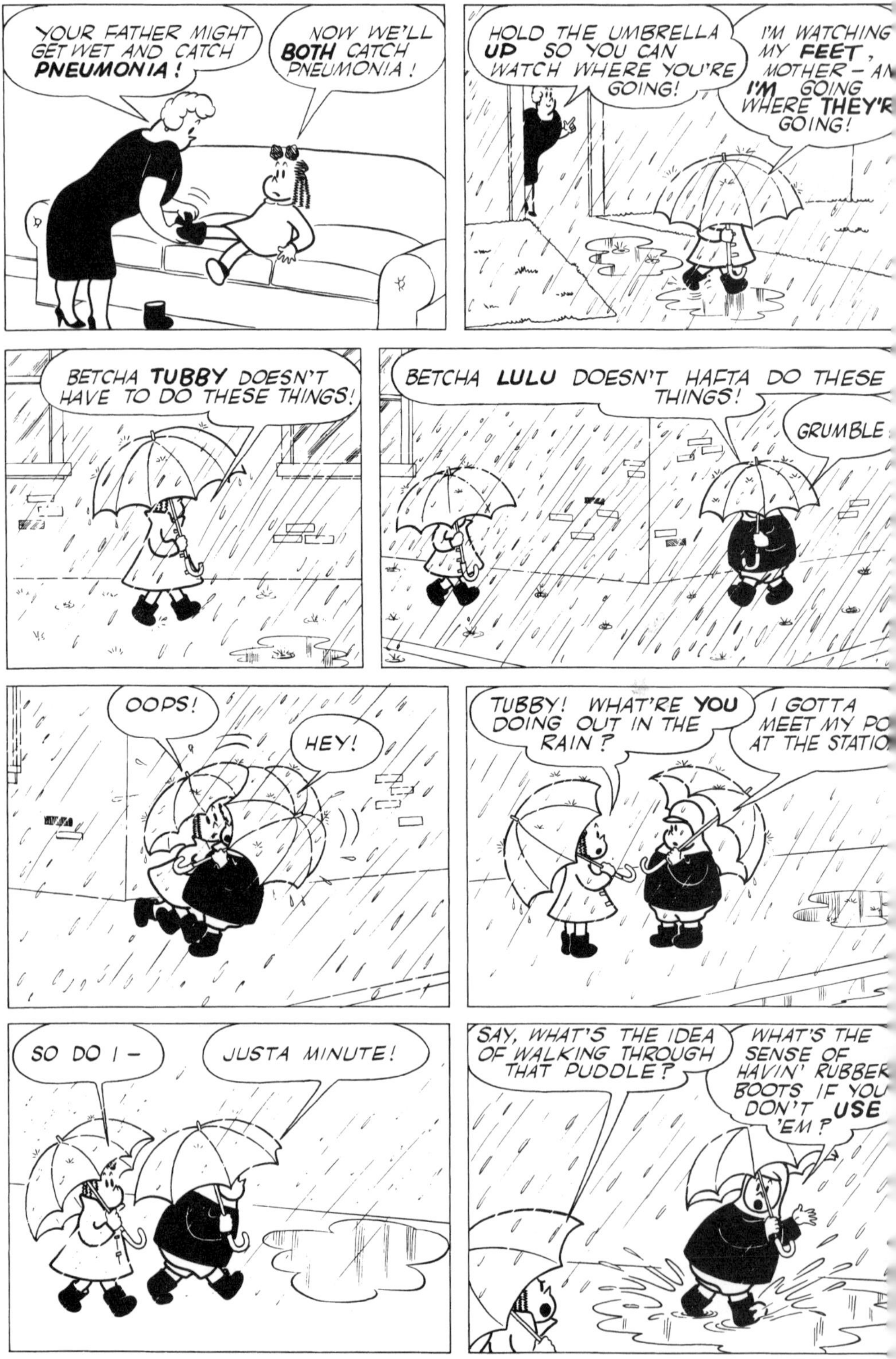
YOUR FATHER MIGHT GET WET AND CATCH PNEUMONIA!
NOW WE'LL BOTH CATCH PNEUMONIA!
HOLD THE UMBRELLA UP SO YOU CAN WATCH WHERE YOU'RE GOING!
I'M WATCHING MY FEET, MOTHER – AN I'M GOING WHERE THEY'R GOING!
BETCHA TUBBY DOESN'T HAVE TO DO THESE THINGS!
BETCHA LULU DOESN'T HAFTA DO THESE THINGS!
GRUMBLE
OOPS!
HEY!
TUBBY! WHAT'RE YOU DOING OUT IN THE RAIN?
I GOTTA MEET MY PO AT THE STATIO
SO DO I –
JUSTA MINUTE!
SAY, WHAT'S THE IDEA OF WALKING THROUGH THAT PUDDLE?
WHAT'S THE SENSE OF HAVIN' RUBBER BOOTS IF YOU DON'T USE 'EM?

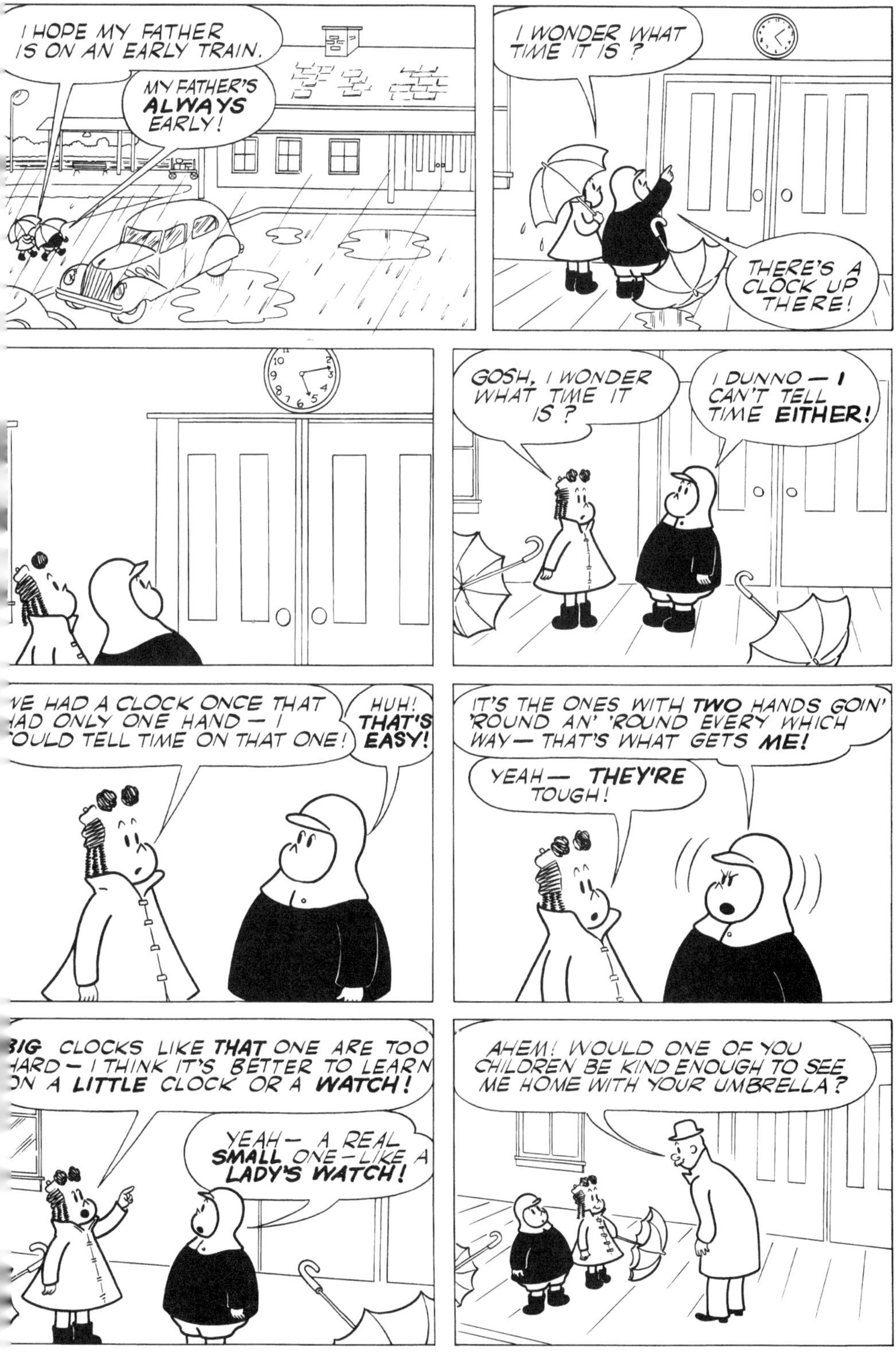
I HOPE MY FATHER IS ON AN EARLY TRAIN.
MY FATHER'S **ALWAYS** EARLY!
I WONDER WHAT TIME IT IS ?
THERE'S A CLOCK UP THERE!
GOSH, I WONDER WHAT TIME IT IS ?
I DUNNO — I CAN'T TELL TIME **EITHER!**
VE HAD A CLOCK ONCE THAT HAD ONLY ONE HAND — I OULD TELL TIME ON THAT ONE!
HUH! **THAT'S EASY!**
IT'S THE ONES WITH **TWO** HANDS GOIN' 'ROUND AN' 'ROUND EVERY WHICH WAY — THAT'S WHAT GETS **ME!**
YEAH — **THEY'RE** TOUGH!
BIG CLOCKS LIKE **THAT** ONE ARE TOO HARD — I THINK IT'S BETTER TO LEARN ON A **LITTLE** CLOCK OR A **WATCH!**
YEAH — A REAL **SMALL** ONE — LIKE A **LADY'S WATCH!**
AHEM! WOULD ONE OF YOU CHILDREN BE KIND ENOUGH TO SEE ME HOME WITH YOUR UMBRELLA?

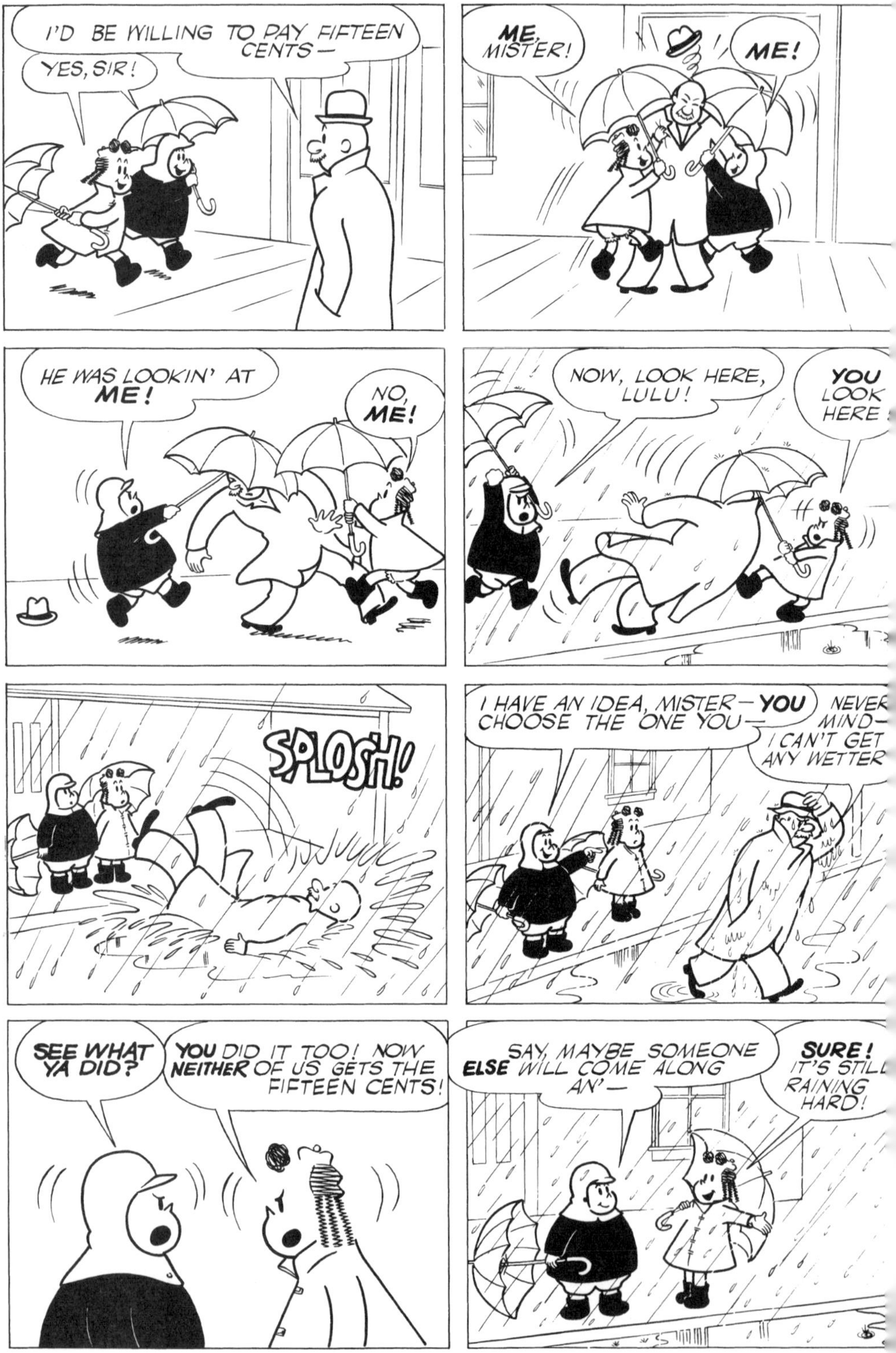
I'D BE WILLING TO PAY FIFTEEN CENTS—
YES, SIR!
ME, MISTER!
ME!
HE WAS LOOKIN' AT ME!
NO, ME!
NOW, LOOK HERE, LULU!
YOU LOOK HERE
SPLOSH!
I HAVE AN IDEA, MISTER—YOU CHOOSE THE ONE YOU—
NEVER MIND—I CAN'T GET ANY WETTER
SEE WHAT YA DID?
YOU DID IT TOO! NOW NEITHER OF US GETS THE FIFTEEN CENTS!
SAY, MAYBE SOMEONE ELSE WILL COME ALONG AN'—
SURE! IT'S STILL RAINING HARD!

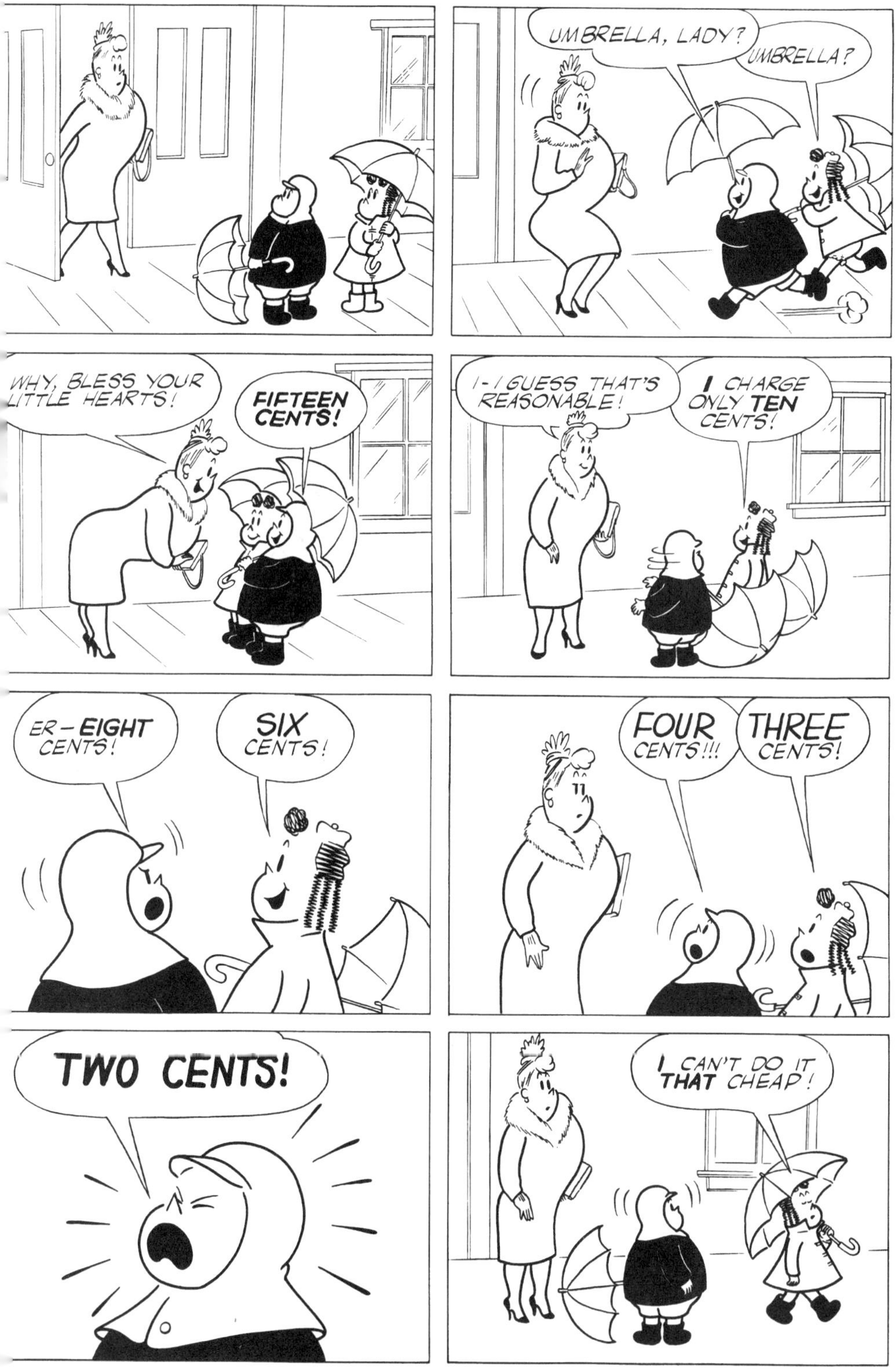
UMBRELLA, LADY?
UMBRELLA?
WHY, BLESS YOUR LITTLE HEARTS!
FIFTEEN CENTS!
I-I GUESS THAT'S REASONABLE!
I CHARGE ONLY TEN CENTS!
ER—EIGHT CENTS!
SIX CENTS!
FOUR CENTS!!!
THREE CENTS!
TWO CENTS!
I CAN'T DO IT THAT CHEAP!

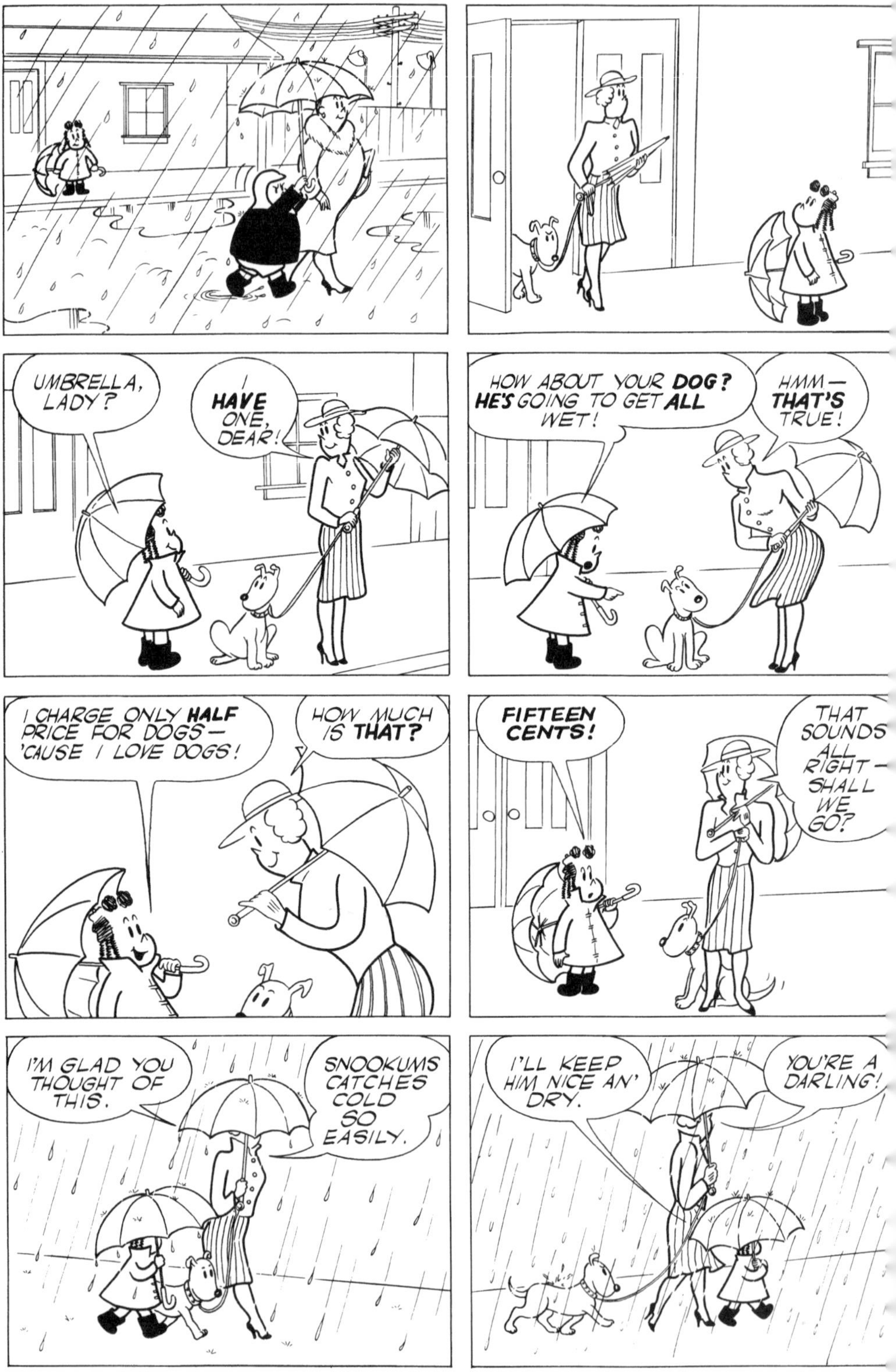

UMBRELLA, LADY?
I **HAVE** ONE, DEAR!
HOW ABOUT YOUR **DOG? HE'S** GOING TO GET **ALL** WET!
HMM— **THAT'S** TRUE!
I CHARGE ONLY **HALF** PRICE FOR DOGS— 'CAUSE I LOVE DOGS!
HOW MUCH IS **THAT?**
FIFTEEN CENTS!
THAT SOUNDS ALL RIGHT— SHALL WE GO?
I'M GLAD YOU THOUGHT OF THIS.
SNOOKUMS CATCHES COLD SO EASILY.
I'LL KEEP HIM NICE AN' DRY.
YOU'RE A DARLING!

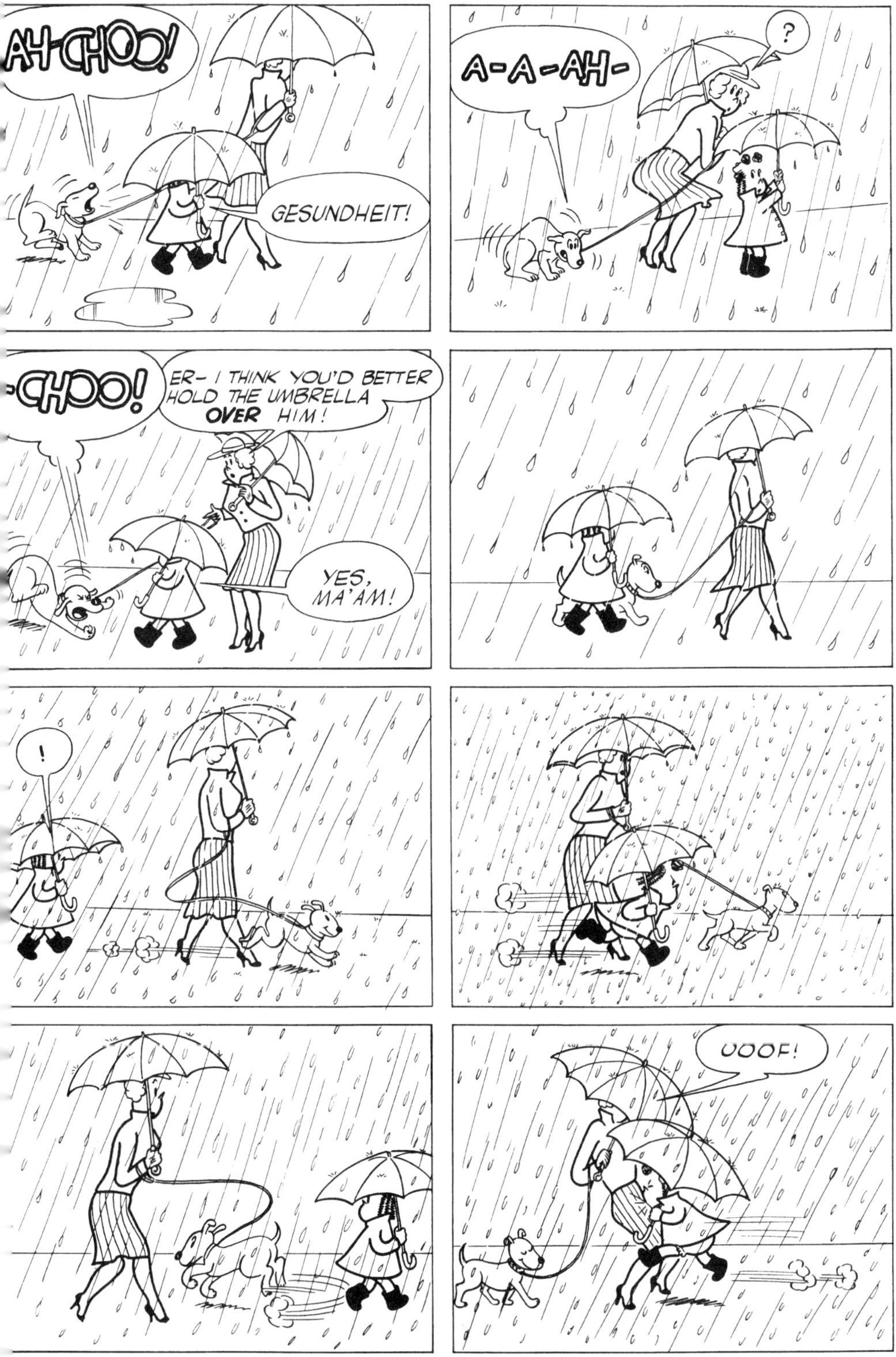
AH-CHOO!
GESUNDHEIT!
A-A-AH-
?
-CHOO!
ER- I THINK YOU'D BETTER HOLD THE UMBRELLA **OVER** HIM!
YES, MA'AM!
!
OOOF!

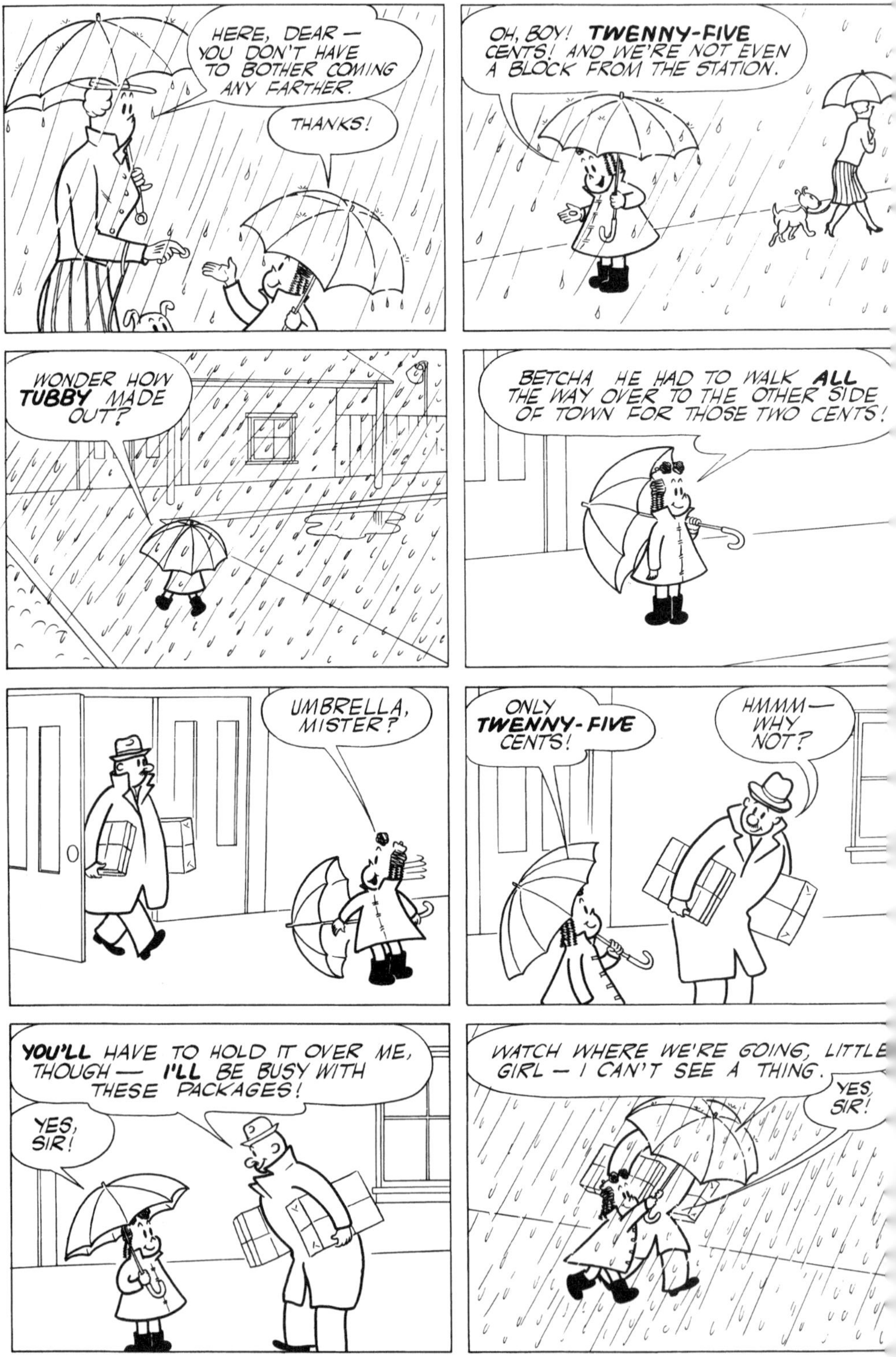
HERE, DEAR — YOU DON'T HAVE TO BOTHER COMING ANY FARTHER.
THANKS!
OH, BOY! TWENNY-FIVE CENTS! AND WE'RE NOT EVEN A BLOCK FROM THE STATION.
WONDER HOW TUBBY MADE OUT?
BETCHA HE HAD TO WALK ALL THE WAY OVER TO THE OTHER SIDE OF TOWN FOR THOSE TWO CENTS!
UMBRELLA, MISTER?
ONLY TWENNY-FIVE CENTS!
HMMM— WHY NOT?
YOU'LL HAVE TO HOLD IT OVER ME, THOUGH — I'LL BE BUSY WITH THESE PACKAGES!
YES, SIR!
WATCH WHERE WE'RE GOING, LITTLE GIRL — I CAN'T SEE A THING.
YES, SIR!

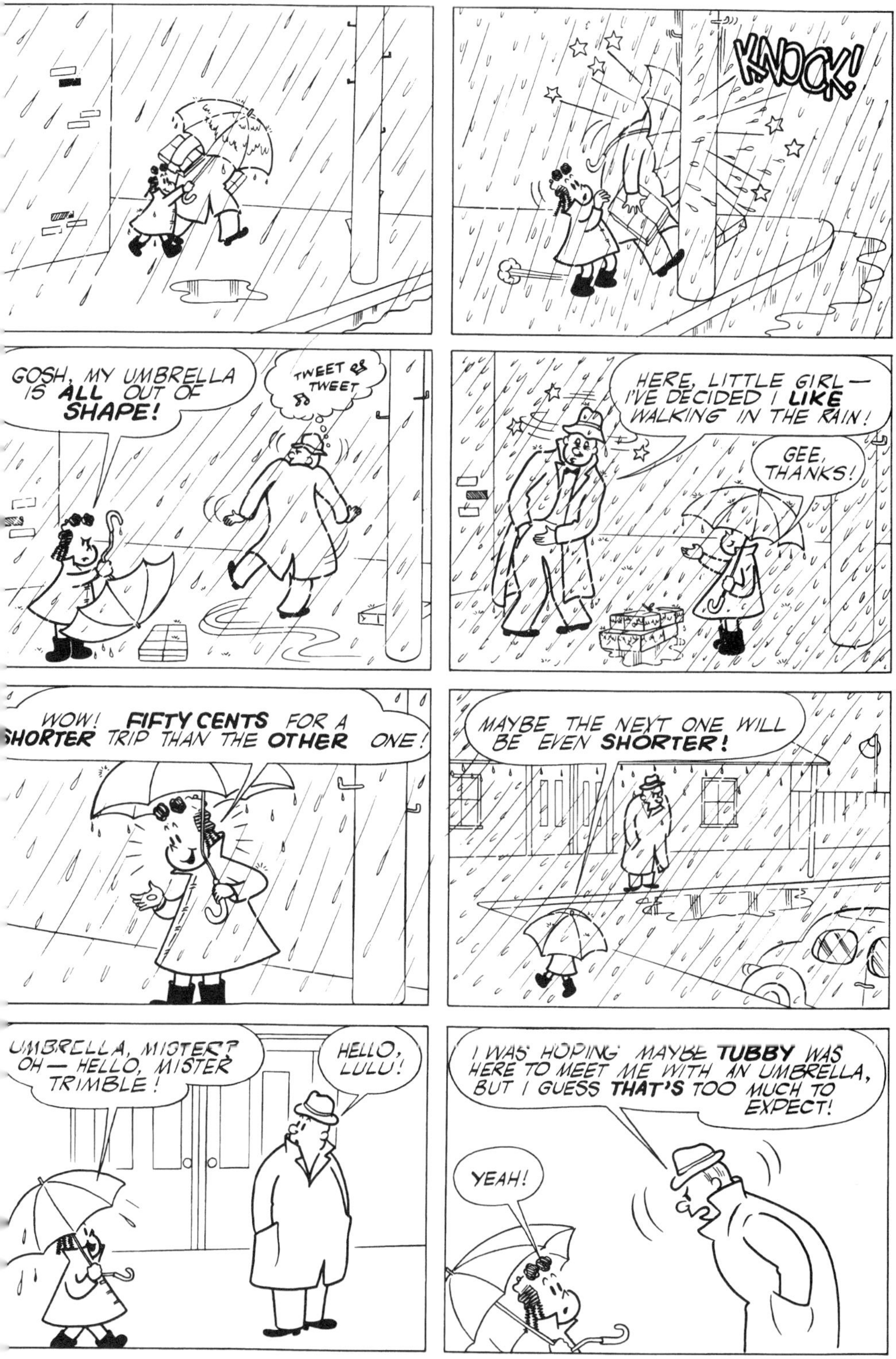
KNOCK!
GOSH, MY UMBRELLA IS ALL OUT OF SHAPE!
TWEET TWEET
HERE, LITTLE GIRL— I'VE DECIDED I LIKE WALKING IN THE RAIN!
GEE, THANKS!
WOW! FIFTY CENTS FOR A SHORTER TRIP THAN THE OTHER ONE!
MAYBE THE NEXT ONE WILL BE EVEN SHORTER!
UMBRELLA, MISTER? OH— HELLO, MISTER TRIMBLE!
HELLO, LULU!
I WAS HOPING MAYBE TUBBY WAS HERE TO MEET ME WITH AN UMBRELLA, BUT I GUESS THAT'S TOO MUCH TO EXPECT!
YEAH!

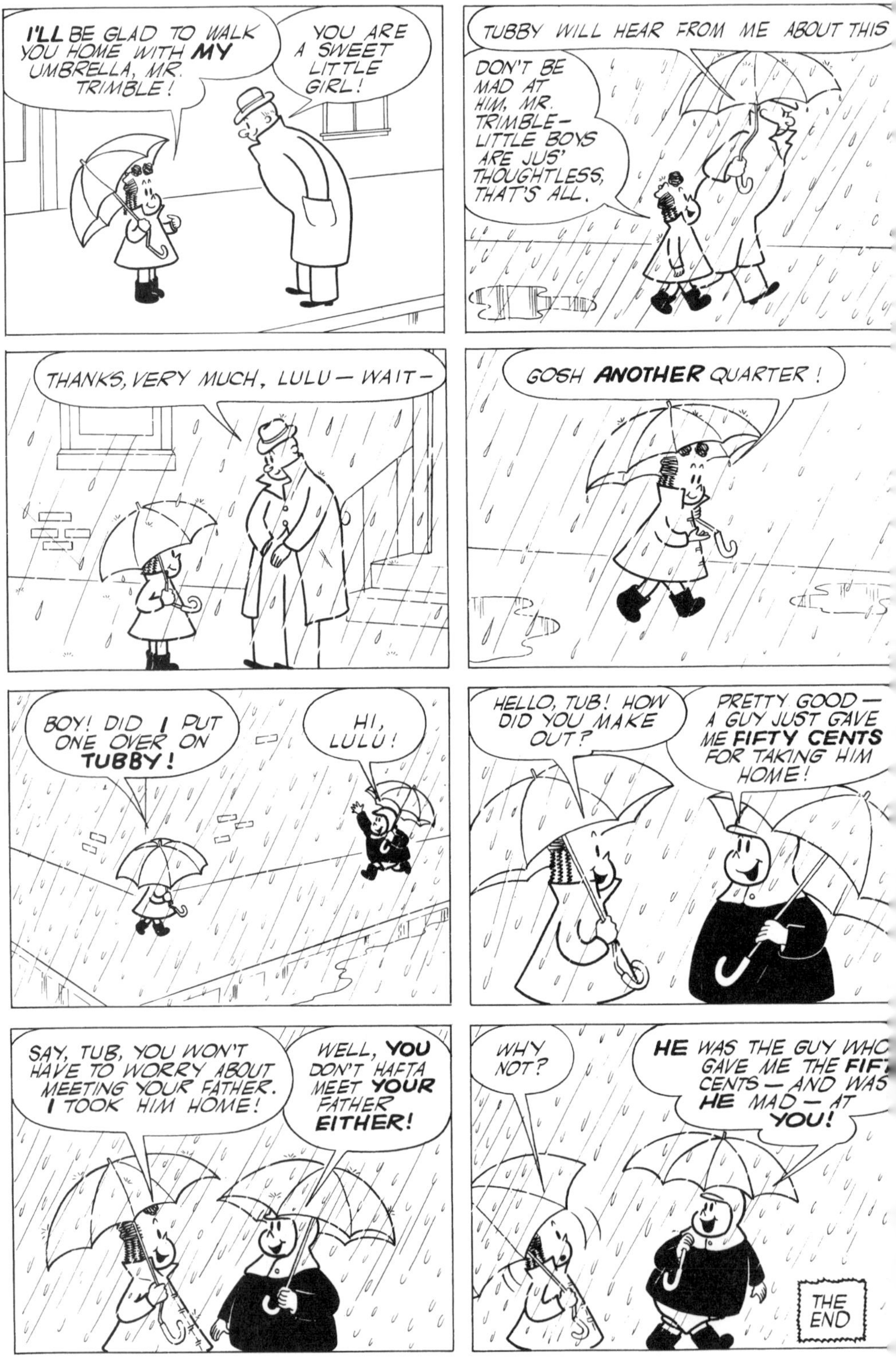
I'LL BE GLAD TO WALK YOU HOME WITH MY UMBRELLA, MR. TRIMBLE!
YOU ARE A SWEET LITTLE GIRL!
TUBBY WILL HEAR FROM ME ABOUT THIS
DON'T BE MAD AT HIM, MR. TRIMBLE– LITTLE BOYS ARE JUS' THOUGHTLESS, THAT'S ALL.
THANKS, VERY MUCH, LULU— WAIT—
GOSH ANOTHER QUARTER!
BOY! DID I PUT ONE OVER ON TUBBY!
HI, LULU!
HELLO, TUB! HOW DID YOU MAKE OUT?
PRETTY GOOD— A GUY JUST GAVE ME FIFTY CENTS FOR TAKING HIM HOME!
SAY, TUB, YOU WON'T HAVE TO WORRY ABOUT MEETING YOUR FATHER. I TOOK HIM HOME!
WELL, YOU DON'T HAFTA MEET YOUR FATHER EITHER!
WHY NOT?
HE WAS THE GUY WHO GAVE ME THE FIFT CENTS— AND WAS HE MAD— AT YOU!
THE END

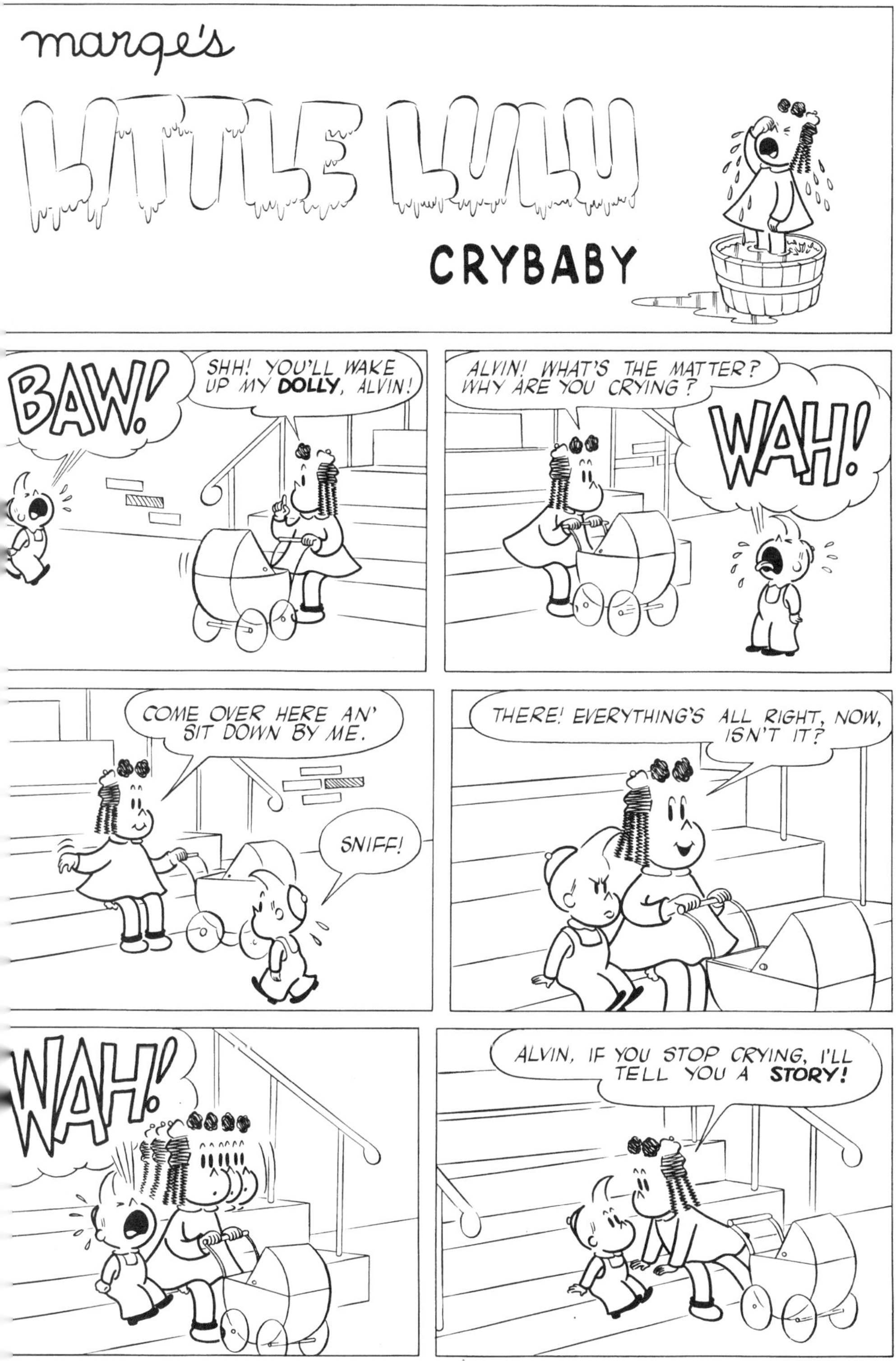
marge's
LITTLE LULU
CRYBABY
BAW!
SHH! YOU'LL WAKE UP MY **DOLLY**, ALVIN!
ALVIN! WHAT'S THE MATTER? WHY ARE YOU CRYING?
WAH!
COME OVER HERE AN' SIT DOWN BY ME.
SNIFF!
THERE! EVERYTHING'S ALL RIGHT, NOW, ISN'T IT?
WAH!
ALVIN, IF YOU STOP CRYING, I'LL TELL YOU A **STORY!**

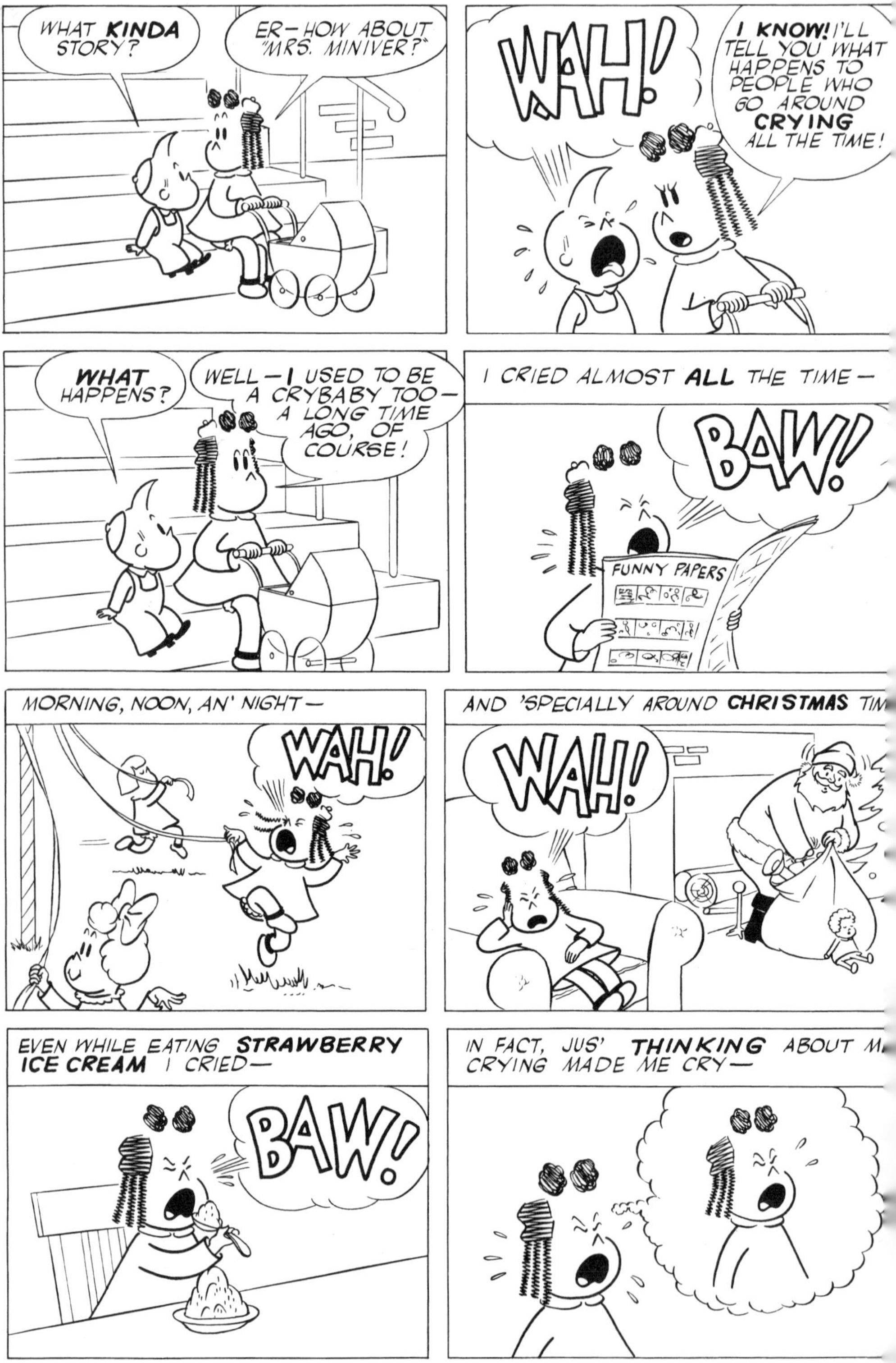
WHAT KINDA STORY?
ER—HOW ABOUT "MRS. MINIVER?"
WAH!
I KNOW! I'LL TELL YOU WHAT HAPPENS TO PEOPLE WHO GO AROUND CRYING ALL THE TIME!
WHAT HAPPENS?
WELL—I USED TO BE A CRYBABY TOO—A LONG TIME AGO, OF COURSE!
I CRIED ALMOST ALL THE TIME—
BAW!
FUNNY PAPERS
MORNING, NOON, AN' NIGHT—
WAH!
AND 'SPECIALLY AROUND CHRISTMAS TIM
WAH!
EVEN WHILE EATING STRAWBERRY ICE CREAM I CRIED—
BAW!
IN FACT, JUS' THINKING ABOUT M
CRYING MADE ME CRY—

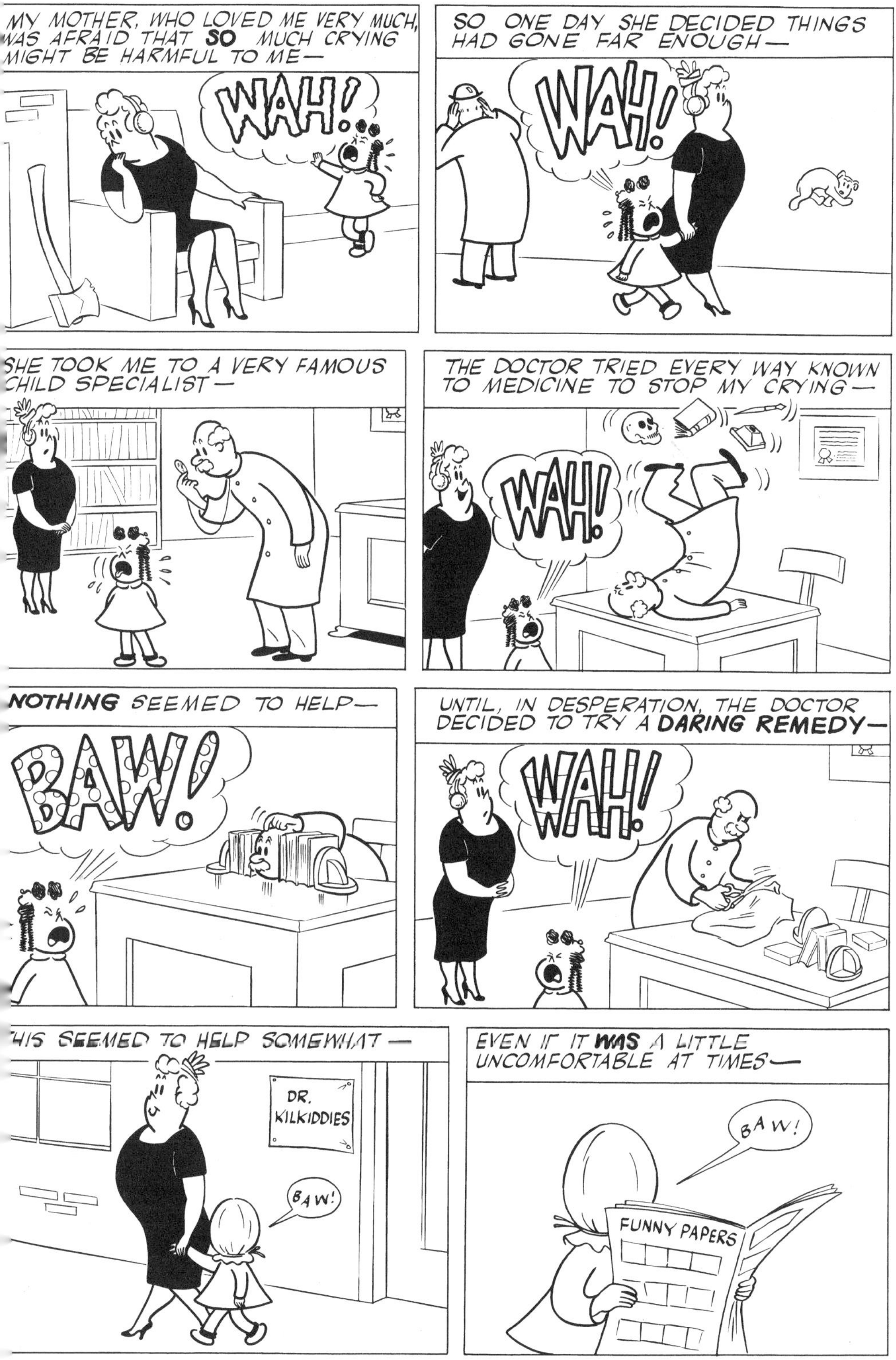
MY MOTHER, WHO LOVED ME VERY MUCH, WAS AFRAID THAT SO MUCH CRYING MIGHT BE HARMFUL TO ME—
WAH!
SO ONE DAY SHE DECIDED THINGS HAD GONE FAR ENOUGH—
WAH!
SHE TOOK ME TO A VERY FAMOUS CHILD SPECIALIST—
THE DOCTOR TRIED EVERY WAY KNOWN TO MEDICINE TO STOP MY CRYING—
WAH!
NOTHING SEEMED TO HELP—
BAW!
UNTIL, IN DESPERATION, THE DOCTOR DECIDED TO TRY A DARING REMEDY—
WAH!
THIS SEEMED TO HELP SOMEWHAT—
DR. KILKIDDIES
BAW!
EVEN IF IT WAS A LITTLE UNCOMFORTABLE AT TIMES—
BAW!
FUNNY PAPERS

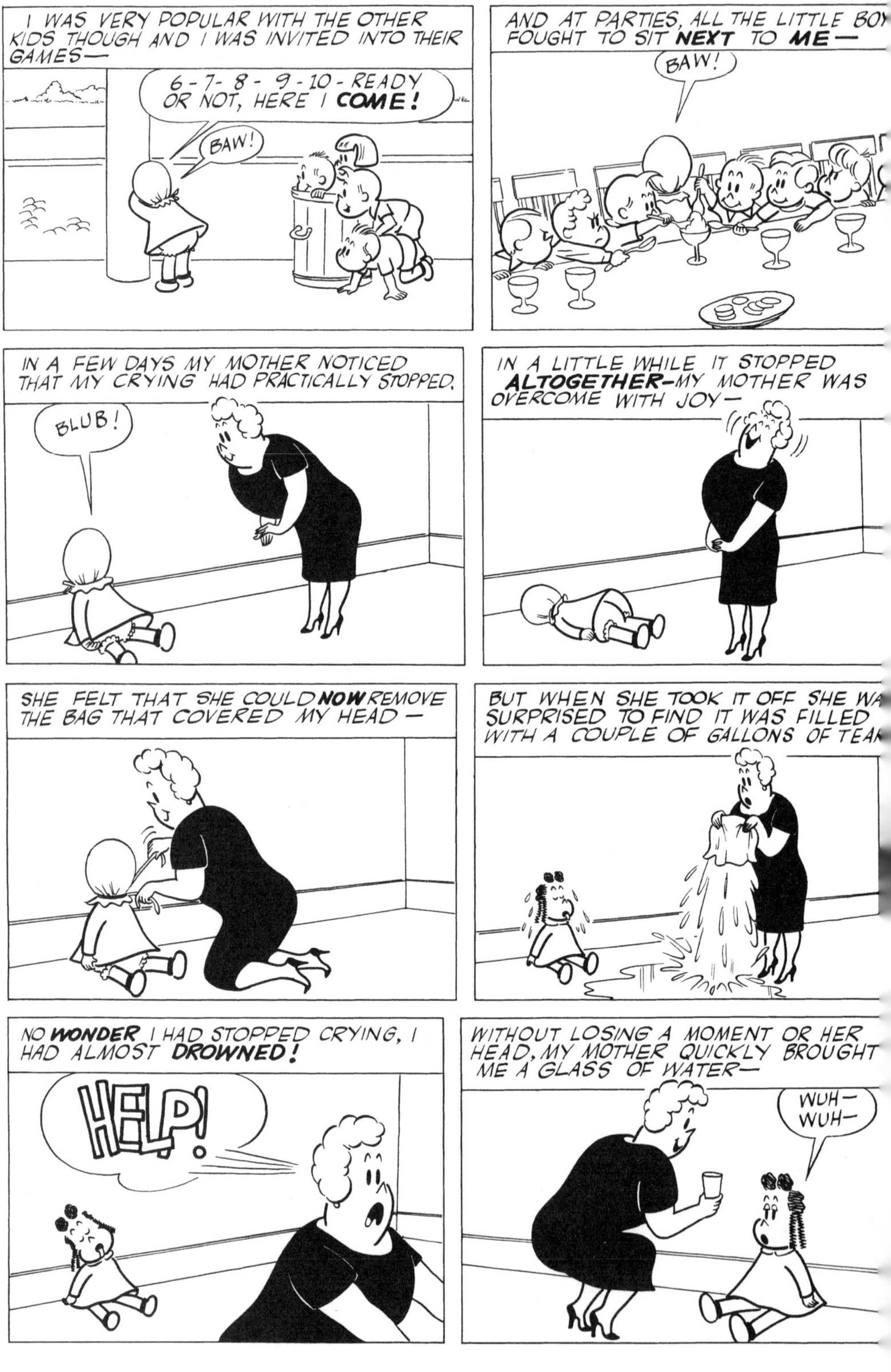
I WAS VERY POPULAR WITH THE OTHER KIDS THOUGH AND I WAS INVITED INTO THEIR GAMES—
6-7-8-9-10-READY OR NOT, HERE I COME!
BAW!
AND AT PARTIES, ALL THE LITTLE BO
FOUGHT TO SIT NEXT TO ME—
BAW!
IN A FEW DAYS MY MOTHER NOTICED THAT MY CRYING HAD PRACTICALLY STOPPED.
BLUB!
IN A LITTLE WHILE IT STOPPED ALTOGETHER–MY MOTHER WAS OVERCOME WITH JOY—
SHE FELT THAT SHE COULD NOW REMOVE THE BAG THAT COVERED MY HEAD—
BUT WHEN SHE TOOK IT OFF SHE WA
SURPRISED TO FIND IT WAS FILLED
WITH A COUPLE OF GALLONS OF TEA
NO WONDER I HAD STOPPED CRYING, I HAD ALMOST DROWNED!
HELP!
WITHOUT LOSING A MOMENT OR HER HEAD, MY MOTHER QUICKLY BROUGHT ME A GLASS OF WATER—
WUH— WUH—

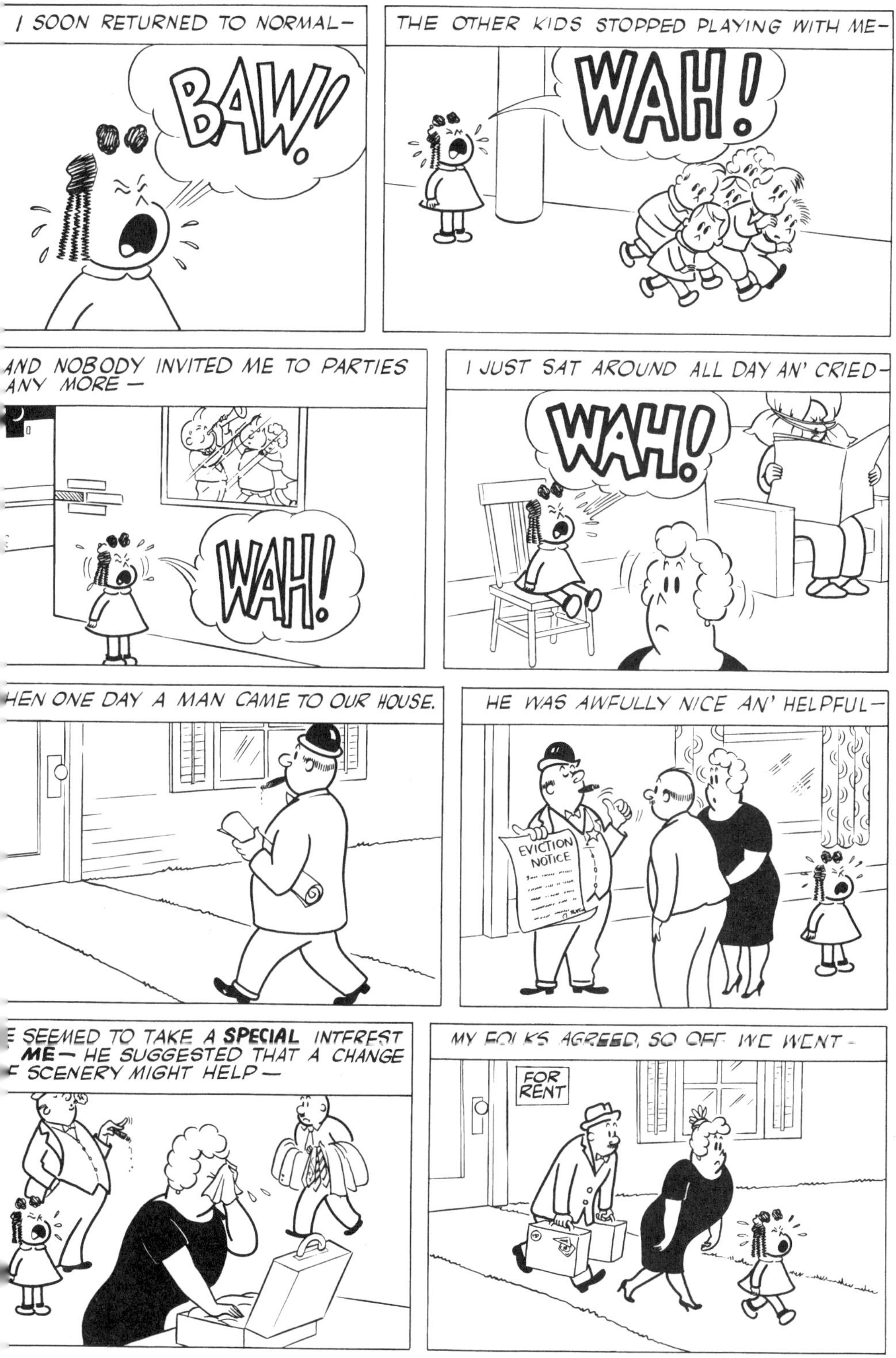

I SOON RETURNED TO NORMAL—
BAW!
THE OTHER KIDS STOPPED PLAYING WITH ME—
WAH!
AND NOBODY INVITED ME TO PARTIES ANY MORE—
WAH!
I JUST SAT AROUND ALL DAY AN' CRIED—
WAH!
HEN ONE DAY A MAN CAME TO OUR HOUSE.
HE WAS AWFULLY NICE AN' HELPFUL—
EVICTION NOTICE
E SEEMED TO TAKE A SPECIAL INTEREST
ME— HE SUGGESTED THAT A CHANGE
F SCENERY MIGHT HELP—
MY FOLKS AGREED, SO OFF WE WENT—
FOR RENT

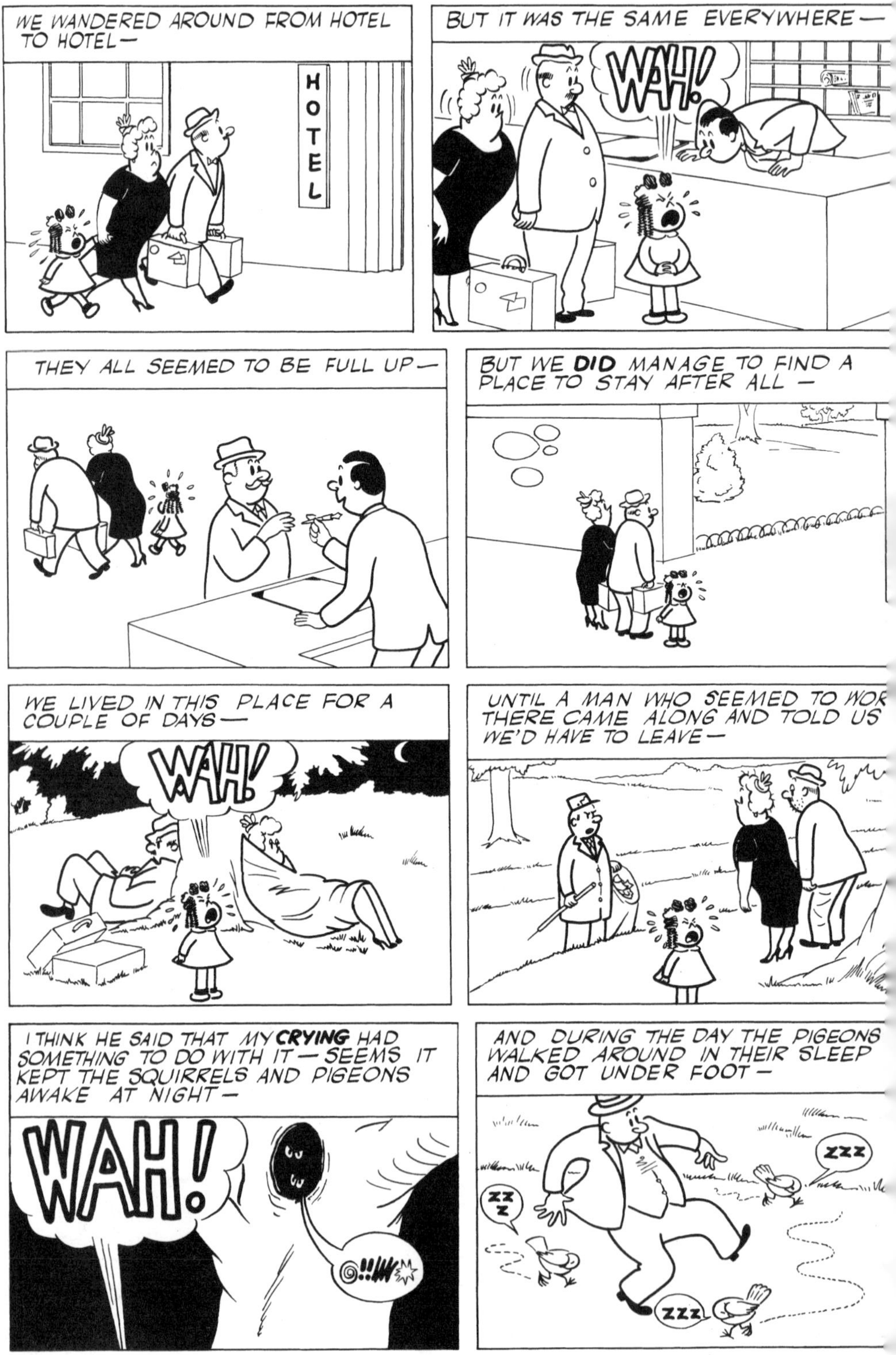
WE WANDERED AROUND FROM HOTEL TO HOTEL—
HOTEL
BUT IT WAS THE SAME EVERYWHERE—
WAH!
THEY ALL SEEMED TO BE FULL UP—
BUT WE DID MANAGE TO FIND A PLACE TO STAY AFTER ALL—
WE LIVED IN THIS PLACE FOR A COUPLE OF DAYS—
WAH!
UNTIL A MAN WHO SEEMED TO WOR
THERE CAME ALONG AND TOLD US
WE'D HAVE TO LEAVE—
I THINK HE SAID THAT MY CRYING HAD SOMETHING TO DO WITH IT—SEEMS IT KEPT THE SQUIRRELS AND PIGEONS AWAKE AT NIGHT—
WAH!
AND DURING THE DAY THE PIGEONS WALKED AROUND IN THEIR SLEEP AND GOT UNDER FOOT—
ZZZ
ZZZ
ZZZ

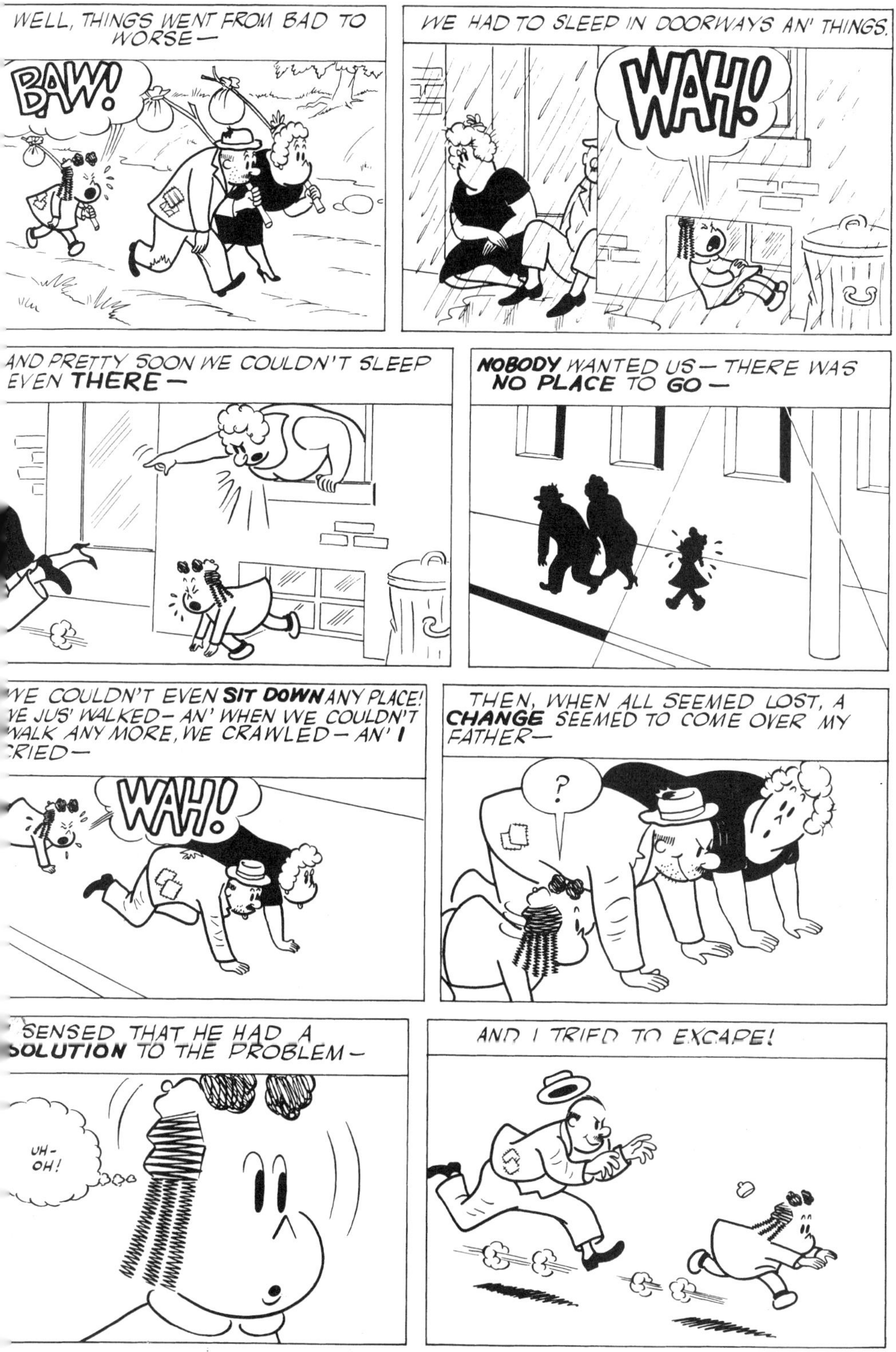
WELL, THINGS WENT FROM BAD TO WORSE—
BAW!
WE HAD TO SLEEP IN DOORWAYS AN' THINGS.
WAH!
AND PRETTY SOON WE COULDN'T SLEEP EVEN THERE—
NOBODY WANTED US—THERE WAS NO PLACE TO GO—
WE COULDN'T EVEN SIT DOWN ANY PLACE! WE JUS' WALKED—AN' WHEN WE COULDN'T WALK ANY MORE, WE CRAWLED—AN' I CRIED—
WAH!
THEN, WHEN ALL SEEMED LOST, A CHANGE SEEMED TO COME OVER MY FATHER—
?
I SENSED THAT HE HAD A SOLUTION TO THE PROBLEM—
UH-OH!
AND I TRIED TO EXCAPE!

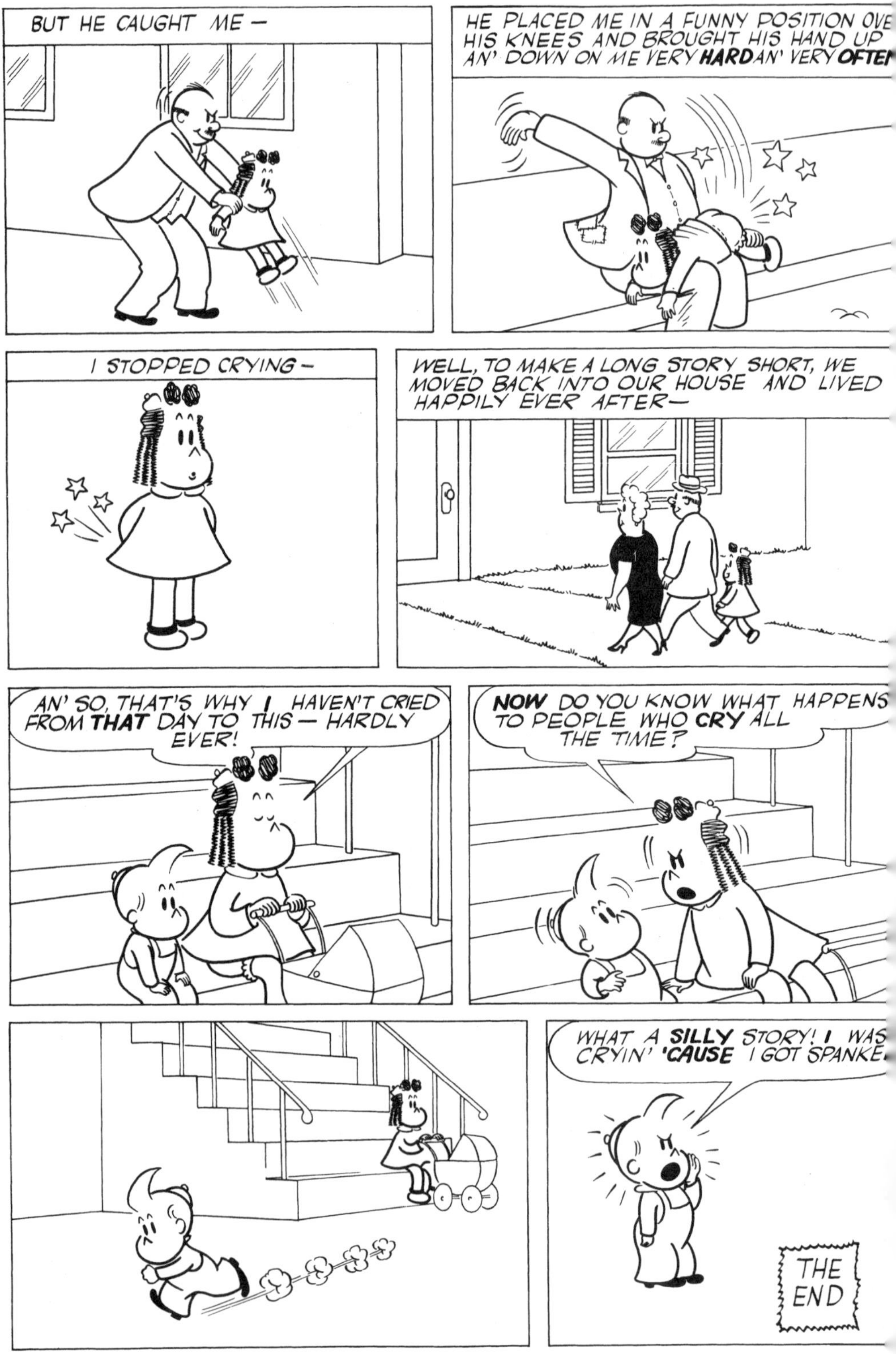
BUT HE CAUGHT ME —
HE PLACED ME IN A FUNNY POSITION OVE
HIS KNEES AND BROUGHT HIS HAND UP
AN' DOWN ON ME VERY **HARD** AN' VERY **OFTE**
I STOPPED CRYING —
WELL, TO MAKE A LONG STORY SHORT, WE MOVED BACK INTO OUR HOUSE AND LIVED HAPPILY EVER AFTER—
AN' SO, THAT'S WHY **I** HAVEN'T CRIED FROM **THAT** DAY TO THIS — HARDLY EVER!
NOW DO YOU KNOW WHAT HAPPENS TO PEOPLE WHO **CRY** ALL THE TIME?
WHAT A **SILLY** STORY! **I** WAS CRYIN' **'CAUSE** I GOT SPANKE
THE END

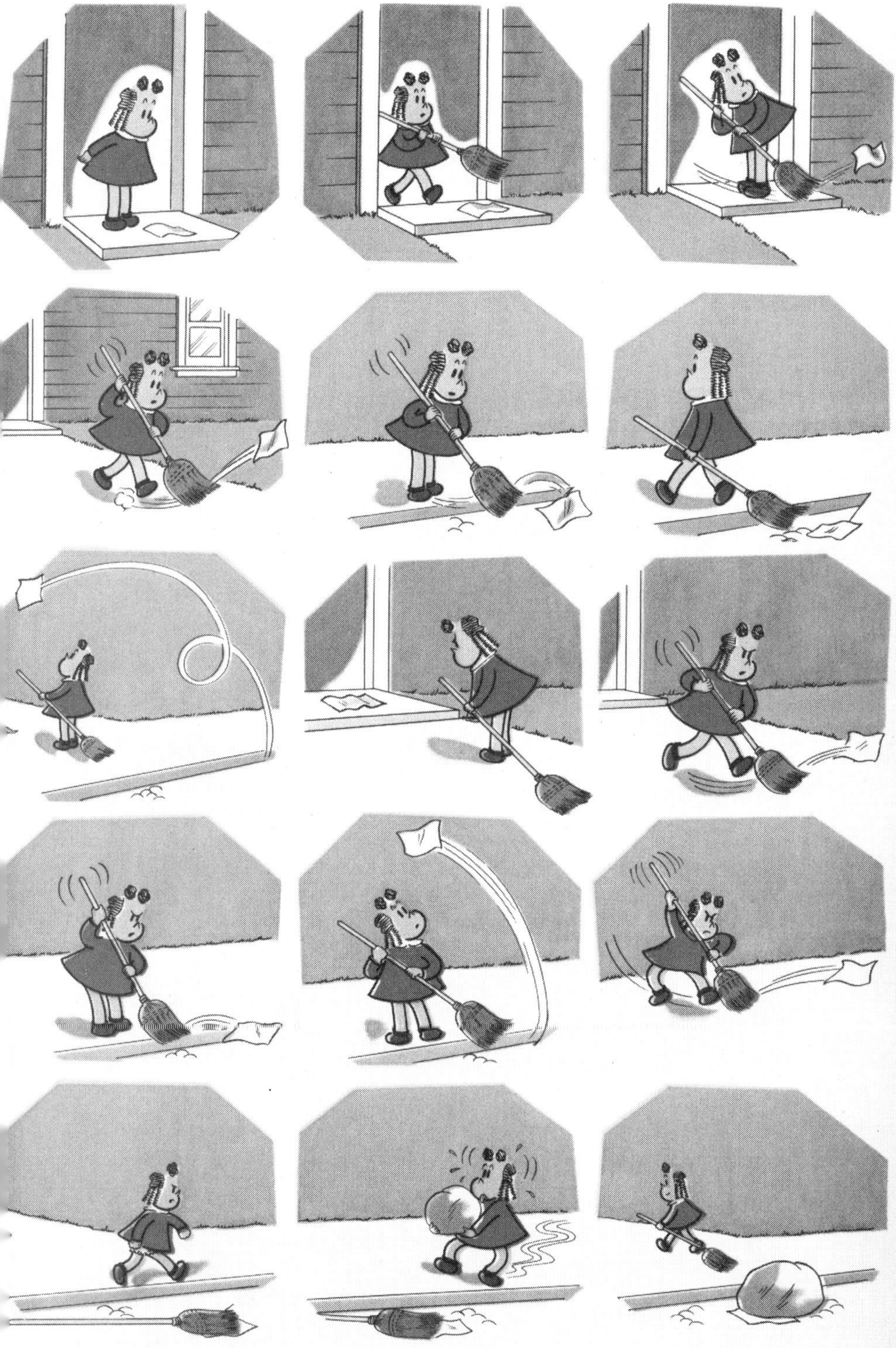

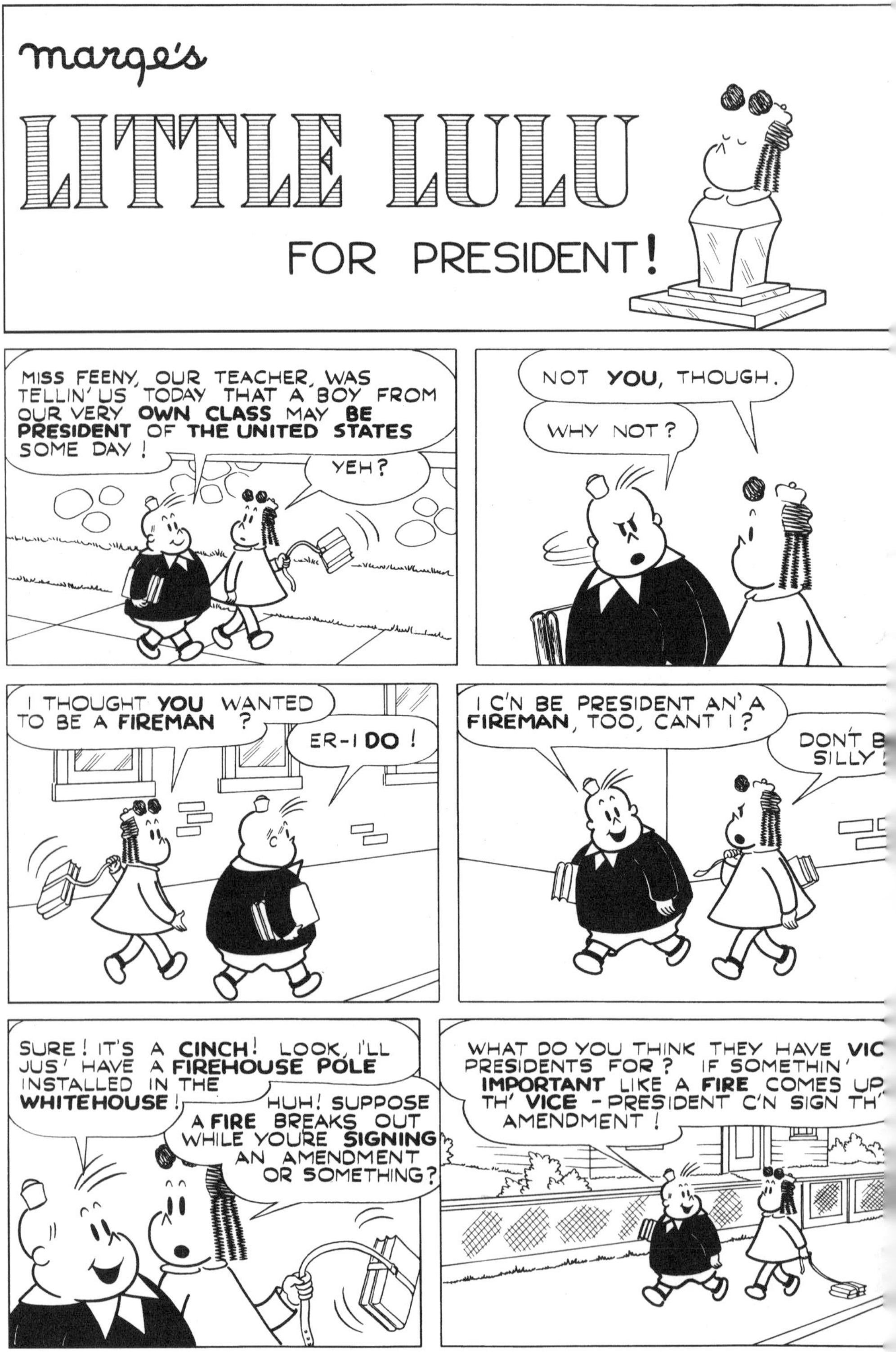
marge's
LITTLE LULU
FOR PRESIDENT!
MISS FEENY, OUR TEACHER, WAS TELLIN' US TODAY THAT A BOY FROM OUR VERY OWN CLASS MAY BE PRESIDENT OF THE UNITED STATES SOME DAY!
YEH?
NOT YOU, THOUGH.
WHY NOT?
I THOUGHT YOU WANTED TO BE A FIREMAN?
ER-I DO!
I C'N BE PRESIDENT AN' A FIREMAN, TOO, CANT I?
DON'T B
SILLY
SURE! IT'S A CINCH! LOOK, I'LL JUS' HAVE A FIREHOUSE POLE INSTALLED IN THE WHITEHOUSE!
HUH! SUPPOSE A FIRE BREAKS OUT WHILE YOURE SIGNING AN AMENDMENT OR SOMETHING?
WHAT DO YOU THINK THEY HAVE VIC
PRESIDENTS FOR? IF SOMETHIN'
IMPORTANT LIKE A FIRE COMES UP
TH' VICE-PRESIDENT C'N SIGN TH'
AMENDMENT!

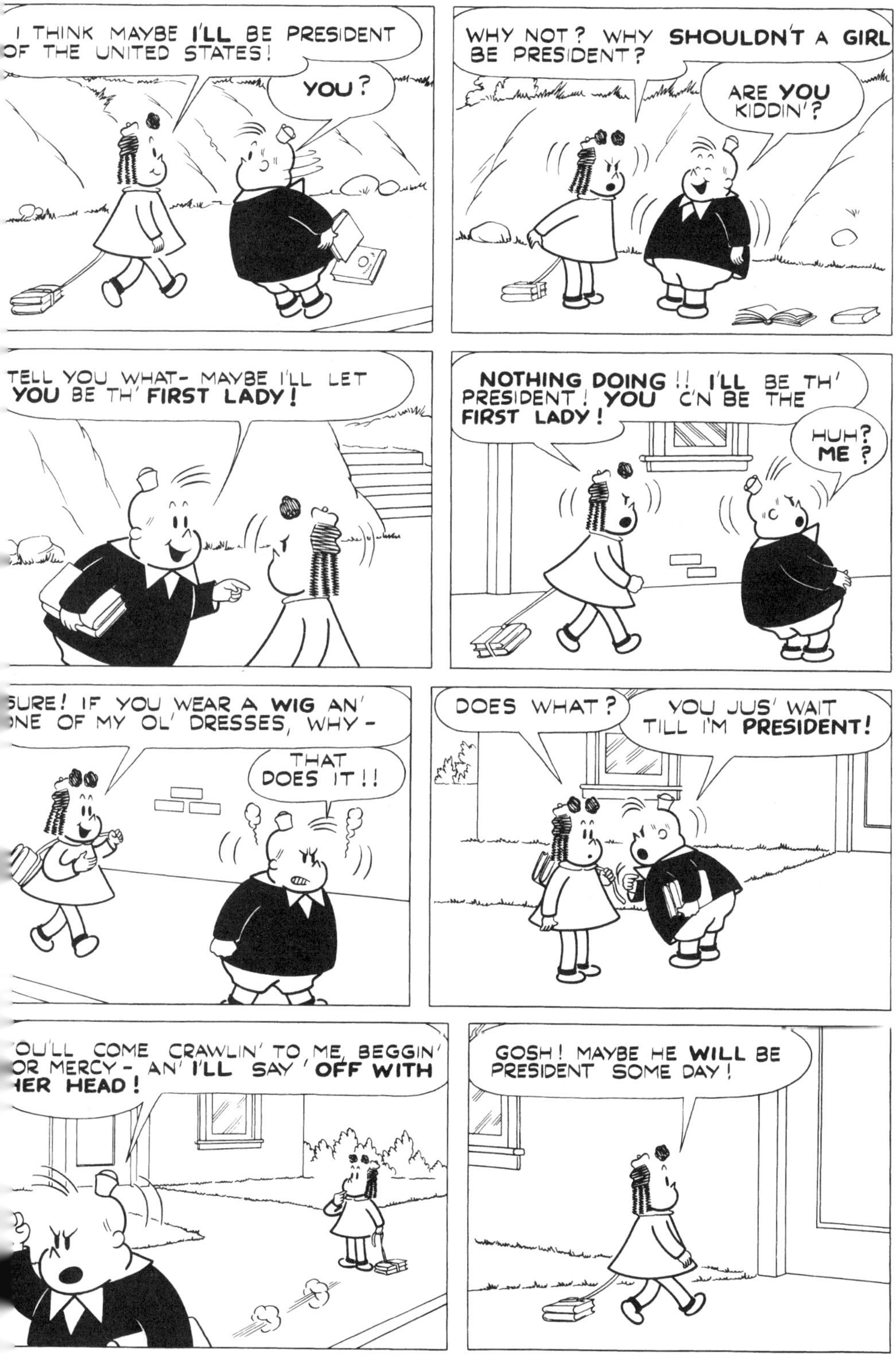
I THINK MAYBE I'LL BE PRESIDENT OF THE UNITED STATES!
YOU?
WHY NOT? WHY SHOULDN'T A GIRL BE PRESIDENT?
ARE YOU KIDDIN'?
TELL YOU WHAT- MAYBE I'LL LET YOU BE TH' FIRST LADY!
NOTHING DOING!! I'LL BE TH' PRESIDENT! YOU C'N BE THE FIRST LADY!
HUH? ME?
URE! IF YOU WEAR A WIG AN' NE OF MY OL' DRESSES, WHY-
THAT DOES IT!!
DOES WHAT?
YOU JUS' WAIT TILL I'M PRESIDENT!
OU'LL COME CRAWLIN' TO ME, BEGGIN' OR MERCY- AN' I'LL SAY 'OFF WITH ER HEAD!
GOSH! MAYBE HE WILL BE PRESIDENT SOME DAY!

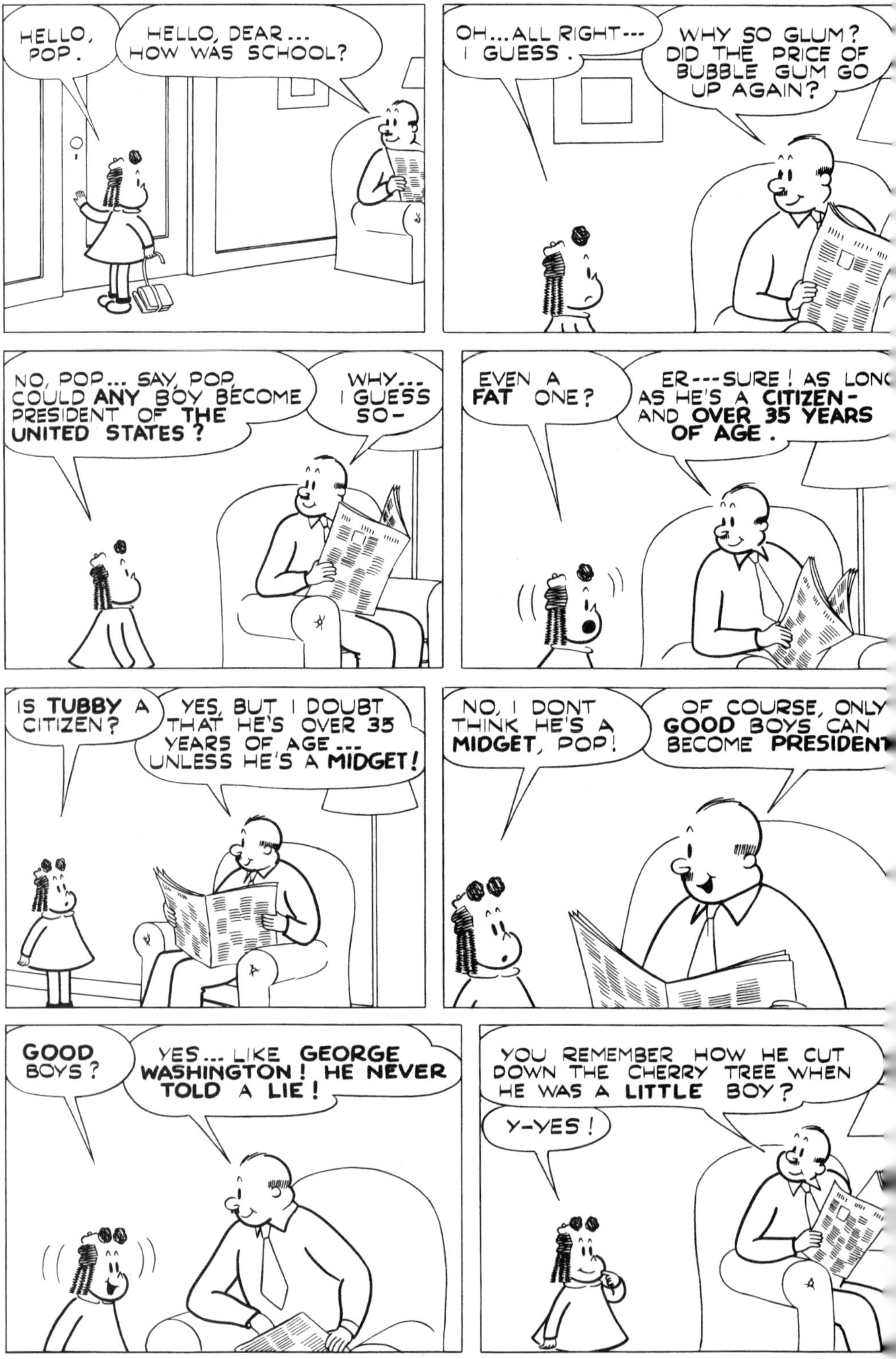
HELLO, POP.
HELLO, DEAR... HOW WAS SCHOOL?
OH...ALL RIGHT--- I GUESS.
WHY SO GLUM? DID THE PRICE OF BUBBLE GUM GO UP AGAIN?
NO, POP... SAY, POP, COULD ANY BOY BECOME PRESIDENT OF THE UNITED STATES?
WHY... I GUESS SO-
EVEN A FAT ONE?
ER---SURE! AS LONG AS HE'S A CITIZEN- AND OVER 35 YEARS OF AGE.
IS TUBBY A CITIZEN?
YES, BUT I DOUBT THAT HE'S OVER 35 YEARS OF AGE... UNLESS HE'S A MIDGET!
NO, I DONT THINK HE'S A MIDGET, POP!
OF COURSE, ONLY GOOD BOYS CAN BECOME PRESIDENT
GOOD BOYS?
YES... LIKE GEORGE WASHINGTON! HE NEVER TOLD A LIE!
YOU REMEMBER HOW HE CUT DOWN THE CHERRY TREE WHEN HE WAS A LITTLE BOY?
Y-YES!

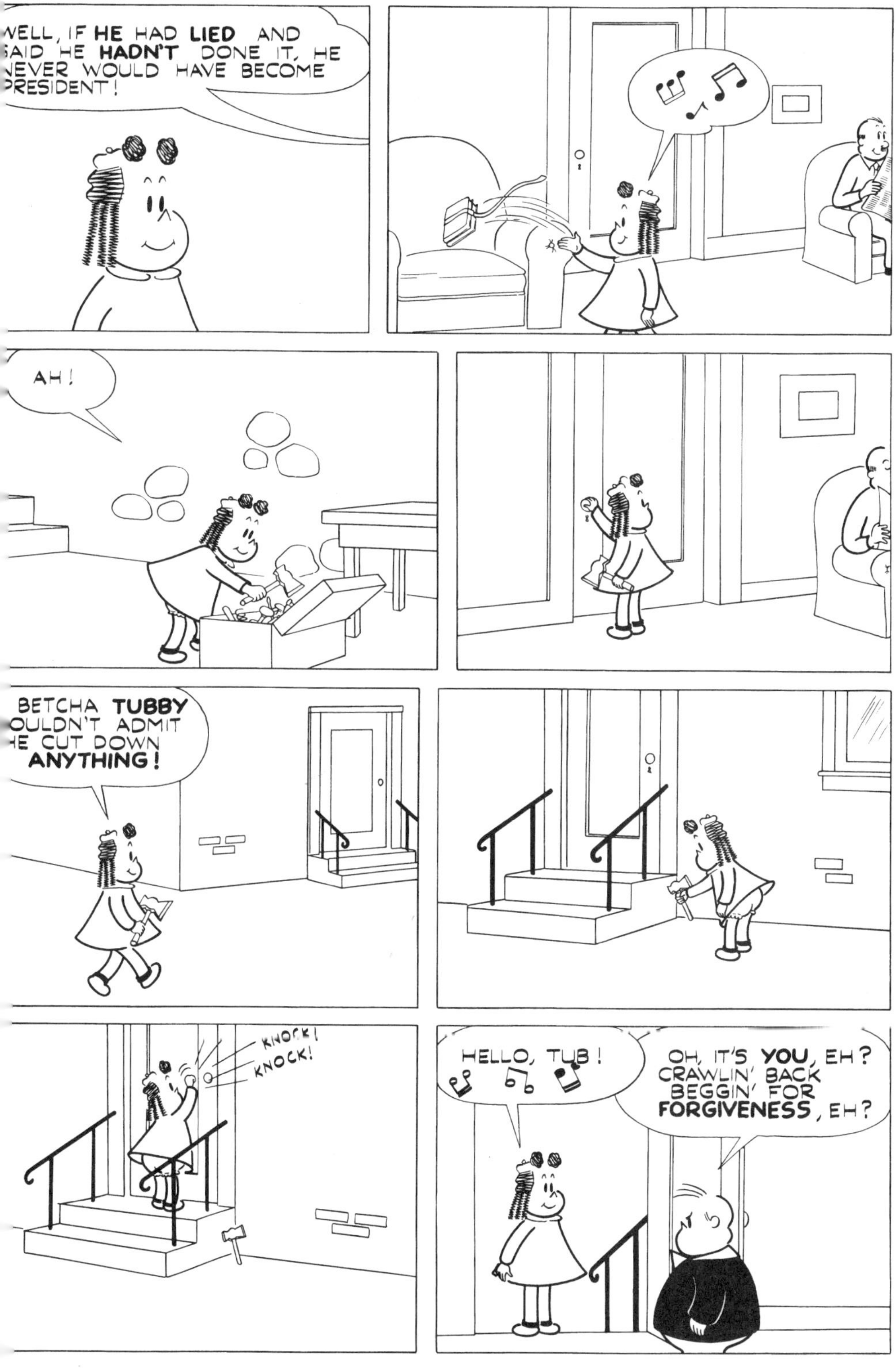

WELL, IF HE HAD LIED AND SAID HE HADN'T DONE IT, HE NEVER WOULD HAVE BECOME PRESIDENT!
AH!
BETCHA TUBBY OULDN'T ADMIT HE CUT DOWN ANYTHING!
KNOCK! KNOCK!
HELLO, TUB!
OH, IT'S YOU, EH? CRAWLIN' BACK BEGGIN' FOR FORGIVENESS, EH?

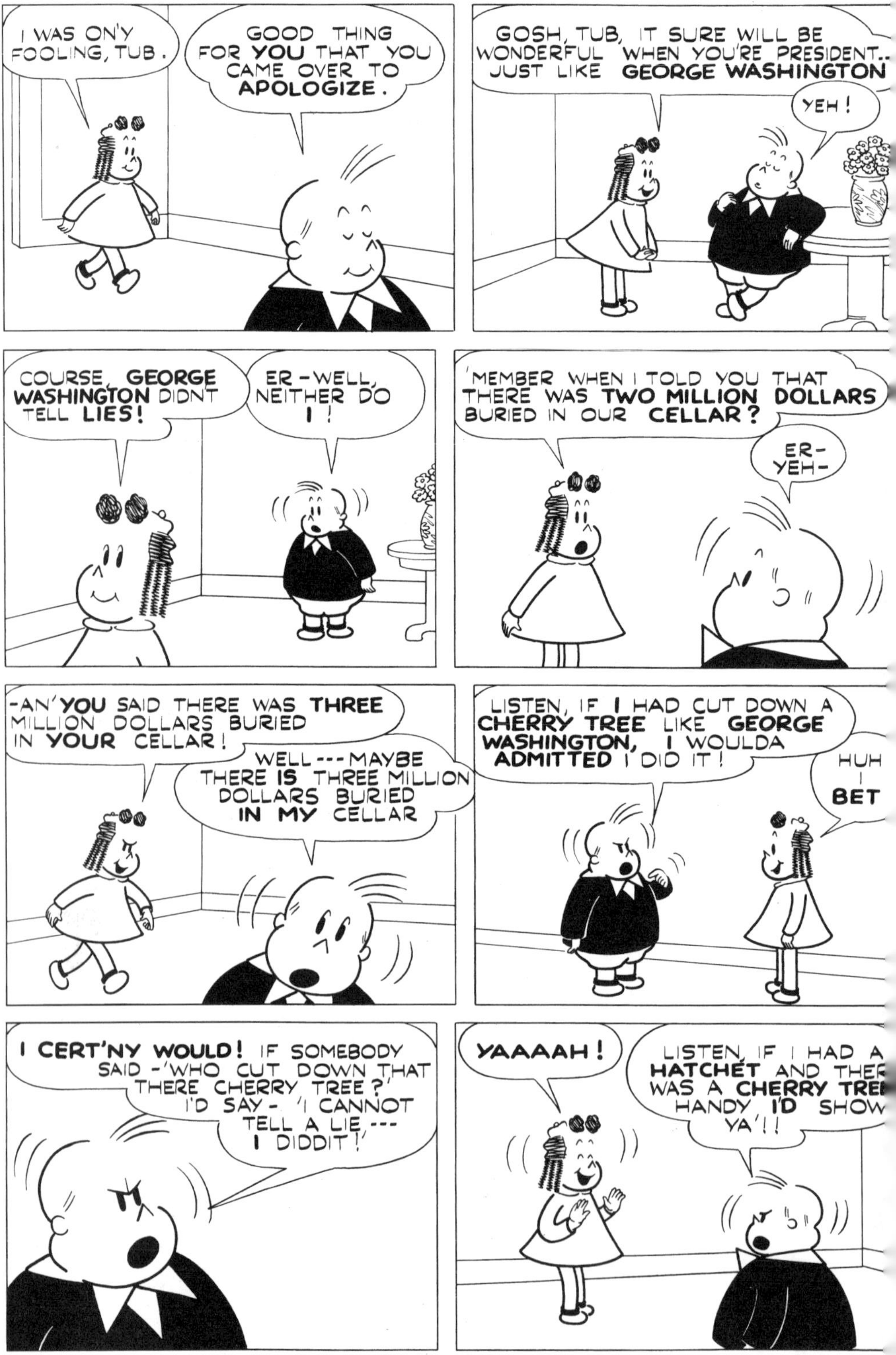

I WAS ON'Y FOOLING, TUB.
GOOD THING FOR **YOU** THAT YOU CAME OVER TO **APOLOGIZE**.
GOSH, TUB, IT SURE WILL BE WONDERFUL WHEN YOU'RE PRESIDENT.. JUST LIKE **GEORGE WASHINGTON**
YEH!
COURSE, **GEORGE WASHINGTON** DIDN'T TELL **LIES**!
ER-WELL, NEITHER DO **I**!
'MEMBER WHEN I TOLD YOU THAT THERE WAS **TWO MILLION DOLLARS** BURIED IN OUR **CELLAR**?
ER-YEH-
-AN' **YOU** SAID THERE WAS **THREE** MILLION DOLLARS BURIED IN **YOUR** CELLAR!
WELL---MAYBE THERE **IS** THREE MILLION DOLLARS BURIED **IN MY** CELLAR
LISTEN, IF **I** HAD CUT DOWN A **CHERRY TREE** LIKE **GEORGE WASHINGTON**, **I** WOULDA **ADMITTED** I DID IT!
HUH I **BET**
I CERT'NY WOULD! IF SOMEBODY SAID-'WHO CUT DOWN THAT THERE CHERRY TREE?' I'D **SAY**- 'I CANNOT TELL A LIE--- **I** DIDDIT!'
YAAAAH!
LISTEN, IF I HAD A **HATCHET** AND THER WAS A **CHERRY TRE** HANDY **I'D** SHOW YA'!!

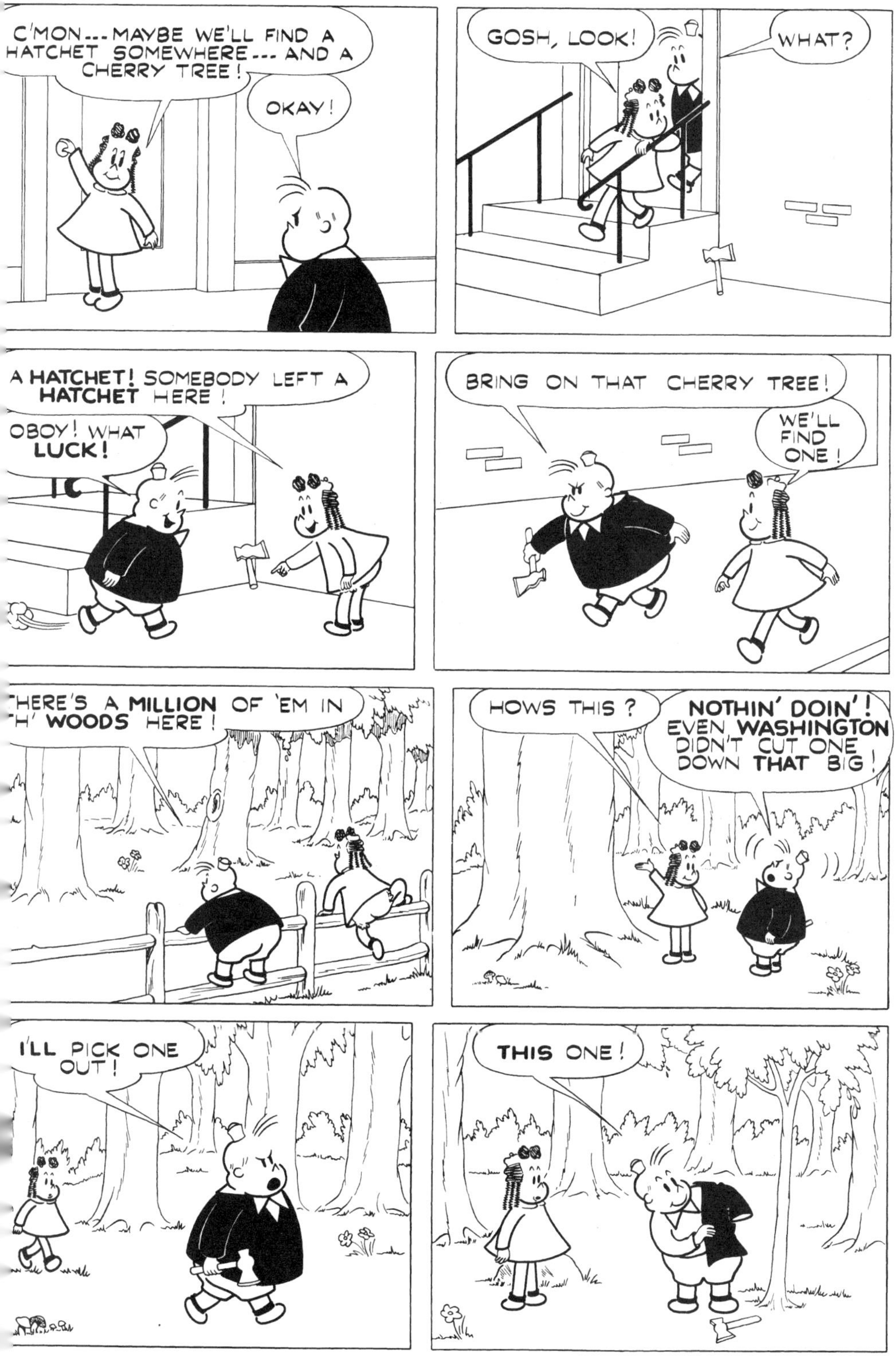
C'MON--- MAYBE WE'LL FIND A HATCHET SOMEWHERE--- AND A CHERRY TREE!
OKAY!
GOSH, LOOK!
WHAT?
A HATCHET! SOMEBODY LEFT A HATCHET HERE!
OBOY! WHAT LUCK!
BRING ON THAT CHERRY TREE!
WE'LL FIND ONE!
THERE'S A MILLION OF 'EM IN TH' WOODS HERE!
HOWS THIS?
NOTHIN' DOIN'! EVEN WASHINGTON DIDN'T CUT ONE DOWN THAT BIG!
I'LL PICK ONE OUT!
THIS ONE!

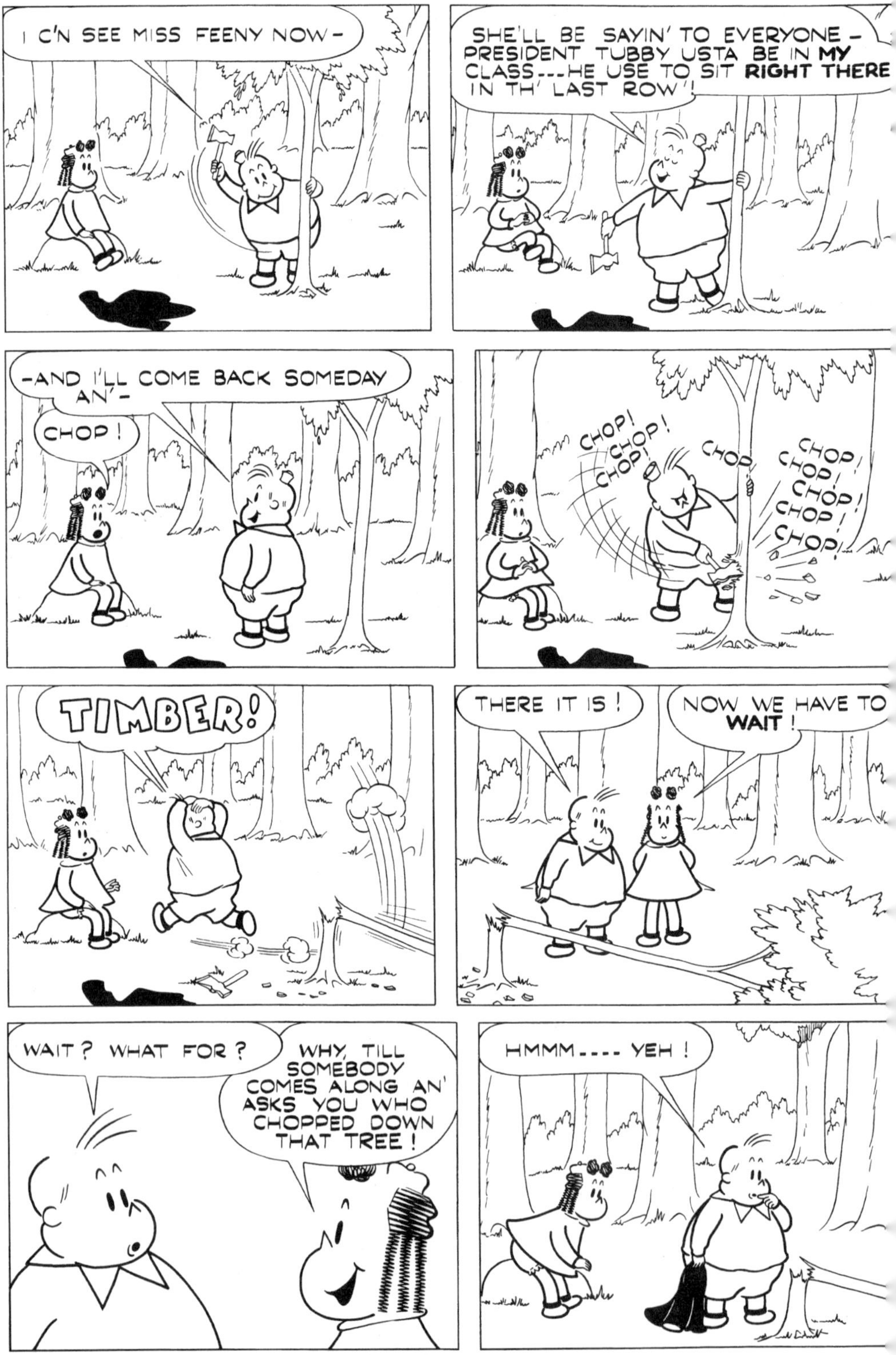
I C'N SEE MISS FEENY NOW -
SHE'LL BE SAYIN' TO EVERYONE - PRESIDENT TUBBY USTA BE IN **MY** CLASS---HE USE TO SIT **RIGHT THERE** IN TH' LAST ROW'!
-AND I'LL COME BACK SOMEDAY AN'-
CHOP!
CHOP! CHOP! CHOP! CHOP! CHOP! CHOP! CHOP! CHOP! CHOP!
TIMBER!
THERE IT IS!
NOW WE HAVE TO **WAIT**!
WAIT? WHAT FOR?
WHY, TILL SOMEBODY COMES ALONG AN' ASKS YOU WHO CHOPPED DOWN THAT TREE!
HMMM.... YEH!

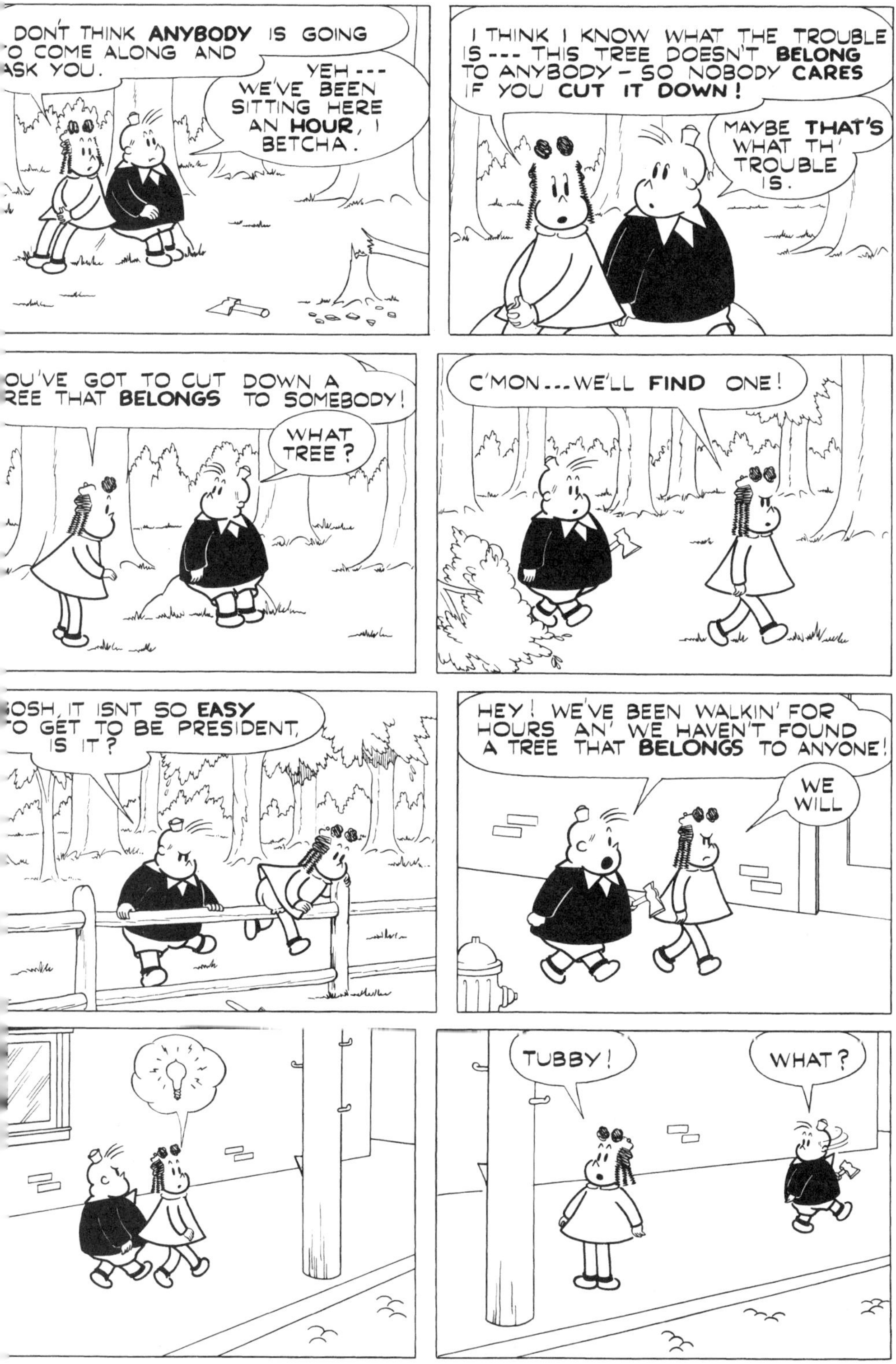
DON'T THINK ANYBODY IS GOING O COME ALONG AND ASK YOU.
YEH --- WE'VE BEEN SITTING HERE AN HOUR, I BETCHA.
I THINK I KNOW WHAT THE TROUBLE IS --- THIS TREE DOESN'T BELONG TO ANYBODY - SO NOBODY CARES IF YOU CUT IT DOWN!
MAYBE THAT'S WHAT TH' TROUBLE IS.
OU'VE GOT TO CUT DOWN A REE THAT BELONGS TO SOMEBODY!
WHAT TREE?
C'MON ... WE'LL FIND ONE!
OSH, IT ISNT SO EASY O GET TO BE PRESIDENT, IS IT?
HEY! WE'VE BEEN WALKIN' FOR HOURS AN' WE HAVEN'T FOUND A TREE THAT BELONGS TO ANYONE!
WE WILL
TUBBY!
WHAT?

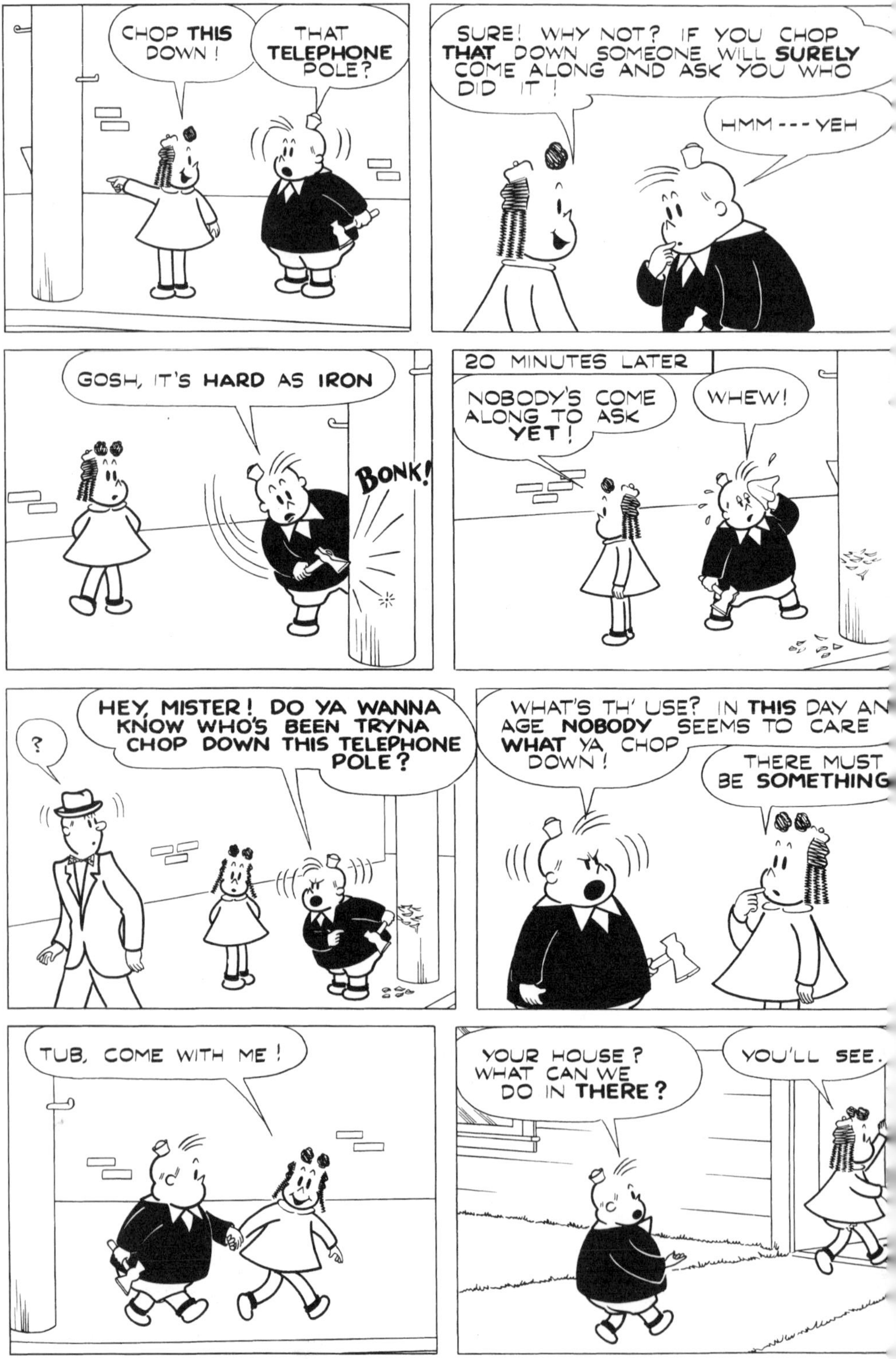
CHOP **THIS** DOWN!
THAT **TELEPHONE** POLE?
SURE! WHY NOT? IF YOU CHOP **THAT** DOWN SOMEONE WILL **SURELY** COME ALONG AND ASK YOU WHO DID IT!
HMM---YEH
GOSH, IT'S **HARD** AS **IRON**
BONK!
20 MINUTES LATER
NOBODY'S COME ALONG TO ASK **YET**!
WHEW!
?
HEY, MISTER! DO YA WANNA KNOW WHO'S BEEN TRYNA CHOP DOWN THIS TELEPHONE POLE?
WHAT'S TH' USE? IN **THIS** DAY AN AGE **NOBODY** SEEMS TO CARE **WHAT** YA CHOP DOWN!
THERE MUST BE **SOMETHING**
TUB, COME WITH ME!
YOUR HOUSE? WHAT CAN WE DO IN **THERE**?
YOU'LL SEE.

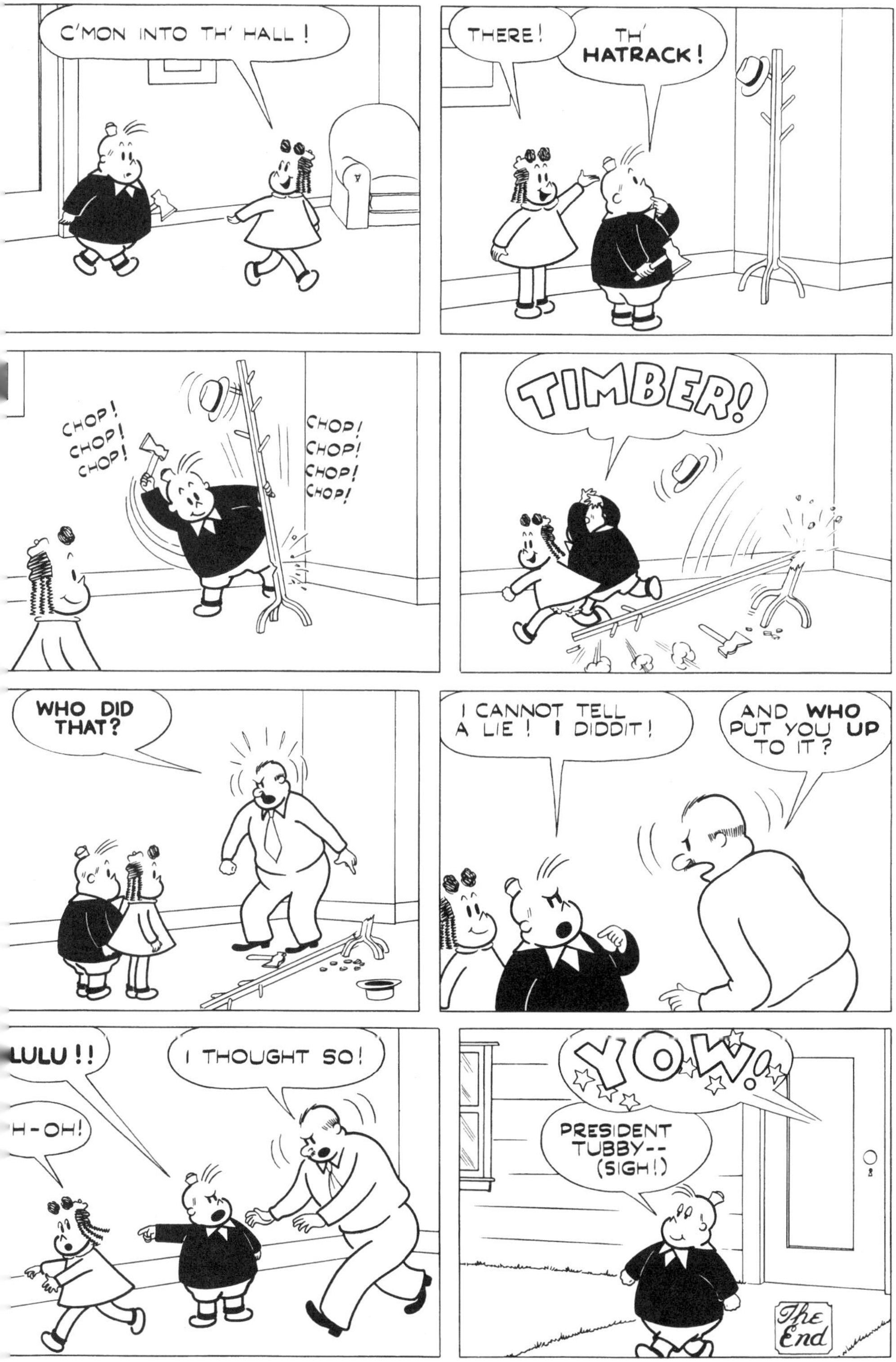

C'MON INTO TH' HALL!
THERE!
TH' HATRACK!
CHOP! CHOP! CHOP!
CHOP! CHOP! CHOP! CHOP!
TIMBER!
WHO DID THAT?
I CANNOT TELL A LIE! I DIDDIT!
AND WHO PUT YOU UP TO IT?
LULU!!
I THOUGHT SO!
H-OH!
YOW!
PRESIDENT TUBBY-- (SIGH!)
The End

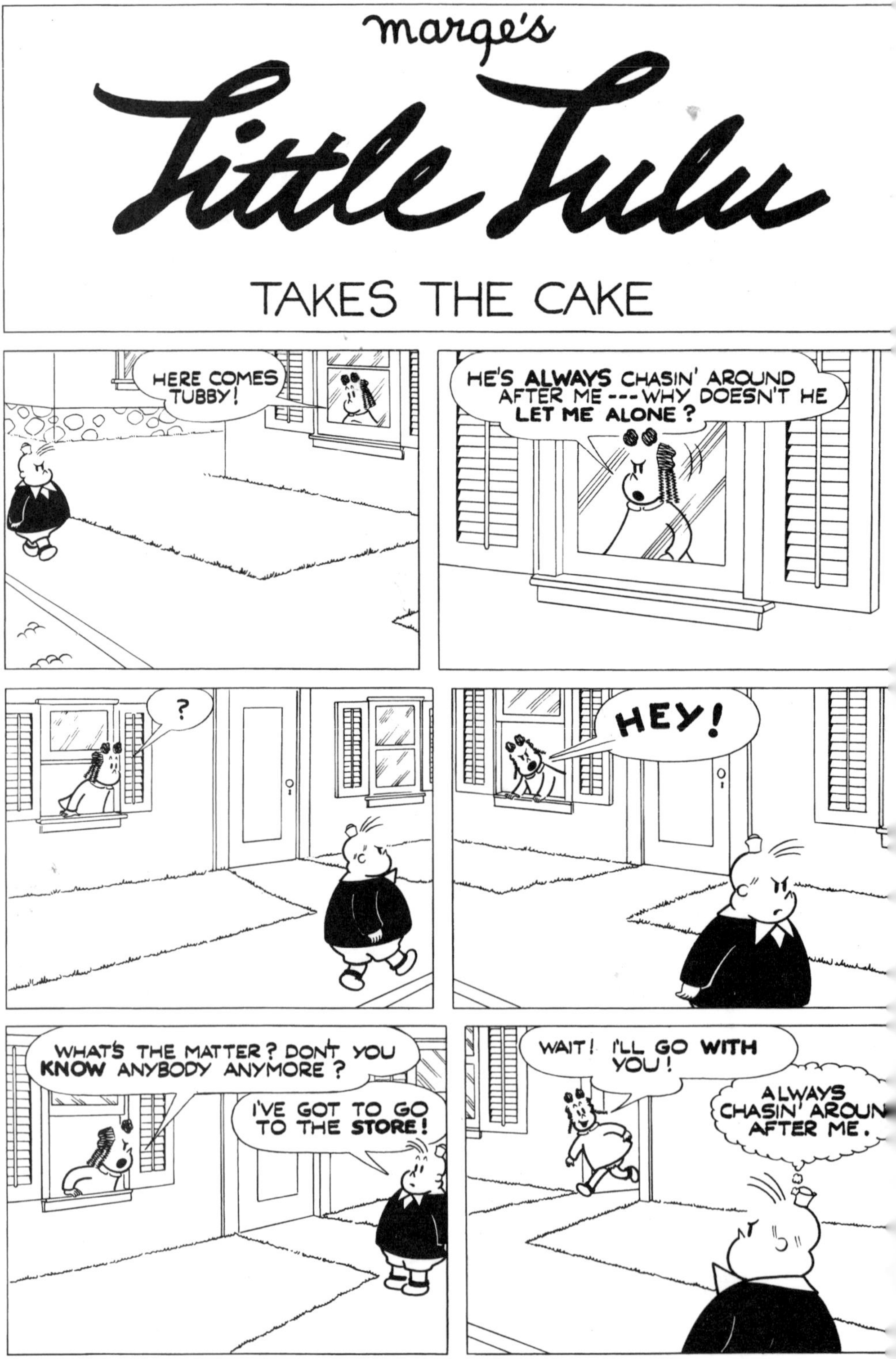
marge's
Little Lulu
TAKES THE CAKE
HERE COMES TUBBY!
HE'S ALWAYS CHASIN' AROUND AFTER ME --- WHY DOESN'T HE LET ME ALONE?
?
HEY!
WHAT'S THE MATTER? DON'T YOU KNOW ANYBODY ANYMORE?
I'VE GOT TO GO TO THE STORE!
WAIT! I'LL GO WITH YOU!
ALWAYS CHASIN' AROUN AFTER ME.

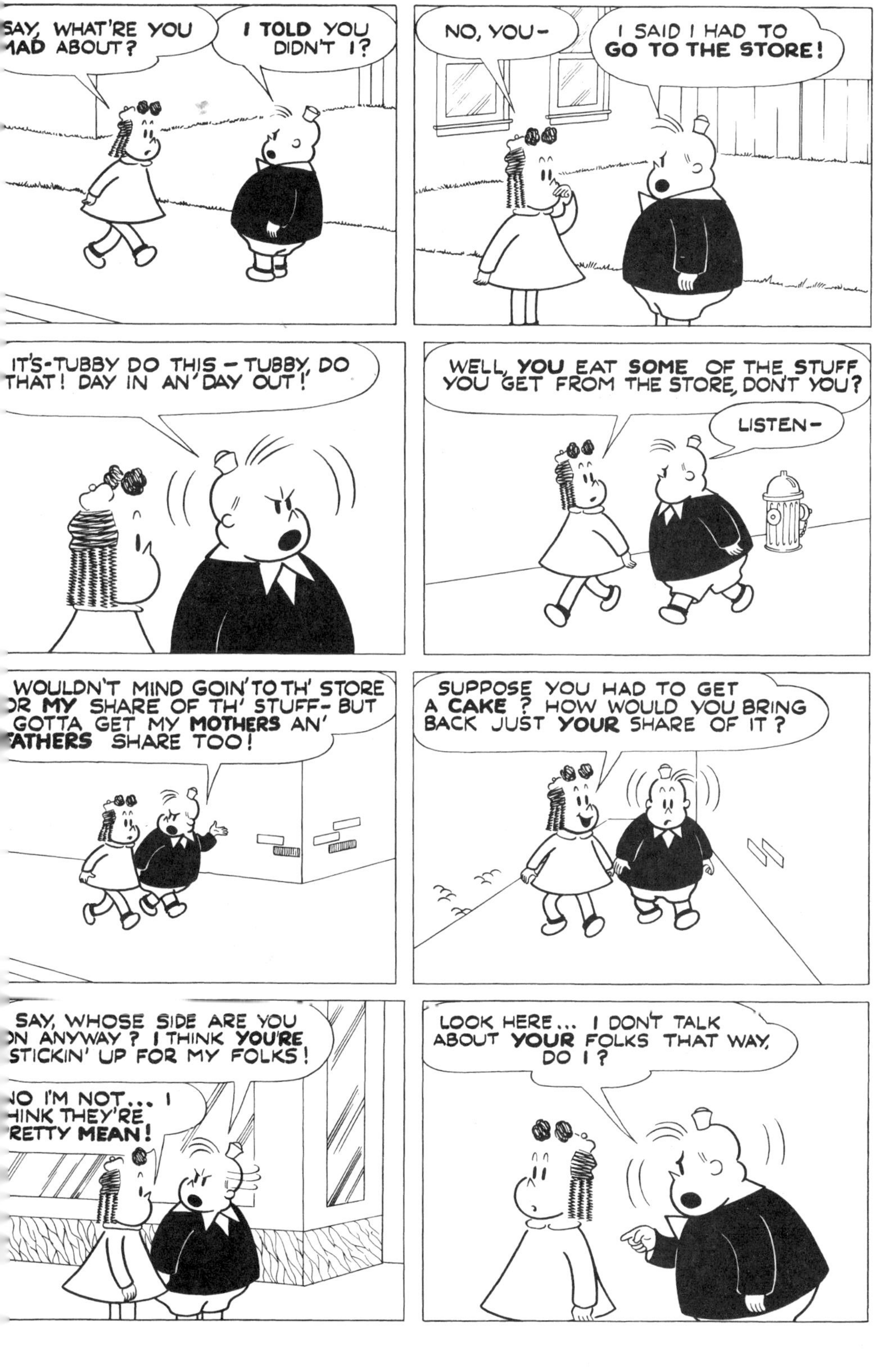
SAY, WHAT'RE YOU MAD ABOUT?
I TOLD YOU DIDN'T I?
NO, YOU-
I SAID I HAD TO GO TO THE STORE!
IT'S-TUBBY DO THIS — TUBBY, DO THAT! DAY IN AN' DAY OUT!
WELL, YOU EAT SOME OF THE STUFF YOU GET FROM THE STORE, DON'T YOU?
LISTEN-
WOULDN'T MIND GOIN' TO TH' STORE OR MY SHARE OF TH' STUFF- BUT GOTTA GET MY MOTHERS AN' FATHERS SHARE TOO!
SUPPOSE YOU HAD TO GET A CAKE? HOW WOULD YOU BRING BACK JUST YOUR SHARE OF IT?
SAY, WHOSE SIDE ARE YOU ON ANYWAY? I THINK YOU'RE STICKIN' UP FOR MY FOLKS!
NO I'M NOT... I THINK THEY'RE PRETTY MEAN!
LOOK HERE... I DON'T TALK ABOUT YOUR FOLKS THAT WAY, DO I?

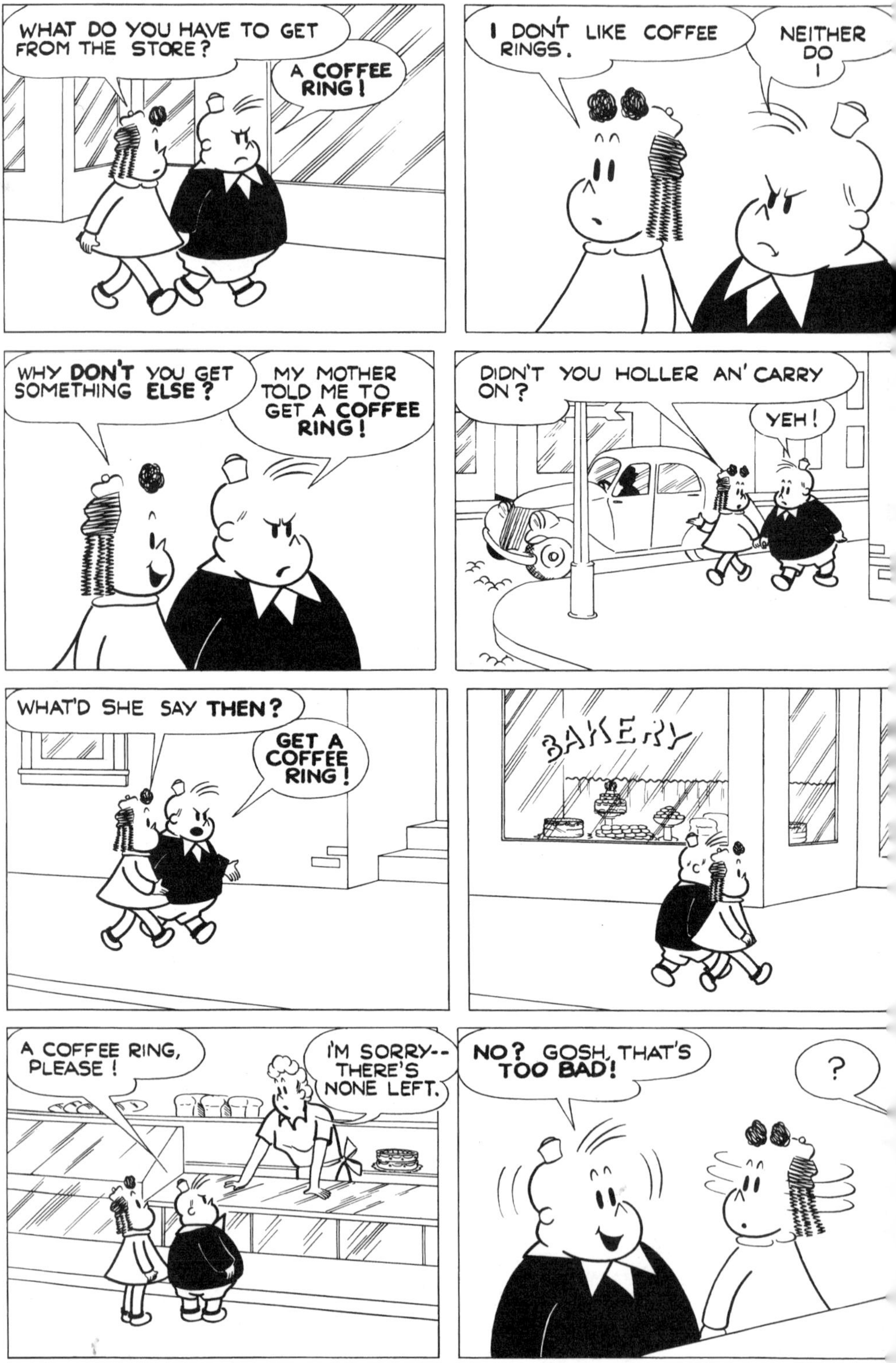
WHAT DO YOU HAVE TO GET FROM THE STORE?
A **COFFEE RING!**
I DON'T LIKE COFFEE RINGS.
NEITHER DO I
WHY **DON'T** YOU GET SOMETHING **ELSE?**
MY MOTHER TOLD ME TO GET A **COFFEE RING!**
DIDN'T YOU HOLLER AN' CARRY ON?
YEH!
WHAT'D SHE SAY **THEN?**
GET A COFFEE RING!
BAKERY
A COFFEE RING, PLEASE!
I'M SORRY-- THERE'S NONE LEFT.
NO? GOSH, THAT'S **TOO BAD!**
?

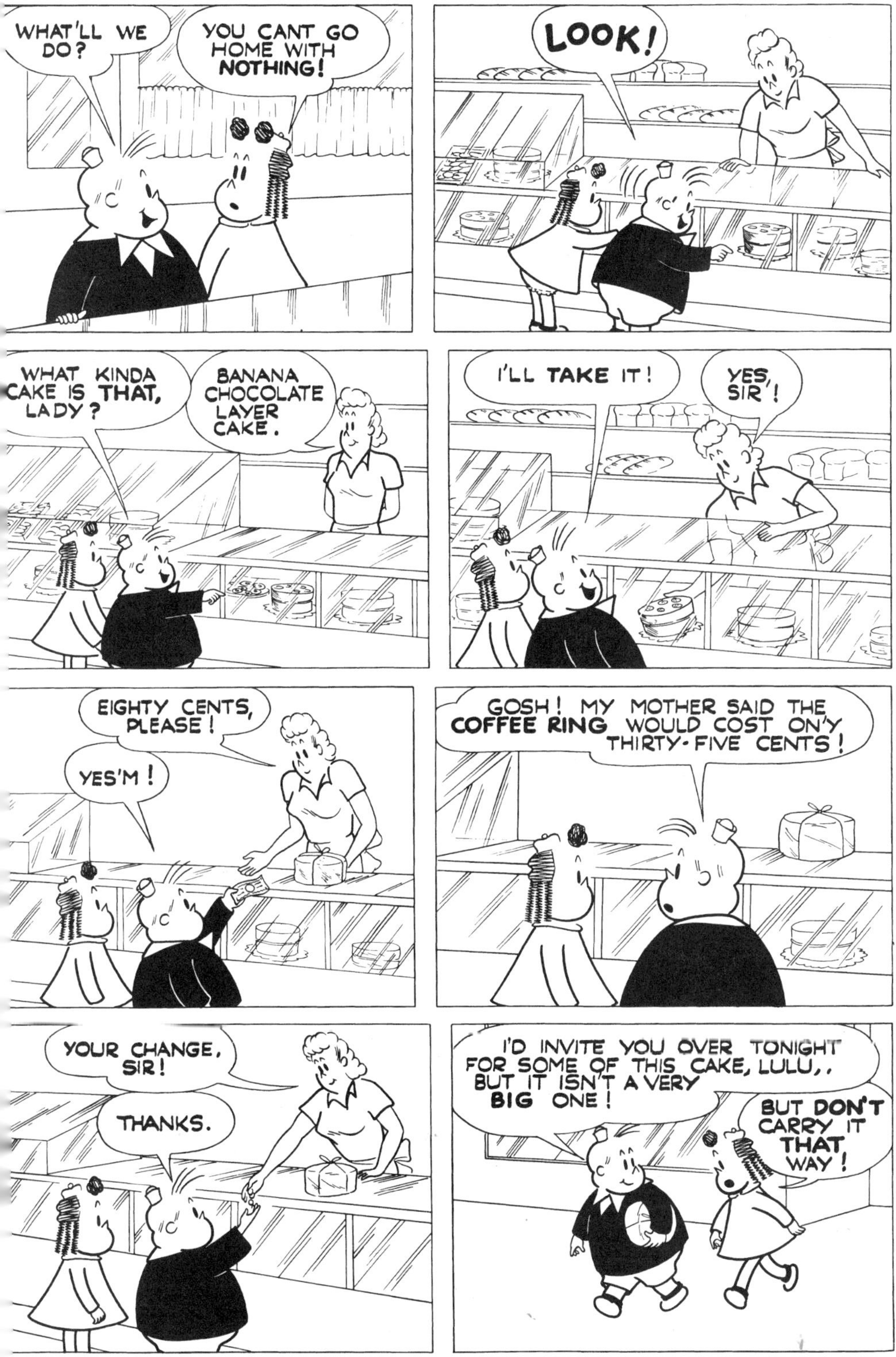
WHAT'LL WE DO?
YOU CANT GO HOME WITH **NOTHING**!
LOOK!
WHAT KINDA CAKE IS **THAT**, LADY?
BANANA CHOCOLATE LAYER CAKE.
I'LL **TAKE** IT!
YES, SIR!
EIGHTY CENTS, PLEASE!
YES'M!
GOSH! MY MOTHER SAID THE **COFFEE RING** WOULD COST ON'Y THIRTY-FIVE CENTS!
YOUR CHANGE, SIR!
THANKS.
I'D INVITE YOU OVER TONIGHT FOR SOME OF THIS CAKE, LULU,, BUT IT ISN'T A VERY **BIG** ONE!
BUT **DON'T** CARRY IT **THAT** WAY!

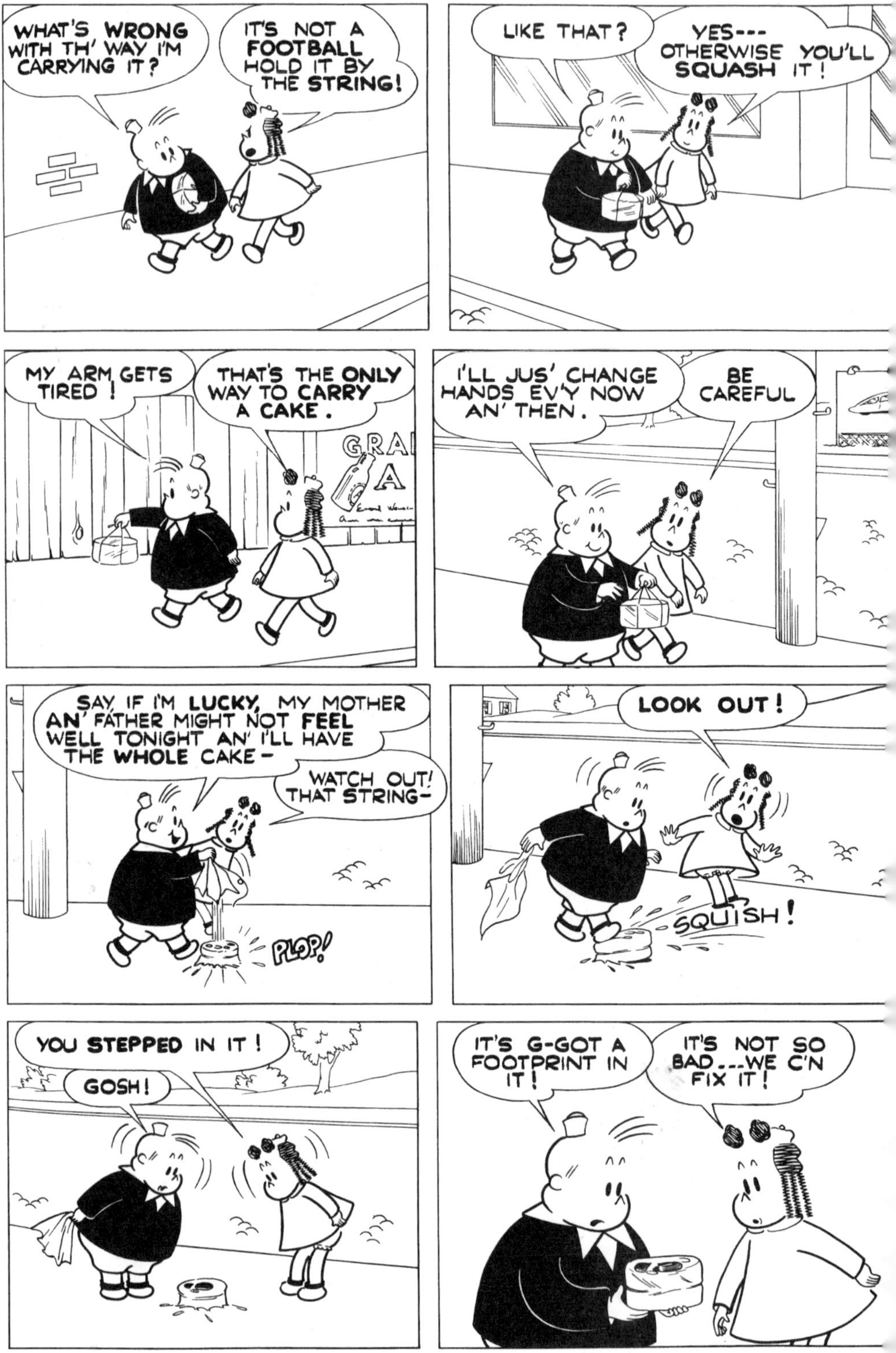
WHAT'S WRONG WITH TH' WAY I'M CARRYING IT?
IT'S NOT A FOOTBALL HOLD IT BY THE STRING!
LIKE THAT?
YES--- OTHERWISE YOU'LL SQUASH IT!
MY ARM GETS TIRED!
THAT'S THE ONLY WAY TO CARRY A CAKE.
I'LL JUS' CHANGE HANDS EV'Y NOW AN' THEN.
BE CAREFUL
SAY IF I'M LUCKY, MY MOTHER AN' FATHER MIGHT NOT FEEL WELL TONIGHT AN' I'LL HAVE THE WHOLE CAKE-
WATCH OUT! THAT STRING-
PLOP!
LOOK OUT!
SQUISH!
YOU STEPPED IN IT!
GOSH!
IT'S G-GOT A FOOTPRINT IN IT!
IT'S NOT SO BAD...WE C'N FIX IT!

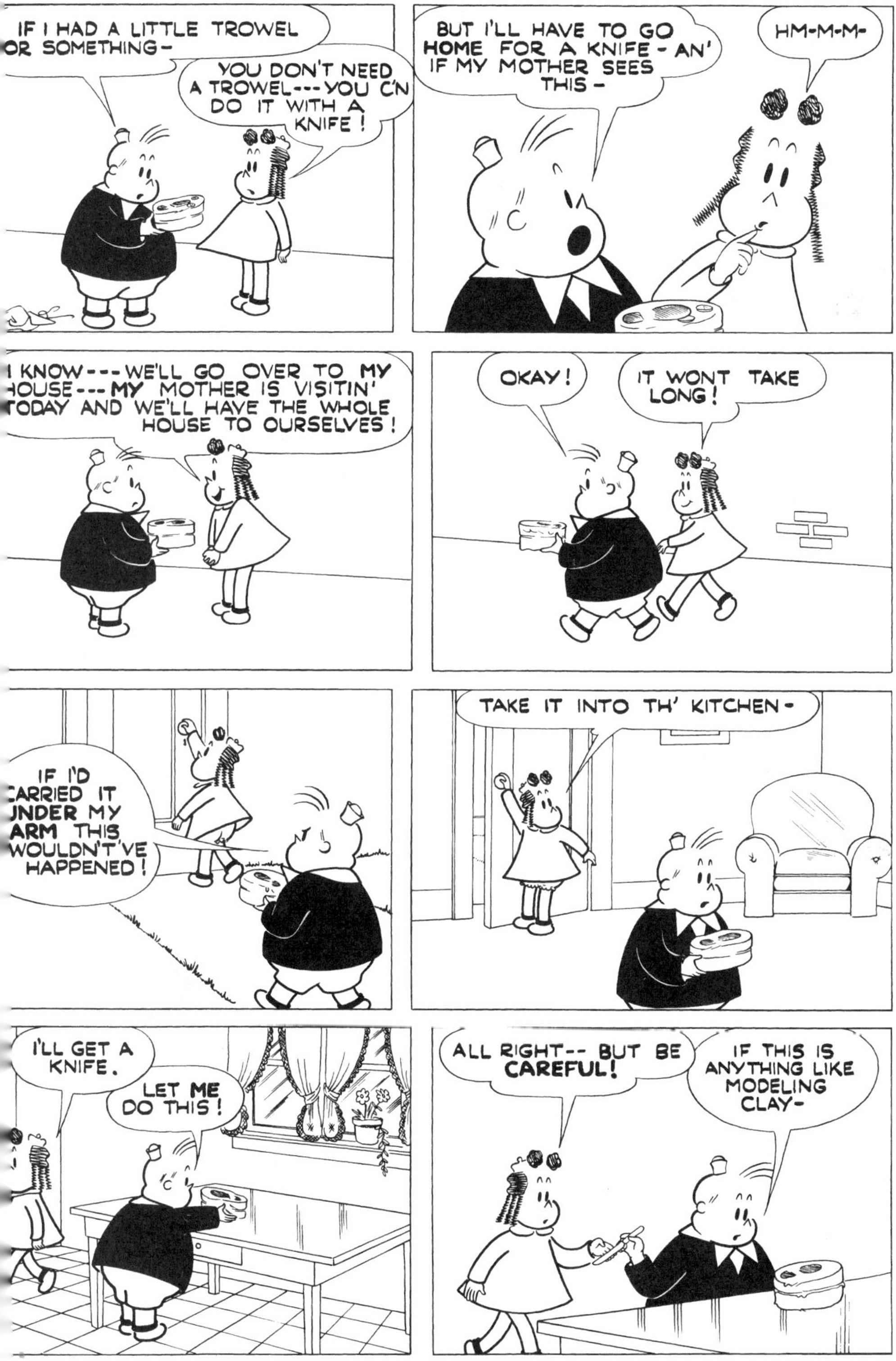
IF I HAD A LITTLE TROWEL OR SOMETHING-
YOU DON'T NEED A TROWEL---YOU C'N DO IT WITH A KNIFE!
BUT I'LL HAVE TO GO HOME FOR A KNIFE - AN' IF MY MOTHER SEES THIS -
HM-M-M-
I KNOW---WE'LL GO OVER TO MY HOUSE---MY MOTHER IS VISITIN' TODAY AND WE'LL HAVE THE WHOLE HOUSE TO OURSELVES!
OKAY!
IT WONT TAKE LONG!
IF I'D CARRIED IT UNDER MY ARM THIS WOULDN'T'VE HAPPENED!
TAKE IT INTO TH' KITCHEN-
I'LL GET A KNIFE.
LET ME DO THIS!
ALL RIGHT-- BUT BE CAREFUL!
IF THIS IS ANYTHING LIKE MODELING CLAY-

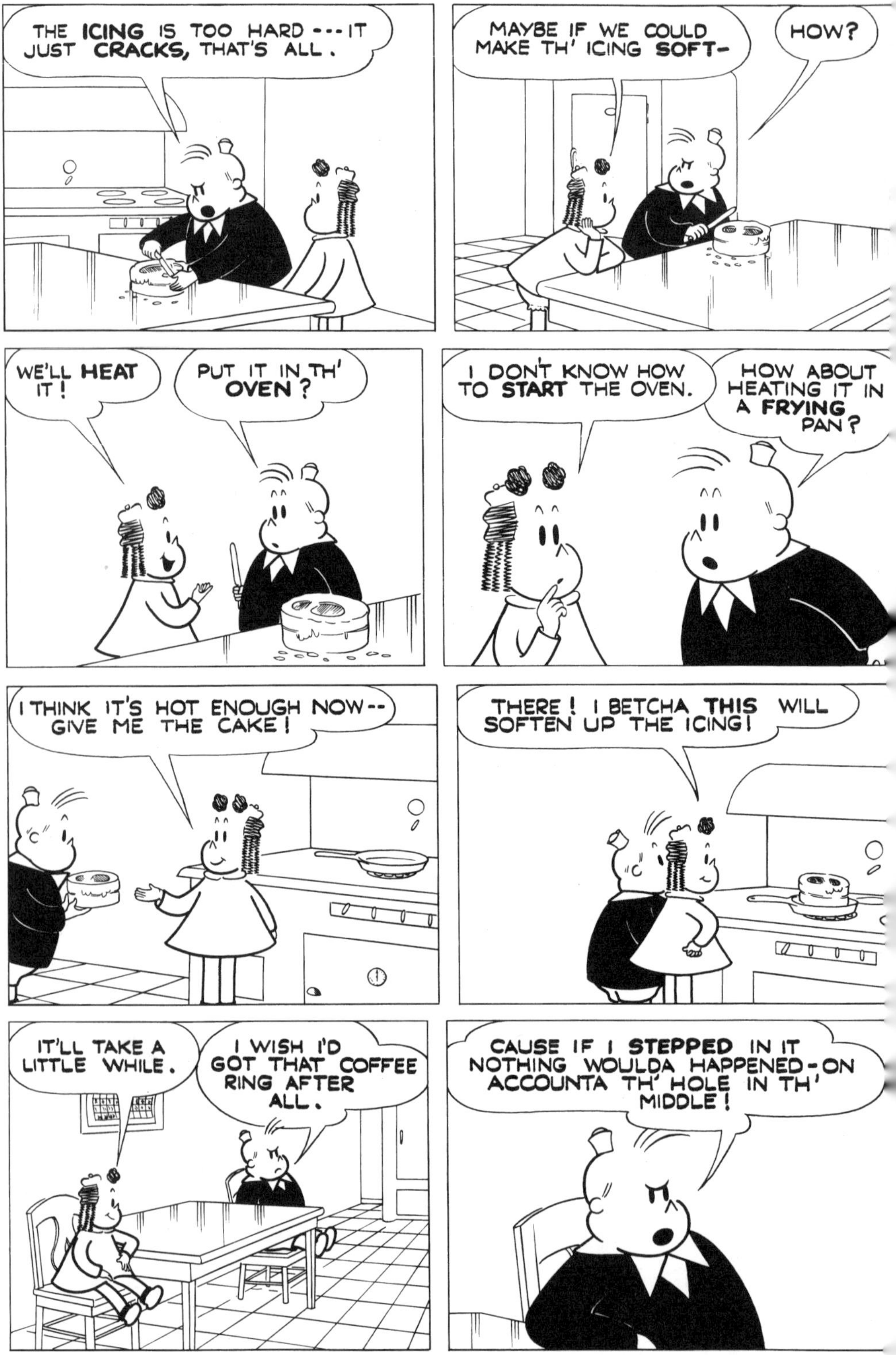
THE ICING IS TOO HARD --- IT JUST CRACKS, THAT'S ALL.
MAYBE IF WE COULD MAKE TH' ICING SOFT-
HOW?
WE'LL HEAT IT!
PUT IT IN TH' OVEN?
I DON'T KNOW HOW TO START THE OVEN.
HOW ABOUT HEATING IT IN A FRYING PAN?
I THINK IT'S HOT ENOUGH NOW-- GIVE ME THE CAKE!
THERE! I BETCHA THIS WILL SOFTEN UP THE ICING!
IT'LL TAKE A LITTLE WHILE.
I WISH I'D GOT THAT COFFEE RING AFTER ALL.
CAUSE IF I STEPPED IN IT NOTHING WOULDA HAPPENED-ON ACCOUNTA TH' HOLE IN TH' MIDDLE!

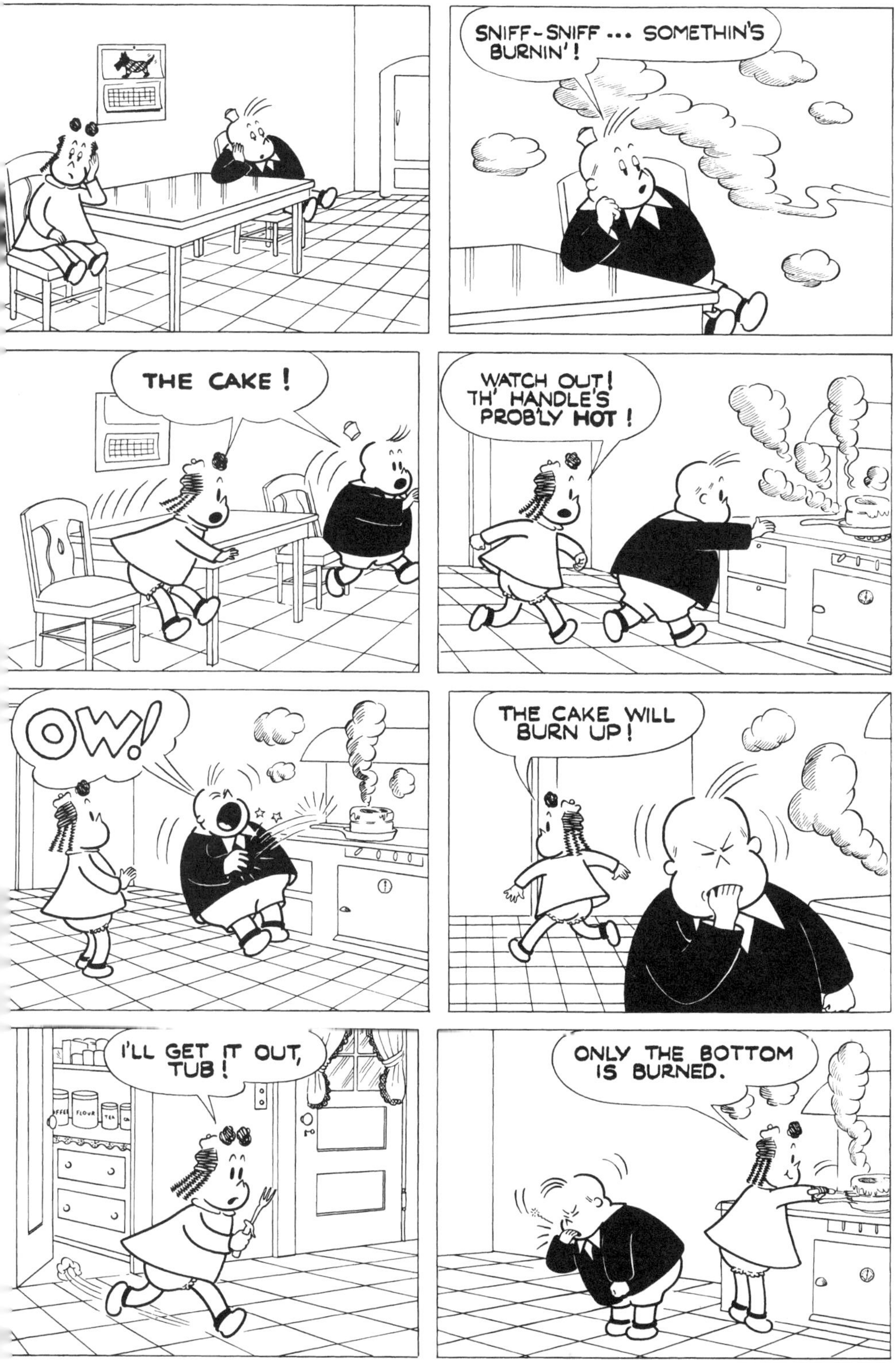
SNIFF-SNIFF ... SOMETHIN'S BURNIN'!
THE CAKE!
WATCH OUT! TH' HANDLE'S PROB'LY HOT!
OW!
THE CAKE WILL BURN UP!
I'LL GET IT OUT, TUB!
FLOUR
TEA
ONLY THE BOTTOM IS BURNED.

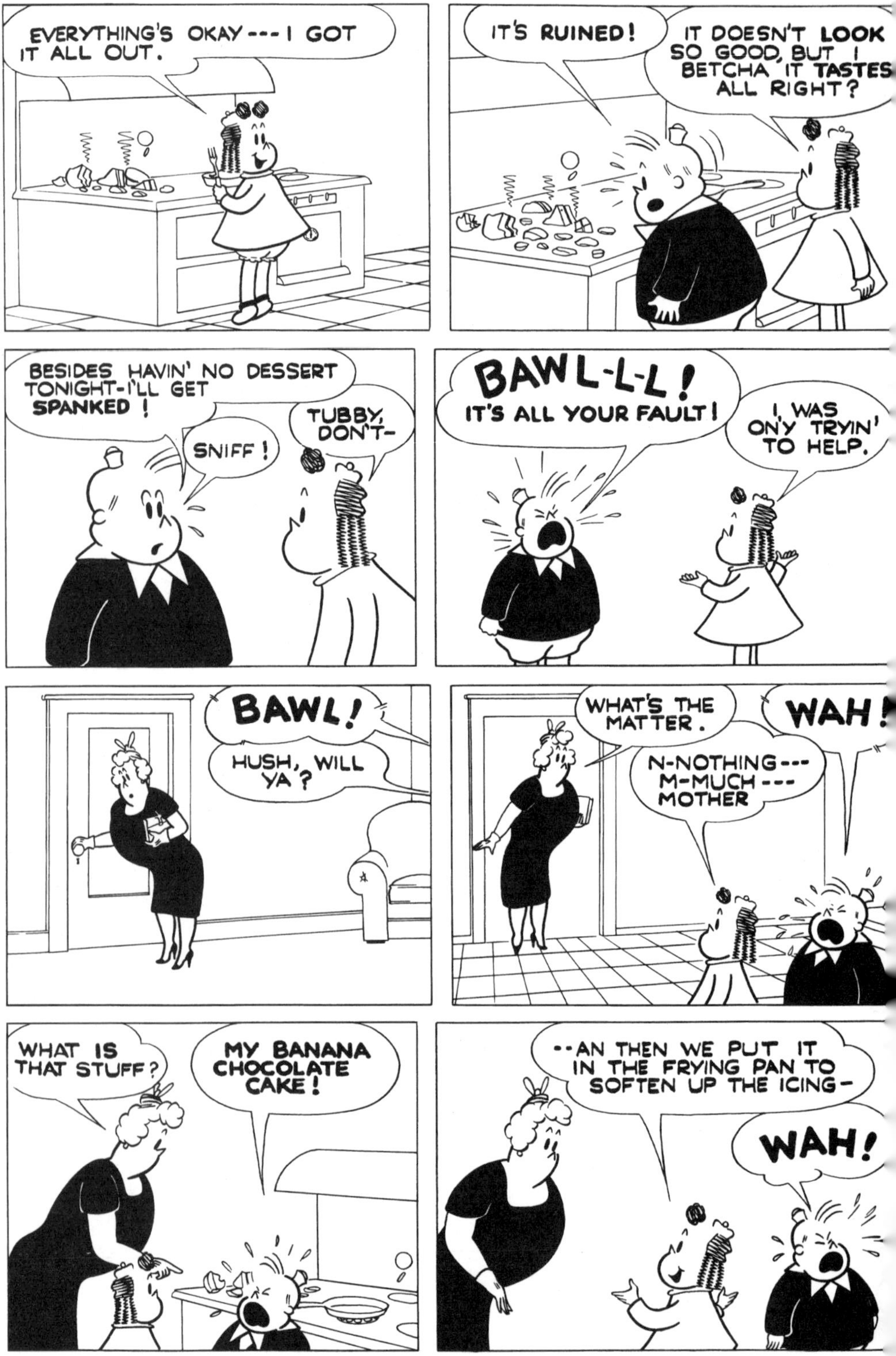
EVERYTHING'S OKAY --- I GOT IT ALL OUT.
IT'S RUINED!
IT DOESN'T LOOK SO GOOD, BUT I BETCHA IT TASTES ALL RIGHT?
BESIDES HAVIN' NO DESSERT TONIGHT-I'LL GET SPANKED!
SNIFF!
TUBBY, DON'T-
BAWL-L-L! IT'S ALL YOUR FAULT!
I WAS ON'Y TRYIN' TO HELP.
BAWL!
HUSH, WILL YA?
WHAT'S THE MATTER.
WAH!
N-NOTHING --- M-MUCH --- MOTHER
WHAT IS THAT STUFF?
MY BANANA CHOCOLATE CAKE!
--AN THEN WE PUT IT IN THE FRYING PAN TO SOFTEN UP THE ICING-
WAH!

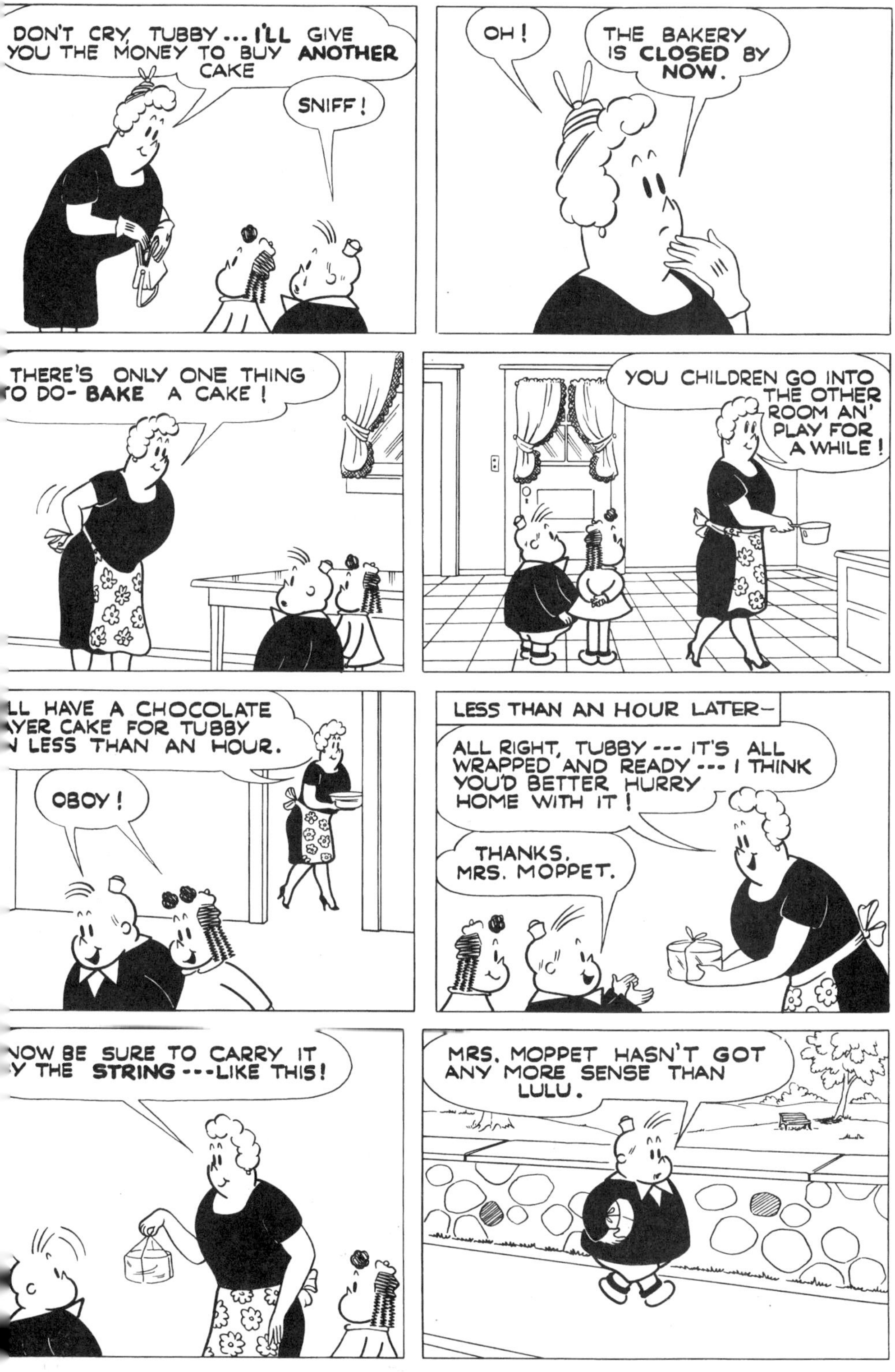
DON'T CRY, TUBBY... I'LL GIVE YOU THE MONEY TO BUY ANOTHER CAKE
SNIFF!
OH!
THE BAKERY IS CLOSED BY NOW.
THERE'S ONLY ONE THING TO DO- BAKE A CAKE!
YOU CHILDREN GO INTO THE OTHER ROOM AN' PLAY FOR A WHILE!
LL HAVE A CHOCOLATE AYER CAKE FOR TUBBY N LESS THAN AN HOUR.
OBOY!
LESS THAN AN HOUR LATER—
ALL RIGHT, TUBBY --- IT'S ALL WRAPPED AND READY --- I THINK YOU'D BETTER HURRY HOME WITH IT!
THANKS, MRS. MOPPET.
NOW BE SURE TO CARRY IT Y THE STRING ---LIKE THIS!
MRS. MOPPET HASN'T GOT ANY MORE SENSE THAN LULU.

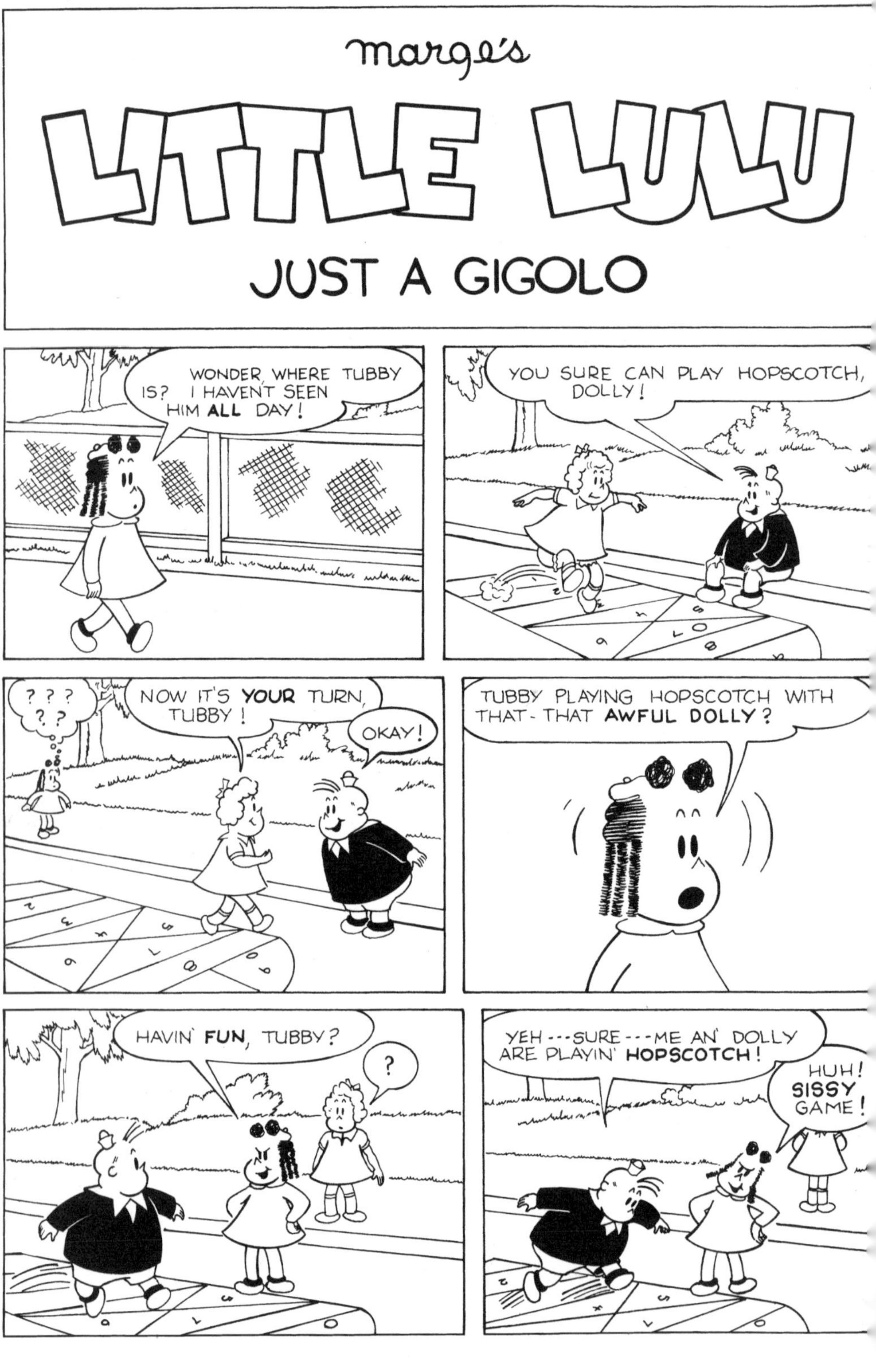
marge's
LITTLE LULU
JUST A GIGOLO
WONDER WHERE TUBBY IS? I HAVEN'T SEEN HIM **ALL** DAY!
YOU SURE CAN PLAY HOPSCOTCH, DOLLY!
? ? ? ? ?
NOW IT'S **YOUR** TURN, TUBBY!
OKAY!
TUBBY PLAYING HOPSCOTCH WITH THAT-THAT **AWFUL DOLLY**?
HAVIN' **FUN**, TUBBY?
?
YEH---SURE---ME AN' DOLLY ARE PLAYIN' **HOPSCOTCH**!
HUH! **SISSY** GAME!

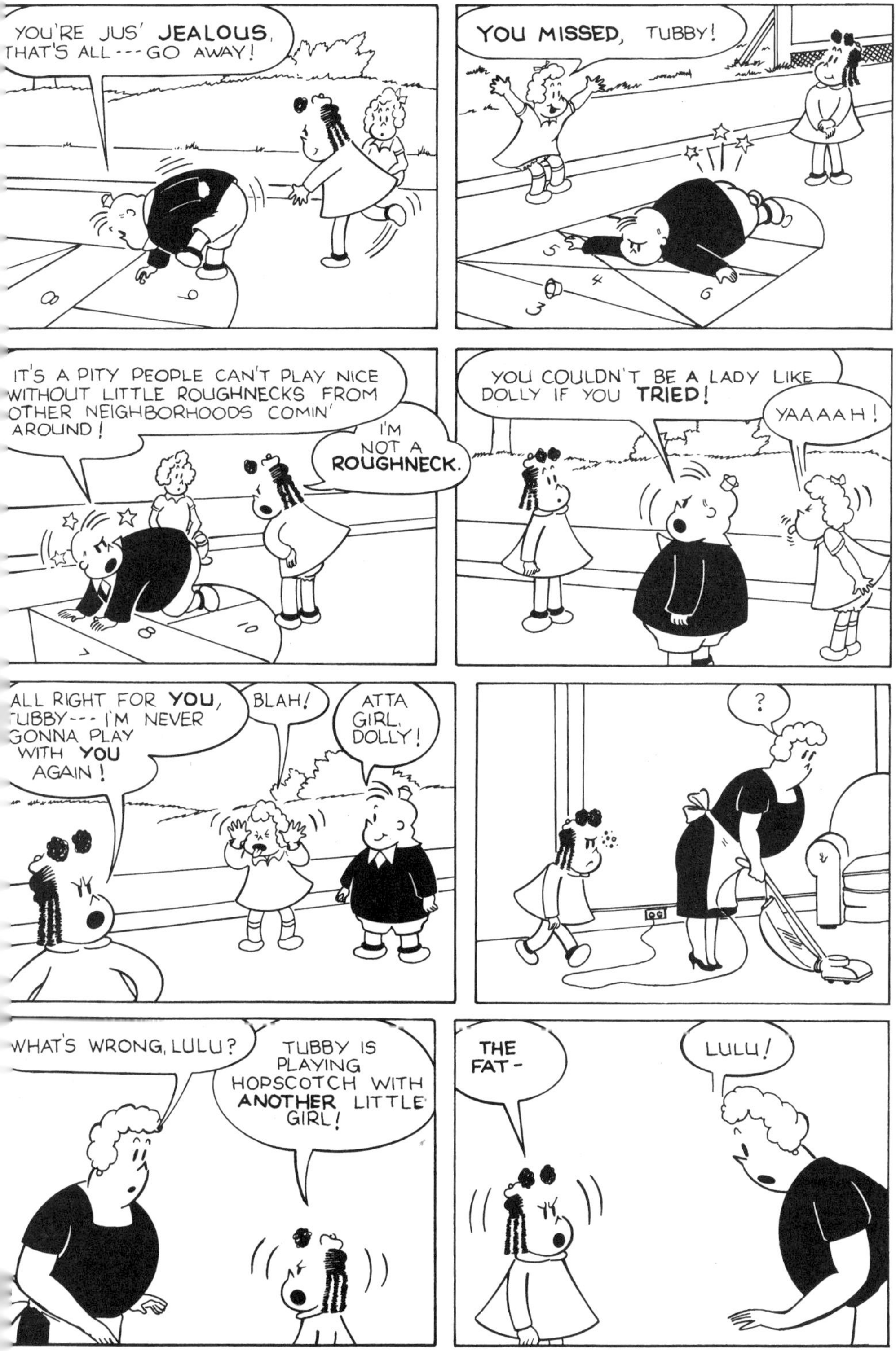
YOU'RE JUS' JEALOUS, THAT'S ALL --- GO AWAY!
YOU MISSED, TUBBY!
IT'S A PITY PEOPLE CAN'T PLAY NICE WITHOUT LITTLE ROUGHNECKS FROM OTHER NEIGHBORHOODS COMIN' AROUND!
I'M NOT A ROUGHNECK.
YOU COULDN'T BE A LADY LIKE DOLLY IF YOU TRIED!
YAAAAH!
ALL RIGHT FOR YOU, TUBBY--- I'M NEVER GONNA PLAY WITH YOU AGAIN!
BLAH!
ATTA GIRL, DOLLY!
?
WHAT'S WRONG, LULU?
TUBBY IS PLAYING HOPSCOTCH WITH ANOTHER LITTLE GIRL!
THE FAT-
LULU!

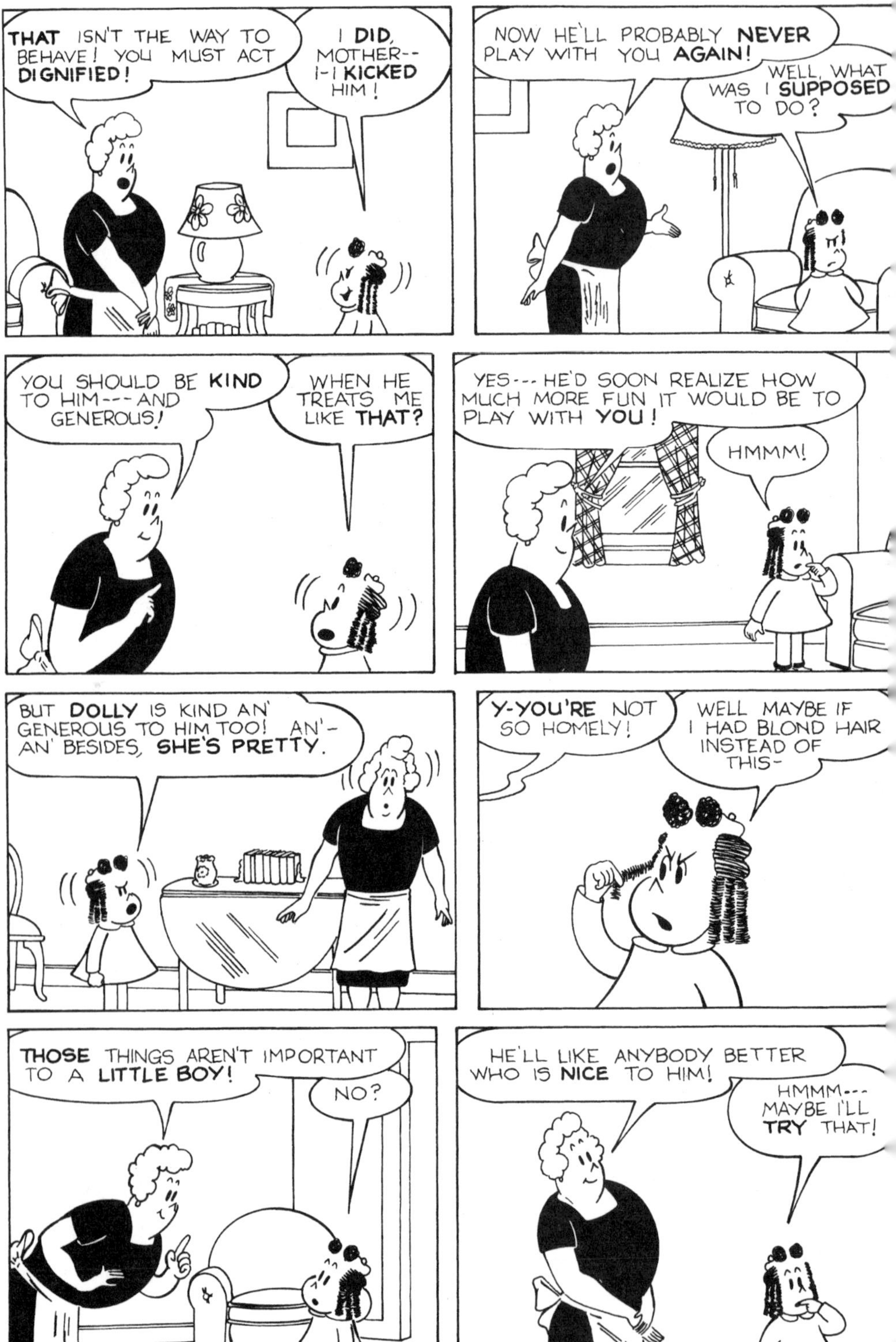
THAT ISN'T THE WAY TO BEHAVE! YOU MUST ACT DIGNIFIED!
I DID, MOTHER-- I-I KICKED HIM!
NOW HE'LL PROBABLY NEVER PLAY WITH YOU AGAIN!
WELL, WHAT WAS I SUPPOSED TO DO?
YOU SHOULD BE KIND TO HIM--- AND GENEROUS!
WHEN HE TREATS ME LIKE THAT?
YES--- HE'D SOON REALIZE HOW MUCH MORE FUN IT WOULD BE TO PLAY WITH YOU!
HMMM!
BUT DOLLY IS KIND AN' GENEROUS TO HIM TOO! AN'- AN' BESIDES, SHE'S PRETTY.
Y-YOU'RE NOT SO HOMELY!
WELL MAYBE IF I HAD BLOND HAIR INSTEAD OF THIS-
THOSE THINGS AREN'T IMPORTANT TO A LITTLE BOY!
NO?
HE'LL LIKE ANYBODY BETTER WHO IS NICE TO HIM!
HMMM--- MAYBE I'LL TRY THAT!

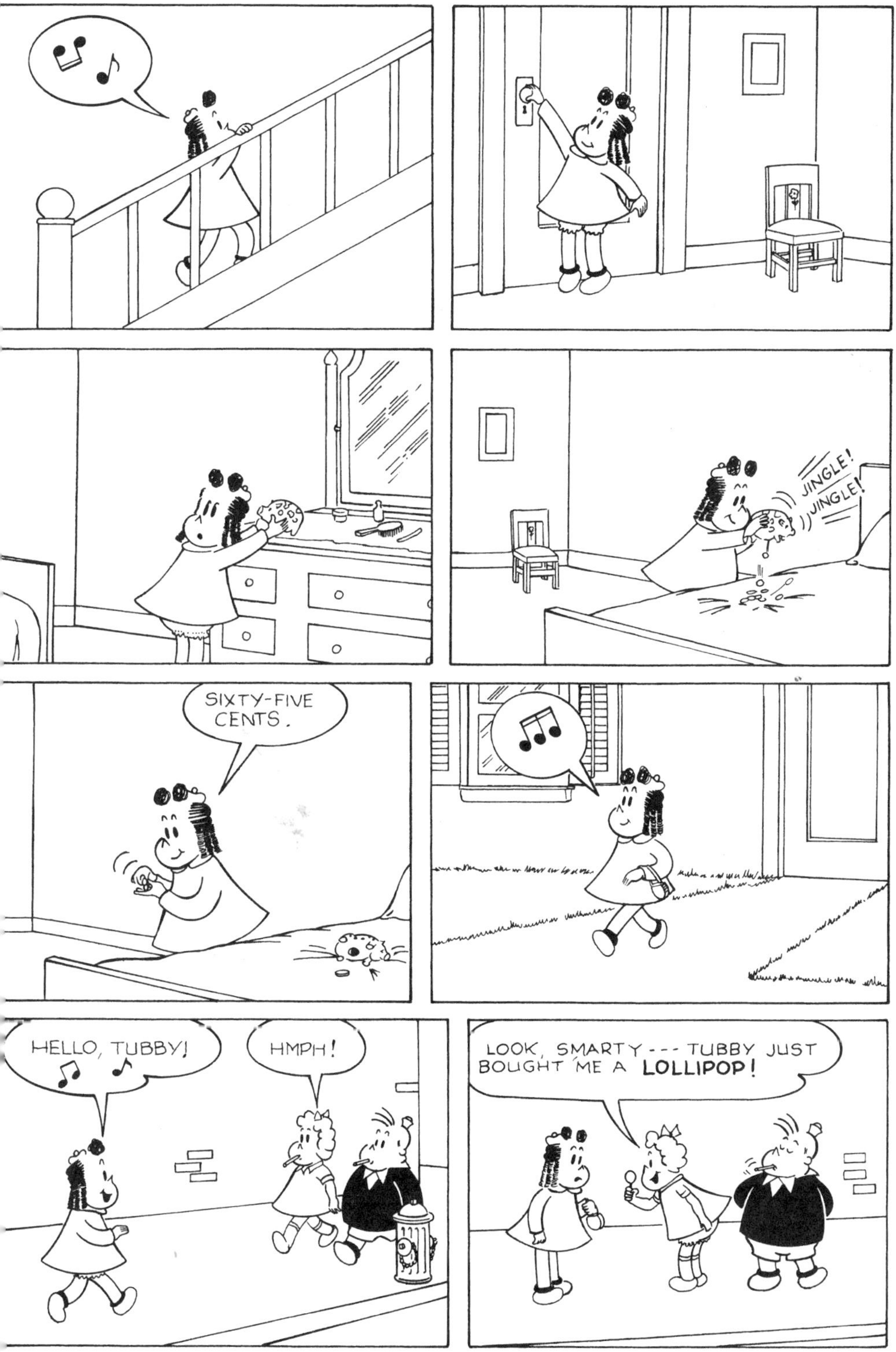
JINGLE!
JINGLE!
SIXTY-FIVE CENTS.
HELLO, TUBBY!
HMPH!
LOOK, SMARTY --- TUBBY JUST BOUGHT ME A LOLLIPOP!

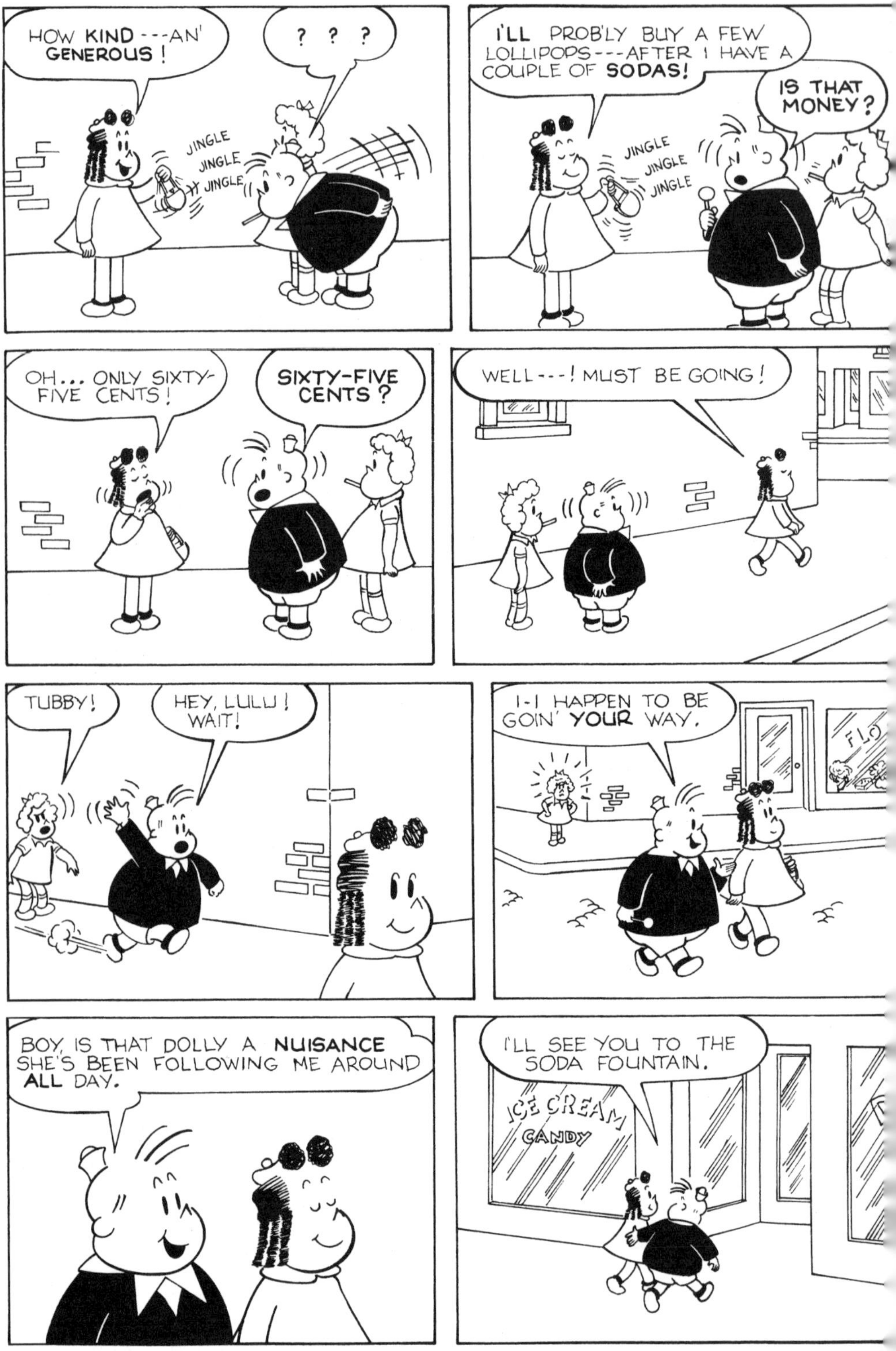
HOW KIND---AN' GENEROUS!
? ? ?
JINGLE JINGLE JINGLE
I'LL PROB'LY BUY A FEW LOLLIPOPS---AFTER I HAVE A COUPLE OF SODAS!
IS THAT MONEY?
JINGLE JINGLE JINGLE
OH... ONLY SIXTY-FIVE CENTS!
SIXTY-FIVE CENTS?
WELL---I MUST BE GOING!
TUBBY!
HEY, LULU! WAIT!
I-I HAPPEN TO BE GOIN' YOUR WAY.
BOY, IS THAT DOLLY A NUISANCE SHE'S BEEN FOLLOWING ME AROUND ALL DAY.
I'LL SEE YOU TO THE SODA FOUNTAIN.
ICE CREAM
CANDY

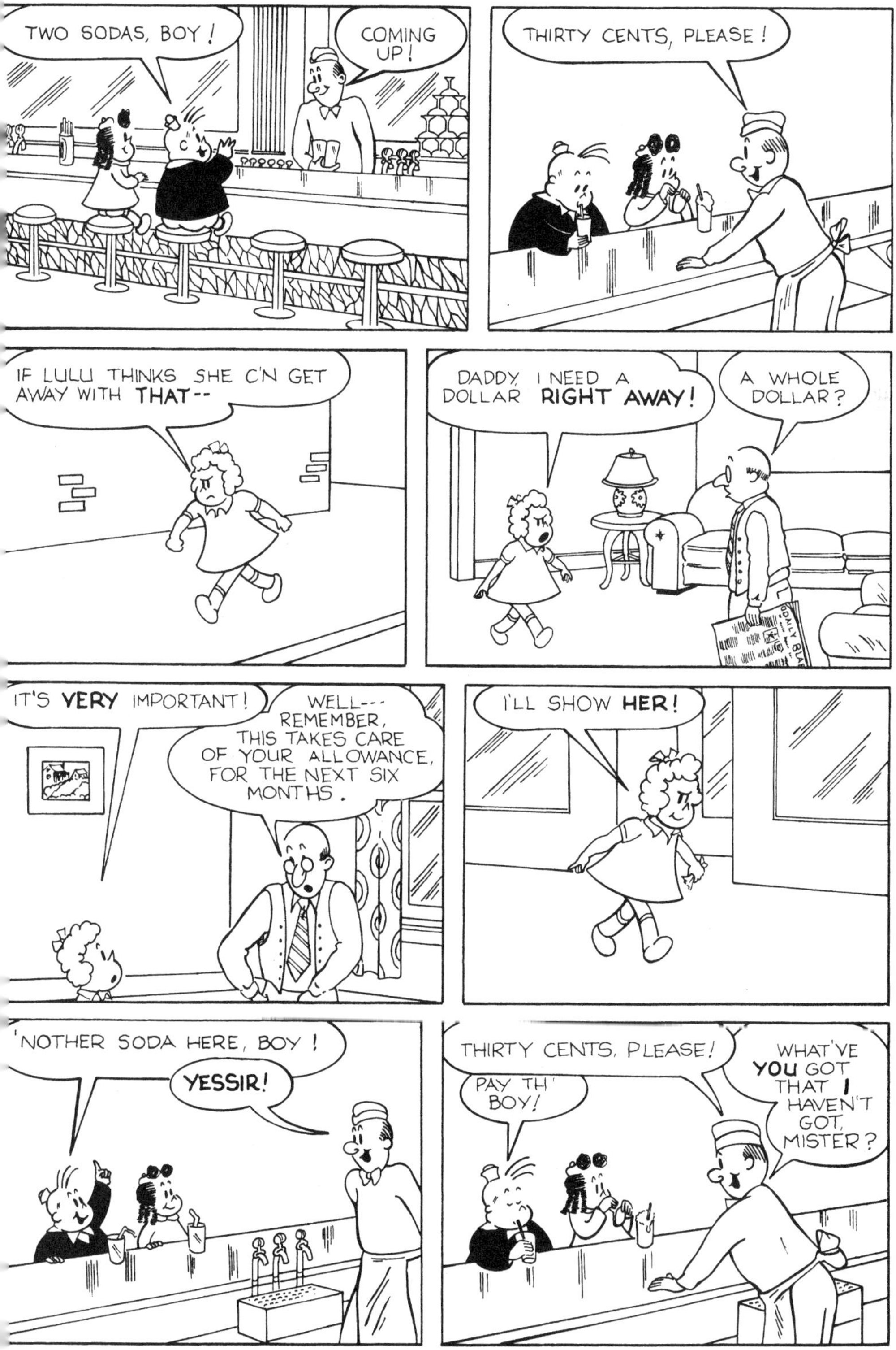
TWO SODAS, BOY!
COMING UP!
THIRTY CENTS, PLEASE!
IF LULU THINKS SHE C'N GET AWAY WITH THAT--
DADDY, I NEED A DOLLAR RIGHT AWAY!
A WHOLE DOLLAR?
DAILY BLAB
IT'S VERY IMPORTANT!
WELL--- REMEMBER, THIS TAKES CARE OF YOUR ALLOWANCE, FOR THE NEXT SIX MONTHS.
I'LL SHOW HER!
'NOTHER SODA HERE, BOY!
YESSIR!
THIRTY CENTS, PLEASE!
PAY TH' BOY!
WHAT'VE YOU GOT THAT I HAVEN'T GOT, MISTER?

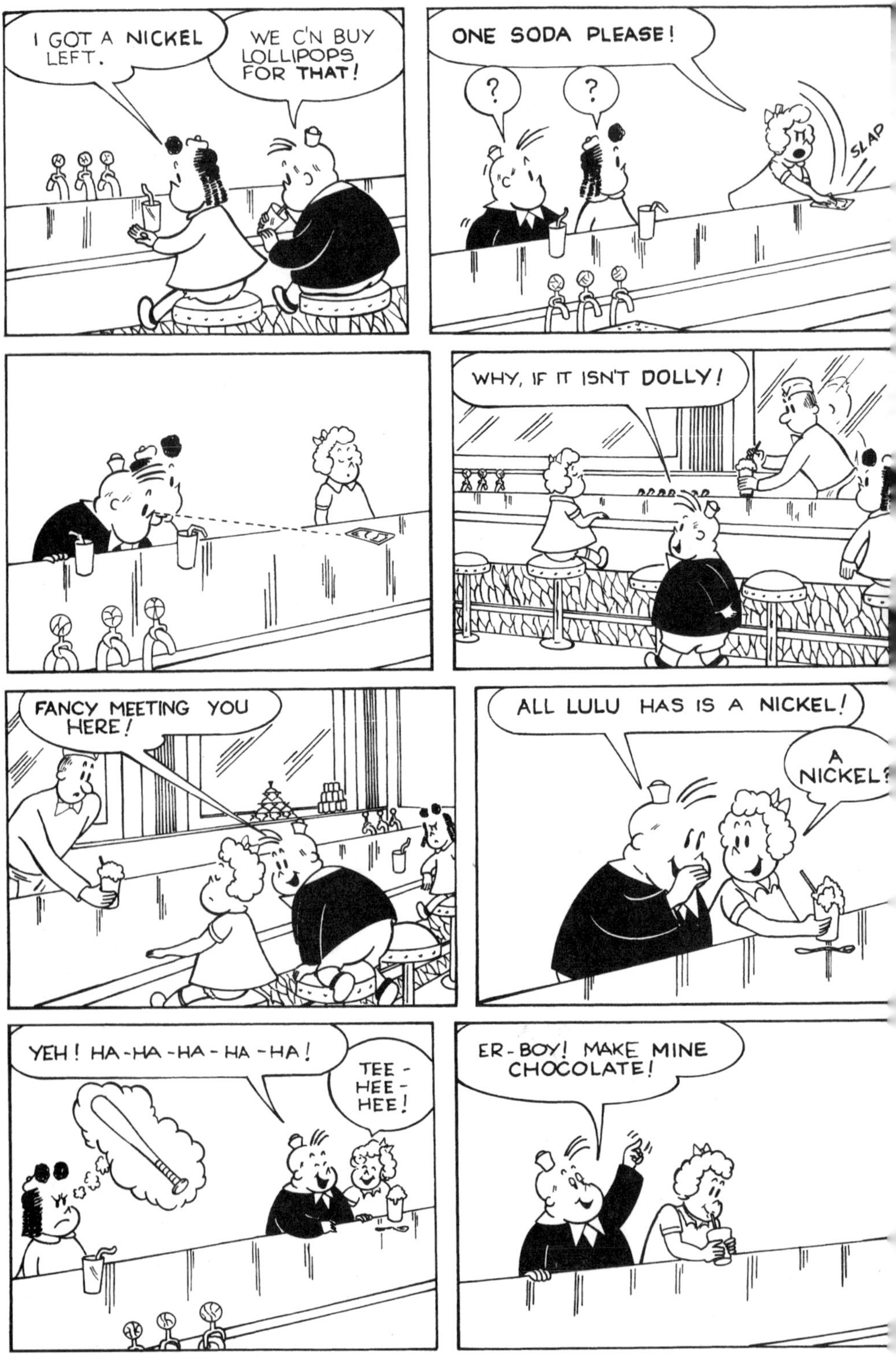
I GOT A NICKEL LEFT.
WE C'N BUY LOLLIPOPS FOR THAT!
ONE SODA PLEASE!
?
?
SLAP
WHY, IF IT ISN'T DOLLY!
FANCY MEETING YOU HERE!
ALL LULU HAS IS A NICKEL!
A NICKEL?
YEH! HA-HA-HA-HA-HA!
TEE-HEE-HEE!
ER-BOY! MAKE MINE CHOCOLATE!

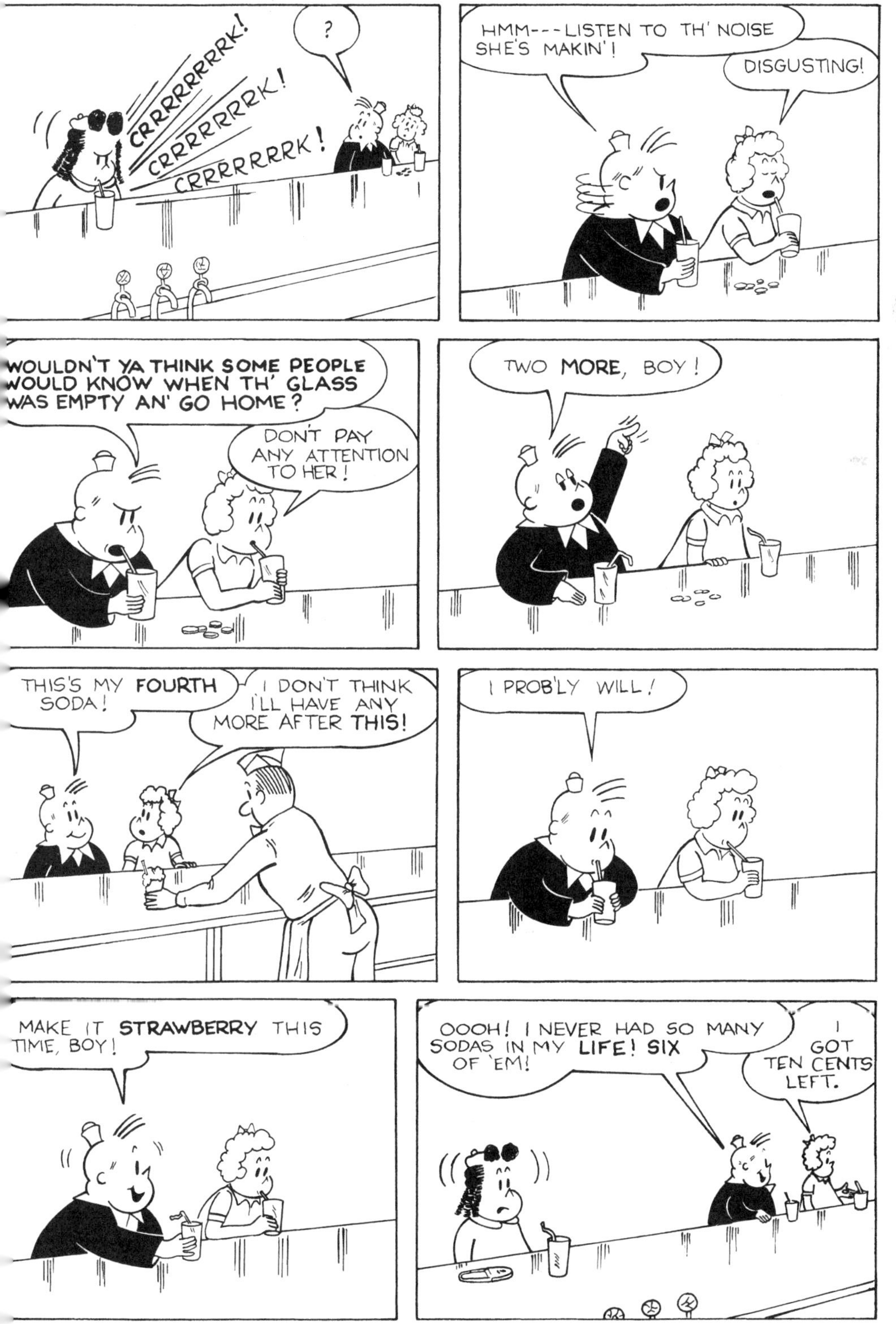
CRRRRRRRK!
CRRRRRRRK!
CRRRRRRRK!
?
HMM---LISTEN TO TH' NOISE SHE'S MAKIN'!
DISGUSTING!
WOULDN'T YA THINK SOME PEOPLE WOULD KNOW WHEN TH' GLASS WAS EMPTY AN' GO HOME?
DON'T PAY ANY ATTENTION TO HER!
TWO MORE, BOY!
THIS'S MY FOURTH SODA!
I DON'T THINK I'LL HAVE ANY MORE AFTER THIS!
I PROB'LY WILL!
MAKE IT STRAWBERRY THIS TIME, BOY!
OOOH! I NEVER HAD SO MANY SODAS IN MY LIFE! SIX OF 'EM!
I GOT TEN CENTS LEFT.

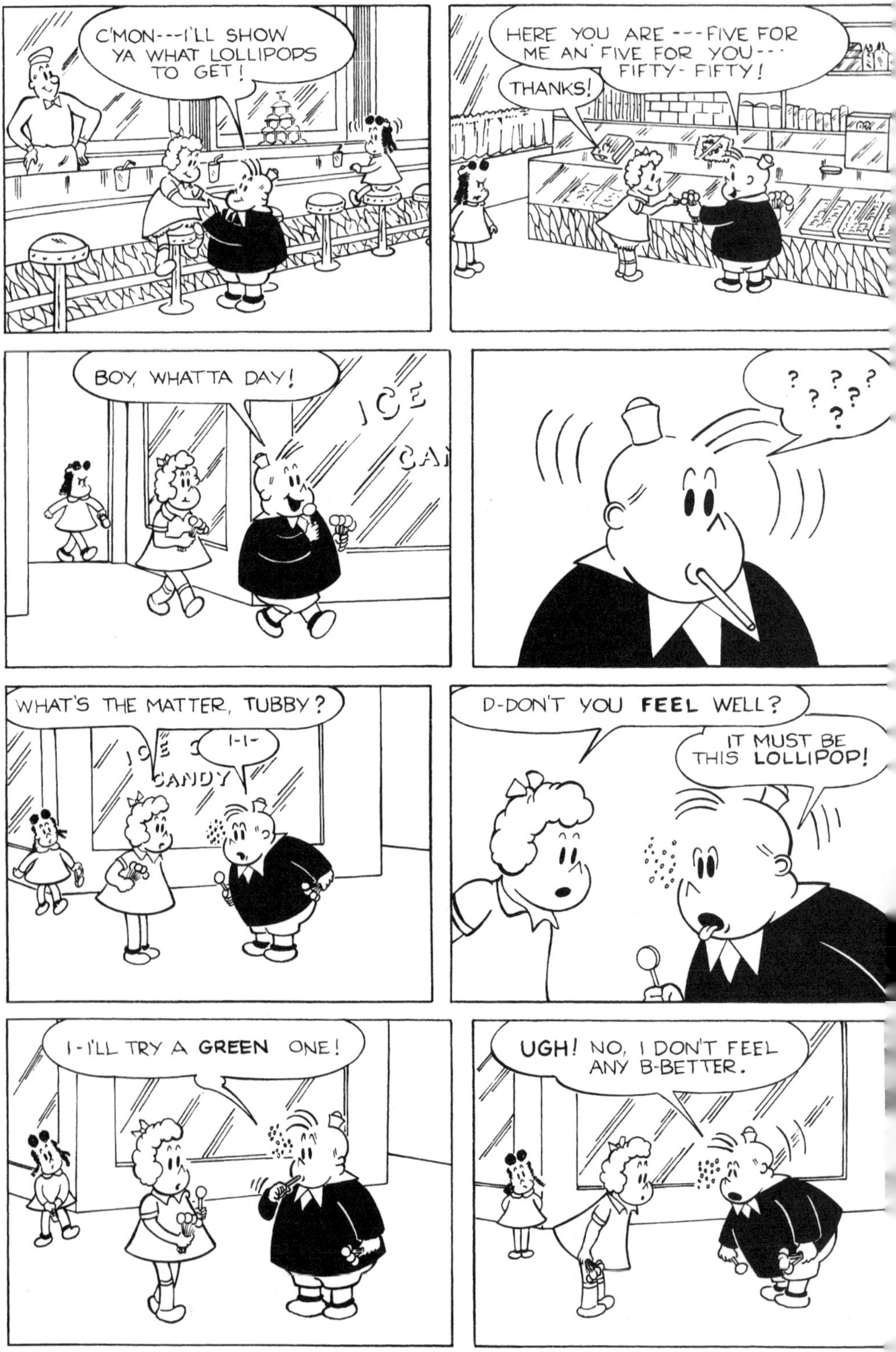
C'MON---I'LL SHOW YA WHAT LOLLIPOPS TO GET!
HERE YOU ARE---FIVE FOR ME AN' FIVE FOR YOU---FIFTY-FIFTY!
THANKS!
BOY, WHATTA DAY!
? ? ? ? ? ?
WHAT'S THE MATTER, TUBBY?
I-I-
D-DON'T YOU FEEL WELL?
IT MUST BE THIS LOLLIPOP!
I-I'LL TRY A GREEN ONE!
UGH! NO, I DON'T FEEL ANY B-BETTER.

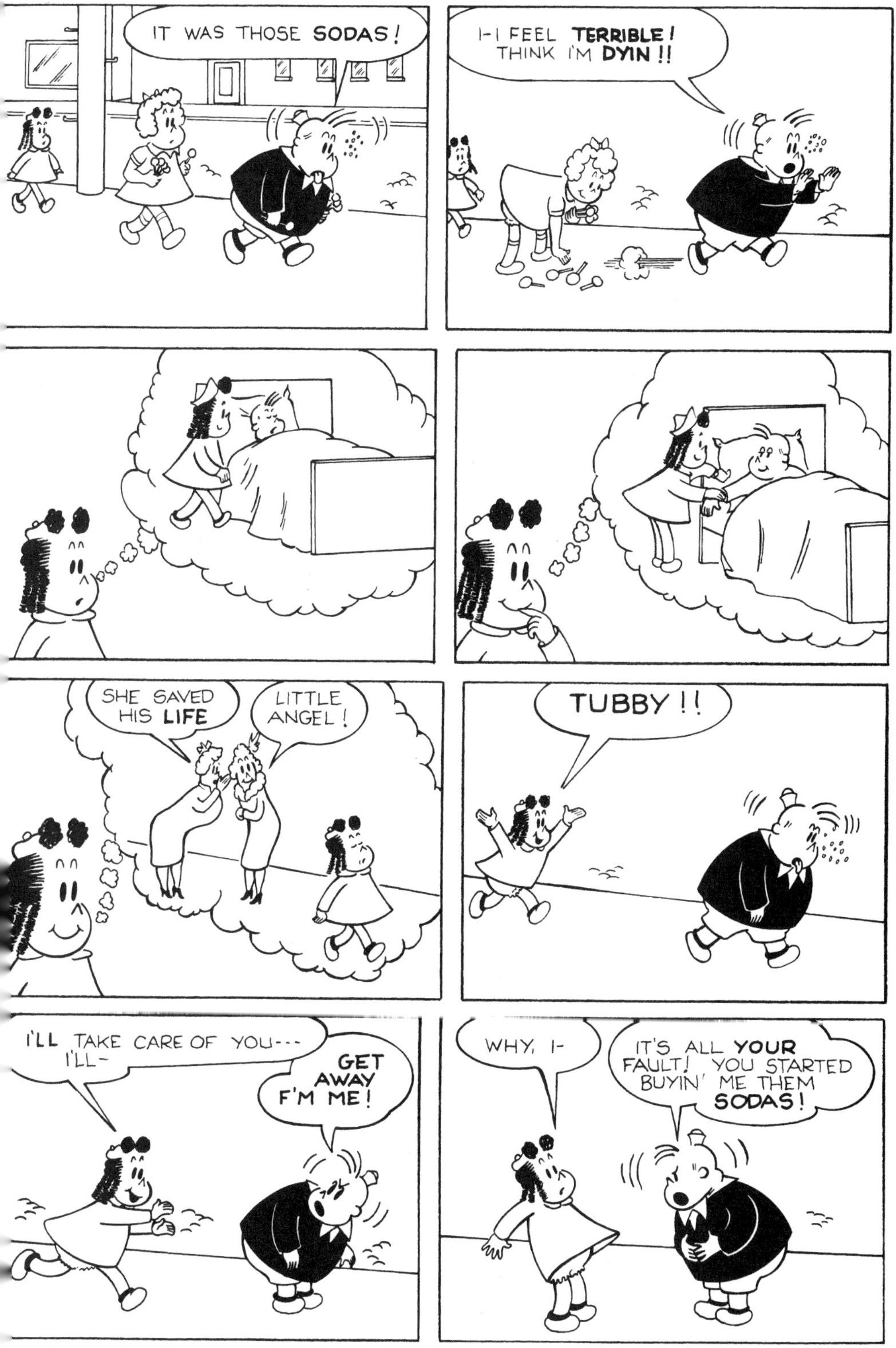

IT WAS THOSE SODAS!
I-I FEEL TERRIBLE! THINK I'M DYIN!!
SHE SAVED HIS LIFE
LITTLE ANGEL!
TUBBY!!
I'LL TAKE CARE OF YOU--- I'LL-
GET AWAY F'M ME!
WHY, I-
IT'S ALL YOUR FAULT! YOU STARTED BUYIN' ME THEM SODAS!

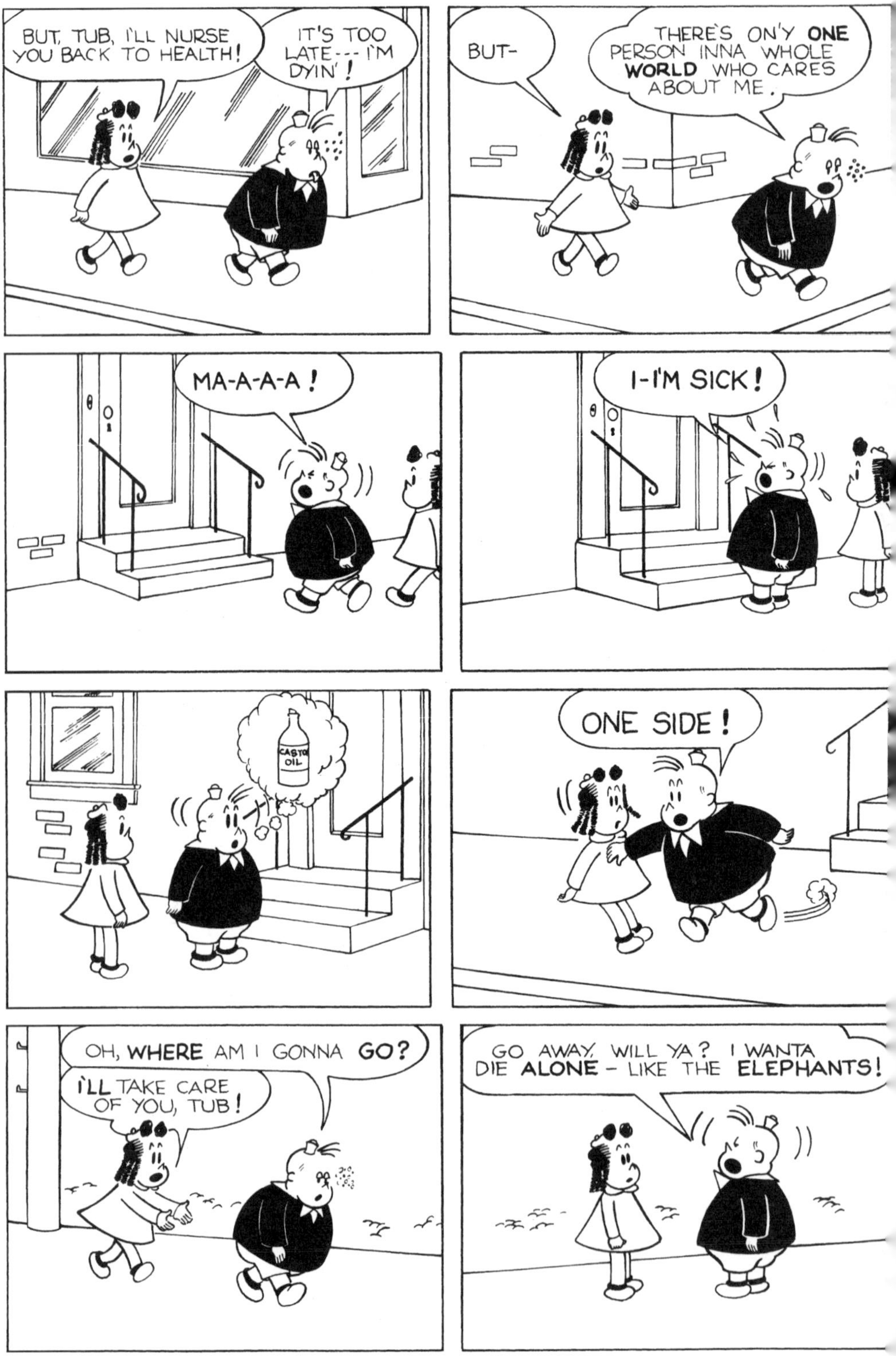
BUT, TUB, I'LL NURSE YOU BACK TO HEALTH!
IT'S TOO LATE--- I'M DYIN'!
BUT-
THERE'S ON'Y ONE PERSON INNA WHOLE WORLD WHO CARES ABOUT ME.
MA-A-A-A!
I-I'M SICK!
CASTO OIL
ONE SIDE!
OH, WHERE AM I GONNA GO?
I'LL TAKE CARE OF YOU, TUB!
GO AWAY, WILL YA? I WANTA DIE ALONE - LIKE THE ELEPHANTS!

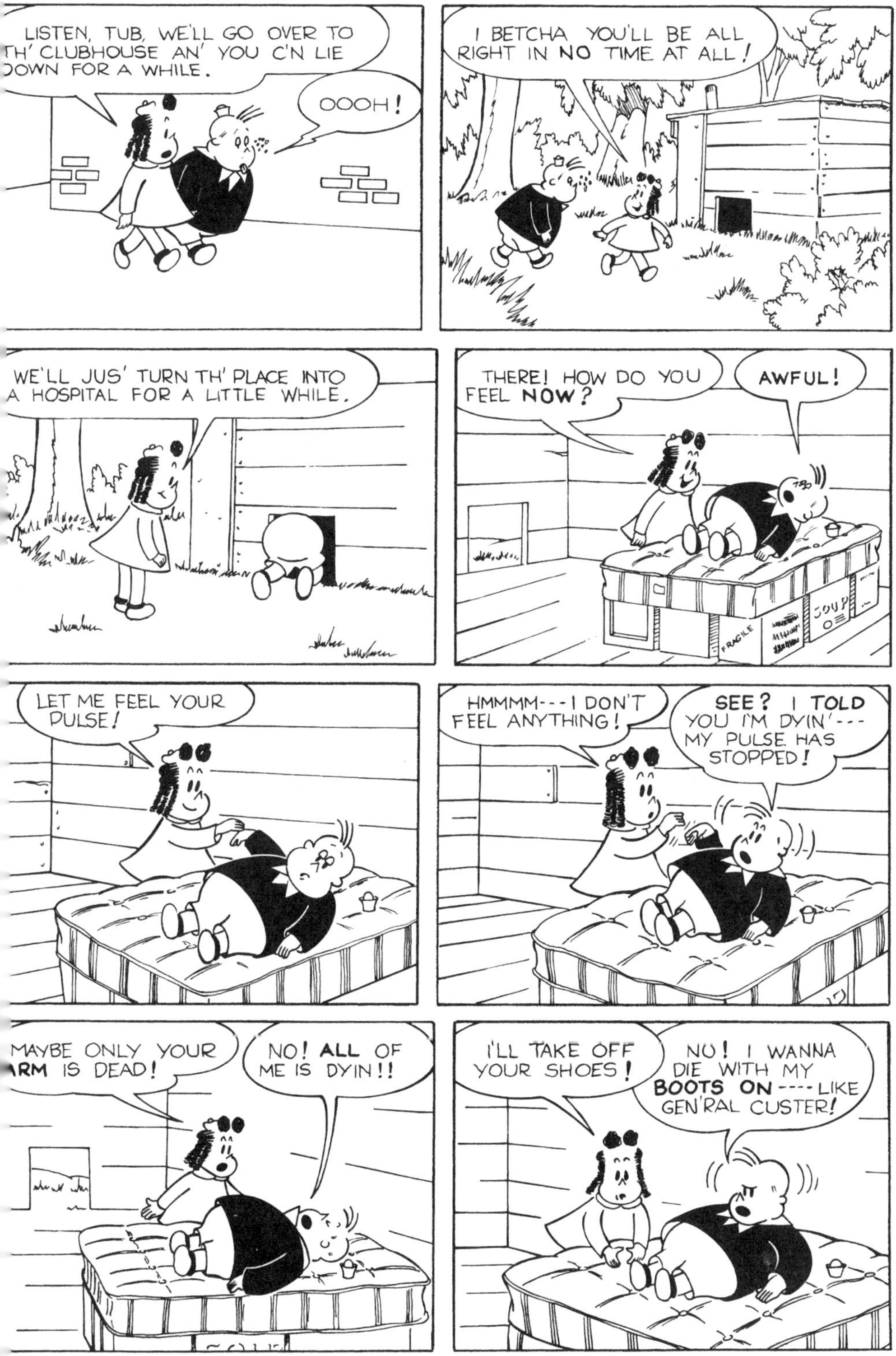

LISTEN, TUB, WE'LL GO OVER TO TH' CLUBHOUSE AN' YOU C'N LIE DOWN FOR A WHILE.
OOOH!
I BETCHA YOU'LL BE ALL RIGHT IN NO TIME AT ALL!
WE'LL JUS' TURN TH' PLACE INTO A HOSPITAL FOR A LITTLE WHILE.
THERE! HOW DO YOU FEEL NOW?
AWFUL!
FRAGILE
SOUP
LET ME FEEL YOUR PULSE!
HMMMM---I DON'T FEEL ANYTHING!
SEE? I TOLD YOU I'M DYIN'--- MY PULSE HAS STOPPED!
MAYBE ONLY YOUR ARM IS DEAD!
NO! ALL OF ME IS DYIN!!
I'LL TAKE OFF YOUR SHOES!
NO! I WANNA DIE WITH MY BOOTS ON ---- LIKE GEN'RAL CUSTER!

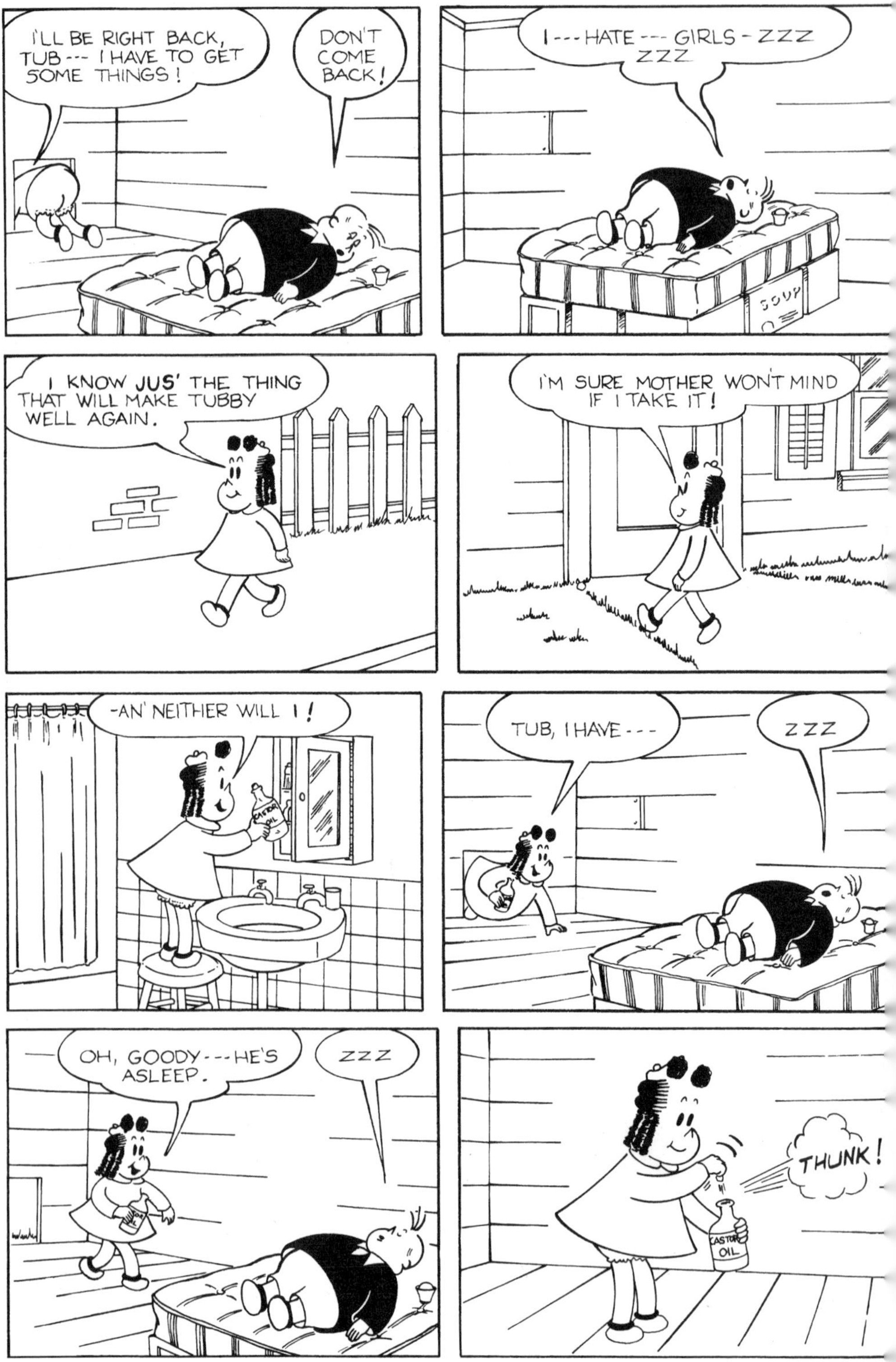
I'LL BE RIGHT BACK, TUB --- I HAVE TO GET SOME THINGS!
DON'T COME BACK!
I --- HATE --- GIRLS - ZZZ ZZZ
SOUP
I KNOW JUS' THE THING THAT WILL MAKE TUBBY WELL AGAIN.
I'M SURE MOTHER WON'T MIND IF I TAKE IT!
-AN' NEITHER WILL I!
CASTOR OIL
TUB, I HAVE ---
ZZZ
OH, GOODY --- HE'S ASLEEP.
ZZZ
THUNK!
CASTOR OIL

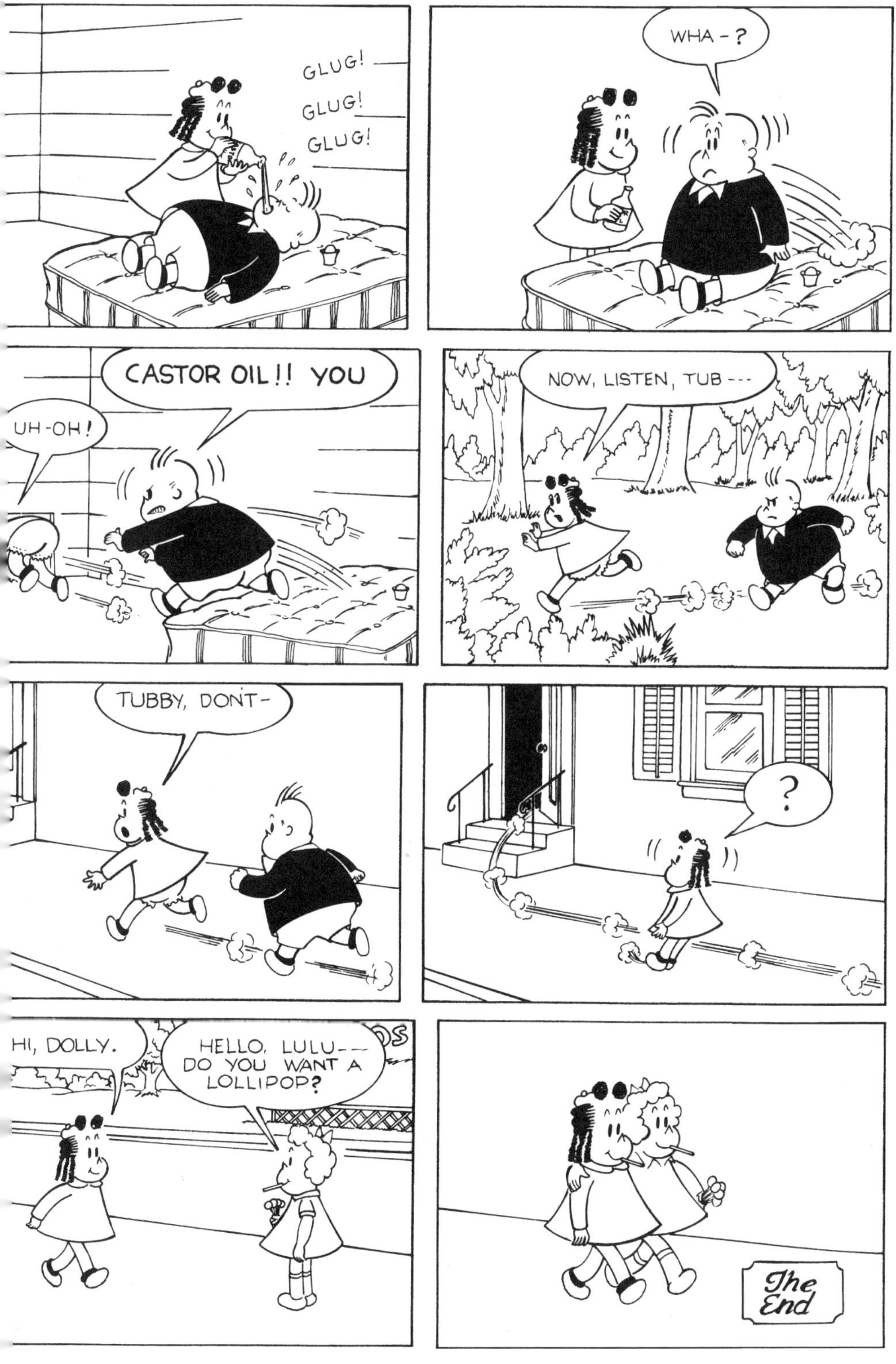
GLUG!
GLUG!
GLUG!
WHA-?
CASTOR OIL!! YOU
UH-OH!
NOW, LISTEN, TUB---
TUBBY, DON'T-
?
HI, DOLLY.
HELLO, LULU---
DO YOU WANT A
LOLLIPOP?
The End

marge's

Little Lulu

LULU'S LAMP

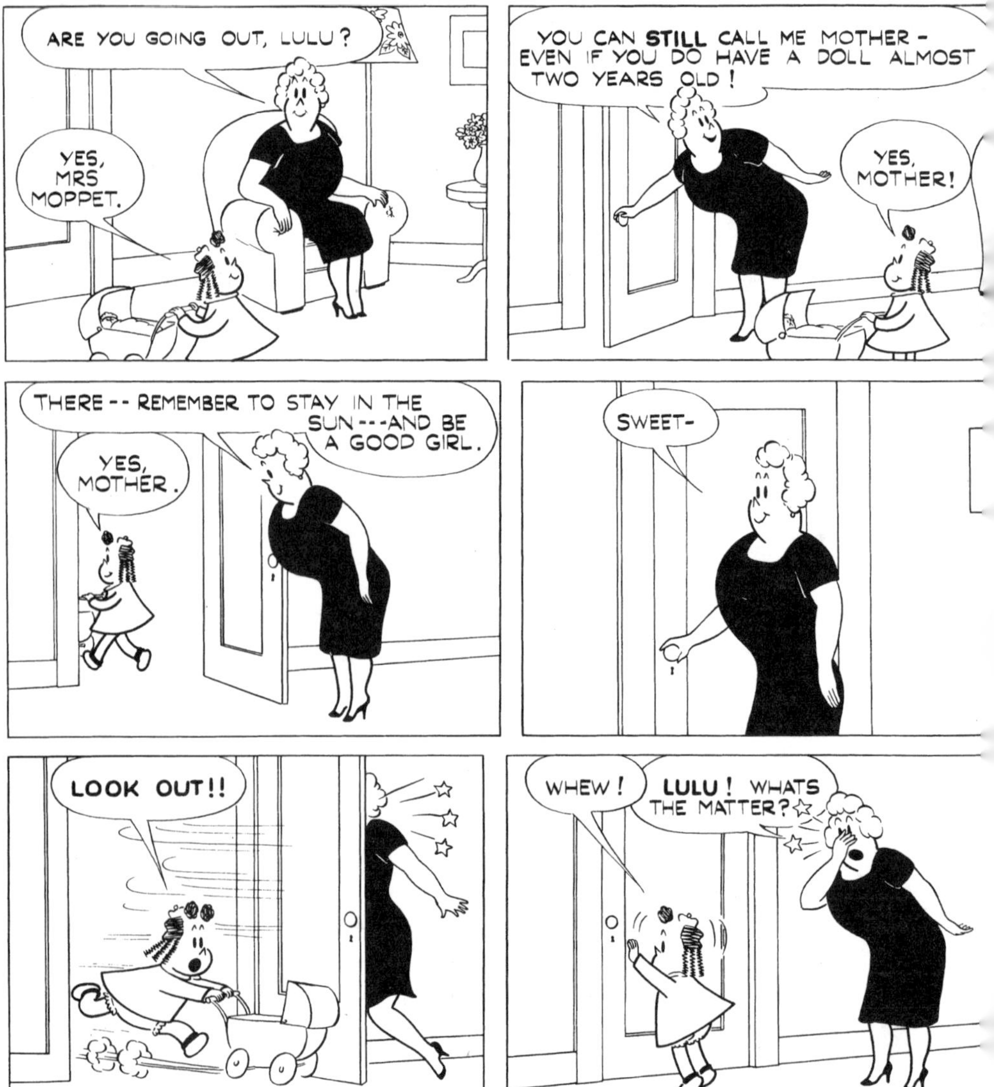
ARE YOU GOING OUT, LULU?
YES, MRS MOPPET.
YOU CAN **STILL** CALL ME MOTHER - EVEN IF YOU DO HAVE A DOLL ALMOST TWO YEARS OLD!
YES, MOTHER!
THERE -- REMEMBER TO STAY IN THE SUN---AND BE A GOOD GIRL.
YES, MOTHER.
SWEET-
LOOK OUT!!
WHEW!
LULU! WHATS THE MATTER?

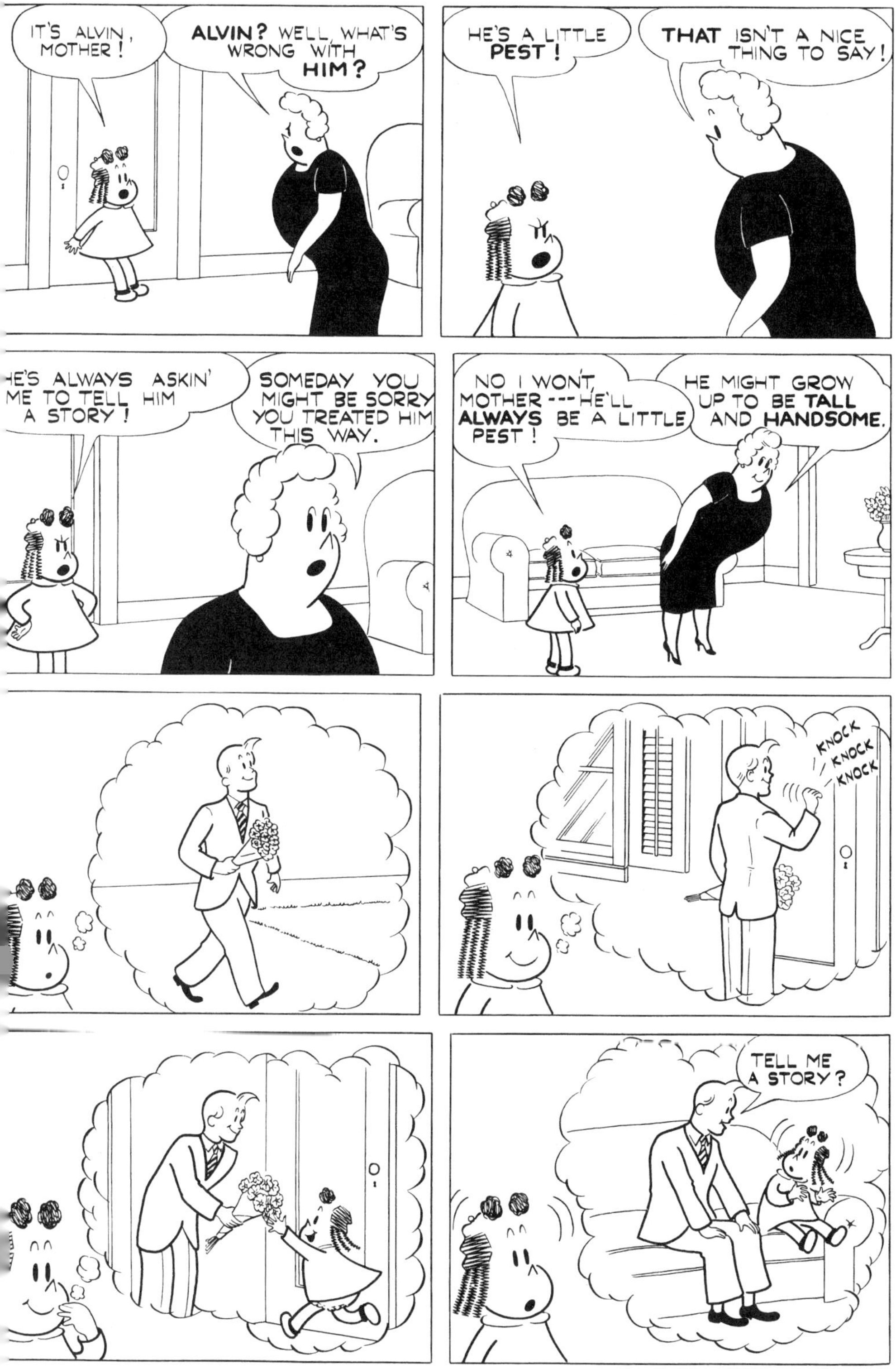
IT'S ALVIN, MOTHER!
ALVIN? WELL, WHAT'S WRONG WITH HIM?
HE'S A LITTLE PEST!
THAT ISN'T A NICE THING TO SAY!
HE'S ALWAYS ASKIN' ME TO TELL HIM A STORY!
SOMEDAY YOU MIGHT BE SORRY YOU TREATED HIM THIS WAY.
NO I WON'T, MOTHER --- HE'LL ALWAYS BE A LITTLE PEST!
HE MIGHT GROW UP TO BE TALL AND HANDSOME.
KNOCK
KNOCK
KNOCK
TELL ME A STORY?

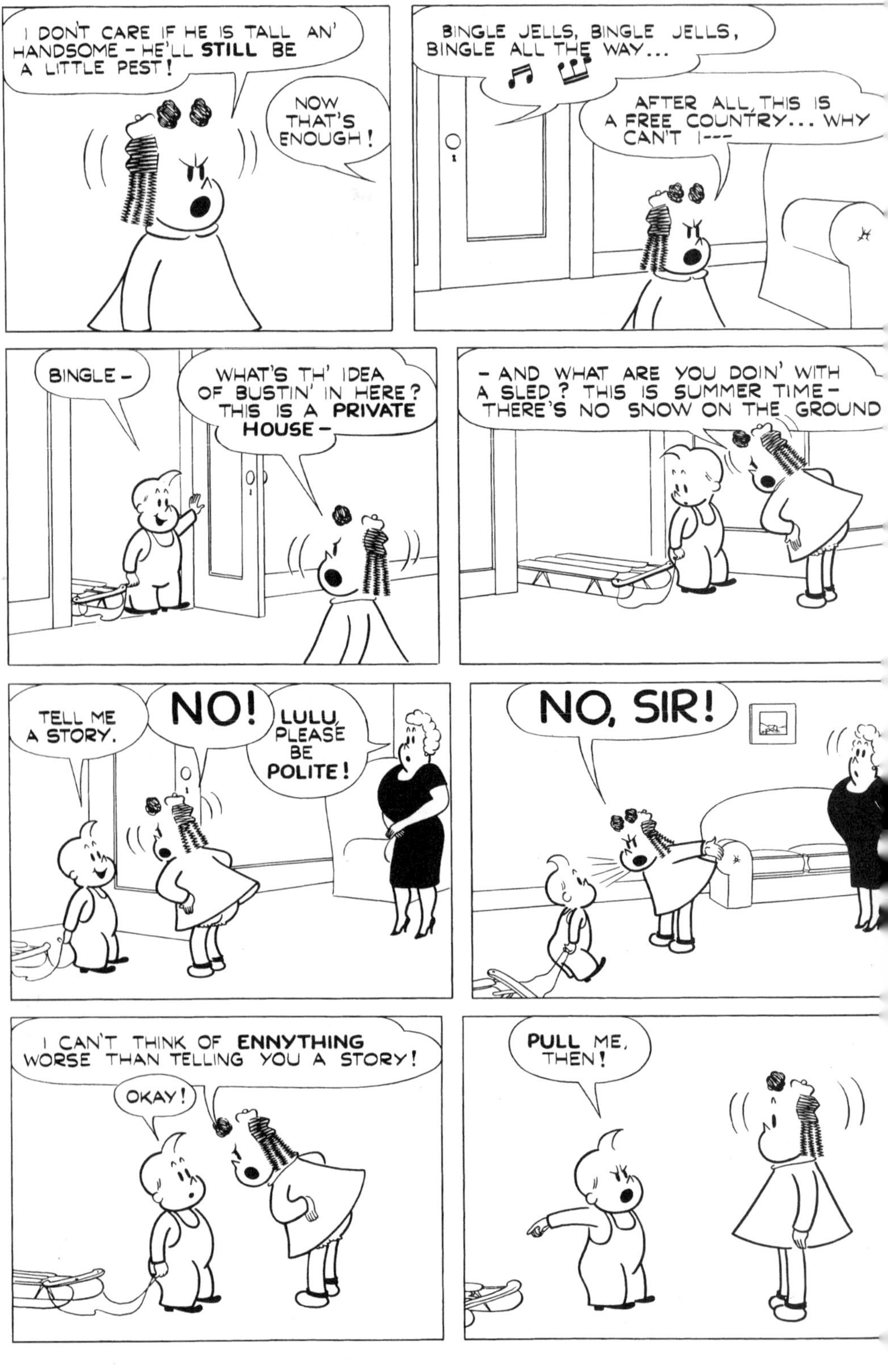
I DON'T CARE IF HE IS TALL AN' HANDSOME - HE'LL **STILL** BE A LITTLE PEST!
NOW THAT'S ENOUGH!
BINGLE JELLS, BINGLE JELLS, BINGLE ALL THE WAY...
AFTER ALL, THIS IS A FREE COUNTRY... WHY CAN'T I---
BINGLE -
WHAT'S TH' IDEA OF BUSTIN' IN HERE? THIS IS A **PRIVATE HOUSE** -
- AND WHAT ARE YOU DOIN' WITH A SLED? THIS IS SUMMER TIME - THERE'S NO SNOW ON THE GROUND
TELL ME A STORY.
NO!
LULU, PLEASE BE **POLITE**!
NO, SIR!
I CAN'T THINK OF **ENNYTHING** WORSE THAN TELLING YOU A STORY!
OKAY!
PULL ME, THEN!

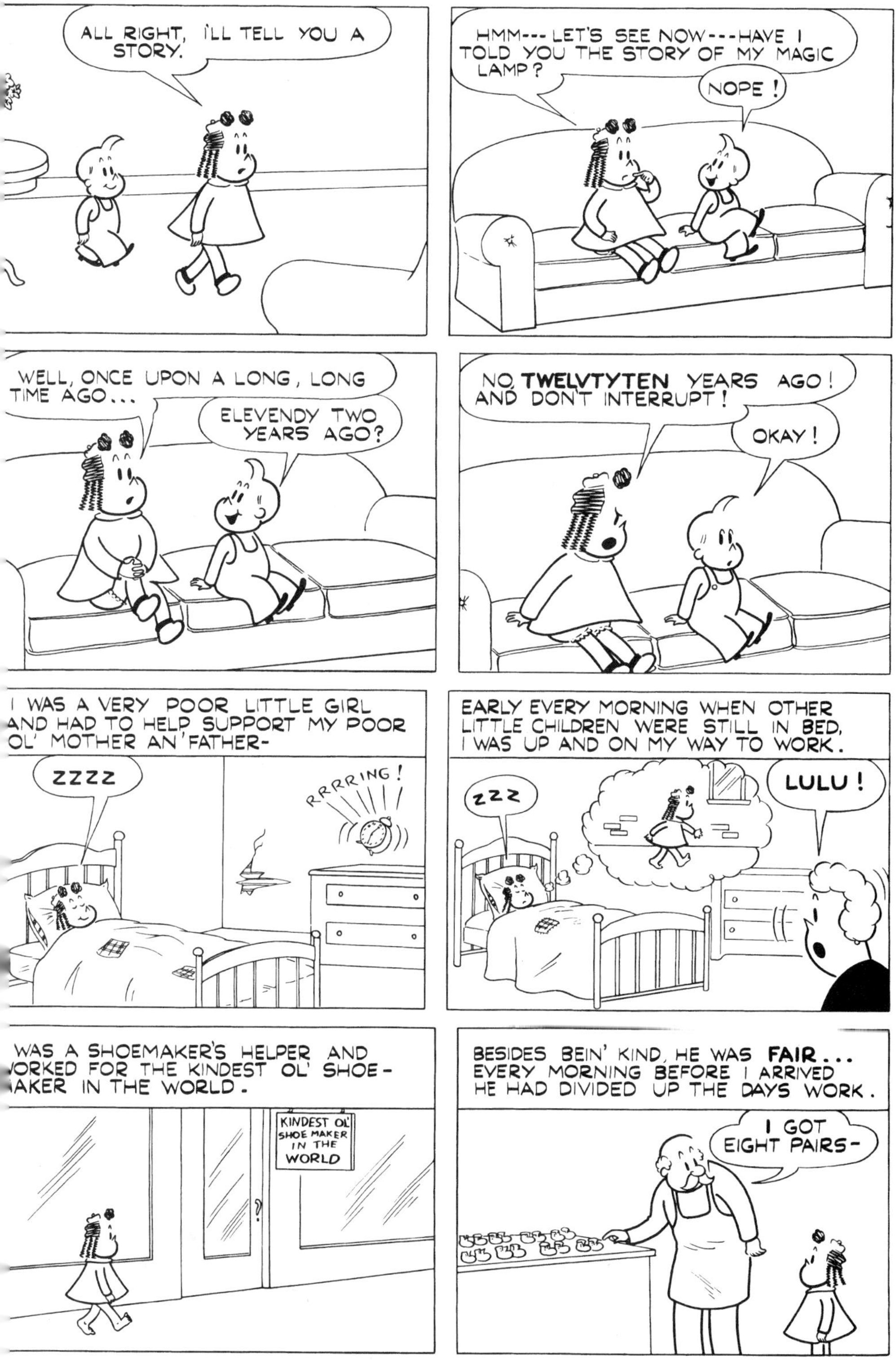
ALL RIGHT, I'LL TELL YOU A STORY.
HMM--- LET'S SEE NOW---HAVE I TOLD YOU THE STORY OF MY MAGIC LAMP?
NOPE!
WELL, ONCE UPON A LONG, LONG TIME AGO...
ELEVENDY TWO YEARS AGO?
NO, TWELVTYTEN YEARS AGO! AND DON'T INTERRUPT!
OKAY!
I WAS A VERY POOR LITTLE GIRL AND HAD TO HELP SUPPORT MY POOR OL' MOTHER AN' FATHER-
ZZZZ
RRRRING!
EARLY EVERY MORNING WHEN OTHER LITTLE CHILDREN WERE STILL IN BED, I WAS UP AND ON MY WAY TO WORK.
ZZZ
LULU!
WAS A SHOEMAKER'S HELPER AND WORKED FOR THE KINDEST OL' SHOE-MAKER IN THE WORLD.
KINDEST OL' SHOE MAKER IN THE WORLD
BESIDES BEIN' KIND, HE WAS FAIR... EVERY MORNING BEFORE I ARRIVED HE HAD DIVIDED UP THE DAYS WORK.
I GOT EIGHT PAIRS-

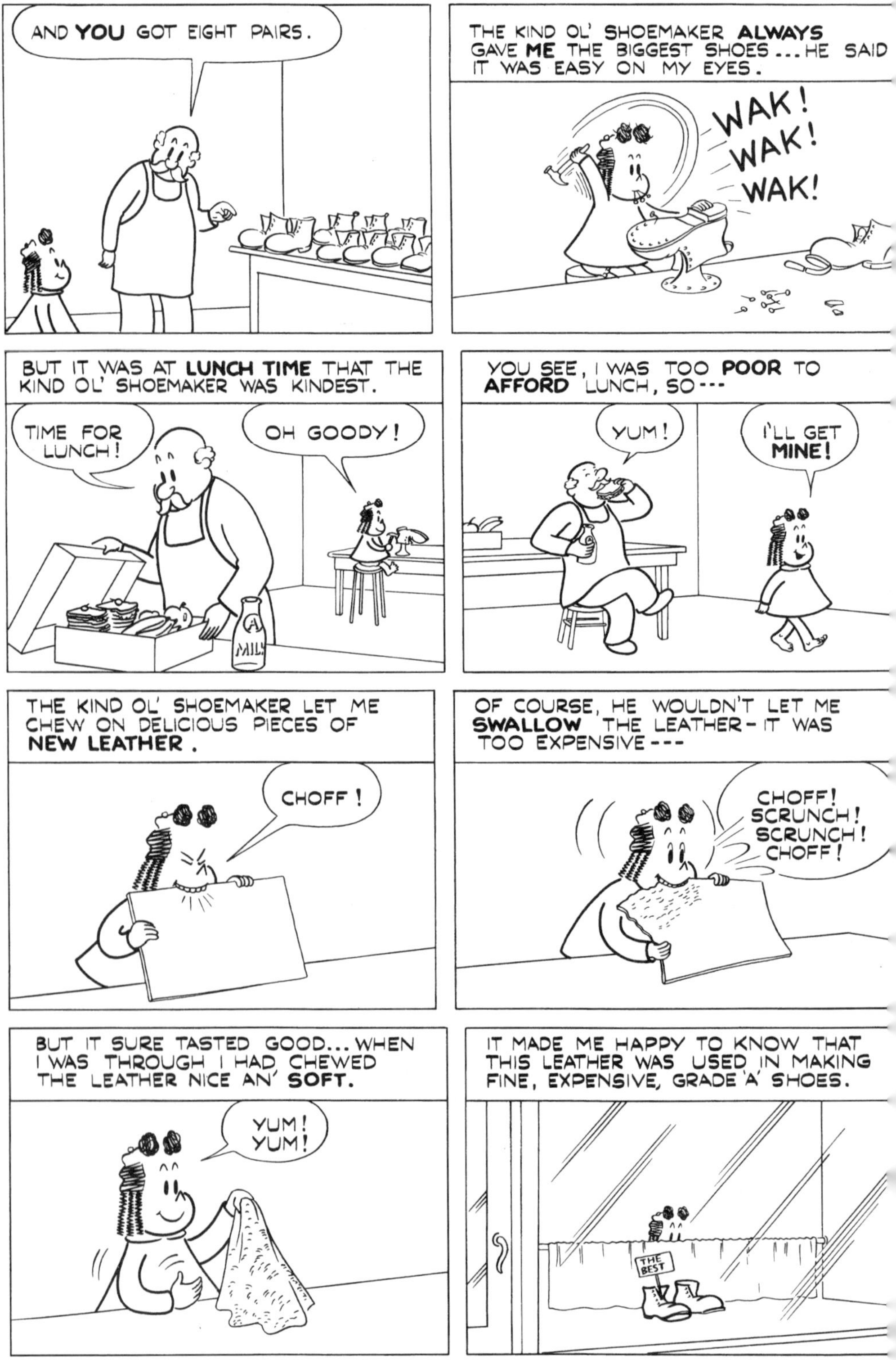

AND YOU GOT EIGHT PAIRS.
THE KIND OL' SHOEMAKER ALWAYS GAVE ME THE BIGGEST SHOES... HE SAID IT WAS EASY ON MY EYES.
WAK! WAK! WAK!
BUT IT WAS AT LUNCH TIME THAT THE KIND OL' SHOEMAKER WAS KINDEST.
TIME FOR LUNCH!
OH GOODY!
YOU SEE, I WAS TOO POOR TO AFFORD LUNCH, SO---
YUM!
I'LL GET MINE!
THE KIND OL' SHOEMAKER LET ME CHEW ON DELICIOUS PIECES OF NEW LEATHER.
CHOFF!
OF COURSE, HE WOULDN'T LET ME SWALLOW THE LEATHER – IT WAS TOO EXPENSIVE---
CHOFF! SCRUNCH! SCRUNCH! CHOFF!
BUT IT SURE TASTED GOOD... WHEN I WAS THROUGH I HAD CHEWED THE LEATHER NICE AN' SOFT.
YUM! YUM!
IT MADE ME HAPPY TO KNOW THAT THIS LEATHER WAS USED IN MAKING FINE, EXPENSIVE, GRADE 'A' SHOES.
THE BEST

ONE DAY AFTER I HAD MENDED 26 PAIRS OF SHOES, THE KIND OL' SHOEMAKER NOTICED THAT I LOOKED A LITTLE TIRED.

HIS HEART MUST HAVE BEEN FULL OF PITY BECAUSE HE SUGGESTED THAT WHAT I PROB'LY NEEDED WAS A LITTLE FRESH AIR.

···FRESH AIR! OH··KIND OL' SHOEMAKER.

AND EVEN THOUGH IT WAS **TWO WHOLE MINUTES** BEFORE CLOSING TIME, HE TOLD ME TO GO HOME.

GO AHEAD, GO AHEAD! DON'T THANK ME!

OH!

AND ON YOUR WAY YOU CAN DELIVER THESE NEW SHOES TO MR. GIGGLEWIG.

OH, I'D BE **GLAD** TO!

MR. GIGGLEWIG LIVED MILES AWAY IN THE OPPOSITE DIRECTION TO WHERE I LIVED.

BUT I WAS HAPPY TO RUN THE ERRAND FOR THE KIND OL' SHOEMAKER.

IMAGINE LETTING ME OFF **TWO WHOLE** MINUTES EARLY!

THE FALLING SNOW MADE IT DIFFICULT TO SEE WHERE I WAS GOING.

BUT THEN I REMEMBERED THAT THE TROLLEY CAR RAN RIGHT TO MR. GIGGLEWIG'S DOOR, TEN MILES AWAY.

SNAP!

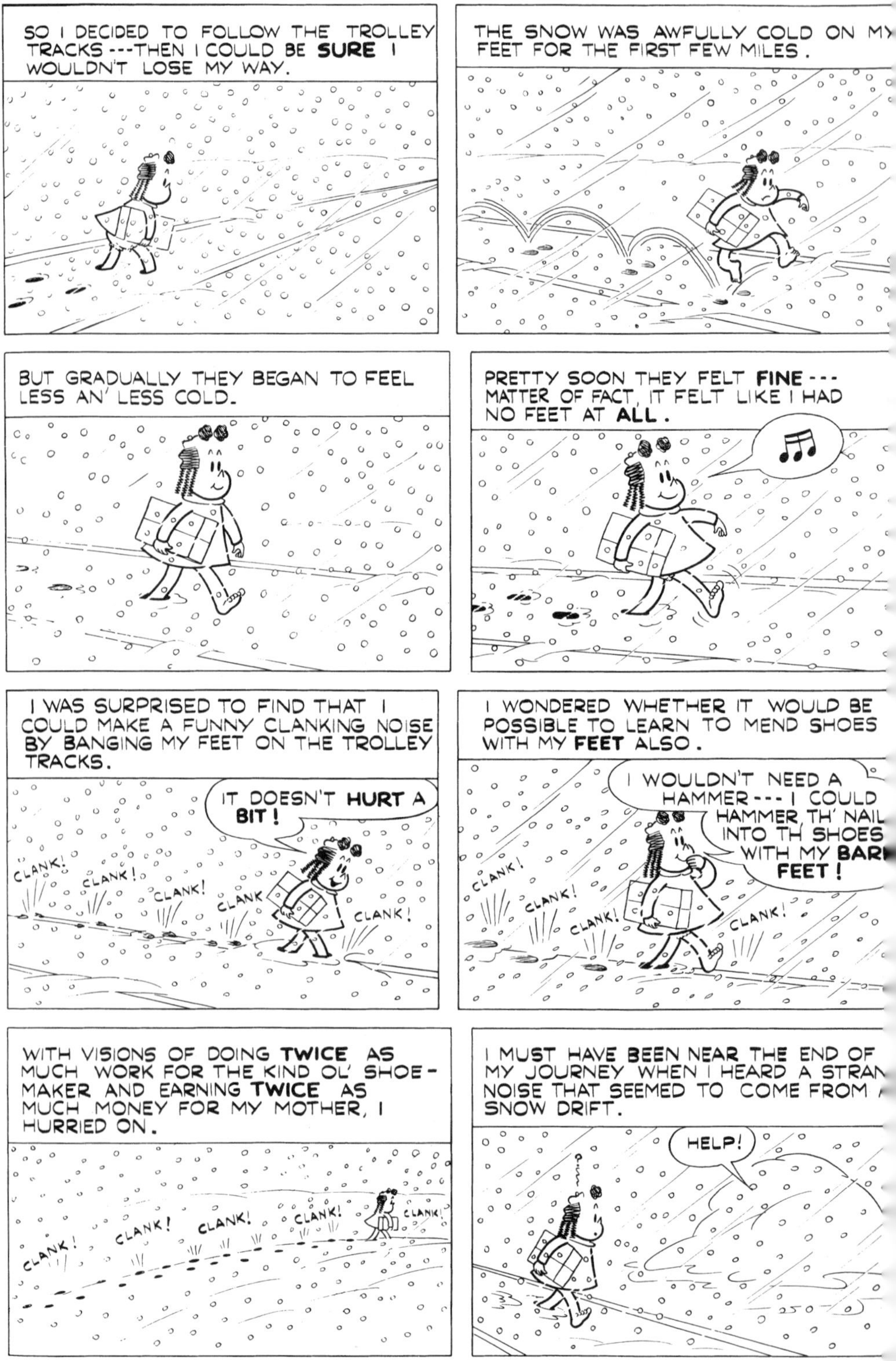
SO I DECIDED TO FOLLOW THE TROLLEY TRACKS---THEN I COULD BE **SURE** I WOULDN'T LOSE MY WAY.
THE SNOW WAS AWFULLY COLD ON MY FEET FOR THE FIRST FEW MILES.
BUT GRADUALLY THEY BEGAN TO FEEL LESS AN' LESS COLD.
PRETTY SOON THEY FELT **FINE**--- MATTER OF FACT, IT FELT LIKE I HAD NO FEET AT **ALL**.
I WAS SURPRISED TO FIND THAT I COULD MAKE A FUNNY CLANKING NOISE BY BANGING MY FEET ON THE TROLLEY TRACKS.
IT DOESN'T **HURT** A **BIT**!
CLANK! CLANK! CLANK! CLANK CLANK!
I WONDERED WHETHER IT WOULD BE POSSIBLE TO LEARN TO MEND SHOES WITH MY **FEET** ALSO.
I WOULDN'T NEED A HAMMER--- I COULD HAMMER TH' NAIL INTO TH SHOES WITH MY **BAR** **FEET**!
CLANK! CLANK! CLANK! CLANK!
WITH VISIONS OF DOING **TWICE** AS MUCH WORK FOR THE KIND OL' SHOE-MAKER AND EARNING **TWICE** AS MUCH MONEY FOR MY MOTHER, I HURRIED ON.
CLANK! CLANK! CLANK! CLANK! CLANK!
I MUST HAVE BEEN NEAR THE END OF MY JOURNEY WHEN I HEARD A STRAN NOISE THAT SEEMED TO COME FROM SNOW DRIFT.
HELP!

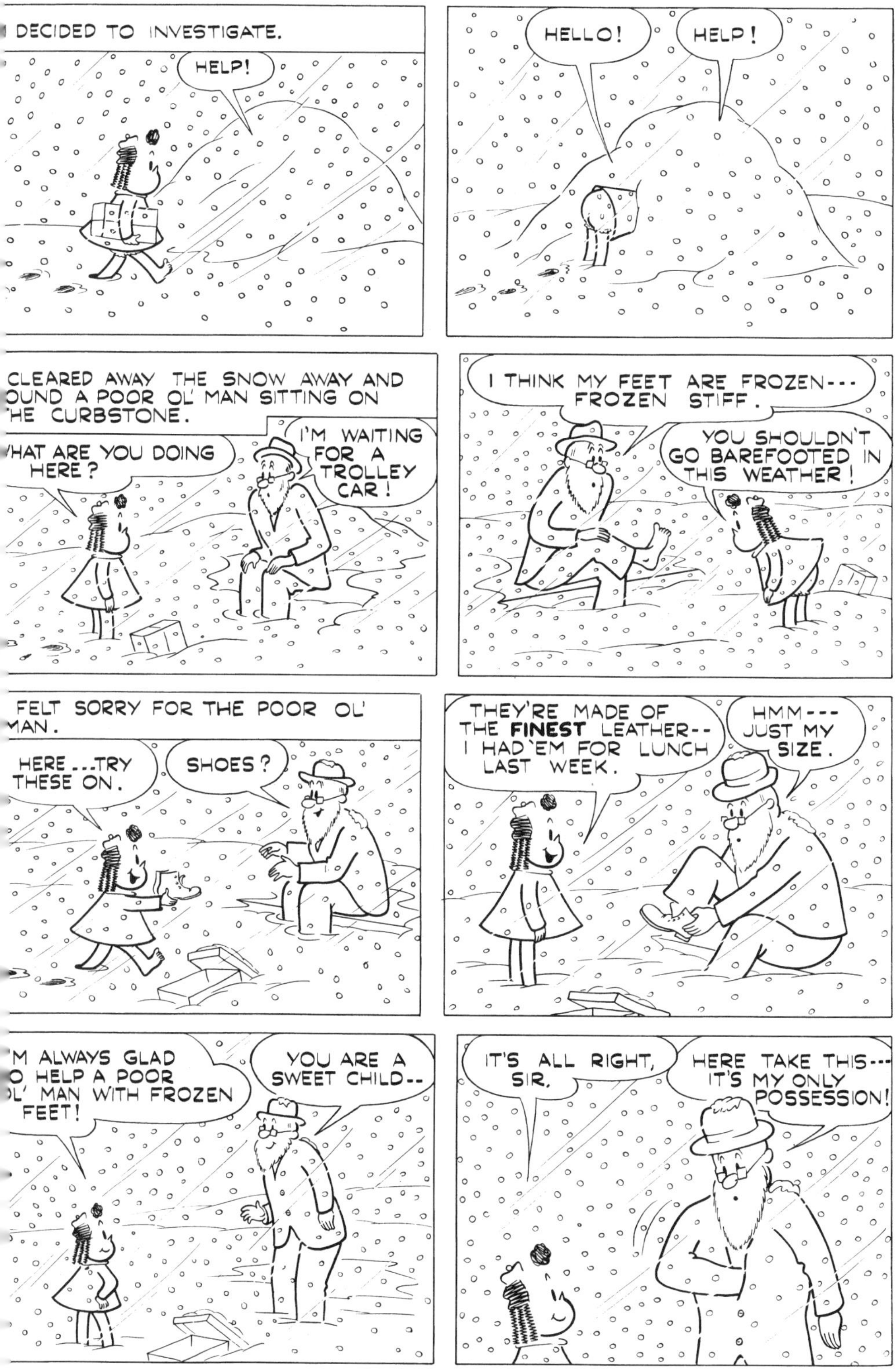

DECIDED TO INVESTIGATE.
HELP!
HELLO!
HELP!
CLEARED AWAY THE SNOW AWAY AND
OUND A POOR OL' MAN SITTING ON
HE CURBSTONE.
HAT ARE YOU DOING HERE?
I'M WAITING FOR A TROLLEY CAR!
I THINK MY FEET ARE FROZEN--- FROZEN STIFF.
YOU SHOULDN'T GO BAREFOOTED IN THIS WEATHER!
FELT SORRY FOR THE POOR OL' MAN.
HERE...TRY THESE ON.
SHOES?
THEY'RE MADE OF THE FINEST LEATHER-- I HAD'EM FOR LUNCH LAST WEEK.
HMM--- JUST MY SIZE.
M ALWAYS GLAD O HELP A POOR L' MAN WITH FROZEN FEET!
YOU ARE A SWEET CHILD--
IT'S ALL RIGHT, SIR.
HERE TAKE THIS--- IT'S MY ONLY POSSESSION!

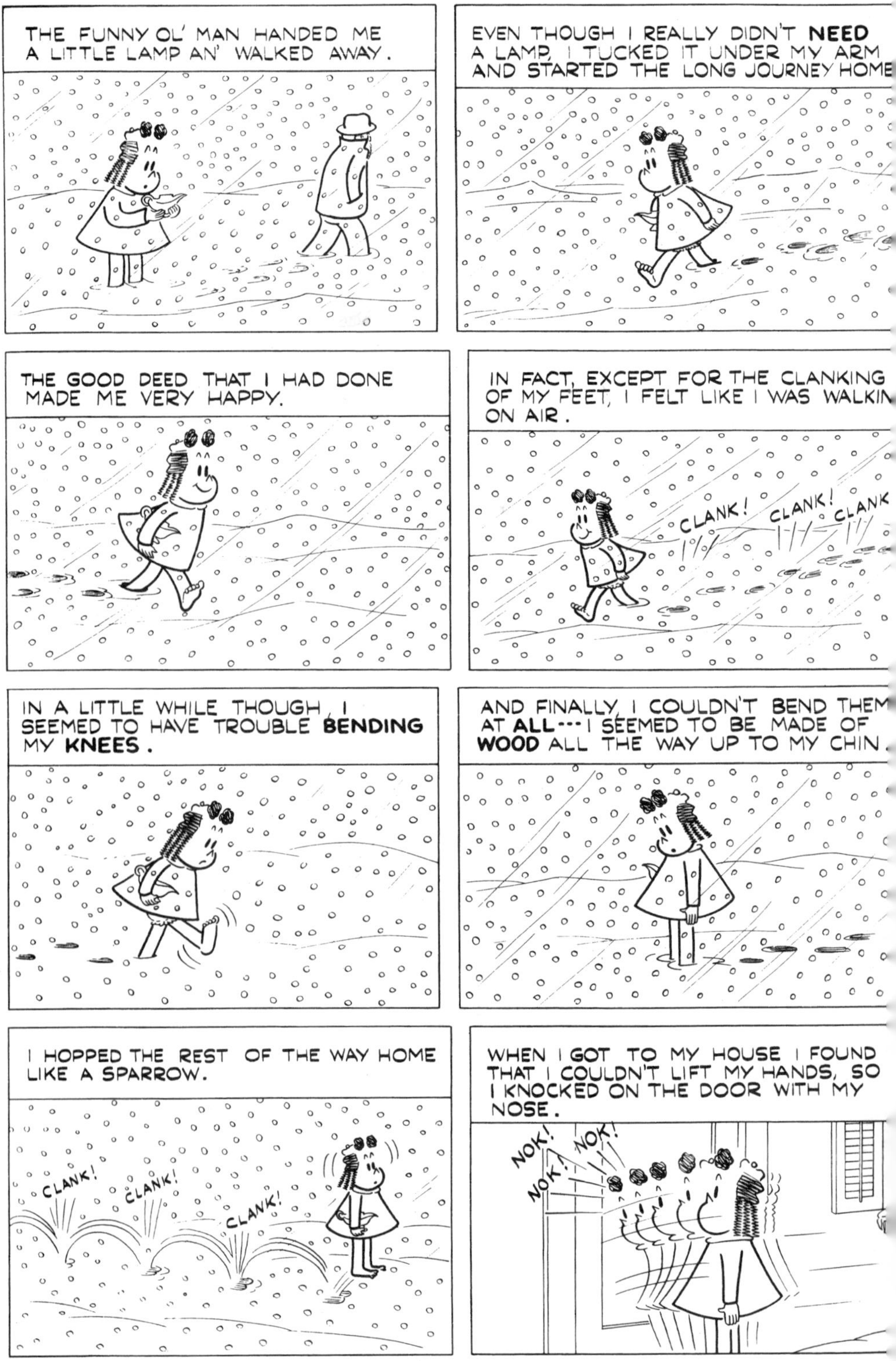
THE FUNNY OL' MAN HANDED ME A LITTLE LAMP AN' WALKED AWAY.
EVEN THOUGH I REALLY DIDN'T NEED A LAMP, I TUCKED IT UNDER MY ARM AND STARTED THE LONG JOURNEY HOME
THE GOOD DEED THAT I HAD DONE MADE ME VERY HAPPY.
IN FACT, EXCEPT FOR THE CLANKING OF MY FEET, I FELT LIKE I WAS WALKIN ON AIR.
CLANK!
CLANK!
CLANK
IN A LITTLE WHILE THOUGH, I SEEMED TO HAVE TROUBLE BENDING MY KNEES.
AND FINALLY, I COULDN'T BEND THEM AT ALL··· I SEEMED TO BE MADE OF WOOD ALL THE WAY UP TO MY CHIN.
I HOPPED THE REST OF THE WAY HOME LIKE A SPARROW.
CLANK!
CLANK!
CLANK!
WHEN I GOT TO MY HOUSE I FOUND THAT I COULDN'T LIFT MY HANDS, SO I KNOCKED ON THE DOOR WITH MY NOSE.
NOK!
NOK!
NOK!

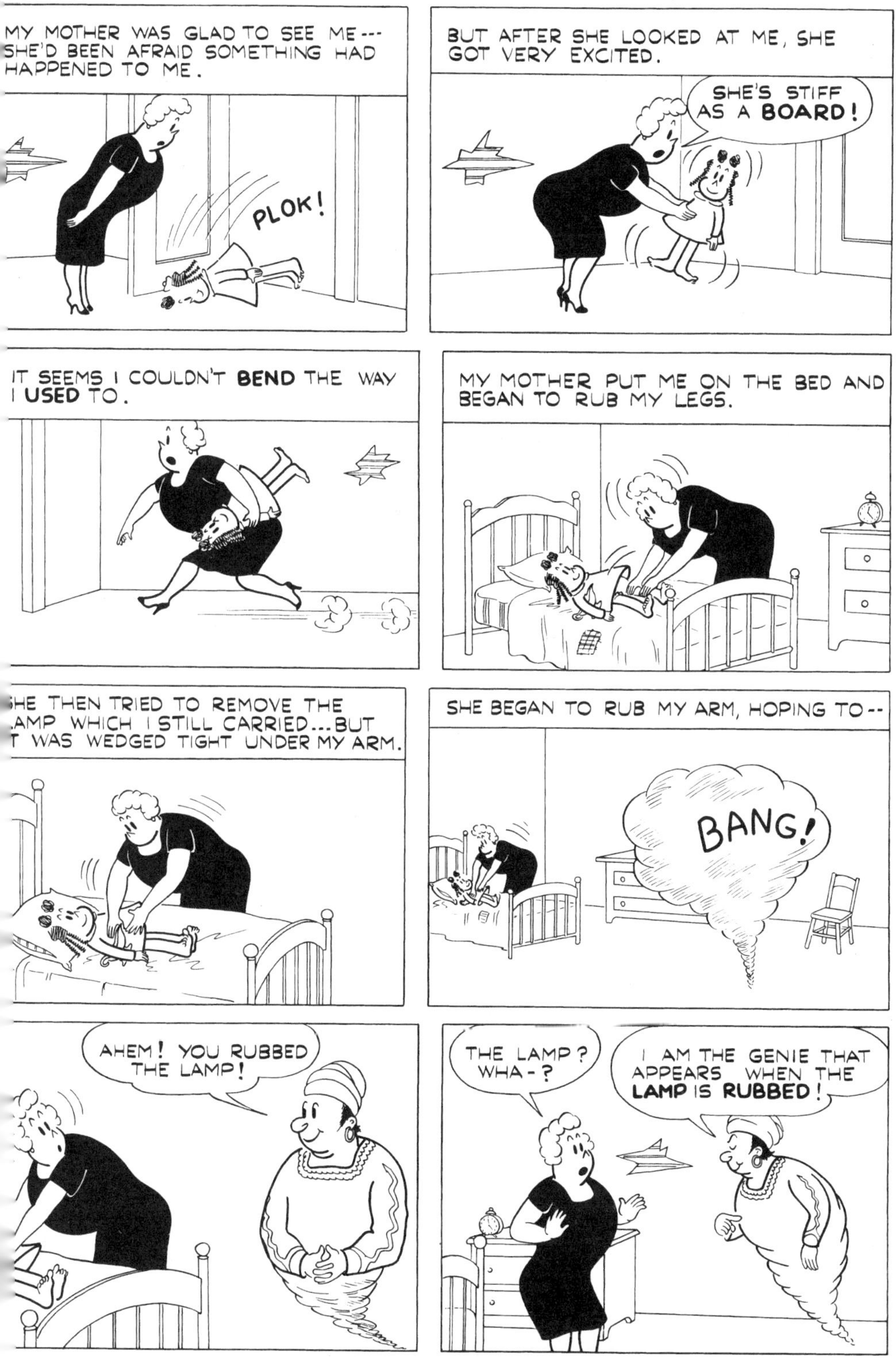

MY MOTHER WAS GLAD TO SEE ME--- SHE'D BEEN AFRAID SOMETHING HAD HAPPENED TO ME.
PLOK!
BUT AFTER SHE LOOKED AT ME, SHE GOT VERY EXCITED.
SHE'S STIFF AS A **BOARD**!
IT SEEMS I COULDN'T **BEND** THE WAY I **USED** TO.
MY MOTHER PUT ME ON THE BED AND BEGAN TO RUB MY LEGS.
HE THEN TRIED TO REMOVE THE AMP WHICH I STILL CARRIED...BUT T WAS WEDGED TIGHT UNDER MY ARM.
SHE BEGAN TO RUB MY ARM, HOPING TO--
BANG!
AHEM! YOU RUBBED THE LAMP!
THE LAMP? WHA-?
I AM THE GENIE THAT APPEARS WHEN THE **LAMP** IS **RUBBED**!

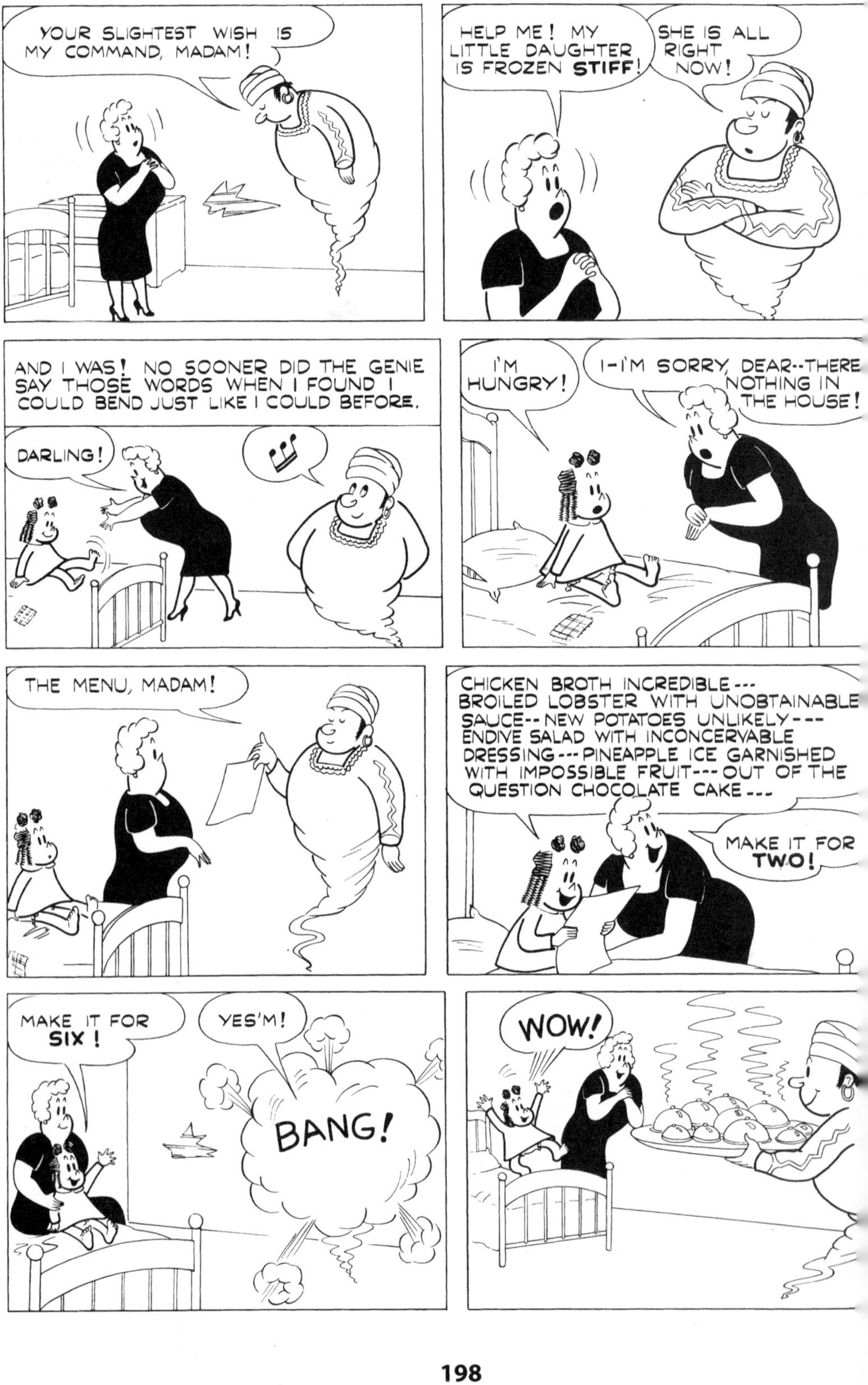
YOUR SLIGHTEST WISH IS MY COMMAND, MADAM!
HELP ME! MY LITTLE DAUGHTER IS FROZEN STIFF!
SHE IS ALL RIGHT NOW!
AND I WAS! NO SOONER DID THE GENIE SAY THOSE WORDS WHEN I FOUND I COULD BEND JUST LIKE I COULD BEFORE.
DARLING!
I'M HUNGRY!
I-I'M SORRY, DEAR--THERE NOTHING IN THE HOUSE!
THE MENU, MADAM!
CHICKEN BROTH INCREDIBLE--- BROILED LOBSTER WITH UNOBTAINABLE SAUCE-- NEW POTATOES UNLIKELY--- ENDIVE SALAD WITH INCONCERVABLE DRESSING--- PINEAPPLE ICE GARNISHED WITH IMPOSSIBLE FRUIT--- OUT OF THE QUESTION CHOCOLATE CAKE---
MAKE IT FOR TWO!
MAKE IT FOR SIX!
YES'M!
BANG!
WOW!

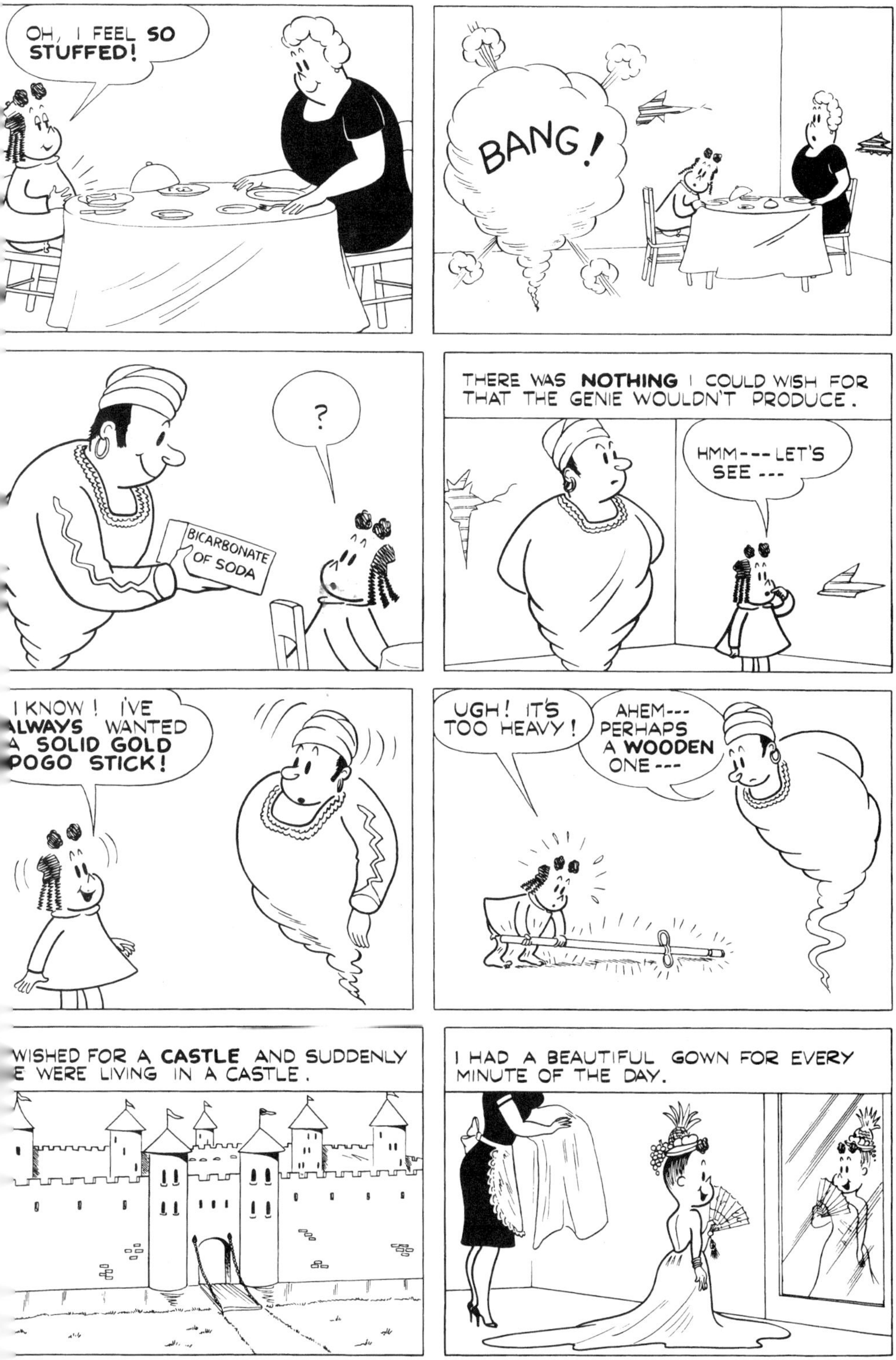
OH, I FEEL SO STUFFED!
BANG!
?
BICARBONATE OF SODA
THERE WAS NOTHING I COULD WISH FOR THAT THE GENIE WOULDN'T PRODUCE.
HMM--- LET'S SEE ---
I KNOW! I'VE ALWAYS WANTED A SOLID GOLD POGO STICK!
UGH! IT'S TOO HEAVY!
AHEM--- PERHAPS A WOODEN ONE ---
WISHED FOR A CASTLE AND SUDDENLY E WERE LIVING IN A CASTLE.
I HAD A BEAUTIFUL GOWN FOR EVERY MINUTE OF THE DAY.

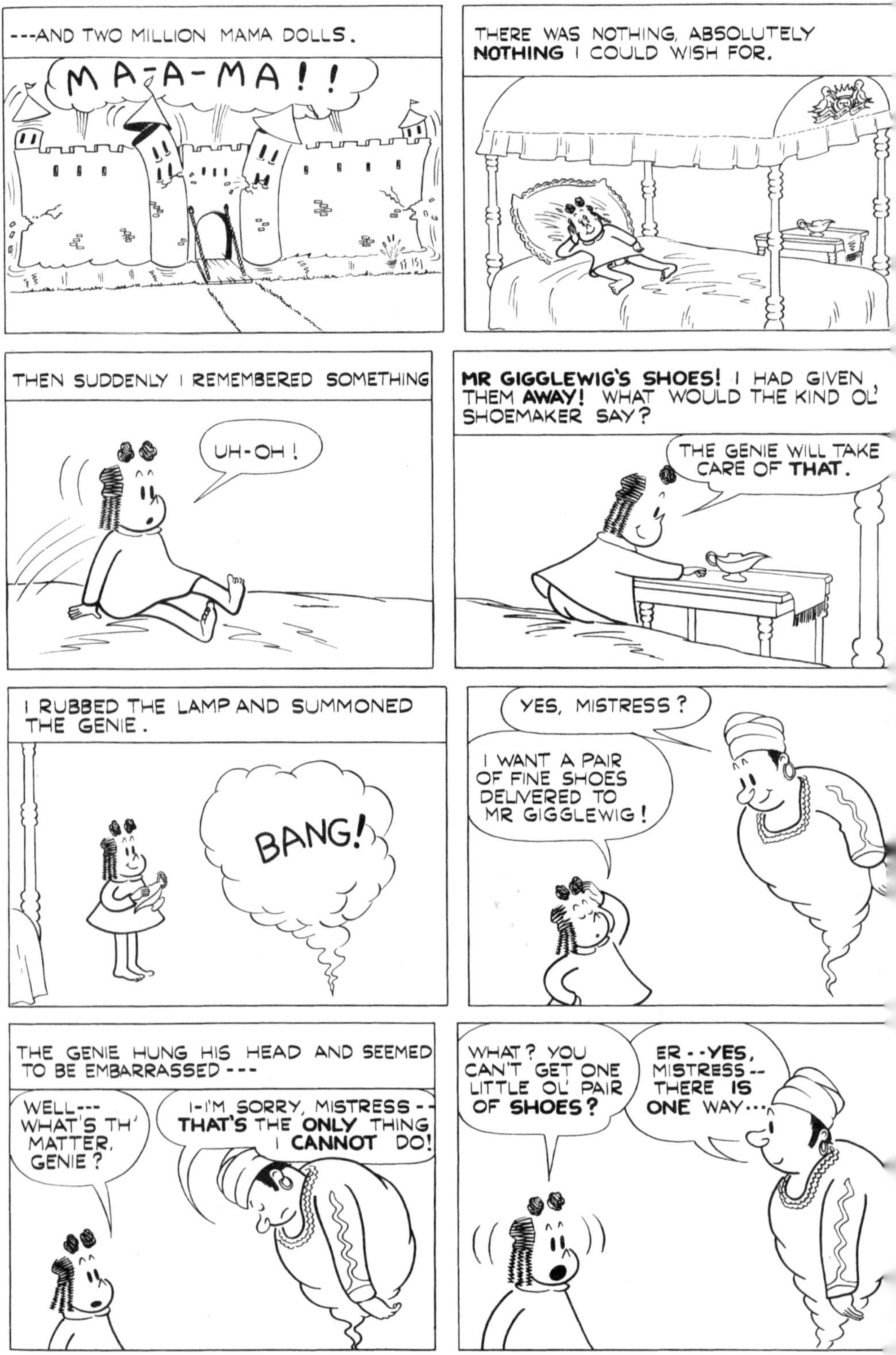
---AND TWO MILLION MAMA DOLLS.
MA-A-MA!!
THERE WAS NOTHING, ABSOLUTELY NOTHING I COULD WISH FOR.
THEN SUDDENLY I REMEMBERED SOMETHING
UH-OH!
MR GIGGLEWIG'S SHOES! I HAD GIVEN THEM AWAY! WHAT WOULD THE KIND OL' SHOEMAKER SAY?
THE GENIE WILL TAKE CARE OF THAT.
I RUBBED THE LAMP AND SUMMONED THE GENIE.
BANG!
YES, MISTRESS?
I WANT A PAIR OF FINE SHOES DELIVERED TO MR GIGGLEWIG!
THE GENIE HUNG HIS HEAD AND SEEMED TO BE EMBARRASSED---
WELL--- WHAT'S TH' MATTER, GENIE?
I-I'M SORRY, MISTRESS-- THAT'S THE ONLY THING I CANNOT DO!
WHAT? YOU CAN'T GET ONE LITTLE OL' PAIR OF SHOES?
ER--YES, MISTRESS-- THERE IS ONE WAY...

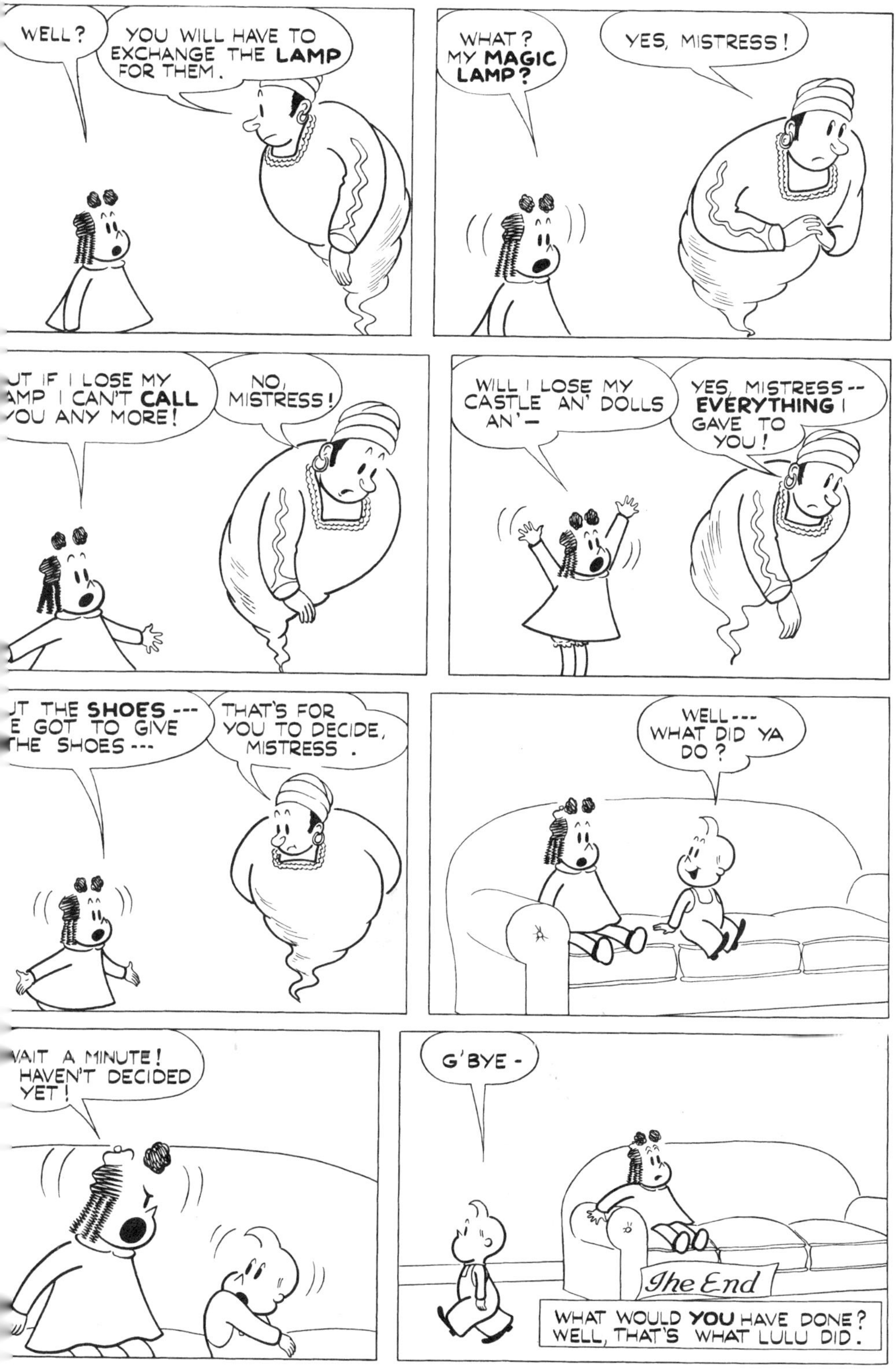
WELL?
YOU WILL HAVE TO EXCHANGE THE LAMP FOR THEM.
WHAT? MY MAGIC LAMP?
YES, MISTRESS!
UT IF I LOSE MY AMP I CAN'T CALL YOU ANY MORE!
NO, MISTRESS!
WILL I LOSE MY CASTLE AN' DOLLS AN'—
YES, MISTRESS-- EVERYTHING I GAVE TO YOU!
UT THE SHOES --- E GOT TO GIVE THE SHOES ---
THAT'S FOR YOU TO DECIDE, MISTRESS.
WELL--- WHAT DID YA DO?
VAIT A MINUTE! HAVEN'T DECIDED YET!
G'BYE -
The End
WHAT WOULD YOU HAVE DONE? WELL, THAT'S WHAT LULU DID.

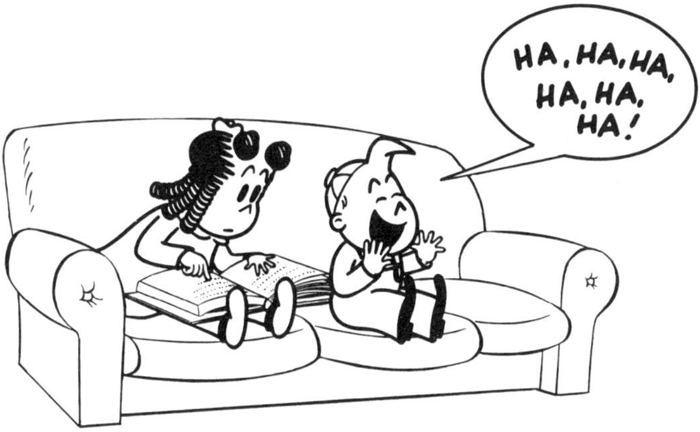
HA, HA, HA,
HA, HA,
HA!

Little Lulu®

Lulu Goes Shopping
ISBN: 1-59307-270-8 / $9.95

Lulu Takes a Trip
ISBN: 1-59307-317-8 / $9.95

My Dinner with Lulu
ISBN: 1-59307-318-6 / $9.95

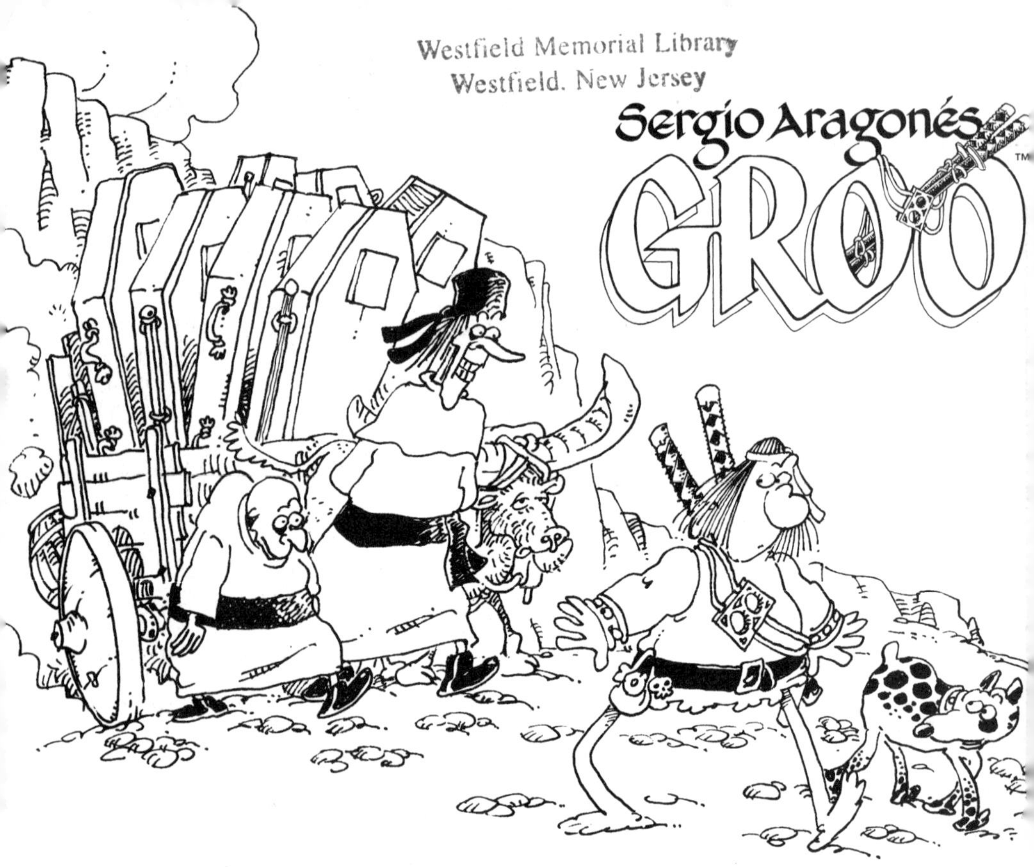
Sergio Aragonés
GROO

The Groo Houndbook
ISBN: 1-56971-385-5 / $9.95

The Groo Inferno
ISBN: 1-56971-430-4 / $9.95

The Groo Jamboree
ISBN: 1-56971-462-2 / $9.95

The Groo Kingdom
ISBN: 1-56971-478-9 / $9.95

The Groo Library
ISBN: 1-56971-571-8 / $12.95

The Groo Maiden
ISBN: 1-56971-756-7 / $12.95

The Groo Nursery
ISBN: 156971-794-X / $11.95

The Groo Odyssey
ISBN: 1-56971-858-X / $12.95

The Most Intelligent Man in the World
ISBN: 1-56971-294-8 / $9.95

Groo and Rufferto
ISBN: 1-56971-447-9 / $9.95

Mightier than the Sword
ISBN: 1-56971-612-9 / $13.95

Death and Taxes
ISBN: 1-56971-797-4 / $12.95

AVAILABLE AT YOUR LOCAL COMICS SHOP OR BOOKSTORE!

To find a comics shop in your area, call 1-888-266-4226.
For more information or to order direct visit Darkhorse.com or call 1-800-862-0052 Mon.-Sat. 9 A.M. to 5 P.M. Pacific Time

*Prices and availability subject to change without notice

DARK HORSE BOOKS

TONY MILLIONAIRE'S
SOCK MONKEY™ COLLECTION

BOOKS

The Adventures of Tony Millionaire's Sock Monkey
1-56971-490-8 $9.95

Tony Millionaire's Sock Monkey A Children's Book
1-56971-549-1 $9.95

The Collected Works of Tony Millionaire's Sock Monkey Volumes 3 and 4
1-59307-098-5 $12.95

Tony Millionaire's Sock Monkey The Glass Doorknob
1-56971-782-6 $14.95

Tony Millionaire's Sock Monkey Uncle Gabby
1-59307-026-8 $14.95

Tony Millionaire's Sock Monkey That Darn Yarn
1-59582-009-4 $7.95

MERCHANDISE

Tony Millionaire's Sock Monkey Journal
1-56971-856-3 $9.99

Tony Millionaire's Sock Monkey Stationery
1-56971-875-X $4.99

Sock Monkey Bendy Toy
1-56971-705-2 $9.99

Sock Monkey Plush
1-56971-708-7 $19.99

Sock Monkey Statue
statue stands 8" tall
item #10-279 $75.00

Sock Monkey Lunch Box (& Postcard)
1-56971-706-0 $14.99

Sock Monkey Zippo® Lighter
item #10-149 $29.99

Sock Monkey Magnet Set
1-56971-707-9 $9.99

Sock Monkey Shot Glass
item #10-134 $6.99

Mr. Crow Shot Glass
item #10-137 $6.99

Sock Monkey T-Shirt
youth tee, white
Small	item #11-191
Medium	item #11-196
Large	item #11-200
X-Large	item #11-203
S-XL	**$17.99**

Sock Monkey T-Shirt
adult tee, white
Medium	item #11-207
Large	item #11-212
X-Large	item #11-216
XX-Large	item #11-220
M-XL	**$17.99**
XXL	**$19.99**

Mr. Crow T-Shirt
youth tee, white
Small	item #11-224
Medium	item #11-228
Large	item #11-231
X-Large	Item #11-234
S-XL	**$17.99**

Mr. Crow T-Shirt
adult tee, white
Medium	item #11-236
Large	item #11-239
X-Large	item #11-242
XX-Large	Item #11-244
M-XL	**$17.99**
XXL	**$19.99**

Sock Monkey Stickers
Sticker #1	item #11-360
Sticker #2	item #11-363
Sticker #3	item #11-366
Sticker #4	item #11-368
all stickers are each	**$1.99**

Tony Millionaire's Maakies: Drinky Crow
comes with interchangeable eyes and a bottle of booze!
1-56971-809-1 $19.99

Uncle Gabby
comes with removable hat and brain!
1-59307-041-1 $24.99

Drinky Crow Coaster Set
item #12-240 $9.99

Tony Millionaire's Sock Monkey™ & © 2005 Tony Millionaire

Westfield Memorial Library
Westfield, New Jersey

JUL 03

YAGN Lulu
Stanley, John.
Sunday afternoon /